WALT
WHITMAN
AND THE
CITIZEN'S EYE

Walt Whitman and the Citizen's Eye

James Dougherty

Louisiana State University Press ❖ *Baton Rouge and London*

Copyright © 1993 by Louisiana State University Press
All rights reserved
Manufactured in the United States of America
First printing
02 01 00 99 98 97 96 95 94 93   5 4 3 2 1

Designer: Rebecca Lloyd Lemna
Typeface: Bembo
Typesetter: Graphic Composition, Inc.
Printer and binder: Thomson-Shore, Inc.

Library of Congress Cataloging-in-Publication Data

Dougherty, James, 1937–
    Walt Whitman and the citizen's eye / James Dougherty.
    p. cm.
    Includes bibliographical references and index.
    ISBN 0-8071-1772-2 (cloth: alk. paper)
    1. Whitman, Walt, 1819–1892—Political and social views.
2. Whitman, Walt, 1819–1892—Knowledge—New York (N.Y.) 3. City and town life in literature. 4. Cities and towns in literature. 5. New York (N.Y.) in literature. I. Title.
PS3242.C56D68 1992
811'.3—dc20   92–14096
                                                                             CIP

The author is grateful to the publishers and agents who granted permission to reprint excerpts contained herein:
Excerpts from *Seize the Day* and *Mr. Sammler's Planet*, by Saul Bellow, reprinted by permission of Penguin USA. Excerpts from *I and Thou*, by Martin Buber, translated from the German by Ronald Gregor Smith, reprinted with permission of The Balkin Agency, Amherst, Mass., and with permission of Charles Scribner's Sons, an imprint of Macmillan Publishing Company. Copyright © 1958 by Charles Scribner's Sons; copyright renewed. Excerpts from "Preludes" and "The Love Song of J. Alfred Prufrock" in *Collected Poems 1909–1962*, by T. S. Eliot, copyright 1936 by Harcourt Brace Jovanovich, Inc., copyright © 1964, 1963 by T. S. Eliot, reprinted by permission of the publisher and by permission of Faber and Faber Ltd. "A Common Ground," "The World Outside," "Six Variations," "From the Roof," "Matins," and "City Psalm," from Denise Levertov, *Poems 1960–1967*. Copyright © 1966 by Denise Levertov Goodman. Reprinted by permission of New Directions Publishing Corporation. "Woman Walking," "Young Sycamore," "View of a Lake," "The Catholic Bells," "Fine Work with Pitch and Copper," "Between Walls," and "Morning," from William Carlos Williams, *The Collected Poems of William Carlos Williams 1909–1939, vol. I.* Copyright 1938 by New Directions Publishing Corporation. Reprinted by permission of New Directions Publishing Corporation and by permission of Carcanet Press Limited. Part of Chapter 7 appeared, in revised form, as "Jacob Riis: Citizenship and Art," in the *Canadian Review of American Studies*, XXII (Winter, 1991), 529–40.

The paper in this book meets the guidelines for permanence and durability of the Committee on Production Guidelines for Book Longevity of the Council on Library Resources. ⊚

For my father and mother
James P. Dougherty, 1890–1977
Cora Smyth Dougherty, 1901–1985

They gave him afterward every day . . .
they and of them became part of him.

At times the man, shuddering at the alienation between the *I* and the world, comes to reflect that something is to be done. As when in the grave night-hour you lie, racked by waking dream—bulwarks have fallen away and the abyss is screaming—and note amid your torment: there is still life, if only I got through to it—but how, how?; so is this man in the hours of reflection, shuddering, and aimlessly considering this and that. And perhaps, away in the unloved knowledge of the depths within him, he really knows the direction of turning, leading through sacrifice. But he spurns this knowledge; "mysticism" cannot resist the sun of electric light. He calls thought, in which he rightly has great confidence, to his aid; it shall make good everything for him again. It is, in truth, the high art of thought to paint a reliable picture of the world that is even worthy of belief. So this man says to his thought, "You see this thing stretched out here with the cruel eyes—was it not my playfellow once? You know how it laughed at me then with these very eyes, and they had good in them then? And you see my wretched *I*—I will confess to you, it is empty, and whatever I do in myself, as a result of experiencing and using, does not fathom its emptiness. Will you make it up between me and it, so that it leaves off and I recover?" And thought, ready with its service and its art, paints with its well-known speed one—no, two rows of pictures, on the right wall and on the left. On the one there is (or rather, there takes place, for the world-pictures of thought are reliable cinematography) the universe. The tiny earth plunges from the whirling stars, tiny man from the teeming earth, and now history bears him further through the ages, to rebuild persistently the ant-hill of the cultures which history crushes underfoot. Beneath the row of pictures is written: "One and all." On the other wall there takes place the soul. A spinner is spinning the orbits of all stars and the life of all creation and the history of the universe; everything is woven on one thread, and is no longer called stars and creation and universe, but sensations and imaginings, or even experiences, and conditions of the soul. And beneath the row of pictures is written: "One and all."

Thenceforth, if ever the man shudders at the alienation, and the world strikes terror in his heart, he looks up (to right or left, just as it may chance) and sees a picture. There he sees that the *I* is embedded in the world and that there is really no *I* at all—so the world can do nothing to the *I*, and he is put at ease; or he sees that the world is embedded in the *I*, and that there is really no world at all—so the world can do nothing to the *I*, and he is put at ease. Another time, if the man shudders at the alienation, and the *I* strikes terror in his heart, he looks up and sees a picture, which picture he sees does not matter, the empty *I* is stuffed full with the world or the stream of the world flows over it, and he is put at ease.

But a moment comes, and it is near, when the shuddering man looks up and sees both pictures in a flash together. And a deeper shudder seizes him.

—Martin Buber, *I and Thou*

Contents

Preface xiii
Acknowledgments xix
Abbreviations xxi

        1 I, Not-Me, You, We 1
Part I: The World in the Self, the Self in the World
        2 The Expanse of Consciousness 39
        3 Satan, Wound-Dresser, Witness 76
        4 Pictorialism 108
Part II: The Citizen of Manhattan
        5 Panoramas 139
        6 The Mystery of the Eyesight 172
Part III: Surface and Depth
        7 Artful Juxtapositions: Jacob Riis and John Sloan 205
        8 Fierce Momentary Tension: T. S. Eliot and William Carlos Williams 236
        9 Surface and Depth: Alfred Stieglitz, Charles Sheeler, Berenice Abbott 264
      10 Angels' Mouths and Existential Space 288

Bibliography 307
Index 317

Illustrations

1. Thomas Crawford, *Armed Freedom*   94
2. Currier & Ives, *The Storming of Fort Donelson, Tenn.*   96
3. Winslow Homer, *Bivouac Fire on the Potomac*   119
4. Edwin Whitefield, *View of Brooklyn, L.I.*   158
5. J. Bachmann, *Bird's Eye View of the City of New York*   159
6. Jacob Riis, *Home of an Italian Ragpicker*   215
7. Jacob Riis, *Street Arabs in the Area of Mulberry Street, ca. 1889*   216
8. Kenyon Cox, after Riis, *In the Home of an Italian Ragpicker*   219
9. Jacob Riis, *Street Arabs*   220
10. John Sloan, *Chinese Restaurant*   229
11. John Sloan, *Three A.M.*   232
12. John Sloan, *The City from Greenwich Village*   265
13. Alfred Stieglitz, *The Terminal*   267
14. Alfred Stieglitz, *Old and New New York*   270
15. Charles Sheeler, *Skyscrapers*   277
16. Berenice Abbott, *A. Zito's Bakery, New York, 1937*   284

Preface

Walt Whitman is often regarded—rightly—as the poet who introduced the city to American literature. Against the grain of his age, he celebrated the inhabitants of New York and the feel of city living, and devised poetic forms that were open to the diversity, pace, and scale of urban life. At the same time—and again rightly—he is often taken as the poet of the individual self, the "solitary singer." The tension between the public and the personal in Whitman's poetry has stimulated critical studies of the almost solipsistic privacy of Whitman's poetics, as well as reflections on the gregarious solitude of modern urban living. Recently, several writers on Whitman have addressed this paradox by showing how Whitman sought to establish himself as a public poet and to imagine and address an American audience. These include C. Carroll Hollis' *Language and Style in "Leaves of Grass"* (1983), M. Wynn Thomas' *The Lunar Light of Whitman's Poetry* (1987), Kerry C. Larson's *Whitman's Drama of Consensus* (1988), Betsy Erkkila's *Whitman the Political Poet* (1989), James Perrin Warren's *Walt Whitman's Language Experiment* (1990), and Ezra Greenspan's *Walt Whitman and the American Reader* (1990).

I believe that Whitman's individualism, in disclaiming affiliation with any person, association, or system that would mediate between the single Person and the All, did result in a state of mind and a poetry in which Self and Cosmos forever engulf each other as Whitman's attention shifts between these two principles of inclusion. Most of Whitman's poems measure and remeasure the Magic Prison of individualist consciousness. The problems of an egotistical poetic have been discussed by many critics of Whitman, of the American Renaissance, and of Romanticism. My first chapter, therefore, recrosses some familiar critical terrain, but does so in order to set the discussion in terms that emphasize how severe the problem is for a poet with Whitman's public temperament, and that will help me show when and how he occasionally resolved that problem. Those terms I derive largely from Martin Buber.

E. Fred Carlisle, in *The Uncertain Self: Whitman's Drama of Identity*, uses Martin Buber's principle of the dialogue between *I* and *Thou* to show that these poems trace passages from "monologic" man to "dialogic" man. Perhaps because I am concerned with the public, or civic, self and its poetry rather than the simply personal, I have emphasized, rather, Buber's account of "modern man," in the later pages of *I and Thou*. As epigraph to this book, I have set three paragraphs from *I and Thou* that describe the ebb and flow of ego in visualist images like those I find in *Leaves of Grass*. Buber's ideas and imagery have helped me to understand why much of Whitman's public poetry seems both undifferentiated and hollowly nationalistic, and why he writes so powerfully in those poems that rejoin a civil community. Reciprocally, I take Whitman as the prototype of that disaffiliation which numbs humans living today in mass society—a disaffiliation that Tocqueville anticipated and that Buber treats in the third section of *I and Thou* and in many of his later essays.

Whitman drew back from the privacy and interiority toward which his poetic thinking tended, recognizing that it reduced his experience to spectacle and illusion. He sought for grounds on which his vision might be both stabilized and communicated. Although some of his poems, like "Song of Myself," rely on an act of faith that the I and the Life-Force are one, others look for a more secular mediation. The forms and images of midnineteenth-century politics might be such a ground; public speech—oratory and rhetoric—might be another. Recent books on Whitman have considered these grounds. Taking my cue from the Preface to the first edition of *Leaves of Grass,* where the poet's "faith" is repeatedly phrased in the imagery of sight, I have looked through Whitman's poetry for those situations in which visual experience, either direct or mediated through popular illustration, serves as the base of communion between Whitman and his readers.[1] These include much of the nationalist poetry published in 1855 and 1856, some of the poems in *Drum-Taps,* and "Crossing Brooklyn Ferry." The latter has long seemed to

---

1. Hyatt Waggoner's *American Visionary Poetry* (Baton Rouge, 1982) appeared after I had formulated my approach to "the mystery of the eyesight" in Whitman's poetry. I have pressed "vision" further into the pictorial and into the visual than he did in that book, which he described as opening the subject for inquiry, not closing it.

me a great poem, and I have tried to show some of the sources of its power in this study.

Whitman might have escaped the vacuity into which most of his nationalist poetry lapses if he had kept his vision more firmly directed toward his own firsthand experience—if the horizon of his poetry had more often coincided with the horizons of New York City and Washington. These cities, especially the former, were the best space within which to try the claims of Self and Mass, One and All. Then and now, the city is where we live out the conflicts in these claims. Before its own horizons became as diffuse as those of "Salut au Monde!" and "Our Old Feuillage," the city was where one might discover how the Self could be nurtured and its claims tempered by such intermediating structures as household, neighborhood, and the communities of shared political, religious, or ethnic faith—all the "free associations" by which, Tocqueville said, Americans seek to lessen the solitude of democratic individualism. I have given most attention to Whitman's poetry of city life. In this, as in my earlier writing on the urban imagination, I have been guided by philosophers of urban space such as Kevin Lynch and Christian Norberg-Schulz, for they are concerned with the imagination as much, or even more, than is the student of literature.[2]

Whitman's poetry cries out his dissatisfaction with the gaps between living and writing, discovery and creation, reader and writer; and with the paired gaps between the writer's experience and his word, between his word and the reader's experience. Men and women, he wrote in his Preface, perceive the beauty and dignity of reality as well as the poet does. What they expect of the poet is that he indicate "the path between reality and their souls." Must the imagination, especially in its visual form, always enforce an aesthetic detachment? In poems like "There was a Child Went Forth" and "Crossing Brooklyn Ferry," and in passages in many other poems, Whitman sought the path linking the poem-making imagination with the practical imagination through which poets and nonpoets alike interpret the worlds in which they dwell. That was the duty of

---

2. Kevin Lynch, *The Image of the City* (Cambridge, Mass., 1960) and *What Time Is This Place?* (Cambridge, Mass., 1972); Christian Norberg-Schulz, *Existence, Space, and Architecture* (New York, 1971). My own writings include *The Fivesquare City: The City in the Religious Imagination* (Notre Dame, Ind., 1980); "Broadacre City: Frank Lloyd Wright's Utopia," *The Centennial Review*, XXV (1981), 239–56; and "Jane Addams: Culture and Imagination," *The Yale Review*, LXXI (1982), 363–79.

the citizen poet. It was not his depicting crowds and omnibuses that made Whitman a poet of city life. Rather, it is those moments when the aesthetic imagination (what Coleridge would have called the "secondary"), creating and re-creating the poem, overlaps the practical (or "primary") imagination through which we shape and share the spaces of city inhabitation.

I am fatigued by studies that conclude that the poet was not writing about Brooklyn, Manhattan, or Rutherford, but about "the city of the mind" or "the poem"—as though these were better addresses. Poetry, of course, is not "the world," but it can bring us to the threshold of the world. In literature we may recognize our world. From literature we may recognize it anew. And that recognition, sometimes, leads not to detachment, "I-It," but to presence, "I-Thou." Buber's reflections on public life suggest that though presence cannot be sustained, it can always be renewed if not foreclosed. At its greatest, in a poem like "Crossing Brooklyn Ferry," Whitman's poetry suggests how these encounters are renewed by citizens sharing a common space. This book speaks not of Whitman's politics but of his citizenship.

Whitman dramatized the tension of public and private, interior and exterior, most intensely in the first phase of his career. By 1860, he had begun to retreat, first toward a purely personal poetry, then toward a conventional public verse. Though I take up poems from all stages of his career, I have preferred the earlier; and I have consistently used the earliest published versions of his poems, though at times these may not be the most familiar or, in a few cases, the most felicitous.

The questions raised by Whitman's poems—about the citizen artist, the aestheticizing of what is seen, and encounters within shared space—have continued to trouble imaginations inspired either by him or by the urban world he celebrated. In my last four chapters, I examine some of the ways in which an urban imagination has developed in American culture in the century since Whitman's death. Still focusing on "the mystery of the eyesight," I consider painters and photographers as well as poets, and one writer of fiction. In the game or out? Spectacle or presence? In a poem called "A Common Ground," Denise Levertov, herself a citizen poet, sets the question once more in urban terms, looking back to the passenger on Fulton Ferry who looked forward to us:

not illusion but what Whitman called
'the path
between reality and the soul'

(*The Jacob's Ladder*, 3)

My quotations from Whitman's poetry almost always use the first published versions—texts sometimes at variance with the familiar readings authorized as the 1891–92 edition. These original versions can be found in modern reprints of the first three editions of *Leaves of Grass* and of *Drum-Taps*. The 1855 edition has been recently reprinted several times: by Viking as *Walt Whitman's Leaves of Grass: His Original Edition,* edited by Malcolm Cowley (1959); by the Eakins Press Foundation (1966); and in the Library of America's *Walt Whitman: Complete Poetry and Collected Prose,* edited by Justin Kaplan (1982). The Folcroft Library published a facsimile of the 1856 edition, with an introduction by Gay Wilson Allen, in 1975. Cornell University Press's facsimile of the 1860 edition, with an introduction by Roy Harvey Pearce, appeared in 1961. *Drum-Taps* and its sequel, edited by F. DeWolfe Miller, were reprinted in 1959 by Scholar's Facsimiles and Reprints (Gainesville, Fla.). Alternatively, the first published versions can be reconstructed from *Leaves of Grass: A Textual Variorum of the Printed Poems,* edited by Sculley Bradley, Harold W. Blodgett, Arthur Golden, and William White (New York, 1980). Because the *Variorum* is easily accessible, I have used it as the text of reference in all my citations. In keeping with the practice of the *Variorum,* I have identified poems by their familiar, final titles, rather than the titles of their first publication: "Crossing Brooklyn Ferry," not "Sun-Down Poem." Further, I have provided section numbers for quotations from "Song of Myself," "Crossing Brooklyn Ferry," and other poems divided into numbered sections in the 1891–92 edition, whether or not the original version of the poem was so divided.

Acknowledgments

The University of Notre Dame helped me write this book. I am grateful to the university and to its College of Arts and Letters for affording me a semester's leave in the spring of 1983, during which I outlined my approach to Whitman, and for providing a word processor. Two deans of the College of Arts and Letters—Robert Burns and Michael Loux—supported my research with travel grants. The college's Institute for Scholarship in the Liberal Arts funded my attendance at a meeting of the Canadian Association for American Studies, at which I presented my work on Jacob Riis; and the institute also met the costs of illustrating this book and paying permissions fees. My thanks to Dean Harold Attridge, Roger Skurski, Jennifer Warlick, and Robert Burke, of the college and the institute. Notre Dame's English Department also helped me by reducing my teaching assignments in several semesters while I was writing this book: I am very grateful to its chairmen—Thomas Werge, Edward Kline, and Joseph Buttigieg—for their patience and their unfailing interest.

My most recent indebtedness is to the staff of Louisiana State University Press for the courtesy and interest they have shown me at every step in the process of publication, most especially John Easterly, Catherine Landry, and Julie Schorfheide. I am very grateful to Professor C. Carroll Hollis, of the University of North Carolina at Chapel Hill, for his attentive reading of my manuscript, his valuable suggestions, and his encouragement. Finally, my thanks to Lois Geehr, who copyedited the text so carefully and so effectively.

Abbreviations

CPE   T. S. Eliot. *Collected Poems, 1909–1962.* New York, 1963.

CPW   *The Collected Poems of William Carlos Williams.* Vol. I. Edited by A. Walton Litz and Christopher MacGowan. New York, 1986. Vol. II. Edited by Christopher MacGowan. New York, 1988.

CRE   Walt Whitman. *Leaves of Grass: Comprehensive Reader's Edition.* Edited by Harold W. Blodgett and Sculley Bradley. New York, 1965.

JL   Denise Levertov. *The Jacob's Ladder.* New York, 1961.

N   Walt Whitman. *Notebooks and Unpublished Prose Manuscripts.* Edited by Edward F. Grier. 6 vols. New York, 1984.

PW   Walt Whitman. *Prose Works, 1892.* Edited by Floyd Stovall. 2 vols. New York, 1963–64.

V   Walt Whitman. *Leaves of Grass: A Textual Variorum of the Printed Poems.* Edited by Sculley Bradley, Harold W. Blodgett, Arthur Golden, and William White. 3 vols. New York, 1980.

WALT WHITMAN AND THE CITIZEN'S EYE

[I]

I, Not-Me, You, We

Clear and sweet is my soul .... and clear and sweet is all that is
   not my soul.

Lack one lacks both .... and the unseen is proved by the seen,
Till that becomes unseen and receives proof in its turn.
                              —"Song of Myself," §3

The Preface to Walt Whitman's first edition of *Leaves of Grass* began conventionally enough. He announced a demand that, in the seventy-ninth year of the American Revolution, had become almost a formula. For a new nation there must be a new literature, forsaking whatever traditions were now lifeless, inventing ways to reveal whatever in America was yet unsung. And given the possibilities of the subject, the task seemed one that could be approached directly enough. "The United States themselves are essentially the greatest poem," he wrote. He began to give examples. The common people—"the picturesque looseness of their carriage," "their good temper and openhandedness—the terrible significance of their elections—the President's taking off his hat to them not they to him—these too are unrhymed poetry." He continued, describing the continent itself, its fauna and flora. So rich and various a subject! A poet who would be truly America's poet need only act reflexively: the land itself, he said, was creative and had "vista." "It awaits the gigantic and generous treatment worthy of it."[1]

Whitman's words at first summon an essentially descriptive, visualist poetry reciting the grandeur of the continent and the vitality and diversity of human life in the democracy that flourished there.

---

1. The most accessible text of the Preface is in *CRE*, 709–10.

Such pictorial and narrative motives had been the heart of national poetry from Homer to Ossian; and they had been the chief recourse of poets who had already assumed the bardic role in America, such as Joel Barlow in his *Columbiad*.

> Thro all the range where shores and seas extend,
> In tenfold pomp the works of peace ascend.
> Robed in the bloom of spring's eternal year
> And ripe with fruits the same glad fields appear,
> O'er hills and vales perennial gardens run,
> Cities unwall'd stand sparkling to the sun;
> The streams all freighted from the bounteous plain
> Swell with the load and labor to the main.
>
> (10.535–42)

Depicting American scenes and stories was the trade of Whitman's contemporary, Henry Wadsworth Longfellow. Longfellow a few years earlier had burlesqued Whitman's sort of literary nationalism, with its calls for "a national literature commensurate with our mountains and rivers, . . . a national epic that shall correspond to the size of the country, . . . a national literature altogether shaggy and unshorn."[2] Still, his recital of American deeds in European verses—the native Indians, the Puritan settlers, the heroes of the Revolution—asserted modestly the claim with which Whitman begins. Once there had been a Matter of Rome (Troy, Aeneas, Alexander), a Matter of France (Charlemagne and Roland), and a Matter of Britain (Arthur). To this the modern poet would add the Matter of America: its geography, the iconic moments from its history, and the present-day doings of its people.[3] This could all be done with simplicity. "What I experience or portray shall go from my composition without a shred of my composition. You shall stand by my side and look in the mirror with me" (*CRE*, 717).

But for Whitman the subject could never be so simply external and "objective," nor his methods naïvely reflexive. First of all,

---

2. Henry Wadsworth Longfellow, *Kavanagh: A Tale* (1849; rpr. Boston, 1872), 115.

3. "The ranges of heroism and loftiness with which Greek and feudal poets endow'd their god-like or lordly born characters—indeed prouder and better based and with fuller ranges than those—I was to endow the democratic averages of America" ("A Backward Glance O'er Travel'd Roads," *PW*, II, 727).

America was not a folk nation like the Hellenes or the Britons. "Here is not merely a nation but a teeming nation of nations." The phrases that follow this announcement describe a new kind of nation: masses . . . space . . . crowds . . . extravagance; the many, made one by the bond of democracy. Looking back in 1872, he described *Leaves of Grass* as "an epic of Democracy" (*PW*, II, 458). America is not simply a people upon a land; it is an ideology.

> I speak the password primeval .... I give the sign of
>   democracy;
> By God! I will accept nothing which all cannot have
>   their counterpart of on the same terms.
>   ("Song of Myself," §24, *V*, I, 32)[4]

Democracy for Whitman has more to do with a religious or moral vision (as Alan Trachtenberg has said) than with the mechanics of Federal government, or extensions of the franchise, or popular sovereignty, though the poet might invoke these matters as symbols of his larger idea.[5] That idea was egalitarianism. These lines from "Song of Myself" espouse it as a social ideal of opportunity and distribution. In "Song of the Open Road," he says it again: "Neither preference nor denial" (§2, *V*, I, 226). Nothing must mediate between the individual and the whole, preferring some persons and excluding others.

> All parts away for the progress of souls,
> All religion, all solid things, arts, governments—all that
>   was or is apparent upon this globe or any globe, falls
>   into niches and corners before the procession of souls
>   along the grand roads of the universe.
>   (§13, *V*, I, 235–36)

---

4. The 1855 version has been reconstructed from the *Variorum*, which serves throughout this book as the source for the first published version of Whitman's poems. For the reader's convenience, poems are identified by their titles in the final version; and quotations from "Song of Myself," "Crossing Brooklyn Ferry," and other poems divided into numbered sections in the 1891–92 edition are referenced to those divisions whether or not the original version of the poem was so divided. Ellipses are Whitman's unless placed in brackets.

5. Alan Trachtenberg, "Whitman's Visionary Politics," *Mickle Street Review*, X (1988), 15.

No parties, no sects, no groupings by region, race, or gender. Nothing but individuals.

> Underneath all are individuals,
> I swear nothing is good that ignores individuals!
> The American compact is with individuals,
> The only government is that which makes minute of individuals.
> ("By Blue Ontario's Shore," §15, *V,* I, 206)

As Tocqueville said of American individualism, "Aristocracy had made a chain of all the members of the community, from the peasant to the king; democracy breaks that chain, and severs every link of it."[6]

When the chain is broken, there is no way to distinguish between its severed links. As Tocqueville also remarked, in democratic communities men are all very much alike.[7] They forfeit those marks of particular identity once provided by social class, national origin, regional loyalties, religious sect—in a word, by their membership in any group that mediates between the One and the All. Although Whitman wrote in a nation where such discriminators had not at all disappeared, he wrote *for* a nation that would have put them behind, uniting in an undifferentiated mass. "Song of Myself" proclaimed that the "word of the modern" was the word "en masse" (§23, *V,* I, 30).

Anticipating some more recent reflections on mass society, Whitman insists that American egalitarianism need not issue in an agglomeration of identical units. In 1867 he began to preface *Leaves of Grass* with an "Inscription" that announced two themes for his chant, one "the word EN-MASSE" but the other "ONE'S-SELF—a simple, separate person" (*V,* II, 557). In his sustained and disillusioned reflection on democracy, the prose work *Democratic Vistas* (1871), Whitman espoused a philosophy of "personalism" that was intended to assert the "centripetal isolation of a human being in himself—identity" (*PW,* II, 391). The term *isolation,* however, suggests the alternate peril of mass societies, the one described also by Tocqueville in a passage often quoted: "[Democracy] throws [man]

---

6. Alexis de Tocqueville, *Democracy in America,* trans. Henry Reeve (New York, 1945), II, 99.
7. *Ibid.,* 73.

back forever upon himself alone, and threatens in the end to confine him entirely within the solitude of his own heart."[8] To save his individuals from an atomistic solitude, Whitman wished them bonded in some force, which he called love, or comradeship, or adhesiveness. But his poetry found democracy as protean and unstable as the nation of nations itself, an uneasily shifting balance between the One and the Many: between the Federal constitution and the incompatible claims of its several states; between artisans and wage laborers; between the conformist mob feared by Emerson and the disaffiliated egotists whom Hawthorne portrayed.[9]

Whitman's egalitarianism, however, was more than a social or political doctrine; it was a habit of thought, a way of perceiving, a compositional style. Structured and hierarchical societies were the outward form and consequence of structured and hierarchical thinking. A democratic mind would think and experience without preference, making minute of every individual fact within the orbit of its intelligence. "The American bard shall delineate no class of persons nor one or two out of the strata of interests nor love most nor truth most nor the soul most nor the body most ... and not be for the eastern states more than the western or the northern states more than the southern" (*CRE*, 718). The poem following the Preface in the 1855 edition was a long free-verse exemplar of American democratic thinking. (In the next edition, he titled it "Poem of Walt Whitman, an American.") It revolts against class and against classification. It does this not so much by professions of social egalitarianism as by inventing an egalitarian poetics, admitting every subject from the conventionally heroic to the conventionally obscene, flouting the decorums of poetic language, modulating his voice from rhapsody to

---

8. *Ibid.*, 99.
9. Quentin Anderson, in *The Imperial Self* (New York, 1971), and Richard Chase, in *Walt Whitman Reconsidered* (New York, 1955), examine the disintegrative individualism of Whitman's poetry. E. Fred Carlisle, in *The Uncertain Self: Whitman's Drama of Identity* (East Lansing, Mich., 1973), Betsy Erkkila, in *Whitman the Political Poet* (New York, 1989), and Kerry C. Larson, in *Whitman's Drama of Consensus* (Chicago, 1988), study his efforts to recover some communitarian base in American democracy. Erkkila, Larson, and M. Wynn Thomas (*The Lunar Light of Whitman's Poetry* [Cambridge, Mass., 1987]) all point out that what threatened Whitman's society most obviously was not the anarchic individualism of single souls, but economic divisions and political schism. Jeffrey Walker, on the other hand, contends that Whitman's Transcendentalist assumptions about poetic authority separated him from the American common reader (*Bardic Ethos and the American Epic Poem* [Baton Rouge, 1989], 13–33).

demotic street slang, and founding the poem's rhythms on a line of unlimited variation in length.[10]

Readers look in vain for a structure in "Song of Myself" (as the poem is now titled), for Whitman's intent is to sabotage structure, insofar as structure implies preference—preference for the beautiful over the ugly, the sonorous over the flippant, the graceful over the bumptious; preference by exclusion; preference in order of presentation, beginning-middle-end. A structured intelligence, like a hierarchical society, would provide schemas for sorting and assimilating experience, categories of comparative relevance, a sense of near and far. But the democratic mind stands open and unbuffered against the press of all reality. In the poem, everything occurs at once; everything demands attention; nothing can be refused. In great unsorted lists the poet ranges his world:

> The pavingman leans on his twohanded rammer—the reporter's lead flies swiftly over the notebook—the signpainter is lettering with red and gold,
> The canal-boy trots on the towpath—the bookkeeper counts at his desk—the shoemaker waxes his thread,
> The conductor beats time for the band and all the performers follow him,
> The child is baptised—the convert is making the first professions,
> The regatta is spread on the bay .... how the white sails sparkle!
> ("Song of Myself," §15, *V*, I, 18)

What contains all these individual things? America. But also, an egalitarian frame of mind. Partly, "Song of Myself" proclaims the manifold vitality of this nation of nations; partly, it celebrates the democratic consciousness that can admit all this heterogeneity. The Matter of America is not just geography, people, and history, but consciousness itself, playing upon that world. Therefore, the true heroes and leaders of a democratic nation should be not its presidents or its warriors, but those who have learned to think democratically—its "poets," he said in the 1855 Preface. "The expression of the American poet is to be transcendent and new," he wrote. "It is

---

10. Most modern critics have made this connection between egalitarian politics and undiscriminating poetics. See, for example, Erkkila, *Whitman the Political Poet*, 88–91.

to be indirect and not direct or descriptive or epic. Its quality goes through these to much more. Let the age and wars of other nations be chanted and their eras and characters be illustrated and that finish the verse. Not so the great psalm of the republic" (*CRE*, 712). The simply pictorial and narrative poetry implied at first in the Preface will not be enough. "The land and sea, the animals fishes and birds, the sky of heaven and the orbs, the forests mountains and rivers, are not small themes ... but folks expect of the poet to indicate more than the beauty and dignity which always attach to dumb real objects ... they expect him to indicate the path between reality and their souls" (*CRE*, 714).

The American hero is not a man of action like Achilles or Roland, but a hero of consciousness. His heroic struggle is to align his inner vision with the outer world; to pioneer the path between reality and the soul. He attempts that alignment in two reciprocal movements, corresponding to the One and the Many in the nation. Whitman called these movements pride and sympathy. In sympathy, the poet gives himself away to his experience, sometimes just so far as a glance of recognition ("The jour printer with gray head and gaunt jaws works at his case, / He turns his quid of tobacco, his eyes get blurred with the manuscript"), but at other times, in a self-forgetful flood of empathy:

> I am the hounded slave ... I wince at the bite of the
>   dogs,
> Hell and despair are upon me .... crack and again crack
>   the marksmen,
> I clutch the rails of the fence .... my gore dribs thinned
>   with the ooze of my skin,
> I fall on the weeds and stones.
>   ("Song of Myself," §15, *V*, I, 16; §33, *V*, I, 52)

"I am the man," says Whitman in this mode; "I suffered .... I was there."

But even as he adverts to his vicarious suffering, he shifts from sympathy to the other mode, pride. The poet exults in his human power to comprehend the world:

> And I know I am solid and sound,
> To me the converging objects of the universe perpetually
>   flow,

> All are written to me, and I must get what the writing
> means.
>
> ("Song of Myself," §20, *V*, I, 25)

So consciousness becomes self-consciousness. "Poem of Walt Whitman, an American" becomes "Song of Myself." No longer simply "in" the world, the Self regards everything as its experience and contemplates itself as experiencer:

> Apart from the pulling and hauling stands what I am,
> Stands amused, complacent, compassionating, idle,
>   unitary,
> Looks down, is erect, bends an arm on an impalpable
>   certain rest,
> Looks with its sidecurved head curious what will come
>   next,
> Both in and out of the game, and watching and
>   wondering at it.
>
> (§4, *V*, I, 5)

The poems of *Leaves of Grass* pulse between other-consciousness and self-consciousness, between United States and state of mind: "The Many in One—what is it finally except myself? / These States—what are they except myself?" (§18, *V*, I, 209). "Starting from Paumanok" begins with a celebration of "persons and places" from Canada to Cuba; but by its end the poem has swallowed its subject:

> See! steamers steaming through my poems!
> See, in my poems immigrants continually coming and
>   landing;
> [. . .]
> See, on the one side the Western Sea, and on the other
>   side the Eastern Sea, how they advance and retreat
>   upon my poems, as upon their own shores.
>
> (§18, *V*, II, 288)

M. Wynn Thomas drew attention to this passage in *The Lunar Light of Whitman's Poetry,* saying that "the lines bespeak Whitman's fear that his writing will simply be autotelic, self-referential rather than referential, self-enclosed rather than debouching onto and affecting the real world."[11] In Whitman's destabilized world, the Matter of Amer-

---

11. Thomas, *Lunar Light*, 39.

ica must shift continually from politic to poetic, from reality to the soul and back again. And with it shifts the poet. Like the Klein bottle, that tubular Moebius strip, he is enclosed by the world and yet he encloses the world.

As mediating institutions had once stood between the individual and the all, so a cultural tradition had once mediated between consciousness and the objects of consciousness. Madison, Jay, and Hamilton had read the prospects of the American experiment against the rise and fall of Mediterranean polities. Freneau, Crevecoeur, and Bryant had used Enlightenment views of nature and of human progress to describe the white man's encounter with a new continent. But in Whitman's America, the inherited culture was of doubtful value, for it perpetuated a European hegemony that bound America to colonial dependency. To inaugurate an indigenous—a modern—frame of thought, America would have to abrogate all reliance on the mediations of culture, for that culture was not only "courtly" and hierarchical, but it had assumed an air of completeness. America would always stand on the margin of the triskelion Old World; modern times would always seem a further lapse from some lost classical or medieval unity. The culture would always come first, and the single individual humbly seek his place within it. The modern American would have to reverse the priority, asserting first of all his own autonomy and his power to establish an independent, original relationship with the universe; then he could draw unto himself whatever he found useful in the culture of the European past.

Whitman proclaimed this reversal of priority in the first paragraph of the first edition of *Leaves of Grass:*

> America [. . .] is not so impatient as has been supposed that the slough still sticks to opinions and manners and literature while the life which served its requirements has passed into the new life of the new forms ... perceives that the corpse is slowly borne from the eating and sleeping rooms of the house ... perceives that it waits a little while in the door ... that it was fittest for its days ... that its action has descended to the stalwart and wellshaped

> heir who approaches ... and that he shall be fittest for his days. (*CRE*, 707)

Some years earlier, in his own first book, *Nature,* Ralph Waldo Emerson had begun with a still more radical gesture of emancipation. He wanted to free himself and his age from a "retrospective" culture so that "we also might enjoy an original relation to the universe." To empower this deliverance from tradition, he invoked a tradition, Idealism, both in its classical platonic form and in the thought of the British and German Romantics. To establish the priority of the inspired autonomous Self, he drew a new line of demarcation, separating "I" from "Not-Me." I was consciousness; all else—"nature and art, all other men and my own body"—was Not-Me: no interpreting culture, no mediating institutions between Self and Other. He then spent the rest of his book, and the rest of his life, seeking to reconcile what he had so absolutely divided.

As Whitman in his Preface distinguished "reality" from "the soul," he embraced the same division, and with it the Romantic struggle to reunite mind and world. As yet unresolved, it is the modern struggle too: to comprehend how the human spirit dwells in the physical order, what place the solitary individual finds among the millions of our kind, and how we humans live mutually in spirit and in matter, in self-consciousness and in other-consciousness. These are not just questions for philosophers and professional readers of poetry. To ask them is to go in search for the grounds of personal and communal morale.

Early in this century, Martin Buber articulated the modern nature of that struggle, in the passage from *I and Thou* that prefaces this book:

> If ever the man shudders at [his] alienation, and the world strikes terror in his heart, he looks up (to right or left, just as it may chance) and sees a picture. There he sees that the *I* is embedded in the world and that there is really no *I* at all—so the world can do nothing to the *I,* and he is put at ease; or he sees that the world is embedded in the *I,* and that there is really no world at all—so the world can do nothing to the *I,* and he is put at ease. Another time, if the man shudders at the alienation, and the *I* strikes terror in his heart, he looks up and sees a picture, which picture he sees does not matter, the empty *I* is

stuffed full with the world or the stream of the world flows over it, and he is put at ease.[12]

First attributing modern man's sense of alienation to the absurdity of the world and then to the insatiable demand of thought, Buber traces within each the reciprocal motions, centrifugal and centripetal, that Whitman had called sympathy and pride. Although *I and Thou* is often thought of as a reflection on the relationships of the individual person, much of the book is given to exploring larger social and religious contexts that might mediate between this isolated sensibility and its seemingly hostile experience.

Although here he poises "soul" (*Seele*) against "world" (*Welt*), Buber characteristically phrased the problem not in terms of entities but of paired pronouns, "*I-It*" or "*I-Thou*." Thomas Carlyle's *Sartor Resartus*—following the example of Fichte—had phrased the agon of his proto-modern hero, Diogenes Teufelsdröckh, in terms of "Me" and "Not-Me," and Emerson adopted his terminology.[13] Whitman in his turn employed "I" and "You" self-consciously, as we will see, as he groped to define the relationship of one consciousness with another. So Buber, in his greatest book, meditated on "I" and "You" and "It" as keys to differences in human relationships. All these writers recognized that it is not things that change—not the mind, not what the mind encounters—but rather the relationships that change; and so it is appropriate to explore a world of relations through a vocabulary of relationships, a vocabulary of pronouns. In this age, the subject is always I and my doings, as Thoreau remarked on the first page of *Walden*. Everything else exists only as the object of those doings: so, Not-Me rather than Not-I.

Modern readers of Whitman, such as Harold Bloom, C. Carroll Hollis, Mitchell Robert Breitweiser, Betsy Erkkila, and Kerry Larson, have thought fruitfully about what Whitman conveys by his pronouns.[14] Throughout his life, Whitman sought for a ground on

---

12. Martin Buber, *I and Thou*, trans. Ronald Gregor Smith (New York, 1958), 71–72.

13. For Carlyle, this was a turn from "The Everlasting No" to "The Centre of Indifference" (*Sartor Resartus*, ed. Charles Frederick Harrold [New York, 1937], 157–68, 169–82). To Buber, they are just alternative forms of alienation.

14. Erkkila, *Whitman the Political Poet*, 95; Larson, *Whitman's Drama of Consensus*, 115; Harold Bloom, *The Ringers in the Tower: Studies in Romantic Tradition* (Chicago, 1971), 219; C. Carroll Hollis, *Language and Style in "Leaves of Grass"* (Baton Rouge, 1983), 94–123; Robert Mitchell Breitweiser, "Who Speaks in Whitman's Poems?" in

which to address "you," his reader, standing now within the I, now within the Not-Me. Once, in "Crossing Brooklyn Ferry," he brought the two together.

Emerson had recognized that his division between consciousness and experience might "unrealize" the splendors of nature and the sweetness of human association. In *Nature,* he spoke of the "noble doubt" that the Not-Me may not exist substantially, but only "in the apocalypse of the mind."[15] In 1836 this seemed not at all a terrible prospect, but by 1843 (in "Experience") it came to be a world-destroying solipsism: "All things swim and glitter. Our life is not so much threatened as our perception. . . . Was it Boscovich who found out that bodies never come in contact? Well, souls never touch their objects. An innavigable sea washes with silent waves between us and the things we aim at and converse with."[16] Emerson's contemporaries explored this sea—or it may be, the abyss—that divides I from Not-Me, in various postures of heroism and isolation: Thoreau at Walden, Dickinson in her "magic prison," Goodman Brown and John Marcher, Captain Ahab and the monologists of Edgar Poe.

In "Song of Myself," Whitman proclaimed his own egotism too, for it freed his poetry from bondage to social hierarchies and cultural convention. But his poems yearned always for contact between bodies, for the touch of one soul with another, for It and They, for You and We. E. Fred Carlisle's *The Uncertain Self* traces in those poems Whitman's effort to pass from the "problematic" of monologic selfhood to an identity confirmed by his dialogic relation with a "Thou"—a person in the poem or its reader.[17] Such a relation would resolve the oppositions of self and world, subject and object, that torment the I. Although, of course, the poems may negotiate these private passages, Carlisle acknowledges the "astounding and ironic" fact that the Poet of Democracy "seldom writes a poem in which he actually dramatizes the relations between the self and the many or the existence of a genuine community."[18] Certainly, the poetics of democratic individualism—like the sexual poetics that shapes many

---

The American Renaissance: New Dimensions, ed. Harry R. Garvin and Peter C. Carafiol (Lewisburg, Pa., 1983), 121–43.

15. Ralph Waldo Emerson, *Selections from Ralph Waldo Emerson,* ed. Stephen E. Whicher (Boston, 1957), 42 (hereinafter cited as *Emerson*).

16. Ibid., 255–56.

17. See, for example, Carlisle on "Crossing Brooklyn Ferry" (*The Uncertain Self,* 59–70) or on "Song of Myself" (177–204).

18. Ibid., 136.

of his poems—accommodated intimate, one-to-one dialogue more readily than communal discourse. But in volunteering as a national poet, Whitman was obliged to find an objective ground on which he could address his fellow citizens.

As C. Carroll Hollis has shown in *Language and Style in "Leaves of Grass,"* Whitman's conception of himself as poet-orator required him to address an audience explicitly identified as "you"—the plural, public "you."[19] None of the classic American writers confronted with more anxiety the cultural consequences of reducing life to subjective "experience" and private "consciousness." There was in Whitman a public self—a civil self—that could not be satisfied by the private discourse of a Poe or a Dickinson, and that sought a common ground on which he could address an imaginable readership. Folks expected that the poet would trace the path between reality and the soul. He looked for ways to affirm the reality of what he experienced and to incorporate himself with his readers upon that reality.

But because he had forsworn the mediation of social alliances and of traditional culture in order to ground his poetry on the I, Whitman frequently was beset by that Cartesian doubt of which Emerson had spoken in the passage from "Experience" quoted above. Consciousness offered him not a common ground, but rather the likelihood of his complete isolation. Both of its movements, sympathy and pride, led back to a solitary self, more truly out of the game than in it. Sympathy might become a mere feat of mind, the ego's willful imposition upon some hapless object. Out of what it took to be love, the Self might devour the World. In the line before he proclaimed "I suffered. . . . I was there," Whitman wrote, "All this I swallow and it tastes good. . . . I like it well, and it becomes mine" ("Song of Myself," §33, *V,* I, 51). For the isolated I, sympathy is a bystander's emotion, the voyeur's caress, ultimately a kind of predation.[20]

---

19. See especially Hollis' third chapter, "Speech Acts and *Leaves of Grass.*"
20. The flirtation with solipsism has been the *donnée* of much interpretation of post-Cartesian or Romantic literature. See, for example, Anderson's *The Imperial Self;* James A. W. Heffernan's *The Re-Creation of Landscape* (Hanover, N.H., 1984); Christopher Collins' *The Uses of Observation* (The Hague, 1971); and Rohn S. Friedman's "A Whitman Primer: Solipsism and Identity" (*American Quarterly,* XXVII [1975], 443–60). Even Ezra Greenspan, who describes Whitman's "attraction to the 'thisness' of the world," concludes that the poet paid a dear price for grounding his vision on "a radically subjective view of life and culture" (*Walt Whitman and the American Reader* [Cambridge, Eng., 1990], 157, 235).

If the dark consort of sympathy is power, the doppelgänger of pride is skepticism.[21] When I becomes the primary reality, then the Not-Me can easily become the Not Real. In this poem from "Calamus," when the "I" questions the appearances, a parenthetical voice assures him that only doubt is doubtless:

> Of the terrible question of appearances,
> Of the doubts, the uncertainties after all,
> That may-be reliance and hope are but speculations after all,
> That may-be identity beyond the grave is a beautiful fable only,
> May-be the things I perceive—the animals, plants, men, hills, shining and flowing waters,
> The skies of day and night—colors, densities, forms—May-be these are, (as doubtless they are,) only apparitions, and the real something has yet to be known,
> (How often they dart out of themselves, as if to confound me and mock me!
> How often I think neither I know, nor any man knows, aught of them;)
> May-be they only seem to me what they are, (as doubtless they indeed but seem,) as from my present point of view—And might prove, (as of course they would,) naught of what they appear, or naught any how, from entirely changed points of view.
> ("Of the Terrible Doubt of Appearances," *V*, II, 377)

In the next line, Whitman turns back from the abyss of alienation to the reassurance of his personal bond with a lover. But this is no resolution. Many of the other Calamus poems testify to bad faith in human relationships. As he says in another poem from the same cluster:

---

21. In this paragraph and later in this chapter, when discussing "There was a Child Went Forth," I draw on the same texts and offer readings similar to those in William Chapman Sharpe's *Unreal Cities: Urban Figuration in Wordsworth, Baudelaire, Whitman, Eliot, and Williams* (Baltimore, 1990), a study that reached me when this book was in its final draft. Although our studies of Whitman are differently directed—his toward the sexual, mine toward the civil—they do overlap at this point and also in Chapter 5, as noted there.

I, Not-Me, You, We

> Do you think the friendship of me would be unalloyed satisfaction?
> Do you suppose I am trusty and faithful?
> Do you see no further than this façade—this smooth and tolerant manner of me?
> Do you suppose yourself advancing on real ground toward a real heroic man?
> Have you no thought, O dreamer, that it may be all maya, illusion?
> ("Are You the New Person Drawn toward Me?"
> *V*, II, 382)

The skepticism that undermines the Not-Me, acting reciprocally, dissolves the I as well. When consciousness becomes self-consciousness, a mirror is held up to a mirror, and an endless regression begins, each new image of the Self accusing the previous of bad faith. In the Calamus sequence, this engulfing doubt seems to arise from Whitman's acknowledgment of his homosexuality: in some of the poems, this self-recognition brings joy; but in others it attunes him to illusions and deceptions both past and future, both public and private.[22] However, this acknowledgment is just the immediate and personal situation through which Whitman confronts the problem of duplicity and illusion endemic to absolute selfhood. In a bleak passage in the otherwise buoyant "Song of the Open Road," Whitman writes:

> Another self, a duplicate of every one, skulking and hiding it goes, open and above-board it goes,
> Formless and wordless through the streets of the cities, polite and bland in the parlors,
> In the cars of rail-roads, in steam-boats, in the public assembly,

---

22. As the many homosexual readings of Whitman's poetry have pointed out, Whitman's "prudential" defense against a homophobic society was to cloak his sexual nature in an ambiguous or even deceptive language. (See, for example, the first chapter in Robert K. Martin's *The Homosexual Tradition in American Poetry* [Austin, Tex., 1979]; Alan Helms's "'Hints . . . Faint Clews and Indirections': Whitman's Homosexual Disguises," in *Walt Whitman Here and Now*, ed. Joann P. Krieg [Westport, Conn., 1985], 61–67; and chapter 3 of M. Jimmie Killingsworth's *Whitman's Poetry of the Body: Sexuality, Politics, and the Text* [Chapel Hill, N.C., 1989].) Unlike most of these critics, I find in the Calamus poems also a theme of past self-deception and present self-doubt, a sense of unresolved conflict between his original program for an American bard and his new insight into his own sexual nature.

> Home to the houses of men and women, among their
> families, at the table, in the bed-room, everywhere,
> Smartly attired, countenance smiling, form upright,
> death under the breast-bones, hell under the skull-
> bones.
>
> (§13, V, I, 236–37)

In any poetics founded on the primary authority of the Self, what is perceived may be illusion, not reality. Efforts to disclose the spiritual world within the visible may end in proclaiming not the spiritual but merely the imaginary.

As this passage suggests, what egotistic bad faith inhibits is candid and mutual speech. Whitman always treated speech as the deliverance from isolation. To do this, however, speech cannot be thought of as the lyric expression of the I or as "direct" description of the Not-Me, for this would only perpetuate a divided and illusory world. Language must address another person, a Listener or Reader, who is able to corroborate the poet's experience by comparing it with his own.[23] In "Song of Myself," Whitman undertakes to stabilize the poem's constant fluctuation from inner to outer consciousness. He introduces a "listener," someone whom he can address as "you," and who can test independently the truth of the poet's utterance. "All I mark as my own you shall offset it with your own, / Else it were time lost listening to me" (§20, V, I, 25).[24] This "listener" may be the god whom the Romantics devised to co-sign their poetic drafts upon a correspondential universe, to guarantee the universal truth of each private vision. But for Whitman, it is also the reader, "up there" above the book he holds.[25] To be delivered from the iso-

---

23. E. Fred Carlisle uses Buber's *I-Thou* to construe in almost all of Whitman's major poems Whitman's successful address to an other, sometimes minimizing his failures of address and the times when he seems to be addressing his own projected image. Kerry C. Larson examines in great detail Whitman's poetic and rhetorical strategies for setting up this contractual relationship between writer and reader. The dialogue he depicts also is a highly private one, operating (by default, given the political disintegration of the 1850s) only within the poems. C. Carroll Hollis discovers in oratory a more public mode of address to "you." My purpose in this writing is to describe another public means Whitman used to corroborate his vision.

24. This passage, early in the poem, anticipates the later development of "you" as a distinct person.

25. See "By Blue Ontario's Shore," §15 (V, I, 206) and "So Long!" (V, II, 452). See also Friedman, "A Whitman Primer," and Paul Bové, *Destructive Poetics: Heidegger and Modern American Poetry* (New York, 1980), 131–79.

lation of I, to pass through "you" to "we," the American bard had to match his words and his reality—his Not-Me—with his reader's.

Furthermore, he must pass from the singular You to the plural. The wistful, defeated Whitman of 1860, abandoning his poems and advancing "personally" from "behind the screen where I hid," would address his reader as a lover ("Is it night? Are we here alone? / It is I you hold" ("So Long!" *V*, II, 452). Some of his poems do speak to the reader so intimately that William H. Shurr has appropriately spoken of them as sexual "seductions," and William Chapman Sharpe has shown how often the invitation is conveyed by an exchange of glances on a city street.[26] But the bardic poet must not so privatize his address. Buber describes the hollowness of a state of mind that divides private feelings ("the province of *I*") from institutional life ("the province of *It*"): "neither of them knows man: institutions know only the specimen, feelings only the 'object'; neither knows the person, or mutual life. . . . Institutions yield no public life, and feelings no personal life."[27] To foster public life, the poet must address a public audience. In Alan Trachtenberg's phrase, Whitman made no separation between poems and politics; he "played out the drama of his self . . . on the stage of otherness," addressing You the reader as "an off-setting presence."[28] At stake is not literature or aesthetics but a nation's capacity for shared imaginative life. In "A Backward Glance O'er Travel'd Roads," he wrote that "the true use for the imaginative faculty of modern times is to give ultimate vivification to facts, to science, and to common life" (*PW*, II, 716). Much earlier he had said that in verse:

> The words of poems give you more than poems,
> They give you to form for yourself poems, religions,
>   politics, war, peace, behaviour, histories, essays,
>   romances, and every thing else.
>   ("Song of the Answerer," §2, *V*, I, 143)

Through an audience's corroboration, the Matter of America (politics and histories alike, poems and behavior) might be objectified and

---

26. William H. Shurr, "Whitman and the Seduction of the Reader," *Mickle Street Review*, XI (1989), 71–79; Sharpe, *Unreal Cities*, 72–78.

27. Buber, *I and Thou*, 44. Carlisle draws from Buber his celebration of the intimate *I-Thou*, passing over both his double-edged treatment of *I-It* and his explorations, later in the book, of one's address to the community and to God.

28. Trachtenberg, "Whitman's Visionary Politics," 23.

made mutual. When, at the end of his Preface, he wrote that "the proof of a poet is that his country absorbs him as affectionately as he has absorbed it," he meant this—not being lionized like a Cambridge poet, or selling ten or twenty thousand copies a year.

Of course, neither proof was to fall within Whitman's grasp. As he wrote in his public letter to Emerson, less than a year later, "the people, like a lot of large boys, have no determined tastes" (*CRE*, 737). Many critics have pondered Whitman's failure to gain general appreciation. Jeffrey Walker has charted the perils of the American "bard," beginning with Whitman, whose "aboriginal and orphic discourse" went unheard by the mass audience he had hoped for; while Ezra Greenspan, in *Walt Whitman and the American Reader,* has shown how Whitman's career as journalist and printer encouraged and empowered him to look beyond any actual readers to an idealized reader and a "new literary culture he hoped to create for and through that reader."[29] In 1855 and 1856, Whitman might sometimes have been willing to concede that there were few actual readers whose sensibilities were truly democratic; but they constituted the readership that he imagined and addressed, and he hoped that someday they would be not the few but the mass. It was only later that he would modify his way of writing poetry to accommodate the actual taste of his time.

Nor did Whitman approach his task with any naïve confidence in the power of poetry to evoke a mutually credible world. From the outset, he was troubled by the gap between language and reality. "Speech is the twin of my vision," he said in "Song of Myself"; but he continued, "it is unequal to measure itself. / It provokes me forever" (§25, *V,* I, 35). Words expand insight for poet and for reader; but because they never fully express it, the gap between I and Not-Me is never altogether closed.

> There is that in me .... I do not know what it is .... but I know it is in me.
> [. . .] I do not know it .... it is without name .... it is a word unsaid,
> It is not in any dictionary or utterance or symbol.
> ("Song of Myself," §50, *V,* I, 81)

---

29. Walker, *Bardic Ethos,* 32; Greenspan, *American Reader,* 110.

"Do you see O my brothers and sisters?" he pleads; but the finale of "Song of Myself," shifting to images of future time and of endless pilgrimage, suggests that the path between the soul and reality may be long and dimly marked.

Further, for all his demand for immediate contact with his experience and with his reader, he was dependent on an instrument, language, that was effective only insofar as it had been made communal by a tradition of usage. Tenney Nathanson has observed Whitman's uneasiness with a simply "representational" theory of language that depends on custom and social agreement: words of that sort could give you only surfaces, illusions.[30] The poet well understood the mediate nature of language: he compiled vocabulary lists, wrote a pamphlet on the history of the American language, and in the 1855 Preface endorsed English as the medium of "American expression" on philological grounds: "On the tough stock of a race who through all change of circumstances was never without the idea of political liberty, which is the animus of all liberty, it has attracted the terms of daintier and gayer and subtler and more elegant tongues. It is the powerful language of resistance ... it is the dialect of common sense" (*CRE*, 727–28). Yet, even as he recognized the dependence of language on a traditionary culture, he exhorted himself: "Poet! beware lest your poems are made in the spirit that comes from the study of pictures of things—and not from the spirit that comes from the contact with real things the[m]selves" (*N*, IV, 1569). "Poems distilled from other poems pass away," he said in "By Blue Ontario's Shore" (§13, *V*, I, 203); but he knew the difficulty—the impossibility—involved in making words refer to reality rather than to poems and pictures; in using words to convey the thing itself rather than ideas about things.[31]

To his contemporaries, he often seemed to have created that sense of immediacy. "It is as if the beasts spoke," Thoreau wrote in 1856 of *Leaves of Grass*.[32] But he continued shrewdly, "If we are shocked, whose experience is it that we are reminded of?" Our own, of course. The "tally" not only must match Whitman's words with re-

---

30. Tenney Nathanson, "Whitman's Tropes of Light and Flood: Language and Representation in the Early Editions of *Leaves of Grass*," *ESQ*, XXXI (1985), 117, 126–27.

31. See Chase, *Walt Whitman Reconsidered*, 94–96.

32. Henry David Thoreau, *The Correspondence of Henry David Thoreau*, ed. Walter Harding and Carl Bode (New York, 1958), 444–45.

ality, but also with his reader's experience of reality. The reader who can offset Whitman's experience with his own must be one who has learned how artistic images can be made to tally with experience—one who has studied pictures and perused other poems. Between the inherent significance of objects and the inborn sensitivity of human subjects, words are a necessarily conventional medium, conductors of the flash of insight that would make I and Not-Me one. So Whitman required the American "poet" to pass over, from words as tokens of an inner and possibly solipsistic consciousness, to words as indicators of substantive beings:

> My words are words of a questioning, and to indicate reality;
> This printed and bound book .... but the printer and the printing-office boy?
> The marriage estate and settlement .... but the body and mind of the bridegroom? also those of the bride?
> The panorama of the sea .... but the sea itself?
> The well-taken photographs .... but your wife or friend close and solid in your arms?
> ("Song of Myself," §42, *V*, I, 67–68)

This passage approaches each "reality" through a cultural intermediary, books and documents, panoramas and photographs. As Paul Zweig and Ezra Greenspan have pointed out, Whitman was at once a great experimental poet and a journalist who knew the reading public: as Zweig put it, Whitman was a "semi-cultivated newspaperman" whose voice passes, again and again, from high poetry to a flat vernacular.[33] Being the American bard, he found, was no simple matter. The modern demand for immediacy—the unmediated vision, the contact of poet with reader, the renunciation of the past, the abrogation of partisan point of view—all confronted him with a dissolving "America," an unstable Self, an unruly language, and an indeterminate audience. This was well enough for a high poet, an Emerson or a Dickinson. But Whitman's platform called for ready passage between reality and the soul, for routes of access between poet and nation. He frequently addressed this need by appealing to a common body of "indirect" visual experience: to a pictorial world

---

33. Paul Zweig, *Walt Whitman: The Making of the Poet* (New York, 1984), 115–16; Greenspan, *American Reader*, 39–88.

familiar to his readers through political oratory or through mechanical reproduction, printing, and engraving; or to sight itself, made self-conscious by the advent of photography. For the audience that he was trying to create, seeing was still believing.

Given his lifelong search for a "listener," it may seem more appropriate for Whitman to have turned to cultural mediators founded on voice. Indeed he did. Kerry Larson's study shows just how often Whitman drew upon rhetorical modes to join the poet with his auditor, and C. Carroll Hollis has traced Whitman's stylistic debt to nineteenth-century oratory. Tenney Nathanson argues that it is the performative power of voice in which Whitman puts his faith, to deliver us into his actual presence.[34] Song summons the poet out of a phase of egoistic isolation near the middle of "Song of Myself." The drama of "Out of the Cradle Endlessly Rocking" springs from the boy's ecstatic response to the bird's operatic song; and in that poem's lesser twin, the elegy for Lincoln, the thrush's carol brings the poet to a visionary acceptance of death.[35] Such predominantly aural experiences, though, seem usually to issue in intensely felt personal insight or union, rather than in a bard's invocation of the Matter of America, addressed to his teeming nation of nations.[36] Rather, Whitman turned repeatedly to rhetorical evocations of a visual or pictorial world as a way of twinning his vision with that of his readers and so invoking a substantive reality in which both could believe.

❖

The world of sight, rather than of speech, was his source of metaphor when in the 1855 Preface he spoke of the poet, in his repre-

34. Nathanson, "Whitman's Tropes," 125–30.

35. For Whitman's use of an auditory metaphor for the faith between poet and audience, see "Song of the Answerer" (*V*, I, 137–43). This is the poem from which Larson's book begins.

36. To explain Whitman's "visionary politics," Trachtenberg studies "the several versions and uses of the eyesight, tropes of vision," in *Democratic Vistas* ("Whitman's Visionary Politics," 24). And Graham Clarke says: "By focusing . . . on Whitman's sense (and use) of the picture and the technology of sight basic to his poetic method we see emerging both his response to his contemporary America . . . and the kind of self he constructs in the poetry: a visual persona which rides history in its search for an ideal representation" ("'To emanate a look': Whitman, Photography and the Spectacle of Self," in *American Literary Landscapes: The Fiction and the Fact,* ed. Ian F. A. Bell and D. K. Adams [London, 1988], 79–80). Clarke's valuable article concentrates on what Whitman depicts and on the implications of the Whitman portraits, whereas I am concerned more with how seeing itself is represented.

sentative and public capacity, as a man of faith: "As he sees the farthest he has the most faith. [. . .] He sees eternity in men and women ... he does not see men and women as dreams or dots. Faith is the antiseptic of the soul ... it pervades the common people and preserves them ... they never give up believing and expecting and trusting." The poet may be beset by the terrible question of appearances; experience may threaten to dissolve into flashes on the retina or solipsistic dreams. But in union with the common people of America, he keeps faith in a visible—and yet a visionary—world. In phrases that seem conned from Emerson's "The Poet," he continues:

> The greatest poet hardly knows pettiness or triviality. If he breathes into any thing that was before thought small it dilates with the grandeur and life of the universe. He is a seer ... he is individual ... he is complete in himself ... the others are as good as he, only he sees it and they do not. He is not one of the chorus ... he does not stop for any regulations ... he is the president of regulation. What the eyesight does to the rest he does to the rest. Who knows the curious mystery of the eyesight? The other senses corroborate themselves, but this is removed from any proof but its own and foreruns the identities of the spiritual world. A single glance of it mocks all the investigations of man and all the instruments and books of the earth and all reasoning. (*CRE*, 713–14)

Here Whitman makes two points. First is the poet's visionary power to discern the marvelous in the commonplace.[37] This aesthetic doctrine Whitman shared with his Romantic predecessors like Blake, Wordsworth, and Emerson. For all of them, especially the Americans, it was part of a political program to democratize literature by demystifying its subjects and so, they hoped, making them recognizable and accessible to a wider, less exclusively educated, readership. Whitman here claims (as had Emerson) that this discernment is not the poet's unique gift but rather a power common to all men and women—active in the poet, latent in them but capable of development if stimulated by a true, egalitarian poet. Midnineteenth-century American writers felt especially the need to demystify liter-

---

37. See Waggoner's *American Visionary Poetry* for a discussion of this power in the American poets descended from Whitman: Crane, Williams, Roethke, Ammons, and Wagoner.

ature and to broaden its audience, because America lacked a cultured leisure class to patronize the arts.[38] They believed that a mass audience would prefer familiar, native subjects—which the esthetics of the time discounted as lacking artistic possibilities. What Whitman and his midcentury peers sought to do was to render inherent what heretofore had been treated as acquired: artistic significance was the innate glory in things, rather than an honor bestowed by tradition and social agreement; and aesthetic sensitivity an inborn faculty rather than a consequence of education.[39]

Whitman's poetics of the commonplace had just such an egalitarian political implication. It is just a few lines later in the Preface when he writes that "folks expect of the poet to indicate more than the beauty and dignity which always attach to dumb real objects .... they expect him to indicate the path between reality and their souls"; and he continues, "Men and women perceive the beauty well enough .. probably as well as he. [. . .] They can never be assisted by poets to perceive ... some may but they never can. The poetic quality is not marshalled in rhyme or uniformity or abstract addresses to things nor in melancholy complaints or good precepts, but is the life of these and much else and is in the soul" (*CRE,* 714). His faith in the infinite artistic resources of "dumb real objects" ("I believe a leaf of grass is no less than the journeywork of the stars") corresponds to a faith in the aesthetic resourcefulness of ordinary men and women ("what I assume you shall assume, / For every atom belonging to me as good belongs to you"); and both rest on a faith in the physical and spiritual vitality of a godly cosmos ("In the faces of men and women I see God [. . .] / I find letters from God dropped in the street") (§31, 1, 48, *V,* I, 41, 1, 79).

Whitman's second point is that eyesight is at once the ideal symbol of his faith and the favored medium by which the poet discovers the path between reality and his own soul, and communicates it to folks:

---

38. David S. Reynolds, in *Beneath the American Renaissance* (New York, 1988), considers the many connections between the "high" literature and the popular culture of Whitman's time. His chapter on Whitman emphasizes the poet's familiarity with, and contributions to, the sensational press of that era.

39. In Emerson's view, these two contentions are metaphysically linked: the divine spirit that is the human soul (that is, the I) discerns the divine spirit that is also within all things (that is, the Not-Me) and intuitively knows its meaning. See *Nature,* 4.2 (*Emerson,* 32), and also "The Poet" (*Emerson,* 233). In Emerson's more solipsistic phases, the soul simply projects meaning onto the objects of its imagination (*Nature,* 6.2 [*Emerson,* 44]).

> What the eyesight does to the rest [*i.e.*, other people] he does to the rest. Who knows the curious mystery of the eyesight? The other senses corroborate themselves, but this is removed from any proof but its own and foreruns the identities of the spiritual world. A single glance of it mocks all the investigations of man and all the instruments and books of the earth and all reasoning. What is marvellous? what is unlikely? what is impossible or baseless or vague? after you have once just opened the space of a peachpit and given audience to far and near and to the sunset and had all things enter with electric swiftness softly and duly without confusion or jostling or jam.
> (*CRE*, 714)

Vision is one of the most natural of metaphors for spiritual discernment. Whitman's moment of ecstatic inspiration early in "Song of Myself" uses other senses—sound and erotic touch—but it culminates as a throb of hyperacute vision in which the myriads of Not-Me stand before the I in their individuated presences:

> And limitless are leaves, stiff or drooping in the fields,
> And brown ants in the little wells beneath them;
> And mossy scabs of the wormfence, and heaped stones,
>   and elder and mullen and pokeweed.
> ("Song of Myself," §5, *V*, I, 6)

However natural or traditional it may have been to identify physical sight with spiritual revelation, the poets of the nineteenth century were loathe to grant that identification unreservedly. Wordsworth's caution against the tyranny of the eye, Blake's resolve to see through, not with the eye—these are touchstones for the many critical studies of the powers of the Romantic eye. As we have seen, the eye separates consciousness from reality, leaving the poet either the slave of mere perception (like Thoreau in his last years) or a spectator inside a magic lantern of correspondences (like Emily Dickinson, like Theodore Roethke). And for twentieth-century criticism, obedient to the dicta of Sartre and then Lacan, it is axiomatic that eyesight reifies the object and alienates the subject. But perhaps that is only a French way of looking at things.

In *The Unmediated Vision*, Geoffrey Hartman discusses the longing of modern consciousness—when deprived of faith in the mediating power of Christ's incarnation—to be assured nevertheless of the reality of its experience. Can some other mediator be found to assure continuity between body and mind, between one mind and another? Hartman argues that "true knowledge," the identification of mind with object, can be attained only through an "intuition . . . that an identical power sustains knower and known"; and that "an account of perception in terms of direct contact would have been of the greatest importance in bridging the gap between sense experience and perfect knowledge." Berkeley approached such an account, in recognizing that a mechanistic explanation of sensation cannot suffice; but he had nothing else to offer except an appeal to God's providential intervention between matter and mind. Hartman, reading Valéry, concludes that the power that will restore the physical world to our imaginations is "perception desired and experienced as the plenary manifestation of a creative presence."[40]

Eyesight, for Whitman, is just such a creative power, doing for men and women just what the poet would do for them. Berkeley's ideas about vision—if he knew them at all—he might have encountered as the still-common wisdom on that subject, conned from some piece of journalism or heard in a lecture hall. Nevertheless, in the passage quoted above, he is straining toward such an understanding of vision as that articulated by Hartman. It is physical as can be, founded on two organs each "the space of a peachpit."[41] Yet through them the whole physical world enters the mind "without confusion," the many becoming one. A commonplace miracle when considered just as sensation, sight becomes even more marvelous when linked with intelligence, for it elicits our recognition of realities that are unmediated by direct physical contact.

Nineteenth-century philosophers and physiologists were searching for ways to resolve Berkeley's dilemma about the relation be-

40. See Geoffrey Hartman, *The Unmediated Vision: An Interpretation of Wordsworth, Hopkins, Rilke and Valéry* (New Haven, Conn., 1954), 150–53. Hyatt Waggoner, comparing Wordsworth and Whitman, says that for both "the world within the mind is blended with the world outside the mind" (*American Visionary Poetry*, 32) through a religious vision of nature that Waggoner relates to Whitehead's idea of God (180–81).

41. An early notebook of Whitman's contains a draft of this passage: "I open two pairs of lids, only as big as peach pits, when lo! the unnamable variety and whelming splendor of the whole world come to me with silence and with swiftness.—In an instant make I fluid and draw to myself, keeping each to its distinct isolation, and no hubbub or confusion, or jam, the whole of physical nature, though rocks are dense and hills are ponderous, and the stars are away off sextillions of miles" (*N*, I, 106–107).

tween eyesight and touch: in what way is there "contact" between the object and the eye? how does touch instruct and correct eyesight?[42] "The other senses corroborate themselves" through some mediating contact between subject and object. But vision, "removed from any proof but its own," conveys its image of reality over long ranges, immediately. Thus it "foreruns the identities of the spiritual world": as mental image is identified with physical sensation, so image can be twinned with idea in a world entirely spiritual. In "Song of the Open Road," published the following year, Whitman affirmed again his faith in the identity of the spiritual and the material, as mediated by the eyesight:

> Wisdom is of the soul, is not susceptible of proof, is its
>   own proof,
> Applies to all stages and objects and qualities, and is
>   content,
> Is the certainty of the reality and immortality of things,
>   and the excellence of things,
> Something there is in the float of the sight of things that
>   provokes it out of the soul.
>
> (§6, *V*, I, 230)

Trusting in our eyes is trusting in the indefinite extension of a miracle. Bringing the far-off Not-Me into the orbit of the I, recognizing the same creative power in each, and discerning God's name embroidered in the corners of grass and pokeweed, seeing is indeed believing—just as folks had said.[43]

And the power of vision is not only creative; it is communicative. What the eyesight does is what the poet does. Summoning up,

---

42. Examples are John Stuart Mill, Johannes Müller, and Hermann von Helmholtz, among others. See Nicholas Pastore, *A Selective History of Theories of Visual Perception, 1650–1950* (New York, 1971), 128–43; and Helmholtz, "Recent Progress in the Theory of Vision," in *Selected Writings*, ed. Russell Kahl (Middletown, Conn., 1971), 196–203. See George Berkeley, "An Essay Towards a New Theory of Vision," §50, 51, 59 (*Works on Vision*, ed. Colin M. Turbayne [Indianapolis, 1963], 41–42, 45–46.

43. Larson notes, briefly, the implications of this passage: "Sight is . . . called forth as that supreme source of acknowledgment, insusceptible to disconfirmation precisely because it tolerates no gap between what it sees and what it confirms. Seeing is believing" (*Whitman's Drama of Consensus,* 125). Waggoner, apropos of "Song of Myself," says that "attentive, receptive, literal *seeing* (not 'scrutinizing') has led to belief, and such belief in turn leads to a further stage of imaginative 'seeing'" (*American Visionary Poetry,* 50–51).

through words, images of the quotidian visible world, he can reveal its marvelousness and so bind himself to his reader in a common faith—a faith in things, a faith in ordinary human faculties like vision, imagination, and language. Whitman had said a paragraph earlier in the Preface, "The time straying toward infidelity and confections and persiflage he withholds by his steady faith [. . .]. As he sees the farthest he has the most faith." He continues: "His thoughts are the hymns of the praise of things. In the talk on the soul and eternity and God off of his equal plane he is silent. He sees eternity less like a play with a prologue and denouement ... he sees eternity in men and women ... he does not see men and women as dreams or dots. Faith is the antiseptic of the soul ... it pervades the common people and preserves them ... they never give up believing and expecting and trusting" (*CRE*, 713). I, the poet, and You, the reader, are incorporated into the American communion of individuals through a secular faith in a fund of visual images called into the mind through language. In his poetry, Whitman was seldom fully the equal of this heroic challenge. Often he finds himself confined to a subjectivized private vision; at other times he surrenders to the givenness of sensation and of the conventional ways of reporting it. But in some passages and in a few poems, resorting to "indirect" forms of mediation, he reveals an incorporative visual world.

❖

"This is the city," said Walt Whitman; "and I am one of the citizens; / Whatever interests the rest interests me" ("Song of Myself," §42, *V*, I, 67). It is commonplace to describe Whitman as the first (perhaps the premier) poet of the American city. As we will see in the central chapters of this study, there is good reason to do so. But the city and urban life confronted Whitman with a severe challenge to his ambitions to be America's bard. The adventurous life on the frontier and the bucolic virtues of the farm had already established their ethos in American culture, along with appropriate modes of artistic representation. James Fenimore Cooper and the writers of the old Southwest had immortalized the rude but noble frontiersman; Crevecoeur, Irving, and Whittier had romanticized the husbandman; the Hudson River painters, the Luminists, and the humbler artists of engraving and lithograph had established the painterly image of the American countryside. But the city remained invisible. Benjamin Franklin had used it as the stage for his New World version of the legend of the Successful Apprentice; and George Lippard had transformed Philadelphia into a gothic menace in *The Quaker City*. There were painted and engraved "views" of every metropolis. But little in American literature and painting suggested the dynamic and complex presence of expanding cities in the midnineteenth-century American landscape. To turn from the rural world to the life of cities was like abandoning the comfortable literary traditions of Europe for the unformulated possibilities of America. What was there to see? how to see it? how to say what you saw?

But the bard of egalitarian consciousness cannot be one whose vision is confined to the countryside or whose poetic resources are inapt for rendering city life. "Song of Myself" leaps effortlessly from rural to urban scenes:

> The machinist rolls up his sleeves .... the policeman
>   travels his beat .... the gate-keeper marks who pass,
> The young fellow drives the express-wagon .... I love
>   him though I do not know him;
> The half-breed straps on his light boots to compete in
>   the race,
> The western turkey-shooting draws old and young ....
>   some lean on their rifles, some sit on logs,
> Out from the crowd steps the marksman and takes his
>   position and levels his piece;
> The groups of newly-come immigrants cover the wharf
>   or levee.
>
> (§15, *V*, I, 16–17)

But this ease of passage is accomplished by keeping attention focused on the consciousness through which these pictures flash. They are simply mental images, altogether the possession of the Self. So long as they pass rapidly across the mind, the I need not acknowledge them as presences, as Not-Me. When the attention lingers, though, the differing qualities of each locale must be acknowledged. The machinist and the driver and the shopgirl form a city, and the city forms them. And their life is not like that of trapper and milkmaid. Some of Whitman's poems are formed upon the juxtaposition of city and country life. "Give Me the Splendid Silent Sun," from *Drum-Taps* (1865), reveals that the characteristics of urban life aggravated those difficulties that Whitman found inherent in the democratic poet's task.

In this poem, Whitman sets city against country to argue a political issue of the Civil War, and the political question raises an aesthetic one. The poem confronts the war-weariness of 1863 and 1864, when a peace party was urging a truce with the Confederacy so that the Union could turn its energies to the agricultural resources of the West. Whitman, himself divided between pressing the war's righteous cause and putting an end to the slaughter, opens his poem with a rhetorical gambit: he states the best case for making peace. He summons up the American agrarian paradise:

> Give me the splendid silent sun, with all his beams full-dazzling;
> Give me juicy autumnal fruit, ripe and red from the orchard;
> Give me a field where the unmow'd grass grows;
> Give me an arbor, give me the trellis'd grape;
> Give me fresh corn and wheat—give me serene-moving animals, teaching content.
>
> (§1, *V*, II, 497)

And so, Whitman paints country life with all the enhanced coloration prepared by seventy-five years of American Romanticism. Then he sweeps it all away, as a mere dream of those "tired with ceaseless excitement, and rack'd by the war-strife." In its place he sets an image of city life, in which the anxieties of war do not seem discordant:

> Give me faces and streets! give me these phantoms incessant and endless along the trottoirs!
> Give me interminable eyes! give me women! give me comrades and lovers by the thousand!
> Let me see new ones every day! let me hold new ones by the hand every day!
> Give me such shows! give me the streets of Manhattan!
> Give me Broadway, with the soldiers marching—give me the sound of the trumpets and drums!
> [. . .]
> The dense brigade, bound for the war, with high piled military wagons following;

> People, endless, streaming, with strong voices, passions,
>   pageants;
> Manhattan streets, with their powerful throbs, with the
>   beating drums, as now;
> The endless and noisy chorus, the rustle and clank of
>   muskets, (even the sight of the wounded;)
> Manhattan crowds with their turbulent musical
>   chorus—with varied chorus and light of the sparkling
>   eyes;
> Manhattan faces and eyes forever for me.
>
> (§2, *V,* II, 498–99)

Rather than endorsing directly the cause of continued war, Whitman turns from rural life to the city. For the harmony of the pastoral myth is achieved unrealistically, by acknowledging only features of peace, whereas heterodox New York City can assimilate the war as part of its intense and ever-changing spectacle.[44] (Also, this turn implicitly rejects the agricultural South for the urban North, the agrarian past in favor of a commercial and industrial future.)

But Whitman is not just arguing against the Copperheads. He is also waging a revolution against the poetic resources of his heretofore pastoral culture.[45] He draws together the materials for a new artistic schema, using the stuff that pastoralism had found repugnant: streets . . . crowds . . . faces . . . noise. This is a true revolution, Have-Not against Have. Pitted against the lavishly sensuous opening lines of his poem, Whitman's endorsement of his city has little except exclamatory fervor. The serenity of his rural landscape outpromises

---

44. A noncombatant, Whitman experienced the war mainly in its urban guises: parades, politics, manufactures, munitions, transport, hospitals. See "First O Songs for a Prelude," "Beat! Beat! Drums!," "City of Ships," and "How Solemn as One by One." See Chapter 3. In the summer and fall of 1864, while the peace Democrats contested Lincoln's presidency, Whitman was in New York recuperating from his hospital service in Washington.

45. Richard Chase (*Walt Whitman Reconsidered*, 78–80) and James L. Machor ("Pastoralism and the American Urban Ideal: Hawthorne, Whitman, and the Literary Pattern," *American Literature*, LIV [1982], 333) argue that, in "Give Me the Splendid Silent Sun" and elsewhere, Whitman is assimilating the city into an essentially pastoral vision. On the contrary: he is opening a breach between them that is not only aesthetic but epistemological. Bové says: "The poet not only testifies to man's being present in the world, but 'he places himself where the future becomes present,' at the point where 'sight' and 'eyes' are retrieved from metaphysics and coercion. In other words, the poet lives on the verge, on the boundary between what-is and has been within life and tradition and what is not yet" (*Destructive Poetics,* 147).

the city's novelty and excitement. Country life is rich with specific adjectival detail, whereas the city cannot muster an intensity of vocabulary to affirm its intensity of life. Further, and most tellingly, the countryside offers substantive things, each seen in its own integrity of being: sun, fruit, orchard, grass, woman, child. In the city we meet not substance but appearance: shows, pageants, theatrics. Integral beings are displaced by fragments and surfaces—by streets, faces, and eyes; by "phantoms."

The city is a world of phantoms. For Whitman, this term, akin to "fantasy," commonly denotes a revenant, an event yet to come or a spiritual being such as a muse. But in his urban poems, it refers to ordinary men and women—casting on them a special significance that is linked to his sense of the dissociation of the Self from its world, expressed in some of the Calamus poems quoted above. In a drafted poem, never finished, which extends the Calamus mood into the early war years, Whitman made this significance clear. He describes himself seated in the vaulted cellar of Pfaff's restaurant on Broadway. He compares the cellar to a vaulted tomb, as he looks out at the flood of life around him and on the street above:

> The thick crowds, well-dressed—the continual crowds
>   as if they would never end
> The curious appearance of the faces—the glimpses first
>   caught of the eyes and expressions, as they flit along.
> (You phantoms! oft I pause, yearning, to arrest some one
>   of you!
> Oft I doubt your reality [whether] you are real—I
>   suspect all is but a pageant.
>
>   (N, I, 455)

Amid the crowds and wares of the city, cut off from the support of a communal ethos (such as that which sustained the rural poets like Whittier), Whitman was most profoundly struck by his Cartesian doubt: maybe the things one perceives are only apparitions (as doubtless they are). Deprived of reality, they become phantoms or shams, solid only on the side that the viewer sees.[46] These are the egotists he addressed in "Song of the Open Road," who walk form-

---

46. Even in the crowds hasting over Fulton Ferry, Whitman said in an editorial, "you get a swift view of the phantom-like semblance of humanity, as it is sometimes seen in dreams" (*The Gathering of the Forces,* ed. Cleveland Rodgers and John Black [New York, 1920], II, 161).

less and wordless through the streets of the city, urbane pageant figures with hell under their skull bones. Baudelaire and Whitman were contemporaries.

The experience of the street—the dissociated life of the man in the crowd—is for Whitman the epitome of democratic consciousness.[47] This man is the individual standing over against the All. He can meet it only with the resources of his own imagination. In the face of its unsorted and unsortable variety, "Sympathy" is quickly spent, "Pride" reduced to narcissism. Consciousness of reality yields to Self-consciousness. The urban spectacle forces Whitman to recognize the insubstantiality of his "experience" and to ask whether a world of mind (I) and a world of fact (Not-Me) can indeed be reconciled. Is there truly a path between reality and the soul? a bridge of words from one soul to another, from I to You? The more intense the city's "show," the more keenly Whitman felt the alienation of the experiencer, the spectator.[48]

Whitman shaped this doubt of appearances and of Self into a contrast of country and city in an important short poem in the first edition of *Leaves of Grass*, "There was a Child Went Forth" (*V*, I, 149–52). This poem epitomizes the entire journey of consciousness in Whitman's poetic scheme, from engagement to withdrawal to a renewed confidence in reality founded on a faith in the power of words to transmit a visual experience. Like "Give Me the Splendid Silent Sun," this poem begins amid the comfortably substantial beings of the rural world:

> There was a child went forth every day,
> And the first object he looked upon and received with
>   wonder or pity or love or dread, that object he
>   became,

---

47. Thomas, *Lunar Light*, 155, 161. Thomas' ideology obliges him to treat Whitman's early euphoria for city life as strained by adverse economic and social forces after 1860; but in the first edition of *Leaves of Grass*, Whitman already is dramatizing both the possibilities and the terrors of urban consciousness. William Chapman Sharpe (*Unreal Cities*), linking Blake, Baudelaire, and Whitman with more recent poets, conceives their common experience of alienation—the felt gap between Self and Other—not as a consequence of democratization but of modernity, for which the city is likewise the epitome.

48. "From the deep, secure observatory of the self, the observer looks out at his body and its futile commerce with the world and then, as Emerson wrote, 'oversees himself.' Thus art becomes a way to deal with external reality, to subject it, *as phenomena*, to the dominion of the transcendent self" (Collins, *The Uses of Observation*, 121).

> And that object became part of him for the day or a
> certain part of the day .... or for many years or
> stretching cycles of years.

> The early lilacs became part of this child,
> And grass, and white and red morningglories, and
> white and red clover, and the song of the phoebe-
> bird.

However, consciousness has already begun to prey upon this innocence. The child's powers of vision and of sympathy make him one with reality, but reality in fact thus becomes "part of him." Advancing through his rural springtime, the child goes from total absorption in nature to an awareness of human beings—strangers and passing schoolchildren—and then to recognition of the particular personalities of his parents (the father "mean, angered, unjust"; the mother "quietly placing the dishes on the suppertable"). But just when the child and the poem are entering into socialized consciousness, self-consciousness arises, and in just the hesitation of an ellipsis the "real" world is reduced to "unreal" phantoms—to "flashes and specks."

> The family usages, the language, the company, the
> furniture .... the yearning and swelling heart,
> Affection that will not be gainsayed .... The sense of
> what is real .... the thought if after all it should prove
> unreal,
> The doubts of daytime and the doubts of nighttime ...
> the curious whether and how,
> Whether that which appears so is so .... Or is it all
> flashes and specks?
> Men and women crowding fast in the streets .. if they
> are not flashes and specks what are they?

So the poem arrives in the unsheltered spaces of the city—streets, facades, shopwindows, wharves, and ferries—numbed by an alienating sense of their inaccessibility. It is as if the maturing child had been cast back into earliest infancy. How does the mind discern continuity in the "flashes and specks" of light that play upon the retina? How can we winnow essence from experience and call it by name, a name that You, the reader, can recognize? (The poet, we were told in the Preface, is the man of faith; he does not see men and women as dreams or dots.[49])

Whitman does not directly answer these poem-destroying skepticisms, but proceeds with a detailed description of sunset over a city's harbor:

> Vehicles .. teams .. the tiered wharves, and the huge
>   crossing at the ferries;
> The village on the highland seen from afar at sunset ....
>   the river between,
> Shadows .. aureola and mist .. light falling on roofs and
>   gables of white or brown, three miles off[.]

Then Whitman ends the poem as he had begun it:

> These became part of that child who went forth every
>   day, and who now goes and will always go forth
>   every day,
> And these become of him or her that peruses them now.

The poem's final assertion is more daring than its first, for now Whitman drafts the reader into that bond of sympathy that earlier he had created between the boy and his experience. As the child once engulfed his world, so now the reader is to engulf the poem about the child, including the "doubts of night" about the reality and reliability of the Self, and the "doubts of day" that would render experience altogether private, sympathy an act of aggression, and language a blind-man's-buff.

But Whitman's poem somehow has crossed over from doubt to faith, a faith in the imagination's ability to construe truthfully the play of light upon the optic nerves, a faith in the poet's power to translate that construction into words, a faith in the reader's ability to replicate the process in reverse order. And the ground of this faith is visual. Eyesight, removed from any proof but its own, foreruns the identities of the spiritual world. Eyesight, the predator of all it looks upon; eyesight, the connoisseur's sense; eyesight yet has somehow the power to bind the poet with reality and to link him with his

---

49. *CRE*, 713. Larson speaks of this poem as an "idyll" "untouched by nostalgia for a lost harmony" (*Whitman's Drama of Consensus*, 130); but William Sharpe, more acutely, remarks that these lines "open up a phantom world dissolving his apparently substantial cities, a kind of Cartesian enchantment" ("City/Body/Text: Walt Whitman's Urban Incarnation," *Cycnos* [Nice], I [1984], 44).

reader. Before the mystical insights about the divinity in the grass, before the ecstatic discovery of God in the faces of men and women, an image from the common miracle of eyesight goes as forerunner. Metaphysics only confirms what the eye has already discovered. In "There was a Child Went Forth," Whitman first dramatizes the child's burgeoning confidence in the power and accuracy of his senses; then introduces into this paradise the serpent of doubt about those senses and the seeming world they project; and then, finally, resolves the child's doubt with another visual image and, passing from singular to plural, objectifies and communicates his vision. The individualist strain in his poetics necessitates the doubt; and yet the nationalist strain—the need to speak for all America—requires that the doubt be overcome. But by what sleight of words?

PART I

The World in the Self, the Self in the World

> A spinner is spinning the orbits of all stars and the life of all creation and the history of the universe, everything is woven on one thread, and is no longer called stars and creation and universe, but sensations and imaginings, or even experiences, and conditions of the soul. And beneath the row of pictures is written: "One and all."
> —Martin Buber, *I and Thou*

> With the twirl of my tongue I encompass worlds and volumes of worlds.
> —"Song of Myself," §25

[2]

The Expanse of Consciousness

It would seem that the words have an easier time when their mimetic function is inward rather than outward; when they hold up a mirror to the activity of the mind rather than to nature; when, as Buber would say, the world is embedded in the I. In an apprentice poem whose imagery foreruns Buber's portrait of modern man, Whitman wrote:

> In a little house pictures I keep, many pictures hanging
>   suspended—It is not a fixed house,
> It is round—it is but a few inches from one side of it to
>   the other side,
> But behold! it has room enough—in it, hundreds and
>   thousands,—all the varieties;
> —Here! do you know this? This is cicerone himself;
> And here, see you, my own States—and here the world
>   itself, bowling / rolling through the air;
> And there, on the walls hanging, portraits of women
>   and men, carefully kept.
>   ("Pictures," *CRE,* 642)

In the six score lines that follow, Whitman carefully describes a series of "pictures" hanging in the gallery inside his skull, some of them personal memories, but most of them depictions of scenes or events or personages from world history or American history, briefly noted and randomly arranged. In this very early poem, seeing is not the opening of a passage between reality and the soul or between I and You. Rather, it has been turned into a commodity that can be gloatingly hoarded: "such pictures have I—and they are but little. / For wherever I have been, has afforded me superb pictures" (*CRE,* 648–

49). And within the gallery stands the collector, its "cicerone," ready to point out his treasures and comment on them.

And among the "views"—standing between a Boston truckman and "melancholy Dante" and Shakespeare:

> Who is this, with rapid feet, curious, gay—going up and down Mannahatta, through the streets, along the shores, working his way through the crowds, observant and singing?
>
> (*CRE*, 645)

Who but Whitman himself?—one of the roughs and yet cheek and jowl with Dante and Shakespeare. Within the poet's brain-gallery stands both the poet as cicerone and the poet portrayed as a sketchbook artist, for whom every moment is potentially a picture. Even before "Song of Myself," Whitman recognized the seductive recessions of self-consciousness: this is the Self who stands apart from the pulling and hauling, out of the game; this is a portrait of the Self who stands apart; this is the Self who portrays the Self who stands apart.

Although Whitman had no intention of being caught in such a recession, the Matter of America was founded on democratic consciousness: a national poet would have to celebrate both the objects of consciousness and its heroic power to absorb all things, including itself. The 1855 Preface announced, first thing, that the United States themselves are the greatest poem, and supported this claim with an inventory of the behavior of the American people, all instances of "unrhymed poetry." But these gave way, at once, to the American poet, one "commensurate" with that people, one who "encloses" his country and "incarnates" its geography. Then began the first visual catalog in *Leaves of Grass*: "On him rise solid growths that offset the growths of pine and cedar and hemlock and liveoak [. . .] and tangles as tangled as any canebrake or swamp .... and forests coated with transparent ice and icicles hanging from the boughs and crackling in the wind .... and sides and peaks of mountains .... and pasturage sweet and free as savannah or upland or prairie." (*CRE*, 711). So the poet becomes America, the landmarks of his inner life indistinguishable from the housed images of his experience. Within the galleries of the mind, the cicerone leads his visitor from landscape to portrait to history, each visual detail stimulating some personal sentiment, some public reflection.

The Expanse of Consciousness

Tours of such inward museums were a commonplace of nineteenth-century American poems by such writers as Bryant ("Green River"), Longfellow ("My Lost Youth"), and Whittier ("Snow-Bound"). As explorations of intense personal feeling, they looked back to the masterful use of memory as a principle of poetic form in the work of Wordsworth—in "Michael," with its ruined sheepfold, in "Resolution and Independence," and especially in the Intimations Ode, with its mysterious tree and field. It is not clear that Whitman as a young poet had read Wordsworth, but he had read the other Romantic poet of memories, Byron, and he had read the Americans influenced by Wordsworth.[1] Whitman drew on these resources, personal and poetic, for many of the poems he added to *Leaves of Grass* in 1860, including "As I Ebb'd with the Ocean of Life," "Out of the Cradle Endlessly Rocking," and many of the Calamus poems. At their best, these poems depend on some intensely recreated eidetic image:[2]

> I saw in Louisiana a live-oak growing,
> All alone stood it, and the moss hung down from the branches,
> Without any companion it grew there, uttering joyous leaves of dark green,
> And its look, rude, unbending, lusty, made me think of myself,
> But I wondered how it could utter joyous leaves, standing alone there, without its friend, its lover near—for I knew I could not,
> And I broke off a twig with a certain number of leaves upon it, and twined around it a little moss,
> And brought it away—and I have placed it in sight in my room,
> It is not needed to remind me as of my own dear friends,
> (For I believe lately I think of little else than of them,)

---

1. Floyd Stovall, *The Foreground of "Leaves of Grass"* (Charlottesville, 1974), 128, 242; 121, 283. For a general discussion of Whitman's relationship to the Romantics, see Robert Weisbuch's *Atlantic Double-Cross: American Literature and British Influence in the Age of Emerson* (Chicago, 1986), and Kenneth M. Price, *Whitman and Tradition* (New Haven, Conn., 1990).

2. So they are well termed in Reese Alexander Bond's "Whitman's Visual Imagination" (Ph.D. dissertation, University of Minnesota, 1971).

> Yet it remains to me a curious token—it makes me think
>   of manly love;
> For all that, and though the live-oak glistens there in
>   Louisiana, solitary, in a wide flat space,
> Uttering joyous leaves all its life, without a friend, a
>   lover, near,
> I know very well I could not.
>
> <div align="right">(<i>V</i>, II, 390)</div>

The live-oak is a token of his memories of manly love; the twig is a token of the oak; and the poem is a token of both. The poem depends upon—even dramatizes—a characteristic power of the memory to select and stylize a visual image so that an extended episode can be entwined around it. The poem, though, does not avow much about that private episode (to the chagrin of his biographers); whatever disinclination he may have felt for such avowals, his interest here is not in the past event itself but rather in the way that a powerfully visualized image can serve as the occasion and the symbol of that event.

"The Wound-Dresser," one of the most powerful poems from *Drum-Taps* (1865–66), is structured as a reminiscence, long after the Civil War, in which images from Whitman's hospital service are placed in dreamlike juxtaposition. As in "Tintern Abbey," the poem alternates between present and past, with the more commanding visual details found in memory:

> On, on I go—(open, doors of time! open, hospital
>   doors!)
> The crush'd head I dress, (poor crazed hand, tear not the
>   bandage away;)
> The neck of the cavalry-man, with the bullet through
>   and through, I examine;
> Hard the breathing rattles, quite glazed already the eye,
>   yet life struggles hard;
> (Come, sweet death! be persuaded, O beautiful death!
> In mercy come quickly.)
>
> <div align="right">(§3, <i>V</i>, II, 481)</div>

While the poem describes the soldiers and Whitman's tending them, it enacts his remembering these things; and through the poem float private feelings, which might be past or present.

The originary Whitman of 1855 and 1856, however, was less concerned with the retrieval of private emotions and situations—with the act of recall, yes, but a more public kind of memory. Here the reliable precedent was Byron, whom he was quoting during his New Orleans sojourn. He would have found everywhere in *Childe Harold* the practice of founding upon a graphic image a range of emotional association that is not simply private reminiscence, but the common experience of educated Europeans:

> Tully was not so eloquent as thou,
> Thou nameless column with the buried base!
> What are the laurels of the Caesar's brow?
> Crown me with ivy from his dwelling-place.
> Whose arch or pillar meets me in the face,
> Titus' or Trajan's? No—'t is that of Time:
> Triumph, arch, pillar, all he doth displace
> Scoffing; and apostolic statues climb
> To crush the imperial urn whose ashes slept sublime.
> (4.110)

Byron spoke for the commonwealth of gentlemen who had made the Grand Tour and for whom the campaigns against the French were fresh memories. (Fifty years later, Henry James would notice how arriviste Americans were using Byron's poems as a guidebook.) But the American Democrat also can ground his public poetry on such a use of visual images, by declaring that the memory containing the places and events is that of an average American, one of the roughs, a kosmos:

> All the acts, scenes, ways, persons, attitudes of These
>   States—reminiscences, all institutions,
> All These States, compact—Every square mile of These
>   States, without excepting a particle—you also—me
>   also,
> Me pleased, rambling in lanes and country fields,
>   Paumanok's fields,
> Me, observing the spiral flight of two little yellow
>   butterflies, shuffling between each other, ascending
>   high in the air;
> [. . .]
> The country boy at the close of the day, driving the herd

> of cows, and shouting to them as they loiter to
> browse by the road-side;
> The city wharf—Boston, Philadelphia, Baltimore,
> Charleston, New Orleans, San Francisco,
> The departing ships, when the sailors heave at the
> capstan;
> Evening—me in my room—the setting sun,
> [. . .]
> Factories, machinery, the mechanical forces—the
> windlass, lever, pulley—All certainties,
> The certainty of space, increase, freedom, futurity,
> In space, the sporades, the scattered islands, the stars—
> on the firm earth, the lands, my lands,
> O lands! all so dear to me—what you are, (whatever it
> is,) I become a part of that, whatever it is.
> ("Our Old Feuillage," *V*, II, 297–98)

Although some of these objects depend upon Whitman's direct, personal experience, some do not—and need not. The memory that comprehends all these "reminiscences" enfolds (with very little mnemonic sorting) all America's social and geographical diversity. Capacious and undiscriminating, its attention shifts instantly from the bucolic to the maritime, from New York to San Francisco, from the concreteness of two gyring butterflies to the universal principles of simple machines. Untrammeled by the narrowness of personal experience, it draws upon the wealth of America's own egalitarian self-consciousness, a repository supported by oratory, journalism, popular amusement (like P. T. Barnum's own American Museum)—"cheap literature, maps, charts, lithographs, daily and weekly newspapers," as Whitman said in "A Song for Occupations"; "The column of wants in the one-cent paper .. the news by telegraph .... the amusements and operas and shows" (§5, *V*, I, 96).

Many of the poems that Whitman added to *Leaves of Grass* in 1856 and 1860 must be understood as exhibits from that museum—and as exhibitions of its capaciousness and unselectivity.[3]

---

3. See Miles Orvell, "Reproducing Walt Whitman: The Camera, the Omnibus and *Leaves of Grass*," in *Prospects: An Annual of American Cultural Studies*, ed. Jack Salzman (New York, 1987), XII, 321–46; and Malcolm Andrews, "Whitman and the American City," in *The American City: Literary and Cultural Perspectives*, ed. Graham Clarke (New York, 1988), 195–96.

> Here is the profound lesson of reception, neither preference or denial,
> The black with his woolly head, the felon, the diseased, the illiterate person, are not denied,
> The birth, the hasting after the physician, the beggar's tramp, the drunkard's stagger, the laughing party of mechanics,
> The escaped youth, the rich person's carriage, the fop, the eloping couple,
> The early market-man, the hearse, the moving of furniture into the town, the return back from the town,
> They pass, I also pass, any thing passes, none can be interdicted.
> ("Song of the Open Road," §2, *V*, I, 226–27)

As C. Carroll Hollis has pointed out, what binds these compendia is a principle of metonymy, according to which objects are linked not by their similarity but by their contiguity in some context.[4] Thus, in these lines a diversity of people are united in the context of their excluded or pariah status, and then a group of people and activities associated with a road. These are necessarily very general and capacious contexts; and in some of Whitman's more dazzling passages, the images seem to have been utterly deprived of any context of contiguity except that provided by the poem itself. With the effacement of context, there disappears all possibility of categorizing or arranging them. They are, simply, pictures in an utterly eclectic gallery of the mind:

> By the city's quadrangular houses .... in log-huts, or camping with lumbermen,
> Along the ruts of the turnpike .... along the dry gulch and rivulet bed,
> Hoeing my onion-patch, and rows of carrots and parsnips .... crossing savannas .... trailing in forests,
> Prospecting .... gold-digging .... girdling the trees of a new purchase,

---

4. Hollis, *Language and Style*, 154–203.

> Scorched ankle-deep by the hot sand .... hauling my
> boat down the shallow river.
>
> ("Song of Myself," §33, *V*, I, 44)

Even the mediation of voice is lost, for these poems talk all sorts of English, from the colloquial to the grotesquely highfalutin. The only intermediary context for these images is the poet's mind, as displayed by his poem.

However, in many of these poems, the representative and inclusive mode produces not poetry but assertive recitation. What encloses America is not a bard's imagination, but a catalog of personages, events, and places so well secured in the American museum that a recital of their names alone, or at most a conventional phrase or epithet, invokes the state of mind for which they are a composite metonym. "A Song of Joys," "Our Old Feuillage," and a dozen other poems from the 1860 edition inventory whaleships, factories, machinery, plantations, the farm boy, the "athletic American matron," the banks of the Brazos and the Saskatchewan, illimitable names:

> Lands scorning invaders! Interlinked, food-yielding
> lands!
> Land of coal and iron! Land of gold! Lands of cotton,
> sugar, rice!
> Odorous and sunny land! Floridian land!
> Land of the spinal river, the Mississippi! Land of the
> Alleghanies! Ohio's land!
> Land of wheat, beef, pork! Land of wool and hemp!
> Land of the potato, the apple, and the grape!
> Land of the pastoral plains, the grass-fields of the world!
> Land of those sweet-aired interminable plateaus!
> Land there of the herd, the garden, the healthy house of
> adobie! Land there of rapt thought, and of the
> realization of the stars! Land of simple, holy, untamed
> lives!
>
> ("Starting from Paumanok," §14, *V*, II, 285)

This is the landscape across which, it was said, the American eagle had traveled so often, in political oratory, that its shadow had worn a trench from the Alleghenies to the Rocky Mountains.[5] Sometimes

---

5. See, for example, the journalist William Gilpin's address to emigrants bound for California (July 4, 1849): "Overland sweeps this tidal wave of population, absorb-

The Expanse of Consciousness 47

the galleries within the skull are not restricted by national political boundaries, but encompass the world; for as America dreams today, so every nation will think tomorrow. In "Salut au Monde!" and "Passage to India," the tally of peoples and places spans not a continent only but the earth, that "vast Rondure, swimming in space" (§5, V, III, 567).

But in every case the rhetoric is the same. A fast-paced litany of names invokes a vision of indiscriminate membership among the objects and between the reader and the objects. But the heterogeneity is so great and the pace so rapid that such membership requires a measure of participation that is, literally, only nominal. It is founded entirely on sequences of nouns and their modifiers, like those constituting the two quotations just above. As they are decontextualized, these persons and things lose as well their substantial being, their right to be themselves—even to govern a syntactical arrangement of their own. Reduced from subject to object, each merits at most a brief notation that appropriates it for the poem's utterance. Dependent noun phrases are massed into the assertion of a national ego so powerful that an individual being is no match for it; is forbidden to assert itself on its own terms; becomes so phantasmal, so lacking in substance, that great masses of its kind can be devoured all at once, unsorted, as a whale takes in britt.[6]

Correspondingly, the reader is caught in the flow also; the catalog does not ask for an indwelling response—in which a personal experi-

---

ing in its thundering march the glebe, the savages, and the wild beasts of the wilderness: scaling the mountains, and debouching down upon the seaboard. . . . Will this cease or slacken? Has the pouring forth of the stream from Europe ever ceased since the day of Columbus? Has the grass obliterated the trails down the Alleghanies, or across the Mississippi? Rather let him who doubts seat himself upon the bank of the supreme Missouri River, and await the running dry of his yellow waters!" (*The Mission of the North American People* [Philadelphia, 1873], 112–13). Whitman's debt to the political oratory of his time, noted by Paul Zweig in *Walt Whitman*, has been carefully studied by Hollis, *Language and Style*, 1–27, 233–52.

6. Lawrence Buell, in *Literary Transcendentalism* (Ithaca, 1973), concludes his study of catalog by saying that "the catalogue is prized chiefly by the Transcendentalists as the closest verbal approximation they were able to achieve to the boundless vitality of nature" (187). In Whitman, however, the catalogs approximate the vitality of the mind, not of external nature. As Buell says on the previous page, in Whitman's catalogs "the spirit triumphs over chaos by sheer energy." Likewise, Graham Clarke remarks that "the panoramic sweep of the Whitman epic is . . . dependent upon the moving image which both sustains the mystique of energy and denies us the attempt to gaze, to contemplate, to 'penetrate into the depths of the picture'" ("'To emanate a look,'" 96).

ence is matched and recreated out of the suggestions of the verbal image; in which the poem and the reader acknowledge the mediated presence of the person or object portrayed. Rather, it demands an inclusive assent to the force of will—poetic and national—that has compelled all of these items into the matrix of one declaration, one "America," one "song." Parataxis en masse may be the grammar of egalitarianism, all objects accepted without reservation or discrimination; but it is also the rhetoric of untempered expansionism, whether psychological or political.

A pair of poems written just before 1860 manifest the power of the mind to absorb its world as a catalog of words. In "Mannahatta" (*V*, II, 419–20), Whitman writes, "I was asking for something specific and perfect for my city, and behold! here is the aboriginal name!" The poem that follows is a performance of civic memory, this time on the municipal level. "Manhattan"—Whitman believed that the Indian word referred to the island's swift currents—summons up in the poet's mind the image of a seaport, which Whitman elaborates here in the style of guidebook and editorial. He takes the visual perspective of a "balloon view," the aerial encompassment that was the nineteenth century's standard tool for municipal publicity:

> [. . .] I see that word nested in nests of water-bays,
>   superb, with tall and wonderful spires,
> Rich, hemmed thick all around with sailships and
>   steamships—an island sixteen miles long, solid-
>   founded,
> Numberless crowded streets—high growths of iron,
>   slender, strong, light, splendidly uprising toward
>   clear skies;
> Tides swift and ample, well-loved by me, toward
>   sundown,
> The flowing sea-currents, the little islands, the larger
>   adjoining islands, the heights, the villas,
> The countless masts, the white shore-steamers, the
>   lighters, the ferry-boats, the black sea-steamers, well-
>   model'd;
> The down-town streets, the jobbers' houses of
>   business—the houses of business of the ship-
>   merchants, and money-brokers—the river-streets

The Expanse of Consciousness 49

—and so on, the massed phrases never coalescing into a sentence other than the original "I see." What the poet sees are the standard pictorial sights just named, with their assimilating descriptives: summer suns, winter sleighing, the "shows" of the streets—parades, processions, shopwindows, "manly" drivers, "well-formed" mechanics, handsome men and women along Broadway. Each visual image is clear enough, but without texture, a sort of fixed epithet, like Homer's wine-dark sea or the balladeers' blood-red wine. What the "aboriginal name" summons onto the screen of the mind is not a city of actual men and women, but "a word nested in nests of water-bays," a verbal construction to which the reader is invited to subscribe, as he might to a real estate prospectus. Although all these images are not labeled "phantoms," as in "Give Me the Splendid Silent Sun," such indeed they are—façades, spectacles, appearances, particles in the flux of consciousness. The word has engulfed the city; Manhattan extends no further than the bard's encompassing mind.

In "A Broadway Pageant," Whitman takes an even more expansive, and no less reductive, view. The poem begins in a journalist's Manhattan, on the occasion of the arrival of the first embassies from Japan. Tall-topped iron and marble façades festooned with bunting, flags on the forest of shipmasts, fire-flashing guns: million-footed Manhattan greets the courteous, swart-cheek'd princes of Asia. Then the writer lifts away to envision that Orient:

> The countries there, with their populations—the
>   millions en-masse, are curiously here;
> The swarming market places—the temples, with idols
>   ranged along the sides, or at the end—bonze,
>   brahmin, and lama;
> The mandarin, farmer, merchant, mechanic, and
>   fisherman;
> The singing-girl and the dancing-girl—the ecstatic
>   person—the divine Buddha;
> The secluded Emperors—Confucius himself—the great
>   poets and heroes—the warriors, the castes, all,
> [. . .] These, and whatever belongs to them, palpable,
>   show forth to me, and are seiz'd by me.
>
>   (§2, *V*, II, 515–16)

Swarming markets, dancing-girls, secluded emperors—thus Whitman appropriates a formulaic Orient conned from travel books, illustrations, and museum exhibits. If this is seeing, it is indeed that rapacious, it-making power feared by Blake, Poe, and their descendants and interpreters. And the next stanza confirms that this imaginative grasping foreruns a more substantial absorption:

> I chant the new empire, grander than any before—As in
>   a vision it comes to me;
> I chant America, the Mistress—I chant a greater
>   supremacy;
> I chant, projected, a thousand blooming cities yet, in
>   time, on those groups of sea-islands;
> I chant my sail-ships and steam-ships threading the
>   archipelagoes;
> I chant my stars and stripes fluttering in the wind;
> I chant commerce opening, the sleep of ages having
>   done its work—races, reborn, refresh'd.

This poem began at the very center of Whitman's experience, with a harbor festival and street parade in New York. But, quickly reducing that scene to verbiage, the poem develops as a tour of the Oriental pictures archived in his memory—on loan from a National Gallery of such images—accompanied by a cicerone from the New York *Herald*. The space it opens is not the existential space of Manhattan's streets and waterways, but the decontextualized volume of consciousness. Its vision is not physical but political, focusing not on crowds milling in the streets of New York but rather on those thousand commercial metropolises projected on the archipelagoes of Cathay. Façades, pageantry, phantasmagoria.

A more substantial seeing can be found in "Song of the Broad-Axe." Whitman portrays the axe not only as the instrument by which Americans were hewing out the physical forms of a democratic culture, but also as a symbol of the spirit of that culture—its moral self-reliance, political insubordination, and mechanical ingenuity.[7] Describing the physical tool-work of America, Whitman celebrates this spiritual *civitas* as the culmination of human history and the antagonist of the tyrannies of Europe (also symbolized by the

---

7. On the axe as a symbol in American painting and writing, see Barbara Novak, *Nature and Culture: American Landscape and Painting, 1825–1875* (New York, 1980), 157–65.

The Expanse of Consciousness 51

axe, for its meaning is as variable as its use). A hymn to humanity's tool-making and form-creating genius and a prophecy of the eventual triumph of democracy worldwide, this poem makes some expansionist gestures comparable to those that climax "A Broadway Pageant." And one passage marks the perigee of Whitman's propensity for milling reality down into opaque words:

> The axe leaps!
> The solid forest gives fluid utterances,
> They tumble forth, they rise and form,
> Hut, tent, landing, survey,
> Flail, plough, pick, crowbar, spade,
> Shingle, rail, prop, wainscot, jamb, lath, panel, gable,
> Citadel, ceiling, saloon, academy, organ, exhibition-
>   house, library,
> Cornice, trellis, pilaster, balcony, window, shutter,
>   turret, porch
>
> (§9, *V*, I, 185)

—and so on, not a teeming nation of nations but the index of a woodworker's catalog. As Manhattan became a "word," the forest here becomes "utterances." When the poem rises above these inventories, still its imagery often resorts to those readily assimilated phrases seen in "A Broadway Pageant." We read of "the snow-covered hills of Scandinavia" and "the European headsman / masked, clothed in red, with huge legs, and strong naked arms," gallery images of foreign parts like those depicting Asia in "A Broadway Pageant." Often the American scenes are equally conventional. "The murderer with haggard face," "dwellers in cabins among the California mountains," "the home of the friendly parents and children," and so forth. However, "Song of the Broad-Axe" also includes one of Whitman's most striking visualist passages, a long description of building-men:

> The house-builder at work in cities or anywhere,
> The preparatory jointing, squaring, sawing, mortising,
> The hoist-up of beams, the push of them in their places,
>   laying them regular,
> Setting the studs by their tenons in the mortises,
>   according as they were prepared,

> The blows of mallets and hammers, the attitudes of the men, their curved limbs,
> Bending, standing, astride the beams, driving in pins, holding on by posts and braces,
> The hooked arm over the plate, the other arm wielding the axe,
> The floor-men forcing the planks close, to be nailed,
> Their postures bringing their weapons downward on the bearers,
> The echoes resounding through the vacant building;
> The huge store-house carried up in the city, well under way,
> The six framing-men, two in the middle and two at each end, carefully bearing on their shoulders a heavy stick for a cross-beam,
> The crowded line of masons with trowels in their right hands rapidly laying the long side-wall, two hundred feet from front to rear,
> The flexible rise and fall of backs, the continual click of the trowels and bricks,
> The bricks, one after another, each laid so workman-like in its place, and set with a knock of the trowel-handle.
>   (§3, *V,* I, 178–79)

These lines, part of a catalog describing men working with tools, are the incarnation of Whitman's ideas about *homo faber americanus* and the city of self-reliance. Here the catalog pauses, as it did not in the carpenter's handbook quoted earlier. The centripetal tide of Whitman's imagination temporarily slacks, balanced by the pull of sympathetic recognition. Catalog yields to narrative, a description governed not by the force of Whitman's assimilative will, but by the rhythms of what he sees. Tracing several phases of construction, first in a framed house and then in a timber-and-masonry warehouse, the eye follows the inherent sequences of the builders' actions, both individual (the mason's trowel-stroke setting the brick) and collective (the undulation of the line of stooping bricklayers; the concerted strokes of the floor-men). When consciousness desists from inventorying what it has accumulated, there is a space for reality to act on its own terms. In that interval, we are delivered from the long recesses of the picture-gallery into the streets of Manhattan; the images are recontextualized in the city and in the building process in which they are involved. Recontextualized, they appear not as phantoms in a private theater of the mind or as commodities to be owned; rather, they must be recognized as presences dwelling in a world of their own. In that world, events occur not in any random order, but in the order demanded by their cooperative work. This may be still a poetry of consciousness; but what it dramatizes is not the arabesques of memory or the power of national assertion, but the experiential encounter of mind with realities other than itself. Although the description still rests on noun phrases rather than independent predications, these phrases do not depend on an explicit or implicit *I see*. Rather, as James Perrin Warren has said of this passage, the present participles, standing as both verb and noun, merge identity and activity.[8] The activity is hammering, not looking-on, and the carpenters set their own pace.

The poem can open this space because Whitman, a sometime carpenter and a perennial spectator, knew his subject with a physical intimacy—as he did not know the cabins of California, the snow-covered mountains of Scandinavia, or the sartorial practices of European headsmen. Whitman chooses to retard the speed of his catalog and to linger over details, diverting the attention from words to the meanings of words. "The words of poems give you more than poems," he wrote; "They are not the finish, but rather the outset" ("Song of the Answerer," §2, V, I, 143). As the poem dilates, the reader can respond not conventionally but imaginatively, recognizing the human skill and integrity of the builders' actions.[9] By stimulating this imaginative response, Whitman dramatizes the very subject about which he orates elsewhere in the poem: the creative intelligence of mankind, which builds both the material city and the democratic *civitas*—and which builds poems, too, and sympathetic readings of poems. In such a passage as this, Whitman becomes the

---

8. James Perrin Warren, *Walt Whitman's Language Experiment* (University Park, Pa., 1990), 63–66.

9. My term *dilation* refers to those moments in Whitman's poetry when the glance dwells, the poem's pace lingers, and the object of consciousness becomes the subject of its own activity. Rohn Friedman used the term, with Whitman's authority, to describe the centrifugal sympathetic phase of Whitman's imagination ("A Whitman Primer," 447). My usage is closer to that of Geoffrey Hartman, who in *The Unmediated Vision* discusses how in moments of "dilation" Wordsworth found some visible being transformed numinously into symbol (164ff.).

citizen bard, using the mysterious power of the eyesight to awaken his reader to the unrhymed poetry of America and to point out the path between that reality and the soul. Whatever he may have claimed in "Salut au Monde!," Whitman was not a habitan of Vienna (§9, *V,* I, 170);[10] but his deeply experienced inhabitation of New York allowed him to enfranchise his reader, for this brief interval, as a fellow citizen.

Such intervals are more likely to occur when Whitman is working with situations in which he could match his phrasing not just with public formulas but with his own personal experience. The city world is not only the scene with which he is most familiar; it is also one most likely to afford him that sense of the Many in One which distinguished the Matter of America and the poetics of the American bard.[11] In "Pictures," he painted himself "going up and down Mannahatta, through the streets, along the shores." "Every hour of the day and night has given me copious pictures," he wrote at the end of that poem (*CRE,* 649). In "Faces," he discovers his subject while "sauntering the pavement or crossing the ceaseless ferry" (§1, *V,* I, 133). Whitman's visualizing, descriptive power leads him into the role of the *flâneur,* the walker of streets and receptor of experience.[12] When, as in "Song of the Broad-Axe," the recitation slows and begins to follow the sequence of the action, as though the saunterer had paused to watch a lovers' quarrel in a restaurant, or the process of milling grain, the poet is brought closer to acknowledging the Not-Me. A similar lingering attentiveness, more completely developed, contributes to the power of "Song of Myself":

> The butcher-boy puts off his killing-clothes, or sharpens
>   his knife at the stall in the market,
> I loiter enjoying his repartee and his shuffle and
>   breakdown,

---

10. In 1856, it was "I am a habitan of St. Petersburgh" (*V,* I, 114). In a sequence of thirty cities, itself only a detail in a vaunt of poetic voraciousness, discriminations between the Hapsburg capital and the Romanov are rather finespun.

11. M. Wynn Thomas points out the special propriety of the paratactic style when it conveys the heterogeneity of urban experience (*Lunar Light,* 154).

12. In "Nineteenth-century Paris: Vision and Nightmare," Peter Collier develops Walter Benjamin's comments on the Parisian *flâneur,* describing him as both a "voyeuristic observer and idle gossip" and a consumer of sights reduced to commodities (*Unreal City: Urban Experience in Modern European Literature and Art,* ed. Edward Timms and David Kelley [New York, 1985], 26). William Chapman Sharpe expands on Benjamin's insight throughout *Unreal Cities.*

The Expanse of Consciousness 55

> Blacksmiths with grimed and hairy chests environ the anvil,
> Each has his main-sledge .... they are all out .... there is a great heat in the fire.
> From the cinder-strewed threshold I follow their movements,
> The light sheer of their waists plays even with their massive arms,
> Overhand the hammers roll—overhand so slow—overhand so sure,
> They do not hasten, each man hits in his place.
>
> (§12, *V*, I, 13)

But the centrifugal pulse of sympathy, with its recognition of the integrity and independence of the Not-Me, is in all these cases still contained within poems that celebrate the inclusive power of consciousness. Even the apparently passive *flâneur* asserts the priority of his power to collect pictures while remaining safely out of the game. And close personal experience with his subjects could not save them from being reduced to epithets and swallowed en masse. The poetics of "Mannahatta" and "A Broadway Pageant" admitted us to no sense of the real being of New York's citizens, no shared civic space. Whitman's personal familiarity with the scene was only a precondition for creating an interval of recognition. What he also needed was a presentational style that would place him and his reader on a mutual footing.

The way out of simply private feelings—the path between the I and the Not-Me, between I and You as fellow citizens—must pass along the route of language, a language invoking visual images in which poet and reader together repose their faith in the power of the eyesight to create a shared world. The task for Whitman is so to use words and visual images that they will awaken the imaginative faculty of his reader, binding poet and reader into a common citizenship founded on that "spiritual world" whose realities the common miracle of eyesight anticipates. So, as Whitman's words must draw upon the communal stock of English, so must his images invoke a familiar way of seeing if he is to pass over from private consciousness to the role of public poet.

In "Pictures," he was beginning to discover that style—not in the form of the poem itself, with its possessive approach to sight, but in the kinds of pictures he describes. They reveal his familiarity with the pictorial art of his time and show him searching for a visual analogue for his democratic poetry. Some of the pictures are linked by an expansionist geography like that in "A Broadway Pageant": the Oregon hunting-hut, Chicago's railroad depots, slave-gangs in the South, the "treeless llanos" east and west of the Rockies, "my woods of Kanada, in winter, with ice and snow," and so on (*CRE*, 648, 646). Others are plainly bookish in origin, such as a series of portraits of religious figures and gods that suggests his acquaintance with Volney's *Ruins,* and an extended representation of the philosophers of ancient Athens drawn from Fanny Wright's *A Few Days in Athens* (1822).[13]

Two lines from the latter picture, though, suggest something different:

> Some, crowded in groups, listen to the harangues or
>   arguments of the elder ones,
> Elsewhere, single figures, undisturbed by the buzz
>   around them, lean against pillars, or within recesses,
>   meditating, or studying from manuscripts.
>
>   (*CRE*, 644)

The reference here, mediated either by engraving or verbal account, is to Raphael's fresco of the Athenian Academy. Although this is his only allusion to a specific painting, many of the other "pictures" refer to classes of paintings and thus reflect the artistic canons of Whitman's time. Some of the "pictures" in Whitman's all-encompassing gallery are European in subject; some are American. The Matter of Europe is rendered just as he would have seen it in academic paintings at the National Gallery or the Academy of Fine Arts in New York. Their themes are biblical, mythological, historical, and oriental: Adam in Paradise, Christ carrying his cross, "imperial Rome, full of palaces," the voyage of Columbus, the storming of the Bastille, a Spanish bullfight, and "an Arab caravan, halting—See you, the palm trees, the camels, and the stretch of hot sand far away" (*CRE*, 646).

When the poem turns to the Matter of America, the subjects reflect not the academic taste but the popular, not the taste of those

---

13. Betsy Erkkila established the provenance of lines 23–37 of "Pictures" (*Whitman the Political Poet,* 17–18).

who subscribed to the American Art Union's annual offering of steel engravings of European masterworks, but of those who bought inexpensive lithographs—Whitman's projected audience.

> O a husking-frolic in the West—see you, the large rude
>   barn—see you, young and old, laughing and joking,
>   as they husk the ears of corn;
> And there in a city, a stormy political meeting—a torch-
>   light procession—candidates avowing themselves to
>   the people;
> [. . .] And there, tall and slender, stands Ralph Waldo
>   Emerson, of New England, at the lecturer's desk
>   lecturing,
> And there is my Congress in session in the Capitol—
>   there are my two Houses in session;
> And here, behold two war-ships, saluting each other—
>   behold the smoke, bulging, spreading in round
>   clouds from the guns and sometimes hiding the
>   ships.
>   (CRE, 647–48)

Images like this—bucolic scenes, seascapes, famous Americans, national politics—hung not just in Whitman's brain-gallery but in most American homes. In "Song of Myself," they crowd out the European material altogether, and Whitman ceases to draw attention to the pictorial quality of the "America" he absorbs.

"Song of Myself," though still a poem dramatizing consciousness, avoids the recessive, picture-of-a-picture quality found in "Pictures" and puts pictorial conventions to a more extroverted use, as a basis for mutuality with his readers. Popular illustration's seeming naïvete and lack of pretension offered a path between the soul and the reality that lay close to his readers and was clearly marked. Some illustrations are given only a glance, like those in the catalogs of the Matter of America noted earlier. Others, though, occupy several lines and allow the subject to assert its own life:

> I saw the marriage of the trapper in the open air in the
>   far-west .... the bride was a red girl,
> Her father and his friends sat near by crosslegged and
>   dumbly smoking .... they had moccasins to their feet

> and large thick blankets hanging from their
> shoulders;
> On a bank lounged the trapper .... he was dressed
> mostly in skins .... his luxuriant beard and curls
> protected his neck,
> One hand rested on his rifle .... the other hand held
> firmly the wrist of the red girl,
> She had long eyelashes .... her head was bare .... her
> coarse straight locks descended upon her voluptuous
> limbs and reached to her feet.
> [. . .]
> The mate stands braced in the whaleboat, lance and
> harpoon are ready,
> The duck-shooter walks by silent and cautious stretches,
> The deacons are ordained with crossed hands at the
> altar,
> The spinning-girl retreats and advances to the hum of
> the big wheel,
> The farmer stops by the bars of a Sunday and looks at
> the oats and rye.
>
> (§10, 15, V, I, 11–12, 16)

Of course, these are still subjective images, phantoms moving on the screen of the Self's consciousness. At the end of the list, Whitman writes, "These one and all tend inward to me, and I tend outward to them." Again the inclusive geographical and historical range, extending beyond the personal experience of Whitman, asserts the omniscience and universal sympathy of the democratic poet, him who stretches long as the Atlantic coast and spans to the Pacific, him who affectionately absorbs his country. But the country that in turn must stretch and absorb this national poet—how is their experience (also limited, also local) to tally with his?

Neither Whitman nor most of his readers had hunted whales or attended an Indian wedding. But his commonfolk audience—the workmen and workwomen to whom he addressed especially the 1856 edition—had all seen the same illustrations, thanks to the proliferation of inexpensive print media in the first half of the nineteenth century. When his images expand beyond the simple epithet, the cabin-dwellers in California or the snowy forests of Kanada, the conventions to which they usually refer are those of the illustration—

usually genre studies, sometimes landscapes or historical painting, rarely (until 1865) the topical. (F. O. Matthiessen suggested this when he identified the affinity between Whitman's "landscapes" and the paintings of William Sidney Mount. Richard Chase later made the same observation negatively, saying that Whitman's visual powers were seldom acute, that his catalogs seemed to have been "culled . . . from books and newspapers" or "observed at an exhibition of paintings."[14]) Whitman is inviting "you" into a shared world through visual experiences that are not direct but indirect, as he said in the 1855 Preface—through culturally mediated pictures. Hollis, arguing that the style of *Leaves of Grass* is essentially metonymic rather than metaphoric, observed that "metonymy tends to remind us of what we already know."[15] Whitman's dilations, assembling a world of contiguous metonymic objects, remind the reader of a familiar, mediated vision of America.

Necessarily then, the visualist passages in "Song of Myself" are founded not on real things but on the pictures of things. Sometimes it is possible to identify the very picture, as it was with the Athenian scene in "Pictures." The trapper's marriage is a painting by Alfred J. Miller.[16] Other scenes have been conjecturally linked with paintings by Miller, Mount, and George Caleb Bingham. Whitman certainly knew the work of Mount, a fellow Long Islander, whom he once reviewed in the New York *Evening Post*.[17] However, in Whitman's time these works of high art would have had such limited currency that they would not have suited his poetic purposes at all. Whitman was invoking not particular paintings and painters, but rather a matter and a style known to his readers through engravings and lithographs that would have included a few reproductions of Bingham, Miller, and Mount, but were mostly the work of humbler, more limited, often anonymous illustrators working in the same traditions.

14. F. O. Matthiessen, *American Renaissance: Art and Expression in the Age of Emerson and Whitman* (New York, 1941), 597–99. Chase associates Whitman's conventionality mainly with his rural scenes, attributing it to his lack of familiarity with the countryside (*Walt Whitman Reconsidered*, 170–71). As we have seen in "Mannahatta," though, Whitman could also be conventional about cityscapes.

15. Hollis, *Language and Style*, 203.

16. Edgeley W. Todd, "Indian Pictures and Two Whitman Poems," *Huntington Library Quarterly*, XIX (November, 1955), 1–11. Miller's watercolor does not correspond exactly to the details of this passage.

17. Emory Holloway, ed., *The Uncollected Poetry and Prose of Walt Whitman* (New York, 1932), I, 236–38.

In a time before the foundation of large public museums of art, before the circulation of inexpensive reproductions of great paintings, before the appearance of glossily illustrated art books and journals, illustrations printed from stone or steel or wood were the principal mediums of popular art. Whitman's art criticism, during his years as a journalist, was mainly devoted to works of this order.[18] (His taste ran to the Matter of America—landscapes, Indians, wild animals, history, topicals.) He owned a print of George Catlin's portrait of Osceola, though the illustrations that Bronson Alcott saw on the walls of his room in 1856 were, anomalously, of classical subjects.[19] As a fellow-traveler of the Transcendentalists, Whitman may have believed that every human soul is part and parcel of the world-soul, and that the untutored reader (properly inspired) might envision directly how all persons and things stood in that spiritual commonweal. But as a delegate of the common people, knowing something of the mind and taste of Americans en masse (even as he idealized them), he must also have understood that the consciousness of each, when it extended beyond immediate experience, was fed not by immediate visions of the All, but by the torrent of images channeled through oratory, press, and cheap illustrations.

It was in just such images, though, that he placed a Transcendentalist's faith in unified, communal vision. "A Song for Occupations," addressing the "workmen and workwomen of these states" and assuring them that they enjoy equal access to this vision, contains a catalog of the "closest, simplest things" that contain "themes and hints" of "the whole," or, as he put it baldly in his final revision, the "objects gross" in which one could discover "the unseen soul." In 1855 this list included (among many other things) cylinder presses and daguerreotypes; in 1856 he added to it a mention of the telegraph and the line quoted earlier about "cheap literature, maps, charts, lithographs, daily and weekly newspapers" (§5, *V,* I, 96). From the eyesight there proceeds another eyesight, he said in the 1855 Preface. If, in rendering the Matter of America, he could present it as the

---

18. Thomas L. Brasher, *Whitman as Editor of the "Brooklyn Daily Eagle"* (Detroit, 1970), 212–15.

19. Bronson Alcott, *The Journals of Bronson Alcott,* ed. Odell Shepard (Boston, 1938), 290. Whitman also owned an original oil by Jesse Talbot: even more anomalously, it was a scene from *The Pilgrim's Progress.* Although an anomaly in Whitman's program for an American art, such a subject was not unusual in American art at that time. See Carl Bode, *The Anatomy of American Popular Culture* (Berkeley, 1959), 70–71.

familiar world of lithographs and woodcuts, not only could he find a common ground on which to meet his readers; he could also show how to trace, through the lineaments of that America, a path leading to the soul.

"Song of Myself" is a mimesis of the activity of democratic consciousness. When from self-consciousness it turns to the Not-Me, it turns usually to the material and method of the popular print, especially to the genre style, which depicted the contemporary rather than the historical, the common rather than the extraordinary.

> American genre of the pre–Civil War period is replete with images that convey the blessings of a democratic society—images that were widely disseminated as illustrations in periodicals and as engravings for sale to the public or to members of art associations. . . . There are scenes of the healthy yeoman tilling the soil and taking delight in music, country dances, and friendly political argument; scenes of his innocent children romping barefoot in green fields, fishing in sparkling streams, sledding on snowy hills; scenes of his unaffected wife sewing, cooking, and caring for family and home. . . . They showed Americans as robust, good-humored, natural folk, while focussing mainly on the rural majority in the population.[20]

In technique, American genre artists emulated the seventeenth-century Dutch painters in their interest in setting and detail, and also in the use of several clearly demarcated planes of attention, foreground to background. The sharp, linear techniques of most methods of mass-producing illustrations fostered in popular art that same concern with detail and with sharp-edged fact rather than clouds of atmosphere. Encouraging the viewer to recognize some universal human trait within the particular event depicted, these illustrations usually implied narrative, a story to which the viewer must imaginatively contribute.[21] In the catalogs of "Song of Myself," and of

20. Edward J. Nygren, "American Genre: Its Changing Form and Content," in *Of Time and Place: American Figurative Art from the Corcoran Gallery* (Washington, D.C., 1981), 8.
21. See Oliver Larkin, *Art and Life in America* (New York, 1960), 214; Barbara Novak, *American Painting of the Nineteenth Century: Realism, Idealism, and the American Experience* (New York, 1969), 115; and Hermann Warner Williams, Jr., *Mirror to the*

"The Sleepers" as well, the implied narrative for each image creates a brief dilation: the characters are arrested in a moment of autonomous action, and for the same moment the reader's imagination is drawn out into the context created by that story:

> The negro holds firmly the reins of his four horses ....
>   the block swags underneath on its tied-over chain,
> The negro that drives the huge dray of the stoneyard ....
>   steady and tall he stands poised on one leg on the
>   stringpiece,
> His blue shirt exposes his ample neck and breast and
>   loosens over his hipband,
> His glance is calm and commanding .... he tosses the
>   slouch of his hat away from his forehead,
> The sun falls on his crispy hair and moustache .... falls
>   on the black of his polish'd and perfect limbs.
> I behold the picturesque giant and love him .... and I do
>   not stop there,
> I go with the team also.
>   ("Song of Myself," §13, *V,* I, 13–14)

Here Whitman explicitly directs his reader to the appropriate way of conceiving this image, calling the drayman "picturesque." In some passages, he can achieve such a dilation in the space of a single line:

> The pedlar sweats with his pack on his back—the
>   purchaser higgles about the odd cent,
> The camera and plate are prepared, the lady must sit for
>   her daguerreotype,
> The bride unrumples her white dress, the minutehand of
>   the clock moves slowly,
> The opium eater reclines with rigid head and just-
>   opened lips.
>   (§15, *V,* I, 18)

But Whitman's technique is different from painterly genre in one respect. His focus is entirely on the foreground event. In this way, the images in "Song of Myself" resemble sketches or the wood engravings just beginning to appear in the new illustrated weeklies like

---

American Past: A Survey of American Genre Painting, 1750–1900 (Greenwich, Conn., 1973), 16–17.

Harper's and *Leslie's*. Whereas the genre artist on canvas, steel, or stone carefully built up a stagelike background as a physical context for his characters, Whitman concentrates on just the foregrounded action, from whose flow he has snatched the moment that he depicts. Even when he extends the picture through several lines, as in the views of the trapper's marriage, the black drayman, or the blacksmiths at their forge, he does so to review all the foreground figures rather than to place them in an elaborated setting. Most of the "historical" scenes likewise are strongly foregrounded, like this scene from "The Sleepers," Washington's farewell to his troops (a favorite subject of illustration, rendered more stoically in a famous Currier and Ives lithograph):

> He stands in the room of the old tavern .... the
>   wellbeloved soldiers all pass through,
> The officers speechless and slow draw near in their
>   turns,
> The chief encircles their necks with his arm and kisses
>   them on the cheek,
> He kisses lightly the wet cheeks one after another .... he
>   shakes hands and bids goodbye to the army.[22]
>
> (§5, *V*, I, 115)

In sequences and vignettes like these, Whitman acknowledges the autonomy of his subjects as he did not in the catalogs cited earlier in this chapter. In the catalogs, the emphasis rests first on the authorial assertion ("I see . . ."), second on the nouns or epithets subsumed in that assertion. These passages transfer the major stress to the persons and events by slowing the pace, expanding and concretizing the description, implying a narrative context. But these images are not recontextualized into a developed setting in place and time. Whitman uses the two-dimensional "picture" image to remind us that the context of his images is, ultimately, that of the observer-consciousness that has absorbed them. Even though the poem has acknowledged their reality, by its dilation, it cannot altogether acknowledge their being in place and time. Continuity is found not in the pedlar's trade

22. Just one "historical" view in "Song of Myself" is treated in depth. Recalling the aftermath of the sea battle between the *Serapis* and the *Bonhomme Richard*, Whitman's storyteller—a participant in the fight—looks from John Paul Jones on the quarterdeck to the battered warships and the wounded and dying sailors, and then on to the moonlit sea and the distant shore (§36, *V*, I, 57–58).

or in Washington's life, but in the comments of the inward cicerone. The context and continuity are, finally, not those of the "real" world of four dimensions, where a gang of flooring-men and bricklayers might actually lay out their own context of act and being, identity, and membership. Rather, they proceed from the random, dimensionless world of consciousness—the poet's consciousness, "America's," and (if the poet has truly found in popular illustration a pathway between reality and their souls) the readers' as well.

❖

Whitman's visualist poems, though, do not simply ratify the people's taste in popular illustration. He sought to improve and broaden that taste, because it was an index of the range of their consciousness:

> Now I wash the gum from your eyes,
> You must habit yourself to the dazzle of the light and of
> every moment of your life.
> ("Song of Myself," §46, V, I, 76)

The democratic poet undertakes to expand the imagination of his audience, to include matters hitherto thought unworthy, obscene, contemptible, beyond the range of what was deemed decorous in poetry—or in society. Whitman's attentions to the pedlar, the construction workers, and the black drayman square with the democratic pronouncements of such poems as "A Song for Occupations" and "Song of the Broad-Axe," asserting the worthiness of unhonored and unnoticed occupations and the characteristic humanity of workers with their tools. It was the liberal doctrine of the age. In the "cetology" chapters of *Moby-Dick,* Melville asserted that it was decorous for the *Pequod*'s mongrel crew to figure in the epic, or the tragedy, of democracy:

> This august dignity I treat of, is not the dignity of kings and robes, but that abounding dignity which has no robed investiture. Thou shalt see it shining in the arm that wields a pick or drives a spike; that democratic dignity which, on all hands, radiates without end from God Himself! The great God absolute! The centre and circumference of all democracy! . . . If I shall touch that

workman's arm with some ethereal light . . . then against all mortal critics bear me out in it, thou just Spirit of Equality, which hast spread one royal mantle of humanity over all my kind!"[23]

For the democratic poet, every human arm shines with that same light: Whitman saw it on the faces that surrounded him on the Fulton Ferry.[24] The capacity to see it rests in a faith in equality that, for these writers at least, implies faith in a divinity whose numinous presence bathes everything under heaven with its intense light. "It is dislocation and detachment from the life of God that makes things ugly," Emerson had written of the supposed ugliness of railroads and factories; "the poet . . . re-attaches things to nature and the Whole."[25]

To reveal the numinous dazzle of the commonplace, further, depends on a faith in the miracle of the eyesight—the power of a visual imagination, schooled in the genre style of popular illustration and guided by poetic language. In the lines quoted above, Whitman wrote that every moment of one's life shines with an unrecognized but dazzling light. "Light" is more than a metaphor. Light, Emerson had said, was "the first of painters": "there is no object so foul that intense light will not make beautiful."[26] His allusion is to the humble subjects and powerful lighting of the Dutch masters. And as well, it is a recognition of the practice of contemporary genre illustrators, who would bathe every surface in a picture with a uniform, undiscriminating light, in which every recorded detail stands forth.

So too for Whitman. Each particular "picture"—for instance, the black man driving a stonemason's dray—is singled out not for its uniqueness, but because it presents a typical, if socially invisible, part of contemporary life in America. *Harper's* would not have published an engraving of so heroically "picturesque" a black workman; in lithograph, "darkies" appeared mainly in comic caricatures. (There was, to be sure, the black man outside the barn door, listening to the violinist, who dominates William Sidney Mount's *The Power of Mu-*

23. Herman Melville, *Moby-Dick,* ed. Harrison Hayford and Hershel Parker (New York, 1967), 104–105 [Chap. 26].
24. M. Wynn Thomas remarks that light not only is "the natural democratic medium," but "actually acts as a democratizing medium" (*Lunar Light,* 101).
25. "The Poet," in *Emerson,* 229.
26. *Nature,* 3 (*Emerson,* 26).

sic, a painting frequently reproduced in several media.[27]) Whitman catches the drayman as brilliant sunlight "falls on the black of his polish'd and perfect limbs." By his pose he might be a New York fireman, a farmer in the western settlements, a pioneer on the Oregon trail, all suitable subjects for lithograph. There is implied narrative in Whitman's "going with" him and his horses. And, whether or not there was a paying clientele for his lithographed image, he epitomized American democracy and self-reliance. Limning him in the mode of genre, Whitman made him visible.

Throughout "Song of Myself" and "The Sleepers," subjects familiar from genre illustration are juxtaposed with subjects also treated in the style of genre, but that could never have been the subject of actual illustrations. The image of the waiting bride, in the lines quoted above, is followed instantly by that of an opium addict; and the next image is more disreputable yet:

> The prostitute draggles her shawl, her bonnet bobs on
>   her tipsy and pimpled neck,
> The crowd laugh at her blackguard oaths, the men jeer
>   and wink to each other,
> (Miserable! I do not laugh at your oaths nor jeer you)
>   ("Song of Myself," §15, *V,* I, 18–19)

And the next image is back to standard lithographic fare, a meeting of the President with his cabinet. The repertoire of popular prints has expanded by Whitman's inclusion, in a genre style, of a glimpse into the depths: the human wolfpack, the abandonment of their scapegoat.

Not that the sordid was altogether missing from the popular art of that time. It might appear as scandal, as prostitution had been portrayed in a lithographed series, *New York by Gas-light,* published a few years before *Leaves of Grass.* Or it might be caricatured for political or reformist purposes, as tenement and tavern life among the blacks and the Irish was depicted in the illustrated weeklies of the

---

27. A number of Mount's paintings feature black men or women: besides his portraits of musicians, there are the fisherwoman in *Eel Spearing at Setauket* and the man in *Farmers Nooning.* But these are oil paintings, aimed at the few, not engravings or lithographs for the many. Later, during the Civil War, Currier and Ives did publish at least one lithograph depicting the black infantry of the 54th Massachusetts in the heroic poses of hand-to-hand combat (Walton Rawls, ed., *The Great Book of Currier and Ives' America* [New York, 1979], 312).

The Expanse of Consciousness 67

late 1850s.[28] But the parenthetic line in the passage above reveals how such accepted references to the indecorous differ from the state of mind that Whitman is inculcating. This poem affords the prostitute and the drug addict the same dilating recognition that it affords pedlar, bride, and president. The tone of that recognition is as sympathetic as that adopted by the genre illustration toward the more accepted foibles of work or courtship—as Bingham's on the fecklessness of frontier democracy, Mount's on the ways farmhands avoided work, Homer's on the licenses of a husking frolic. Rendering the street mob, the suicide, the drunkard in the characteristic, narrative mode of the genre illustration, Whitman traced some of the grimmer realities of American life in order to throw light on a dark side of the national soul and the single self.

If "Song of Myself" uses the pictorial mode to extend consciousness so that it can recognize what was socially or aesthetically invisible, "The Sleepers" draws in the sexual life, dream, and nocturnal fantasy, illuminating (as Whitman had promised in the 1855 Preface) that deep between the setting and rising sun. At the poem's center are three images that would have been familiar from popular prints: Washington's defeat on Brooklyn Heights; his farewell to his troops, quoted earlier in this chapter; and a red squaw, tall and beautiful, a weaver of rushes, whom the poet's mother had encountered in her girlhood. Around these figures, though, is a network of then-uncustomary sketches that collectively depict the defeat of reason and of will, and the triumph of the passional and physical: couples sleeping or making love; a drowning swimmer and a shipwreck; and a sequence in which time is reversed and America's immigrant nations go back across the sea. The stock pictorial figures thus are drawn into a nonrational, prevoluntary context in which dislocated things are reattached to the Whole, through processes of relinquishment:

> The homeward bound and the outward bound,
> The beautiful lost swimmer, the ennuyee, the onanist,
>   the female that loves unrequited, the moneymaker,
> [. . .]
> The criminal that stood in the box, the judge that sat

---

28. So had the city's darker side figured in the sensationalist press of the mid-nineteenth century. See John A. Kouwenhoven, *The Columbia Historical Portrait of New York* (New York, 1972), 226, 261, 270–72.

> and sentenced him, the fluent lawyers, the jury, the audience,
> The laugher and weeper, the dancer, the midnight widow, the red squaw,
> The consumptive, the erysipalite, the idiot, he that is wronged,
> The antipodes, and every one between this and them in the dark,
> I swear they are averaged now .... one is no better than the other,
> The night and sleep have likened them and restored them.
> I swear they are all beautiful,
> Every one that sleeps is beautiful .... every thing in the dim night is beautiful,
> [. . .]
> The soul is always beautiful,
> The universe is duly in order .... every thing is in its place.
>
> (§7, *V,* I, 117–19)

Light is the best painter; caught in a revelatory moment of action, the seeming ugly, the tabooed, the grotesque, all speak of the fullness of the Self and of America as much as views of farmers nooning or blacksmiths at their forge. Annihilating all traditional poetic decorums, Whitman could string conventional and unconventional into one dazzling sequence:

> The sprawl and fullness of babes .... the bosoms and heads of women .... the folds of their dress .... their style as we pass in the street .... the contour of their shape downwards;
> The swimmer naked in the swimmingbath .. seen as he swims through the salt transparent greenshine, or lies on his back and rolls silently with the heave of the water;
> Framers bare-armed framing a house .. hoisting the beams in their places .. or using the mallet and mortising-chisel,
> The bending forward and backward of rowers in rowboats .... the horseman in his saddle;

The Expanse of Consciousness 69

> Girls and mothers and housekeepers in all their exquisite offices,
> The group of laborers seated at noontime with their open dinnerkettles, and their wives waiting,
> The female soothing a child .... the farmer's daughter in the garden or cowyard,
> The woodman rapidly swinging his axe in the woods .... the young fellow hoeing corn .... the sleighdriver guiding his six horses through the crowd,
> [. . .]
> Suchlike I love .... I loosen myself and pass freely .... and am at the mother's breast with the little child.
> ("I Sing the Body Electric," §2, *V*, I, 122–23)

Although the heterogeneity in such a passage may recall the way in which the catalogs of "Salut au Monde!" and "A Broadway Pageant" marshaled names into an assertion of national purpose, there is a difference. His use of the genre style has opened for each image a moment and a space for autonomous being. His indifference to pictorial decorum has not only cleared the eye for a range of "invisible" subjects. It has created, within the expanse of the poem, a picture plane—albeit a shallow and decontextualized plane—in which it is possible to juxtapose objects utterly incongruous according to conventional hierarchical standards. As we will see in a later chapter, at the end of the nineteenth century this abolition of decorum would make Whitman the implicit ally of a photographer like Jacob Riis and the avowed patron of a painter like John Sloan.

The context of these images is consciousness; the picture is to be seen as an instant in the activity of the mind. Whose mind? In almost all of these poems, Whitman claims the role of thinking and feeling for the American public. When the image remains undeveloped, little but a conventionalized name and epithet, the poem usually reflects uncritically the rhetorical and political expansiveness of midcentury Young America. The more developed images, as they command a constructive imaginative response from the reader, summon forth a sense of the reality for which the words stand; and at their strongest, Whitman uses such visual images to extend his readers' receptivity beyond the range of conventionalized thought, to recognize persons and matters that were "invisible" according to canons of social or literary taste. Whitman's lingering attentiveness exemplifies the attentiveness that every being in a true democracy deserves. The poem's motive is to instruct the reader in the proper way of looking at the world—or, rather, the proper attitude to take toward one's unnoticed process of consciousness. The reader is invited to follow the example of the poet; to walk his own city's streets with the same sketchbook attentiveness; to hang within his own small gallery the images of America; to inspect them with a connoisseur's eye. As E. H. Gombrich put it in *Art and Illusion:* "To read the artist's picture is to mobilize our memories and our experience of the visible world and to test his image through tentative projections. To read the visible world as art we must do the opposite. We must mobilize our memories and experience of pictures we have seen and test the motif again by projecting them tentatively onto a framed view."[29] "There is such a thing as a real visual discovery," Gombrich asserts a few pages later. Painting is not always a matter of "matching" the visual expectations generated by previous painting. He cites the Impressionists: when people had learned how to "read" their experiment, they "found to their delight that the visible world *could* after all be seen in terms of these bright patches and dabs of paint."[30] So Whitman, self-consciously drawing his readers' attention to the picture-making power of consciousness, encouraged them (in some poems and passages) to relax its egotistical grasp and to grant some space and autonomy to what it was they beheld.

❖

No matter how developed the image, though, no matter what foothold is provided it, the main mimetic activity of these poems is directed not toward making words "indicate" an external reality, but toward making them represent the play of images, ideas, and feelings within the mind. There may be objective contexts that might contain these persons and objects, such as "Manifest Destiny," "The United States," or "New York City." But in these poems their status is that of subjective images, less real than the mind that contains them.

As the years went by, Whitman did not desist from the pictorial mode of "Song of the Broad-Axe" and "Our Old Feuillage," in which visual images are used as the game-pieces of consciousness

---

29. E. H. Gombrich, *Art and Illusion: A Study in the Psychology of Pictorial Representation* (New York, 1960), 314.
30. *Ibid.*, 324.

and the poem takes its sequential form from the expansion and contraction of mental attention, while the reader is addressed either as the object of nationalist rhetoric or as one whose imagination has been formed from the material of popular culture. In Whitman's later life, nationalism was his most frequent motive for displaying assemblages of pictures within the skull-gallery of consciousness. "Song of the Exposition," "Thou Mother with Thy Equal Brood," "Song of the Redwood-Tree," and "Passage to India" are all late examples of his assimilatory style. However, after 1860 this style seems gradually to have lost its power for him.

In 1855 Whitman had announced confidently that, as the American bard absorbed his country, so the nation would reciprocally absorb him. In the first decade of his career, the poet did indeed absorb America, digesting its people and landscapes into the meat of his poems. Yet the 1856 edition of *Leaves of Grass,* in its poems and its dedicatory letter to Emerson, hints at its author's impatience to find—or create, or imagine—an audience capable of absorbing these poems. By 1860 his search for an audience was growing desperate; his habitual salutation to "you, whoever you are" suggests less "you, of whatever class or circumstance," more "you, unknown to me."[31] Far from creating a demand for his poetic and spiritual leadership, the sexual frankness of the 1860 edition engendered alarm from well-wishers like Emerson, betrayed its publishers' plans to promote a new poetry, and was to embroil its author in almost two decades of controversy about its, and his, licentiousness. During the Civil War, Whitman began to write a different kind of poetry—still approaching his bardic role in visual and pictorial terms, but in ways that submerged the I within the Not-Me.

An instructive case is found in "Salut au Monde!" First introduced into *Leaves of Grass* in 1856, the poem began by asking, "What widens within you, Walt Whitman?"—and the response was, "Within me latitude widens, longitude lengthens, / Asia, Africa, Europe, are to the east—America is provided for in the west." The ensuing pages illustrate what multitudes Whitman contains within that mental space, until at the end Whitman can exult, "My spirit has passed in compassion and determination around the whole earth" (§1, 2, 13, *V,* I, 162, 175). Midway through the poem, though, in a litany that draws together images of food gathering among many peoples ("I

---

31. Ezra Greenspan discusses this turn of phrase in *American Reader,* 230.

see flocks of goats feeding, I see the fig-tree, tamarind, date [. . .],
I see over the pampas the pursuit of wild cattle"), there occurs one
of those moments of dilation:

> I see two boats with nets, lying off the shore of
>   Paumanok, quite still,
> I see ten fishermen waiting—they discover now a thick
>   school of mossbonkers, they drop the joined seine-
>   ends in the water,
> The boats separate, they diverge and row off, each on its
>   rounding course to the beach, enclosing the
>   mossbonkers,
> The net is drawn in by a windlass by those who stop
>   ashore,
> Some of the fishermen lounge in the boats, others stand
>   negligently ankle-deep in the water, poised on strong
>   legs,
> The boats are partly drawn up, the water slaps against
>   them,
> On the sand, in heaps and winrows, well out from the
>   water, lie the green-backed spotted mossbonkers.
>
>   (§7, *V*, I, 169–70)

This passage is an anomaly in the poem and in the book. "Salut au Monde!" affords no other image more than a single line's attention. The fishermen are not just caught in one moment of typical action, like the pedlar or the prostitute in "Song of Myself," but are followed through an entire cycle of their work. In the early editions of *Leaves of Grass,* even the extended images tend to be focused on the foreground, as the figures of drayman or blacksmith or of Washington; here attention begins with the coast and seascape, passes through the deeds of the fishermen, to rest at last on the spots on the fishes' skins. Not only are these men accorded a dilation of attention in which they take command of their work; they are almost fully recontextualized within the place and the duration of time in which their work actually occurs.

After these lines had for a quarter of a century occupied their place in "Salut au Monde!," Whitman excised them and made of them a separate poem, "A Paumanok Picture" (*V*, III, 689). He deleted the twice-repeated "I see," thus terminating all avowed dependency on the poet's mediating ego. The poem uses its linear sequence of words

The Expanse of Consciousness

not to imitate the flux and expansion of consciousness, but to trace an action from beginning to end. There they are, the Not-Me—boats, ten fishermen, sand, mossbonkers—outlined against the shore and the sky. Delivered from the womb of Whitman's mind, they go resolutely about their business, as though the reader were looking into Achilles' shield.

Still, "A Paumanok Picture" has not entirely escaped from subjectivity. The question that governs most of "Salut au Monde!"—"What do you see, Walt Whitman?"—still haunts this poem, for it is the democratic bard's undiscriminating attention that has made a "poem" out of this otherwise unremarkable scene. The democratic reader is now asked to extend his own categories of aesthetic appreciation, applying to these humble harvesters of the sea the same dignity that genre illustration gave to harvesters in the fields and to the more daring fishers of the whale. By designating their work a "picture," Whitman has defined a way for his reader to associate it with an analogue aesthetic experience, genre illustration. There is no need for the poet to lecture us as he does in "Song of the Broad-Axe," diminishing these men to mere words about them.

❖

Was the world embedded in the I? Whitman's readers were not put at ease. Perhaps the I could appear embedded in the world. A few poems in the 1860 edition attempt that reversal. At some point, he penciled a note on the script of the unpublished "Pictures": "Break all this into several 'pictures'" (*CRE*, 642n). That is, break open the casque of consciousness in which the images floated—as Whitman was eventually to do with the fishing scene in "Salut au Monde!"—and declare its single perceptions to be poems. Several poems from the Calamus sequence, like "I Saw in Louisiana a Live-Oak Growing" and "A Glimpse," are moving toward independence from the sponsoring mind. Elsewhere in that edition appeared a poem about an emigrant train camped on the prairies, told from the perspective of one of the pioneers. And next:

> Sea-water, and all living below it,
> Forests at the bottom of the sea—the branches and
>   leaves,

> Sea-lettuce, vast lichens, strange flowers and seeds—the
>   thick tangle, the openings, and the pink turf,
> Different colors, pale gray and green, purple, white, and
>   gold—the play of light through the water,
> Dumb swimmers there among the rocks—coral, gluten,
>   grass, rushes—and the aliment of the swimmers,
> Sluggish existences grazing there, suspended, or slowly
>   crawling close to the bottom,
> The sperm-whale at the surface, blowing air and spray,
>   or disporting with his flukes,
> The leaden-eyed shark, the walrus, the turtle, the hairy
>   sea-leopard, and the sting-ray;
> Passions there—wars, pursuits, tribes—sight in those
>   ocean-depths—breathing that thick-breathing air, as
>   so many do,
> The change thence to the sight here, and to the subtle air
>   breathed by beings like us, who walk this sphere;
> The change onward from ours to that of beings who
>   walk other spheres.
>   ("The World Below the Brine," *V*, II, 327–28)

These poems entrain a series of actions without absorbing them into some oracular proclamation like "Song of Myself." In such poems, the order of observation implies a statement of sorts. The house-builders passage acknowledges the necessary sequences of skilled labor; "A Glimpse" advances from outside to inside, from noisy bar-room to quiet nook, from coarse camaraderie to silent intimacy. The seascape poem ascends from a remarkably visualized panorama of the ocean floor, through a list of sea creatures, to the philosophic discourse about other spheres in which eyesight is again the symbol of faith in a spiritual world. From the eyesight proceeds another eyesight.

Moreover, the poet is not present here, either in his own person, as in "A Glimpse," or as national bard, as in "Salut au Monde!" In the first eight lines, the language is objectively descriptive, not betraying an attitude, not imputing human characteristics to the thick-breathing swimmers and crawlers. The ocean world is not appropriated by an expansionist rhetoric. There is no mind-gallery and no cicerone. Until the final line offers a motive for the "poem," the reader is simply confronted with visual images, as in the plates of a text on marine biology. Consciousness is of no manifest importance; these undersea apparitions are unquestioned and unquestionable. (The poem's conclusion, that life exists in other, less physical spheres, is presented as equally unquestionable.)

Suitably, this poem inaugurating a new approach to the visual mode depicts an underwater scene: the subject has swallowed up the poet; consciousness has drowned in the dense material world. It was in another poem new to the 1860 edition that Whitman confessed to the terrible question of appearances. Buffeted by that Cartesian doubt, the poet—like the swimmer in "The Sleepers"—here gives up his struggle and submits to the evident, phenomenal order; to that manifest world in which the American people were triumphantly building iron warehouses, tinkering with steam engines, and perfecting the daguerreotype. Seeking a new path between the lonely poet's soul and the bustling reality of America, Whitman was preparing to dedicate his poetry to an entirely different approach to the mystery of the eyesight—to a systematic depiction of conventionally stabilized visual images.

[3]

Satan, Wound-Dresser, Witness

"Cavalry Crossing a Ford," from *Drum-Taps*, offers just such a visual image:

> A line in long array where they wind betwixt green islands,
> They take a serpentine course, their arms flash in the sun—hark to the musical clank,
> Behold the silvery river, in it the splashing horses loitering stop to drink,
> Behold the brown-faced men, each group, each person, a picture, the negligent rest on the saddles,
> Some emerge on the opposite bank, others are just entering the ford—while,
> Scarlet and blue and snowy white,
> The guidon flags flutter gayly in the wind.
>
> (*V*, II, 457)

This is the kind of poem (presented here in its familiar, post-1871 version) that we suppose is typical of *Drum-Taps*. Describing it, writers on Whitman have resorted inevitably to pictorial metaphors, such as "realist," "photographic," or "imagist." But if these metaphors imply an artless and unmediated seeing, they are not accurate. Also, this is not the only kind of poem in Whitman's book about the Civil War. There is a war going on in *Drum-Taps*, a *duellum intestinum* in which several different poets contend, each armed with his own style and point of view. The spare, direct visual poem, which represents *Drum-Taps* to us today, is the medium of one of those poets, but he is a minority presence in the book. And though his style seems innovative because his coming is unforecasted by Whitman's earlier work, there is much in that style that conforms to earlier pictorial conventions; for *Drum-Taps* represents Whitman's bid to be "absorbed" by America not as a radically democratic visionary but as the inheritor and master of a tradition according to which poems were like pictures.

Drum-Taps often speaks with the voice of 1855 and 1856, as though nothing had happened, as though the doubts hinted at in those years had never broken forth in the Calamus poems. Whitman had been writing throughout the war, but he had published no book since 1860. With the war winding down, he was eager to reassert his claims as a national poet.[1] The familiar bardic voice of "Our Old Feuillage" and "Salut au Monde!" speaks first in the book that Whitman published in May of 1865:

> First, O songs, for a prelude,
> Lightly strike on the stretch'd tympanum, pride and joy
>   in my city,
> How she led the rest to arms—how she gave the cue,
> How at once with lithe limbs, unwaiting a moment, she
>   sprang;
> (O superb! O Manhattan, my own, my peerless! [. . .]
>   (*V*, II, 453)

This prelude begins the war as Whitman did, in New York City. Throughout *Drum-Taps* appear other poems from Manhattan's point of view: encamped recruits, parades, wagons of supplies rolling down to the wharves. And most of all, we hear the rhetoric of newspapers and public speakers proclaiming the eagle's-eye view of war:

> Long for my soul, hungering gymnastic, I devour'd
>   what the earth gave me;
> Long I roam'd the woods of the north—long I watch'd
>   Niagara pouring;
> I travel'd the prairies over, and slept on their breast—I
>   cross'd the Nevadas, I cross'd the plateaus;
> I ascended the towering rocks along the Pacific, I sail'd
>   out to sea;
> I sail'd through the storm, I was refresh'd by the storm;

---

1. Whitman hurried *Drum-Taps* into print, anticipating a boom in patriotic poetry at the war's end. "Nothing else meant so much to him as to be accepted by the American people as a poet" (Gay Wilson Allen, *The Solitary Singer* [Rev. ed.; New York, 1967], 357).

> I watch'd with joy the threatening maws of the waves;
> [. . .]
> —These , and such as these, I, elate, saw—saw with
>   wonder, yet pensive and masterful;
> All the menacing might of the globe uprisen around me;
> Yet there with my soul I fed—I fed content,
>   supercilious.
>   ("Rise O Days from Your Fathomless Deeps," §1, *V,* II,
>   483–84)

And together with his continent-encompassing vision, he takes up also the rhetorical devices that support that vision. Like "Song of Myself" and "By Blue Ontario's Shore," these poems are sustained by the poet's declamatory tone and by the strength of a will that can compel disparate things into one poetic line. Whitman asserts once more the power of consciousness to assimilate and unify a discordant nation. His grasp of those things is quick and light: sketchy epithets and a balloon-view perspective are enough to make his claim on Niagara, the rockbound Pacific, and the mountaintop at Chattanooga. An even more glorious future is foreseen:

> Over the carnage rose prophetic a voice,
> Be not dishearten'd—Affection shall solve the problems
>   of Freedom yet;
> Those who love each other shall become invincible—
>   they shall yet make Columbia victorious.
>   ("Over the Carnage Rose Prophetic a Voice," *V,* II, 373)

The expansive, spread-eagle posture of national consciousness has not changed. *Drum-Taps* includes "A Broadway Pageant," that hymn to Manifest Destiny, which Whitman had written five years earlier, with its chant of the "new empire" and its brief descriptive tags for the continents and archipelagoes soon to be united with America. Closer at hand, the Canadians are served notice that the American poet-nation will "absorb Kanada in myself" ("From Paumanok Starting I Fly like a Bird," *V,* II, 468).[2] And the poet declares again his self-conscious delight in consciousness. A short lyric early in the

---

2. The Canadians at that moment were federating themselves into a more formidable political entity. Although they may have been unaware of Whitman's poetic expansiveness, they were alert to its political equivalent in the United States.

book confesses frankly the pleasure of being the connoisseur of one's own experience:

> Beginning my studies, the first step pleas'd me so much,
> The mere fact, consciousness—these forms—the power of motion,
> The least insect or animal—the senses—eyesight;
> The first step, I saw, aw'd me and pleas'd me so much,
> I have never gone, and never wish'd to go, any farther,
> But stop and loiter all my life, to sing it in extatic songs.
> ("Beginning My Studies," *V*, II, 468)

Nor does *Drum-Taps* have the kind of dramatic structure in which the old posture is finally replaced by a new. In the book's finale, the poet, as a just-discharged soldier "forth from my tent emerging for good," resumes the songs that bind together the Alleghenian hills, the tireless Mississippi, the prairie spreading wide, Northern ice and rain, and the hot sun of the South ("To the Leaven'd Soil They Trod," *V*, II, 556). Repeatedly throughout *Drum-Taps,* Whitman proclaims anew the bardic vision of 1855.

But still things were not as they had been in 1855. The nation had been torn apart, and every rank of society riddled with losses. Whitman's faith in his absorbing consciousness and in the rhetoric that gave national utterance to that consciousness had been rebuked. Other styles interrupt and contradict the bard. Whitman made plain the losses and the broken confidence when, reissuing *Drum-Taps* as part of the 1871 *Leaves of Grass,* he set as its epigraph a few lines he later added to "The Wound-Dresser":

> Aroused and angry,
> I thought to beat the alarum, and urge relentless war;
> But soon my fingers fail'd me, my face droop'd, and I resign'd myself,
> To sit by the wounded and soothe them, or silently watch the dead.
> (*V*, III, 630)

These lines, though, simplify the conflict evident in the ensemble of poems comprising the original *Drum-Taps*. Of course, his glimpse of the reality of war, his plentiful experience of death in the military hospitals that surrounded Washington, and the recent break in his own health had made it impossible to renew absolutely his faith in physical and spiritual regeneration, or to entrust his poetic vision altogether to the declamatory style of the original *Leaves of Grass,* or to adapt it to the nation's insatiate demand for patriotic poetry. But the problem was older than that. The 1855 Preface had spoken of infidelity and of the poet's need to keep faith. But the flaws within his original poetic had led him to confess his doubts in "There was a Child Went Forth," in "Song of the Open Road," and in several of the Calamus poems. Remember:

> May-be the things I perceive—the animals, plants, men, hills, shining and flowing waters,
> The skies of day and night—colors, densities, forms—
> May-be these are, (as doubtless they are,) only apparitions, and the real something has yet to be known,
> (How often they dart out of themselves, as if to confound me and mock me!
> How often I think neither I know, nor any man knows, aught of them;)
> May-be they only seem to me what they are, (as doubtless they indeed but seem,) as from my present point of view—And might prove, (as of course they would,) naught of what they appear, or naught any how, from entirely changed points of view.
> ("Of the Terrible Doubt of Appearances," *V,* II, 377)

Words (as we have seen) may fail to render experience accurately or to express the Self truthfully. Experience may prove phantasmal, a flicker of dots and specks; and the Soul may dissolve in self-doubt and in the recognition of one's own hypocrisy.[3]

Many of the poems of *Drum-Taps* renew these doubts, questioning the reality of the Not-Me, confessing the bad faith of the I and its inability to speak frankly to You. Near the center of the book stands "Give Me the Splendid Silent Sun," in which Whitman rededicates himself to the prosecution of the war, by embracing Manhattan with its munitions, its shipping, its military parades—and its

---

3. Richard Chase writes that "by 1859 . . . Whitman's personal troubles and doubts led him to question whether the self really had any dependable psychological or metaphysical status at all, and at the same time the confusion and aimlessness of a nation on the brink of the war gave little assurance that it would continue to be a source of strength and an object of admiration" (*Walt Whitman Reconsidered,* 149).

Satan, Wound-Dresser, Witness 81

illusory "shows" and "pageants": "give me these phantoms incessant and endless along the trottoirs!" (§2, *V*, II, 498). To endorse the Union cause is to turn one's back on the "primal sanities" of Nature and to accept an urban world that seemed as unembraceable as a specter. Again in one of *Drum-Taps'* concluding poems, "How Solemn as One by One," as one of the disbanding regiments marches by him, Whitman observes the soldiers' masklike faces:

> [. . . T]he faces, the masks appear as I glance at the
>   faces, studying the masks;
> (As I glance upward out of this page, studying you, dear
>   friend, whoever you are;)
> How solemn the thought of my whispering soul, to
>   each in the ranks, and to you.
>
> (*V*, II, 554)

So even near the book's end, a street experience in Washington tells him again what the streets had always told him: that identity is a mask draped on an indeterminacy of dreams and dots; that there is forever a mask, or a quarrel, or a book between I and You. Much of the patriotic poetry in *Drum-Taps,* which to modern readers seems illuded or dishonest, the strutting and preening of the spring of 1861 (though doubtless sincerely meant), can be read as a city vision of the Civil War, limited to parades, publicity, and speechmaking—displays of emotion and rhetoric that never dilate into an extended contemplation of the actuality of war. That would come later, in hospital interiors and in the fields.

In *Drum-Taps,* the voice of doubt and of bad faith is not always contained within parentheses nor used to set a question that the rest of the poem will resolve, as it was in the Calamus poems. Often it speaks out unchallenged. "Chanting the Square Deific" identifies this skeptic voice as that of Satan—not the malignant one of *Paradise Lost* but the Satan of Job, of Blake's Milton, and of Byron—a spiritual power for dissent, self-criticism, and rebellion against constraint, here apotheosized as the fourth person of the Godhead: "Aloof, dissatisfied, plotting revolt, / Comrade of criminals, brother of slaves, / Crafty, despised [. . .], brooding, with many wiles" (§3, *V*, II, 544–45). Ever and again in *Drum-Taps,* Satan speaks forth as the voice of subversion, the accents of one who will never be absorbed by America's citizens:

> Did you ask dulcet rhymes from me?
> Did you find what I sang erewhile so hard to follow, to
>   understand?
> Why I was not singing erewhile for you to follow, to
>   understand—nor am I now;
> —What to such as you, anyhow, such a poet as I?—
>   therefore leave my works,
> And go lull yourself with what you can understand;
> For I lull nobody—and you will never understand me.
>   ("To a Certain Civilian," *V*, II, 500)

"Song of Myself" had spoken on behalf of slaves and criminals, to draw them back within the spiritual commonwealth from which they had been excluded. Now Whitman speaks as an outsider himself: a citizen whose democratic anarchism was affronted by the Union's suppression of political dissent and by the elitism of its military leadership, and whose humane impulses were enraged by the suffering and human wastage he saw in the hospitals;[4] a bard whose book had been denied publication, whose poems had caused him to be dismissed from his job, whose volumes would find the library doors closed against them;[5] a homosexual whose secret could never be frankly avowed.[6] He begins to speak not as the president of regulation (as he had called himself in the 1855 Preface), but as the perpetual revolutionary:

> I know I am restless, and make others so;
> I know my words are weapons, full of danger, full of
>   death;
> [. . .]

---

4. George M. Fredrickson, *The Inner Civil War: Northern Intellectuals and the Crisis of the Union* (New York, 1965), 94–95, 148–49.

5. Denise Askin has described *Drum-Taps* as a struggle between a grandiloquent "prophetic" voice, public and assured, and a "private" voice, doubting, "demonic," which sits by the wounded and counts the dead ("Retrievements Out of the Night: Prophetic and Private Voices in Whitman's *Drum-Taps*," *ATQ*, LI [1981], 211–23). Daniel Aaron also describes the split between public and private in *Drum-Taps*, tracing it to the poet's doubts about the war, his inner divisions, and his deepening alienation from his hoped-for readership (*The Unwritten War: American Writers and the Civil War* [New York, 1973], 68). As we will see, there are more than two speakers in *Drum-Taps*.

6. See Joseph Cady, "*Drum-Taps* and Nineteenth-Century Male Homosexual Literature," in *Walt Whitman Here and Now*, ed. Krieg, 56–57.

> For I confront peace, security, and all the settled laws, to
>   unsettle them;
> I am more resolute because all have denied me, than I
>   could ever have been had all accepted me.
>> ("As I Lay with my Head in Your Lap Camerado,"
>> *V*, II, 549)

In the early volumes, Whitman had addressed an idealized reader, an undiscriminating democratic consciousness like his own or one that with some instruction and example could become like his own. As early as the open letter to Emerson, he had recognized that actual readers did not prove so readily sympathetic. Now acknowledging the warfare between the public and himself, he enfranchises "Satan" as his general and spokesman. Mingled with the hymns of national triumph that conclude *Drum-Taps* are poems—some sullen, some filled with bravado—that tell of an "old, incessant war" conducted on two fronts. One front is within the Self:

> You degradations—you tussle with passions and
>   appetites;
> You smarts from dissatisfied friendships, (ah wounds,
>   the sharpest of all;)
> You toil of painful and choked articulations—you
>   meannesses;
> You shallow tongue-talks at tables, (my tongue the
>   shallowest of any;)
>> ("Ah Poverties, Wincings, and Sulky Retreats,"
>> *V*, II, 548)

And the other front is against the American people, both as his subject and as his readers:

> Of the endless trains of the faithless—of cities fill'd with
>   the foolish;
> Of myself forever reproaching myself, (for who more
>   foolish than I, and who more faithless?)
> Of eyes that vainly crave the light—of the objects
>   mean—of the struggle ever renew'd;
> Of the poor results of all—of the plodding and sordid
>   crowds I see around me;
> [. . .]

> The question, O me! so sad, recurring—What good
> amid these, O me, O life?
>
> ("O Me! O Life!" *V*, II, 547)

Both of these poems conclude as did the earlier poem about the doubt of appearances, with a brief, forced reconciliation; but the burden of these pages is Whitman's acknowledgment of an interminable civil war between the poet and his fickle nation, between the poet and the falseness of his own personae. One concluding poem manages to be about both wars: "Spirit whose Work is Done" begins as a patriotic invocation to the American Bellona, celebrating and honorably discharging the spirit of relentless belligerence with which the Civil War had been prosecuted; but it ends by transferring this spirit to Whitman himself:

> Touch my mouth, ere you depart—press my lips close!
> Leave me your pulses of rage! bequeath them to me! fill
>   me with currents convulsive!
> Let them scorch and blister out of my chants, when you
>   are gone;
> Let them identify you to the future in these songs.
>
> (*V*, II, 542–43)

❖

But *Drum-Taps* does not introduce a phase of Whitman's work devoted to shocking the bourgeois or excoriating the hypocritical reader; and though Satan's voice issues from many of the lyrics of this volume, Whitman does not adopt him as exclusive spokesman. For while this book was being written and published, Whitman had acquired another, actual spokesman, in character quite the opposite of his Satan—William Douglas O'Connor, in whose house he boarded during his years in Washington and who defended him when he was turned out of his position in the Department of the Interior. O'Connor's apologia for him, *The Good Gray Poet,* creates an image of the poet somewhat like that proposed early in the 1855 Preface—the bard as curator of a national gallery of attitudes and images, the keeper of the Matter of America. "The nation is in it!" O'Connor wrote of *Leaves of Grass*—probably with Whitman at his elbow. "In form a series of chants, in substance it is an epic of America." There follows one of those patented panoramic catalogs: "the prairie solitudes, the vast pastoral plateaus; the Mississippi; the land dense with villages and farms . . . the august figure of Washington . . . the Federal Mother, seated with more than antique majesty in the midst of her many children." Although O'Connor seems more concerned with defending the benignity of the person than with the wholesomeness of the poetry, nevertheless his Whitman is a poet who could be affectionately absorbed by his people. *Leaves of Grass*, he writes, has a "national character and national purpose": namely, a "vigorous re-enforcement and service to all that we hold most precious."[7] Cooperating—or collaborating—with O'Connor, Whitman in *Drum-Taps* made many concessions to popular literary taste. Roger Asselineau has noted the appearance of poetic archaisms for the first time in this book, and the overtures into regular stanza structure and rhyme, which were to issue in two of his most popular poems: the unrhymed but regular trochaics of "Pioneers! O Pioneers!" and the singsong stanzas of "O Captain! My Captain!"[8] Justin Kaplan speaks of a "Tennysonian sonority and sweetness of diction" even in the Lincoln elegy—evidence of a "retreat from the idiomatic boldness and emotional directness of Whitman's earlier work."[9]

More was involved than matters of diction. Whitman began to create other identities, other points of view. As Richard Chase once put it, "The brash, egotistic Whitman and the troubled, doubting Whitman both give way to the self-sacrificing, even self-annihilating hospital visitor."[10] The former Whitman, the nationalistic bard of 1855 and 1856, had founded his poems on a moment of unmediated vision on a transparent summer morning. So authorized, that poet had detached his Self from all mediating points of view, all merely

---

7. William Douglas O'Connor, *The Good Gray Poet* [1866]; rpr. in Richard Maurice Bucke, *Walt Whitman* (Philadelphia, 1883), 117–18.

8. Roger Asselineau, *The Evolution of Walt Whitman* (Cambridge, Mass., 1960), II, 226, 249–50. Arthur Golden refers to Whitman's assuming, after 1866, a "public personality," though he seems to include *Drum-Taps* within the decade when Whitman was not "assuming postures of one kind or another but concentrating his efforts on writing a number of his most important poems" (Introduction to *Walt Whitman's Blue Book* [New York, 1968], II, xix). James Perrin Warren dates the change later still, from 1871: Whitman's theory of the evolution of language, he says, led him to introduce "archaic, formal, abstract diction" so that *Leaves of Grass* "enacts the cumulative quality of American English, blending the ancient and the modern to form a linguistic 'ensemble'" (*Walt Whitman's Language Experiment*, 138).

9. Justin Kaplan, *Walt Whitman: A Life* (New York, 1980), 309–10.

10. Chase, *Walt Whitman Reconsidered*, 150.

local or partial ways of seeing and saying. The latter Whitman, for whom Satan speaks in *Drum-Taps,* sets himself in explicit defiance of all the mediators of his country's culture—librarians, reviewers, bureaucrats, priests. As we have seen, this professedly unmediated vision is recontextualized in consciousness and in tacit allusions to the conventions of popular visual media, so that the visionary I could communicate his ecstasy to the unenlightened You. In *Drum-Taps,* there are other viewpoints, such as the hospital visitor's, through whom Whitman seeks more frankly to join his readers within a mediating context.

The wound-dresser and mourner sees the war not from Manhattan but from Washington, where Whitman first came in December of 1862. This city was not only the capital and center of military command, but also a fortress at the eastern salient of the Union battle line. It was filled not with the metonymies of war, like New York, but with its actual stuff: troops, convalescents, prisoners, politicians, civil servants, office seekers. What he saw there burst into life in *Specimen Days.* There he would write of a city swarming with convalescent and furloughed soldiers ("Their blue pants and overcoats are everywhere. The clump of crutches is heard up the stairs of the paymasters' offices" [*PW,* I, 85]). There, prowling the city at night, he would come on the "strange scene" of Congress still in session at dawn: "The gas-light, mix'd with the dingy day-break, produced an unearthly effect. The poor little sleepy, stumbling pages, the smell of the hall, the members with heads leaning on their desks, the sounds of the voices speaking, with unusual intonations ... —the grandeur of the hall itself, with its effect of vast shadows up toward the panels and spaces over the galleries—all made a mark'd combination" (*PW,* I, 96). Whitman made himself a citizen of Washington, absorbing it as he had New York, wandering its streets day and night and frequenting its public buildings and saloons as well as the military hospitals that lay on the hills all around it.

But the city experiences of those years were consigned to the anecdotal prose of *Specimen Days.*[11] When he looked at the Civil War

---

11. M. Wynn Thomas has traced through *Specimen Days* the process by which Whitman passed from hostility toward the capital, seen as an epitome of "that other civil war between the people and their estranged officers and institutions," to a recognition of how Lincoln and the common soldiers had made it "a truly American city and a genuine national capital" (*Lunar Light,* 185–90).

with the eye of a poet, his actual citizenship in Washington gave him no ground on which to address the American people. For all its experiential substance, it could not provide him with a mediating context for his own "songs, / Fit for war" ("Not Youth Pertains to Me," *V*, II, 528). It may be that he found the pose of the *flâneur* and saunterer, even in Washington, too remote to acknowledge the reality of awe and of mourning. These required instead his fictive membership in the army, the mostly invisible context of the hospital ward—and an implicit reference to pictorial conventions in popular art and in landscape poetry.

The two mediating groups for Whitman's war book are the army and the hospital. In some of the poems, he speaks in the person of a soldier—in combat, musing by his campfire, or reminiscing after the war's end. In others, what is depicted requires experience available only to a soldier: a troop of cavalry, a bivouac. Adopting this viewpoint allows him to speak directly for the common soldier, eliminating secondary interpreters such as the *flâneur,* the journalist, or the speechmaker. Although these poems are in a way extensions of the feats of empathy found in "Song of Myself," where Whitman spoke for hounded slaves and crushed firemen, now he emphasizes not the poet's power of assimilation but the undistinguished dignity, suffering, and heroism of the soldiers. These poems have the quality of testimonies, experiences retold not for their personal value to the speaker but for what they might contribute to sustaining the faith of a community—the people of America whose soldiers and kin these were; whose poet Whitman desired to be.

Although Whitman's friends from O'Connor's time till today have pressed the claim of his devoted hospital service, relatively few of the poems make explicit use of that setting. Nevertheless, it is implicitly a powerful mediating context, as a liminal place between life and death, military and civilian. In *Specimen Days,* his prose memoranda of the war, he said that "the marrow of the tragedy [was] concentrated in those Army Hospitals—(it seem'd sometimes as if the whole interest of the land, North and South, was one vast central hospital, and all the rest of the affair but flanges)" (*PW,* I, 117). The hospital epitomized the interminable misery and losses of the war, as well as Whitman's doubts about whether the struggle could be justified, and his respect and love for the young men who suffered its wounds in their flesh. Also, it was the context from which Whitman launched his first efforts to mediate between the war and a readership, as he wrote family letters on behalf of the soldiers he nursed, and then as he sought a way to raise funds for their comfort.

Soon after the 1860 *Leaves of Grass* appeared, his publishers announced a sequel, *Banner at Day-Break*. The proposed title, drawn from a poem that eventually appeared in *Drum-Taps,* suggests that Whitman was planning a directly patriotic campaign for recognition by America's readers. By 1863, however, his instinct for self-promotion had been complicated by his need to raise money to buy gifts and treats for the wounded soldiers whom he was visiting. That year he wrote to the Boston publisher James Redpath, who was soliciting funds for this cause: "Do you want to print a little 30 or 50ct book about the scenes, war, camp, hospitals &c (especially the &c)."[12] (Redpath had recently published a popular book of hospital sketches by Louisa May Alcott, contributing part of his profit to the care of children orphaned by the war.[13]) Nine days later he wrote again, proposing more than just a fund-raising pamphlet: "My idea is a book of the time, worthy the time—something considerably beyond mere hospital sketches—a book for sale perhaps in a larger American market—the premises of skeleton memoranda of incidents, persons, places, sights, the past year [. . .] a book full enough of mosaic, but all fused to one comprehensive thing."[14] This project was eventually to be realized as his prose books *War Memoranda* (1873) and *Specimen Days* (1882).

These letters show that as Whitman thought of ways to reach a "larger American market," he thought also about recording his experience of the war in a pictorial way, as "scenes" or "sketches," whether in prose or in poetry. In 1864 he told William Douglas O'Connor he was writing "thumb-nail sketches" of the war for a volume of poems he now called "Drum-Taps."[15] At the end of that year, he wrote that his poems had "photographed" the war (*N,* IV, 1449). No longer restricting himself to his experiences in the hospital, Whitman was now planning to respond to the war comprehensively—and pictorially.

12. Edwin Haviland Miller, ed., *The Correspondence of Walt Whitman (1842–1867)* (New York, 1961), I 164.
13. Louisa May Alcott, *Hospital Sketches* (1863; rpr. Cambridge, Mass., 1960); Kaplan, *Walt Whitman,* 278.
14. Miller, ed., *Correspondence of Walt Whitman,* I, 171.
15. *Ibid.,* 239.

Satan, Wound-Dresser, Witness   89

There were other, competing books of war "sketches" in print. In 1863, as another fund raiser for orphans, John Henry Hayward had compiled *Poetical Pen-Pictures of the War;* and in 1864 Ledyard Bill issued a similar collection of poems and of journalists' eyewitness reports, *Pen-Pictures of the War.*[16] Perhaps the public was hungry for more vivid descriptions of a war that was daily chronicled in the newspapers and whose scenes and combatants were so close to them. However, readers seeking in Hayward or Bill for any specific news of battle, hospital, or camp would have been disappointed by the vagueness of the stock imagery of almost all their poems:

> The march was o'er—the toilsome march,
>   Through forest dark, and tangled wild—
> Each soldier sought his couch of leaves,
>   And slumbered like a wearied child.
> The swift Potomac coursed along
>   Beside them, like a silver thread,
> And mingling with its rushing tide
>   Came echoes of the sentry's tread.[17]

The chief merit of Alcott's *Sketches* was her Dickensian sketches of wounded or dying soldiers. In proposing a book of "sketches" or "photographs," Whitman was marketing his considerable descriptive talents to a reading public that had responded to Alcott, eager for details and feelings, and accustomed to visualizing events through the medium of words. As he urged Redpath to publish his "sketches" in time to catch the Christmastime gift trade, he was preparing to accommodate his bardic role to readers as he took them to be and to their taste for the visual, rather than waiting for the appearance of the idealized disciples whom he had sought to create in the 1855 and 1856 editions of *Leaves of Grass.*

Because *Drum-Taps* is a book divided between several voices and several poetics, not all the visualist poetry in it is of the same sort. Descriptive and narrative poems like "Song of the Banner at Daybreak" and "The Centenarian's Story" consort perfectly with those declamatory poems, quoted above, that spoke with the rhetorical confidence of 1855, to beat the alarum and urge relentless war. Most,

16. John Henry Hayward, ed., *Poetical Pen-Pictures of the War* (1863; rpr. Louisville, 1975).
17. George F. Bourne, "The Night Guard," in Hayward, *Poetical Pen-Pictures,* 214.

though, take a humbler perspective. In a prose passage probably drafted around the time he was completing *Drum-Taps,* he wrote that

> future years will never know the seething hell and the black infernal background of countless minor scenes and interiors, (not the official surface-courteousness of the Generals, not the few great battles) of the Secession war; and it is best they should not—the real war will never get in the books .... Its interior history will not only never be written—its practicality, minutiae of deeds and passions, will never be even suggested. The actual soldier of 1862-65, North and South, with all his ways, his incredible dauntlessness, habits, practices, tastes, language, his fierce friendship, his appetite, rankness, his superb strength and animality, lawless gait, and a hundred unnamed lights and shades of camp, I say, will never be written—perhaps must not and should not be. (*Specimen Days, PW,* I, 116-17)

Here Whitman sets the course that he would follow in those poems that have proven the most important and enduring part of *Drum-Taps*. Disaffiliated, like his Satan, from the war's grand gestures—from the courtly generals and the great battles—Whitman was nevertheless eager to serve as bard for the new, proven America emerging from its struggle. The subversive tones of Satan, heard so clearly in some of the poems of *Drum-Taps,* could modulate into the more acquiescent voice of a citizen who remembers the cost of victory; who stands aside from the triumph to sing dirges for the fallen. In one of the book's last poems, he says that he brings "No poem proud [. . .] nor mastery's rapturous verse," but rather "a little book, containing night's darkness, and blood-dripping wounds, / And psalms of the dead" ("Lo, Victress on the Peaks," *V,* II, 555). Despite this phrase about darkness and wounds, few of the poems would look directly into the seething hell of battlefield death and mutilation; and his hospital sketches, though more candid about delirium and agony than Alcott's sketches, would not tell the worst that he had known.[18] Rather, he would redeem from oblivion the

18. Fredrickson has questioned Whitman's reticence about the extremes of suffering: "It is possible that raw descriptions of the hospital life and battlefield carnage were too jarring and sensational to be suitable material for poetry. . . . He could give no formal expression to his sense of the war as an anonymous 'slaughterhouse,' not

best that the war had produced—the unremarkable virtues and courage of the common soldier in his daily life.

And the mode for this muted commemoration would be pictorial description. The lines from *Specimen Days* emphasize the "background" of "minor scenes and interiors" and of the "lights and shades of camp." He would "sketch" for his readers the "interior" war, the unofficial war of the private soldier in the camps and hospitals that he knew from their own words. Through him the wounded had told their stories to their families. He had attempted to pass along the soldiers' war to the readers of the New York *Times*, as he had heard it from them during his sojourn with the 51st New York Regiment:

> [September] 18 [1862] lay in the neighborhood, (no grub for two days,) expecting an attack from Secesh but they now retired for scores and hundreds and hundreds of miles—all this through mud, rain, heat, snow, cold, woods, bog, fording rivers, slipping down steep descents, climbing upright & hills, . . . amidst an active enemy, in secretiveness, the inhabitants full of treachery and venom, our men often marching without food, often worse, no water, the muddiest water sometimes a precious luxury, dragging their limbs, deadly tiresome, carrying heavy burdens, . . . shoes worn out, feet bleeding, clothing torn, dirty, not only sleeping on the ground in the open air, (that was nothing), sometimes having to scrape away the snow to make a place to lie down.[19]

But the *Times* did not print this. It offered a journalistic translation:

> They were on the march, fighting, advancing or retreating, for nearly four months, with seldom any intermission. It was life on the bivouac in earnest, sleeping on the

---

only because his readers could not assimilate such an insight, but because, ultimately, he could not accept it himself" (*The Inner Civil War*, 95). Timothy Sweet says more harshly that Whitman was obeying "the ideology of Union," which dictated that deaths and wounds be represented only typically, as sacrifice, or through the conventions of elegy or pastoral (*Poetry, Photography, and the Crisis of the Union* [Baltimore, 1990], 11–77). Sweet, however, does not acknowledge the other voices in *Drum-Taps* that gainsay the Unionist bard.

19. Charles I. Glicksberg, ed., *Walt Whitman and the Civil War* (Philadelphia, 1933), 76–77.

ground where night overtook them, and up and on again the next day, with battle or pursuit every week, and often men falling by the road from utter exhaustion. Thus they promenaded by rapid marches, through heat, dust, rain or snow, crossing mountains, fording rivers, etc., often without food to eat or water to drink.[20]

The real war did not even get into the newspapers.

Encountering these soldiers' stories in camps and hospitals, Whitman lent them his powers for empathetic participation and intense visual detail, to throw a democratic light on the commonplace heroism of this war. Thus he would subvert those canons of cultural taste that had rendered "actual soldiers" and their deeds invisible. That was what he had done in the indecorous juxtapositions of "Song of Myself" and the other long poems of 1855 and 1856. And he would present them as he had in "Song of Myself"—in ways that invoked the popular artistic styles with which his readers were familiar.

Those artistic styles were not, of themselves, styles of subversion. *Drum-Taps* contains several poems depicting an altogether "official" war. And despite the epigraph lines claiming that he early abandoned writing verses that urged relentless war, graphic images of bellicose patriotism appear throughout the book. No fewer than four of its poems invoke the Union's iconic image, the Stars and Stripes. Despite his disclaimer in the poem quoted earlier, Whitman was well practiced in the declamatory mode appropriate for rapturous verse proclaiming "mastery."

> Flag of stars! thick-sprinkled bunting!
> Long yet your road, fateful flag!—long yet your road,
>   and lined with bloody death!
> For the prize I see at issue, at last is the world!
> All its ships and shores I see, interwoven with your
>   threads, greedy banner!
>   ("Thick-Sprinkled Bunting," *V*, II, 518)

The cause of democracy now vindicated in war, America is called to extend her virtues to all nations. The flag appears in *Drum-Taps* as it did in the battle tactics, the political cultus, and the songs and the popular art of that time: a visual reference point in combat, a symbol

---

20. New York *Times*, October 29, 1864, p. 2. The translator of Whitman the poet may, of course, have been Whitman the journalist.

of divinely ratified principles, and an emblem of national hegemony. Sight passes into vision, physical description to prophetic interpretation of the banner's meaning and America's character or future.

One of these poems invokes it as "flag like a beautiful woman!" ("Bathed in War's Perfume," *V*, II, 493). *Drum-Taps* abounds with such personifications. In the 1855 *Leaves of Grass*, Whitman's search for a You often had led him to the rhetorical device of apostrophe. By 1860 the apostrophe was beginning to take visual, personal shape: "Democracy! / Near at hand to you a throat is now inflating itself and joyfully singing. / Ma femme!" ("Starting from Paumanok," §12, *V*, II, 282). In *Drum-Taps*, when Whitman invokes "Democracy" and other muses of American heroic poetry, they assume fully pictorial form as the female figures that had become part of the national iconography displayed in public statuary, on governmental seals and on the national coinage, and in printed media such as editorial cartoons and engraved or lithographed prints. The most famous of these figures, Luigi Bartholdi's Liberty, had not yet arisen on Bedloe's Island off Manhattan, but Thomas Crawford's statue of Freedom was mounted on the Capitol dome in 1863 (Fig. 1); and Brumidi's mural on the interior of that dome, completed two years later, displayed many allegorical female figures, among them *Armed Freedom*. In *Drum-Taps*, Whitman addresses a bevy of personifications: Manhattan ("Lady of this teeming and turbulent city"), Democracy, Freedom, Ireland ("at her feet fallen an unused royal harp"), "Libertad" ("be not alarmed—turn your undying face"), Columbia (unnamed), Death ("Dark Mother, always gliding near, with soft feet"), the belligerent "Spirit" quoted some pages earlier, and, most fully set forth in the iconography of popular illustration, victorious America:

> [. . .] Victress on the peaks!
> Where thou standest, with mighty brow, regarding the world,
> [. . .]
> Where thou, dominant, with the dazzling sun around thee,
> Towerest now unharm'd, in immortal soundness and bloom[.]21

21. These figures appear in "First O Songs for a Prelude" (*V*, II, 453), "Rise O Days from Your Fathomless Deeps" (II, 485), "Years of the Modern" (II, 504), "Old

Fig. 1 Thomas Crawford, *Armed Freedom* (plaster model for bronze statue, 1856)
Courtesy Division of Photographic History, National Museum of American History, Smithsonian Institution

In later years, as his energies withered, Whitman would turn more and more frequently to recording the proclamations of Columbia, Freedom, the Star of France, America, Columbus, and other sym-

---

Ireland" (II, 518), "Turn O Libertad" (II, 525), "Pensive on Her Dead Gazing" (II, 526–27), "When Lilacs Last in the Dooryard Bloom'd" §14 (II, 536), "Spirit whose Work is Done" (II, 542–43), and "Lo, Victress on the Peaks" (II, 555).

bolic figures from the nation's scrapbook.²² But never did he draw so explicitly on a popular pictorial idiom, with such a wealth of visual detail, as in the apostrophes of the *Drum-Taps* years.

Also, *Drum-Taps* affords one direct glimpse of the official war, as it might have appeared in a lithograph commemorating the valor of some commander:

> I saw old General at bay;
> (Old as he was, his grey eyes yet shone out in battle like
>   stars;)
> His small force was now completely hemmed in, in his
>   works;
> He call'd for volunteers to run the enemy's lines—a
>   desperate emergency;
> I saw a hundred and more step forth from the ranks
>   [. . .].
>   ("I Saw Old General at Bay," *V*, II, 521)

Although the poem's ending, a few lines later, dwells on the courage of the volunteers making the sortie, nevertheless it implies that the general's example has summoned up or even created this bravery. And so the poem commemorates the official, chivalric Civil War, invoking those illustrations that employed the conventions of historical painting in which the general commands not only the field but the canvas, where he is given foreground space of his own, individualized modeling, and a conventionally heroic stance (Fig. 2). Theodore Davis, one of the artists of the war, remarked that conventional military painting implied "that all battlefields have some elevated spot upon which the general is located, and that from this spot the

---

22. In 1867 he revised "By Blue Ontario's Shore," which had begun its life as the brashly self-confident Preface to the 1855 *Leaves of Grass,* so that it became a dream vision inspired by the muse-mother Democracy:

> Democracy! while weapons were everywhere aim'd at your breast,
> I saw you serenely give birth to children—saw in dreams your dilating
>   form;
> Saw you with spreading mantle covering the world.
>   (§17, *V*, I, 208)

Betsy Erkkila provides a historical background for these feminine personifications in "Whitman as Revolutionary Son," *Prospects,* X (1985), 421–41. Timothy Sweet interprets them as ideologically manipulable substitutes for the actual bodies of soldiers (*Poetry, Photography,* 16–23).

Fig. 2 Detail from *The Storming of Fort Donelson, Tenn., Feb. 15th, 1862* (Currier & Ives lithograph)
Courtesy Museum of the City of New York; The Harry T. Peters Collection, 56.300.464

commander can see his troops, direct all their maneuvers and courteously furnish special artists an opportunity of sketching the scene."[23]

❖

However, most of the pictorial poetry in *Drum-Taps* takes a different approach than this, though it still invokes the schemata of popular art. Some of the most successful poems in *Drum-Taps* represent a compromise between Whitman's original poetic and the conventions of nineteenth-century poetry—not a capitulation, as in "Pioneers! O

23. Quoted in Stephen W. Sears, ed., *The American Heritage Century Collection of Civil War Art* (New York, 1974), 125. For this quotation I am indebted to M. Wynn Thomas, "Whitman and the American Democratic Identity Before and During the Civil War," *Journal of American Studies*, XV (1981), 93.

Pioneers" and "O Captain! My Captain!," but a compromise in which Whitman's rhythm and sensibility are mated with the emotions and situations of popular poetry. The intention is to paint a picture or to tell a story—not a picture confined to the brain-gallery, or a story that has been absorbed by the omnivorous Self, but objects and events presented as objectively real and as the occasion of true and widely accepted emotions. In these poems, invoking poetic and pictorial conventions and often framed in a more traditional poetic idiom, the Good Gray Poet was exploring yet another path between dumb real objects and the souls of common folk, a highway far less challenging than the endless reversals of field, I and Not-Me, in "Song of Myself."

There are several narrative poems in *Drum-Taps,* and they are usually cast in the form of dramatic monologs. In "Song of Myself," Whitman had entered sympathetically the experience of a hounded slave or a dying fireman, but he had done so to demonstrate the expanse and power of the democratic imagination. When the slave spoke, or the sailor, it was from within the protean, encompassing Soul that was the real subject of Whitman's inaugural poem, just as the fishermen in "A Paumanok Picture" began their labors as an image within "Salut au Monde!" Narrative, or sustained description, appeared only as a momentary dilation in the poem's current of catalog or rhetorical invocation. In *Drum-Taps,* the motive is more naïvely mimetic; it is an account told by a defined character. The poet is describing a world, just as real as himself, in which he takes a place. When Whitman thought about Chancellorsville, he did not ask whether it was all flashes and specks.

This transition is yet incomplete in "The Centenarian's Story," one of the early poems in *Drum-Taps.* In it a veteran of the Revolutionary War recounts the battle of Brooklyn Heights, a story Whitman had told in "The Sleepers" (1855). What was five lines in the earlier poem has now become seventy, reviewing the events of several days and developing several visually striking scenes:

> As I talk, I remember all—I remember the Declaration:
> It was read here—the whole army paraded—it was read
>   to us here;
> By his staff surrounded, the general stood in the
>   middle—he held up his unsheath'd sword,
> It glitter'd in the sun in full sight of the army.

> [. . .]
> [. . . D]ull and damp and another day;
> But the night of that, mist lifting, rain ceasing,
> Silent as a ghost, while they thought they were sure of
>   him, my General retreated.
> I saw him at the river-side,
> Down by the ferry, lit by torches, hastening the
>   embarcation.

However, at the end of the old soldier's reminiscence, Whitman self-consciously resumes his encompassing bardic role:

> Enough—the Centenarian's story ends;
> The two, the past and present, have interchanged;
> I myself, as connector, as chansonnier of a great future,
>   am now speaking.
>
>   (*V*, II, 471, 473)

The poem is bound together by its repeated references to the Brooklyn landscape and by the theatrical pictures of Washington, but Whitman is still the presiding consciousness.

In "The Wound-Dresser," Whitman becomes himself the centenarian, an old man reminiscing on his hospital service during the Civil War, now long in the past. Dramatizing the fluid transitions of memory, it is another poem of ego-consciousness. But here the I does not just absorb the Not-Me. Consciousness is set in a specific, double context: one established by the old man talking with young people about the bygone war; the other by the wartime hospital, recalled "in silence, in dream's projections." The dresser's memories flood back in tableaux of great visual power:

> From the stump of the arm, the amputated hand,
> I undo the clotted lint, remove the slough, wash off the
>   matter and blood;
> Back on his pillow the soldier bends, with curv'd neck,
>   and side-falling head;
> His eyes are closed, his face is pale, he dares not look on
>   the bloody stump,
> And has not yet looked on it.
>
>   (§3, *V*, II, 480–82)

The memories are contained within and selected by the schema of "hospital sketches"—the subject he had proposed to Redpath in 1863; and the poem's *mise en scène* binds them, as a "past," with a specific "present." The poem's dramatic movement is that of an old man's memories, not the unfettered caprice of the democratic imagination depicted in "Song of Myself" or "Salut au Monde!"[24] As the wound-dresser moves from ward to ward, from one vivid scene to another, the "doors of time" through which he passes separate each memory from the others and yet unite them as the experiences of a specific place and time.

The hospital is a schema within which these personal reflections can be shared with others—not only the "young men and maidens" around him, but also the reader, You, whom the dresser invites to enter that mediating context, both book and hospital: "[. . .] I enter the doors—(while for you up there, / Whoever you are, follow me without noise, and be of strong heart.)" (§2, *V*, II, 480). That context unites both poet and reader with all other Americans, through their common devotion toward those who had suffered in the war.[25] Such emotions aroused by the war offered Whitman a bond of shared faith by which he might be united with his readers, and he entered some of the common situations of war poetry in order to evoke those emotions and to invoke that faith.

One of those genres plumbed the anxiety and grief of the soldier's loved ones. Because the war's poems were mainly written for civilians, it was a very popular genre. "Come Up from the Fields Father" is Whitman's essay into sentimental narrative. Both in and out of the story, he speaks for the members of an Ohio family as they read a letter, just arrived, about their soldier son Pete; and he sets them in a conventional pastoral setting intended to make their experience representative:

> Lo, 'tis autumn;
> Lo, where the trees, deeper green, yellower and redder,

24. In 1866, a year after *Drum-Taps*, John Greenleaf Whittier was to publish *Snow-Bound*. Though his poem has more narrative structure and the pictorial scenes are longer sustained, Whittier's structural principle, like Whitman's, is the dramatizing of the behavior of memory. Mark Twain's career shows that the Gilded Age found reminiscence more palatable than prevision.

25. The nation responded to the war's death toll through a rhetoric of quasi-religious sacrifice that subsumed personal grief in a bond of national piety. Lincoln's address at Gettysburg is only the most familiar expression of a pervasive communal piety. See Sweet, *Poetry, Photography*, 11–43.

> Cool and sweeten Ohio's villages, with leaves fluttering
>   in the moderate wind;
> Where apples ripe in the orchards hang, and grapes on
>   the trellis'd vines;
> [. . .]
> Above all, lo, the sky, so calm, so transparent after the
>   rain, and with wondrous clouds;
> Below, too, all calm, all vital and beautiful—and the
>   farm prospers well.
>
> (*V*, II, 488)

The scene is one of peace and plenty: it evokes the title of an Inness painting and the implicit subtitle of many a lithograph of Summer or The American Farm. Here calm is invoked as a conventionally ironic prelude to catastrophe. The poem shifts into dramatic utterance:

> Open the envelope quickly;
> O this is not our son's writing, yet his name is sign'd;
> O a strange hand writes for our dear son—O stricken
>   mother's soul!
> All swims before her eyes—flashes with black—she
>   catches the main words only:
> Sentences broken—*gun-shot wound in the breast, cavalry
>   skirmish, taken to hospital,*
> *At present low, but will soon be better.*

Then the poet interrupts, with an insight sharpened by his experience as letter writer for wounded soldiers:

> Alas, poor boy, he will never be better, (nor may-be
>   needs to be better, that brave and simple soul;)
> While they stand at home at the door, he is dead already;
> The only son is dead.

The poem ends, though, not with this irony but with a sentimental anticipation of Pete's mother's untempered grief, her wish to "withdraw unnoticed—silent from life, escape and withdraw, / To follow, to seek, to be with her dear dead son." Although the rhythms of the final stanza are Whitman's own, its events and emotions are entirely conventional, like those of "O Captain!" They preempt the poet's obligation either to respond for his Self, as mediator, or to acknowledge the actions and feelings of the stricken family.

In another poem, "Vigil Strange I Kept on the Field One Night," Whitman depicts another of the conventional situations of the war's poetry—the battlefield at night, littered with the slain. But he does not stop with the convention. He invests himself completely in the person of the soldier who keeps watch beside his dead son:

> Long there and then in vigil I stood, dimly around me
>   the battle-field spreading;
> Vigil wondrous and vigil sweet, there in the fragrant
>   silent night;
> But not a tear fell, not even a long-drawn sigh—Long,
>   long I gazed;
> Then on the earth partially reclining, sat by your side,
>   leaning my chin in my hands;
> Passing sweet hours, immortal and mystic hours with
>   you, dearest comrade—Not a tear, not a word;
> [. . .]
> Till at latest lingering of the night, indeed just as the
>   dawn appear'd,
> My comrade I wrapt in his blanket, envelop'd well his
>   form,
> Folded the blanket well, tucking it carefully over head,
>   and carefully under feet;
> And there and then, and bathed by the rising sun, my
>   son in his grave, in his rude-dug grave I deposited.
>
>   (*V,* II, 492)

The poem has a double subject: the formulaic situation of a soldier's body discovered on the battlefield by a relative or lover and a more individualized evocation of the father's mental quietude during his "vigil." Although less explicitly about memory than "The Wound-Dresser," it is still a poem of reminiscence, promising that the dying and the vigil will not be forgotten. Its implicit context is the camp or the hospital, places where memories are exchanged. The setting of the vigil itself remains unrealized, but the soldier gives a clear sense of his featureless, nightlong meditation, in its mixture of exhaustion, shock, and genuine peace; and so the dearth of visual details supports Whitman's reluctance to violate this inward stillness by setting names to it. Whereas "Come Up from the Fields" clogged its situation with stock figures and stock attitudes in a conventional landscape, "Vigil Strange" enters a space in which the reader can create for himself the soldier's emptiness of mind. That space is, first, the army, which provides both a context for comradeship and also an unsayable explanation for his lassitude. Second, it is the hospital, where the wound-dresser sits, beside men like this, building poems out of silences like his.

In the midst of so many poems that are quick to impose their emotions and opinions on the events of the war, "Vigil Strange" is striking for the reticence of its soldier-persona. His I stands mute and passive in the presence of a Not-Me that exceeds his capacity to respond; and Whitman's imagination embraces that emptiness, not filling its void as he did at the end of "Come Up from the Fields." In *Drum-Taps,* there are about ten poems in which the struggle between the Soul and the World ceases, opening a brief glimpse of an intensely visualized experience. Most of these are the minor scenes of the war's "interior," genre pictures of the commonplaces of march and bivouac. These events had not got into the books: for these "unnamed lights and shades" there was no vocabulary of conventional phrases and emotions. Many of them assume the viewpoint of an eyewitness like the soldier in "Vigil Strange," speaking in the character of that mourner into which "Satan" had modulated. It is for these poems that *Drum-Taps* is known today.

Probably the most powerful poem in *Drum-Taps* is "A March in the Ranks Hard-Prest, and the Road Unknown." In this poem, Whitman unites the visual scene painting of "The Wound-Dresser" with the dramatic realization of an eyewitness point of view like that in "Vigil Strange" or "The Artilleryman's Vision." Whitman developed it from a wounded soldier's story set down in one of his notebooks.[26] Its subject is one unfamiliar in the anthology poetry: defeat and death, not on the field but in the unpoetic wretchedness of a hospital.

> A march in the ranks hard-prest, and the road unknown;
> A route through a heavy wood, with muffled steps in
>   the darkness;

[26]. "Scene in the woods on the peninsula—told me by Milton Roberts, ward G, (Maine)" (Glicksberg, ed., *Walt Whitman and the Civil War,* 123–24). Whitman identifies the battle as that of White Oaks Church, actually White Oak Swamp (June 30, 1862).

Our army foil'd with loss severe, and the sullen remnant
  retreating;
Till after midnight glimmer upon us, the lights of a
  dim-lighted building;
We come to an open space in the woods, and halt by the
  dim-lighted building;
'Tis a large old church, at the crossing roads—'tis now
  an impromptu hospital;
—Entering but for a minute, I see a sight beyond all the
  pictures and poems ever made:
Shadows of deepest, deepest black, just lit by moving
  candles and lamps,
And by one great pitchy torch, stationary, with wild red
  flame, and clouds of smoke;
By these, crowds, groups of forms, vaguely I see, on the
  floor, some in the pews laid down;
At my feet more distinctly, a soldier, a mere lad, in
  danger of bleeding to death, (he is shot in the
  abdomen;)
I staunch the blood temporarily, (the youngster's face is
  white as a lily;)
Then before I depart I sweep my eyes o'er the scene, fain
  to absorb it all;
Faces, varieties, postures beyond description, most in
  obscurity, some of them dead;
Surgeons operating, attendants holding lights, the smell
  of ether, the odor of blood;
The crowd, O the crowd of the bloody forms of
  soldiers—the yard outside also fill'd;
Some on the bare ground, some on planks or stretchers,
  some in the death-spasm sweating;
An occasional scream or cry, the doctor's shouted orders
  or calls;
The glisten of the little steel instruments catching the
  glint of the torches;
These I resume as I chant—I see again the forms, I smell
  the odor;
Then hear outside the orders given, *Fall in, my men,
  Fall in;*

> But first I bend to the dying lad—his eyes open—a half-smile gives he me;
> Then the eyes close, calmly close, and I speed forth to the darkness,
> Resuming, marching, ever in darkness marching, on in the ranks,
> The unknown road still marching.
>
> (V, II, 493–94)

Bursting upon the reader in three lines of urgent phrases that never cohere into a sentence, and then in collecting into syntactic unity, the poem speaks from the midst of firsthand experience. "I am the man .... I suffered .... I was there," Whitman had said in "Song of Myself"; but here the verbs are present tense and the sympathetic immediacy almost complete. ("Almost," because in one parenthetic line, "These I resume as I chant—I see again the forms, I smell the odor," he reveals to his readers that this is a soldier's reminiscence, like "The Artilleryman's Vision"—and that the soldier, with Whitman's aid, is making his memories into a poem.)

The poem is not arranged to imitate the flux of reminiscence, as was "The Wound-Dresser." Rather, it recreates a sequence of physical movements and visual discoveries. Whitman's earlier poems sometimes had dilated into an "experiential" mode, as when "Song of the Broad-Axe" paused to contemplate the motions of the housebuilders, and "A Song for Occupations," the rhythms of the mill and the slaughterhouse. Here the entire poem is set in the experiential mode. It begins and ends with the army's huggermugger retreat, a compelled movement down the road (and through the poem's lines) where nothing is foreknown and expected. Words repeat themselves without plan or provision: *march, dim-lighted building, marching, unknown road, darkness.* Objects appear as the soldier approaches them, then disappear. The poem's motion is the movement of his hard-pressed striding body, his incurious eyes.

Then this motion is arrested. We have entered the church. The viewpoint stands still as the soldier first takes in "a sight beyond all the pictures and poems ever made." As a "sight," it is a lurid impression of light—he has just come in from the night road—contrasted with darkness. Lamps and torch flicker against shadows and smoke, and in the foreground there is the white face of a dying soldier. Two simple planes of attention, with a dramatic contrast in illumination, it is the kind of view that could have been managed very effectively in the wood engravings that newspapers were just beginning to employ in the 1860s. Yet it is beyond pictures and poems. He has opened the door of a church and found hell inside. Here are the unnamed lights and shades and the black infernal background of that "interior" war that Whitman knew would never get into the books. A hundred or two of the "Dying Soldier" poems in Hayward's *Poetical Pen-Pictures* would not make anything in this room intelligible.

The boy at his feet is not his son, not his comrade, but a stranger, like everything he sees. Nevertheless, the soldier's attention focuses on him, for he can be seen distinctly; and as he is seen ("a mere lad, in danger of bleeding to death, . . . shot in the abdomen"), he becomes something on which the poem likewise can focus its attention, as the appropriate subject of a customary emotion. But no emotion is named. As the soldier attends to his hemorrhaging wound, the poem utters its only metaphor: "the youngster's face is white as a lily"—a conventional comparison for pallor, but just as right, in this situation, as the soldier's automatic and ineffectual aid for the boy.

Now the visitor looks again at the church's interior. It resolves into a "scene," and its occupants assume "postures." Not only its lighting but its composition is, for the moment, resolved into tableau.[27] He identifies the middle-ground figures as surgeons and attendants; he connects the crowd inside with the crowd outside awaiting attention; he hears the soldiers' screams and the doctors' calls, and smells the ether and the blood. The officer outside shouts; he focuses again on the foreground; the boy loses consciousness. The "scene" is over. Its sequence of impressions, directed by the visitor's darting eye, gives way to a renewal of the dogged succession of *march . . . darkness . . . road.*

Whitman's imagination has achieved something like the passivity of the father keeping vigil by his son—perhaps the passivity he had attained beside many hospital beds—in which it is not necessary for the Soul to vaunt its powers of absorption or to dominate the experience with its own rhetorical patterning. Rather, the actions of the participants have set the rhythm for the entire poem. This graphic

27. Thomas, noting the "somber use of the picturesque," attributes it to a wish to escape guilt for having survived, so "mastering" the unmanageable pain and suffering of the war (*Lunar Light,* 209–13). The tableau, however, lasts only a moment before dissolving into the shifting immediacy of the experience.

series of movements and glimpses, presented both as mediated reminiscence and as the immediate experience of an *eye*witness, provide for the reader an imaginative path between the war's realities and his own soul. The power of sympathy has allowed Whitman temporarily to forsake his own I for a stranger's point of view and to acknowledge the Not-Me as reality rather than as the phenomena of an omnivorous consciousness. The mystery of the eyesight has brought poet and reader together as ministrants to the young soldier, whose brief glance up at you (whoever you are) is the glance of recognition.

Closest in technique to "A March in the Ranks" is "A Sight in Camp in the Day-Break Gray and Dim," where the succession of images again matches the unfolding physical and visual experience of the speaker—though the sequence is less complex than in the former poem. In this case, it appears that the memory is Whitman's own:[28]

> A sight in camp in the day-break grey and dim,
> As from my tent I emerge so early, sleepless,
> As slow I walk in the cool fresh air, the path near by the
>   hospital-tent,
> Three forms I see on stretchers lying, brought out there,
>   untended lying,
> Over each the blanket spread, ample brownish woolen
>   blanket,
> Grey and heavy blanket, folding, covering all.
>
> Curious, I halt, and silent stand;
> Then with light fingers I from the face of the nearest,
>   the first, just lift the blanket:
> Who are you, elderly man so gaunt and grim, with
>   well-grey'd hair, and flesh all sunken about the eyes?
> Who are you, my dear comrade?
>
> Then to the second I step—And who are you, my child
>   and darling?
> Who are you, sweet boy, with cheeks yet blooming?
>
> Then to the third—a face nor child, nor old, very calm,
>   as of beautiful yellow-white ivory:

---

28. Glicksberg, ed., *Walt Whitman and the Civil War*, 73–74.

> Young man, I think I know you—I think this face of
> yours is the face of the Christ himself;
> Dead and divine, and brother of all, and here again he
> lies.
>
> (*V*, II, 495–96)

Here too the poem means to make you *see,* introducing a visually "dim" setting and then providing a series of disclosures suspended within an account of the speaker's movements. Promised "a sight" in its first words, we are led through several lines of circumstantial motion until the three shrouded bodies appear; and, after a detailed scrutiny of the blankets, we must participate in the discovery of one stranger's face, then another's, knowing that the third will be no stranger and that it will fulfill the promise of the poem's opening. So it does: "brother" (or perhaps "lover") is added to "father" and "son," so that every reader may find his, or her, worst fear embodied here. Sight culminates in recognition, though not of the soldier's individual identity. As in "A March in the Ranks," the pale face suggests a metaphor—this time a reference to art (a crucifix, an ivory diptych), and through art to the story of Christ. Sight culminates in vision, assimilating the soldier's death into a communally accepted story of sacrificial death and of apotheosis. In this poem, Whitman dresses the wounds of his readers, affirming through a series of intensely visual descriptions the spiritual identity of "soldier" with "brother" and "Christ." This process of discovery bonds Whitman with his reader, and the readers with one another. The mystery of the eyesight foreruns the identities of the spiritual world.

[4]

Pictorialism

Most of Whitman's "thumb-nail sketches" of the war seek such a bond with the American people through the mystery of eyesight. While "A March in the Ranks" and "A Sight in Camp" reproduce the immediacy of visual discovery, others invoke the spatial arrangements of pictorial art. They place faith both in an objectively "real" world, validated by the unquestionable public significance of the war itself, and in the reliability of genre illustration as a means of disclosing that world in its three substantial dimensions. In most of them, Whitman not only effaced his own poetic ego; he stepped beyond any need for an explicitly defined witness and reporter such as the nurse in "The Wound-Dresser" or the infantryman in "A March in the Ranks." The events need no validation through an individual consciousness. This escape from the poetic ego can be seen in three poems about troops in bivouac, a commonplace wartime situation and a favorite subject of Civil War art and poetry. The first is from Hayward's *Pen-Pictures;* the others are Whitman's.

>   The camp is all quiet—my comrades are sleeping—
>   They dream of their homes, and loved ones dear,
>   The slow rising moon, with its light gently creeping,
>   Shows eyelids now wet with the slow falling tear,
>
>   There lays a young soldier—in years but a boy—
>   His musket beside him—cold pillow of steel—
>   The weapon to him is a pride and a joy,
>   As he dreams to the traitor a death it will deal.
>
>   And he dreams, too, of hearts that anxiously fear
>   Each bulletin sad with its grim battle story,

> May tell that he, whom they all love so dear,
>   Is in death lying low in his youth—yet in glory.
>
> A stern visaged man is lying near by—
>   Fitfully sleeping, and fitfully dreaming—
> His country he loves—for that country he'll die—
>   His brow this reveals in the moonlight's gleaming.
>
> Thus resting in groups, on this now peaceful spot,
>   Lie father and brother—the lover, the son,
> To-morrow to waken midst rattling of shot,
>   The shrieks of the wounded, and war of the gun.
>
> When the next risen sun shall have sunk in the West,
>   And the next evening stars shine o'er us on high,
> Those sleeping here now, will take their last rest
>   'Neath the sod where they fight but to gallantly die![1]

Although this wakeful soldier notices a few details of his encampment, the poem is mostly concerned with imaginary seeings—what his comrades are thinking and how their campsite will look the following night when the sleepers have become the slain. The soldier describes what he feels, not what he sees. The actual bivouac is less important than the imaginary battlefield, because the poem is based on an unavowed inward conflict. The soldier struggles with his fear of death and transfers it to those who lie around him, calling them by relational epithets—father, son, brother, lover—as Whitman did in "A Sight in Camp." Thus he acknowledges his unnameable emotion, fear, by changing it to its legitimized sentimental variant, the grief of the survivors. He invokes some catch phrases about personal glory, patriotic duty, and the righteousness of the cause, to combat both fear and grief. Although the poem's title—"The Bivouac"—seems to promise a pen-picture of an encampment, the soldiers' campsite is only a context (or a pretext) for rehearsing some familiar wartime emotions. This is the war that got into the books, again and again.[2]

1. Hayward, ed., *Poetical Pen-Pictures*, 117.
2. So a popular song of 1864 began:

> Just before the battle, Mother,
>   I am thinking most of you,

In "By the Bivouac's Fitful Flame," Whitman's soldier is more definite about his surroundings, less specific about what he is thinking:

> By the bivouac's fitful flame,
> A procession winding around me, solemn and sweet and
>   slow;—but first I note,
> The tents of the sleeping army, the fields' and woods'
>   dim outline,
> The darkness, lit by spots of kindled fire—the silence;
> Like a phantom far or near an occasional figure moving;
> The shrubs and trees, (as I lift my eyes they seem to be
>   stealthily watching me;)
> While wind in procession thoughts, O tender and
>   wond'rous thoughts,
> Of life and death—of home and the past and loved, and
>   of those that are far away;
> A solemn and slow procession there as I sit on the
>   ground,
> By the bivouac's fitful flame.
>
>   (*V*, II, 466)

Whitman's attention too is divided, but it is split between the possibility of writing a poem like the anthology poem, with its overt appeal to familiar public emotions, or writing a pictorial "sketch" that will capture some of the unnamed lights and shades of camp life. Beside his fire, the soldier looks inward on a procession of thoughts, vaguely defined as about "life and death"—like the sentimental reflections of the Hayward poet. At the same time, he looks

---

>   While upon the field we're watching
>   With the enemy in view.
>
>   Comrades brave are round me lying,
>   Fill'd with tho'ts of home and God;
>   For well they know, that on the morrow
>   Some may sleep beneath the sod.
>
>   Farewell, Mother, you may never
>   Press me to your heart again;
>   But oh, you'll not forget me, Mother,
>   If I'm numbered with the slain.

The author, George F. Root, also wrote "The Battle-Cry of Freedom" and "Tramp, Tramp, Tramp, the Boys are Marching": his songs caught the "official" temperament of the war years.

about him on a scene that likewise loses its definition as it recedes from the campfire's light. So soldier-phantoms, wandering and disappearing, are likened to his wandering thoughts. Naming the objects that he sees and fixing their relative clarity or obscurity from a viewpoint there beside the fire, Whitman introduces us into the perceptual space of his soldier. The poem bears witness not to the public value to his musings, but rather to his experiential presence, there in the midst of an encamped army.

"Bivouac on a Mountain Side" further develops the sense of physical, visual participation, dispensing almost entirely with both persona and inwardness after its opening phrase:

> I see before me now, a traveling army halting;
> Below, a fertile valley spread, with barns, and the
>   orchards of summer;
> Behind, the terraced sides of a mountain, abrupt in
>   places, rising high;
> Broken, with rocks, with clinging cedars, with tall
>   shapes, dingily seen;
> The numerous camp-fires scatter'd near and far, some
>   away up on the mountain;
> The shadowy forms of men and horses, looming, large-
>   sized, flickering;
> And over all, the sky—the sky! far, far out of reach,
>   studded with the eternal stars.
>
> (*V*, II, 526)

Now presence is everything. Such a poem could hardly suggest that these dumb real objects are only appearances that could be doubted. Nor does it establish their reality by creating a "tally" between them and the identities of the spiritual world—linking phantom soldiers with wandering thoughts or a dead man with Christ. This poem does not depict the Soul making an experience significant by absorbing it into its own patterns of energy. Consciousness here seems just to "see," quietly identifying the contents of a visual field. The army goes about its practical business; the valley and mountains and the stars occupy their spaces, beyond question, beyond interpretation.

What determines the sequence of presentation? Not the steps of a walking man, as in "A Sight in Camp," nor the darting of his eye, as in "A March in the Ranks." Rather, it is a steady movement through several planes of attention, locating each object in relation to the others and with reference to a fixed point of view: "before," "below," "behind," "away," "large-sized" (because near at hand), and "over." Relating details as they would strike the eye from that point, Whitman guides us sequentially to our own corresponding place in this setting. He establishes with his readers a mutual ground, secured on a common orientation in space.

Having established that common ground, the poem explores the implications of a painterly way of seeing. This is a landscape, seen from such a distance and on such a scale that within it an army corps seems only a texture, like the shadow of a cloud. Since the time of Thomas Cole, Americans had been taught the awesome scale of their national scene. Here the landscape stabilizes the activities of the war, which had seemed so fervid in the earliest of Whitman's war poems.[3] At the same time, it is the army's presence that makes this specific scene worthy of artistic rendering. This is not a panel from one of Whitman's nationalistic panoramas of the continent, but the backdrop of an event in a great, awe-inspiring war. What sort of event? An earlier historical painter might have rendered Napoleon capering on an Alp or Washington presiding over his defeat on Brooklyn Heights. But this was a war by and for the people, and it could be rendered only as a massive, featureless military force that invests the landscape as certainly as the earth turns and the stars wheel. And this army is shown not in the histrionics of combat, but in a commonplace business more fit for genre painting—bedding down for the night.

The poem's final shift of focal plane and of painterly style might have introduced the I in personal, sentimental reflection like that in the two previous poems. But in lieu of a direct avowal of consciousness, the poem shifts our gaze upward and outward to "the eternal stars," in their sublime remoteness the absolute Not-Me. Is this gesture an ironic dismissal of sublunary strivings? Or is it an intimation of unity between cosmic power and the armed might of democracy, based on the physical space—immense, but visually apprehensible— that they each occupy? Do the causes of the war stand as firm as mountains and yet move as inexorably as the stars, beyond any question of personal subjectivity? Quieted by the depths into which he looks, the see-er cannot say.

3. Timothy Sweet shows how the earliest photographs of the war assimilated the aftermath of combat into the conventions of landscape painting (*Poetry, Photography,* 107–64).

Pictorialism

In a closely related poem, Whitman enacts the same discoveries from close range:

> A line in long array, where they wind betwixt green islands;
> They take a serpentine course—their arms flash in the sun—Hark to the musical clank;
> Behold the silvery river—in it the splashing horses loitering, stop to drink;
> Behold the brown-faced men—each group, each person, a picture—the negligent rest on the saddles;
> Some emerge on the opposite bank—others are just entering the ford;
> The guidon flags flutter gaily in the wind.
> ("Cavalry Crossing a Ford," *V*, II, 457)

Now it is not even "I see." The poem does not depend on any personal consciousness, the poet's or his fictive delegate's, to authorize this image or to interpret it. We follow the column of troopers, discerned at first vaguely as a long serpentine line, then seen as carrying glinting weapons, and finally scrutinized close up, in some detail: *horses, brown-faced men, saddles, guidon flags* (later, in 1871, retouched in color: scarlet, white, blue). In the eclipse of I, these beings cannot be reduced to Not-Me. The poem's words trace not the round-dance of consciousness but the linear rhythm of the soldiers' approach and passage. Traced through the landscape from a stationary viewpoint near the ford, this rhythm extends beyond the horizons of the valley and of the poem. For a moment, the troopers fill the poem's space, but it does not capture them. At home in their world, sure of their skills, sure of their cause, like the bricklayers in "Song of the Broad-Axe" or the mossbonker fishermen in "Salut au Monde!" they impose their own pattern on the poem. Rather than "absorbing" them, Whitman (emulating the passiveness of the wound-dresser, the musing soldiers of "Vigil Strange" and "By the Bivouac's Fitful Flame") is absorbed into their world, the four dimensions of historically significant action. In no other poem has Whitman so completely entered the war's "interior," seeing the common soldier going about his business without self-consciousness—either Whitman's or the cavalryman's.[4]

4. More critical of Whitman's "photographic" effects, Graham Clarke remarks, "In Whitman the photograph seeks to document history but, at the same time,

Whitman is not just repeating the subjectivist effects of his first poetic phase, when in "Song of Myself" and "The Sleepers" he copied the phenomena found within the poet's skull-gallery. In these new poems, the pictured world appears as an independent power, confronting the mind with its own reality. In "Bivouac on a Mountain Side" and "Cavalry Crossing a Ford," this world could even be said to contain the mind, as the war creates a context and viewstand from which the events can be intelligibly perceived. In the earlier poems, images rapidly appeared and disappeared, replaced by others as the imagination arabesqued among its contents. Here objects are given slower, more devoted attention. One look—one sympathetic surrender to the rhythm of an event—may constitute a poem.

Such poems give new importance to time. In "Song of Myself," time-bound narrative or descriptive passages were only interruptions of an eloquence that was impatient with time—that apprehended all of America simultaneously and would spit it all out in a single syllable if it could. Other poems like "There was a Child Went Forth" and "Crossing Brooklyn Ferry" accepted the time-bound quality of language because they were about the time-bound, maturing experience of the poet or his character: the elapsed time between the poem's beginning and ending was a microcosm of the lapse of time that the poem described. So in "A March in the Ranks" and "A Sight in Camp," the poem's unfolding matches the unfolding acts and visual discoveries of the protagonist. The sense of time in *Drum-Taps* is historical rather than psychological.

Elsewhere in *Drum-Taps,* Whitman uses the poem's time to range through several planes of attention from background to foreground. Placing his soldiers within a fully dimensional setting, he releases his rhetorical authority over them and entrusts them to the reader's recognition of their place in a world in which he has his own corroborating share. So, for example, "Bivouac on a Mountain Side" and "Cavalry Crossing a Ford" advance from far to near, while they invite readers to relate the scene to their own history of the war. Likewise, a pictorial passage in "When Lilacs Last in the Dooryard Bloom'd" leads us away from the viewstand in order to effect, indirectly, a change in our view of Lincoln's death:

---

admonish memory; it wants to image the world in all its depth but, simultaneously, only allow us the illusion of such extension as the eye moves over a surface flatness" ("'To emanate a look,'" 92). Alternative surface and depth will be my subject in Chapters 7–9.

Pictures of growing spring, and farms, and homes,
With the Fourth-month eve at sundown, and the gray-
smoke lucid and bright,
With floods of the yellow gold of the gorgeous,
indolent, sinking sun, burning, expanding the air;
With the fresh sweet herbage under foot, and the pale
green leaves of the trees prolific;
In the distance the flowing glaze, the breast of the river,
with a wind-dapple here and there;
With ranging hills on the banks, with many a line
against the sky, and shadows;
And the city at hand, with dwellings so dense, and
stacks of chimneys,
And all the scenes of life, and the workshops, and the
workmen homeward returning.

(§11, *V*, II, 533)

Here, as in a comparable passage a few stanzas later, the recession in planes aims to move the reader-viewer from his absorption in private emotion to rejoining the life of the nation as a whole.

Often the effect of this movement is to render not the quick glances of a protagonist (as in "A March in the Ranks") but the systematic perspectivism of painting. The succession of words does not trace an action or explore a four-dimensional world, but rather leads the eye over a picture. Treating the field of vision as a fixed image, like a painting, the poem occupies its time in imitation of the process of apprehending that image. For the apprehending of a picture is not instantaneous (G. E. Lessing to the contrary), but sequential, an accumulation and incorporation of details in a sequence directed partly by habits of perception and partly by the artist's own designs. Pictorial poets have comparable designs. Some of Whitman's poems that seem most concerned with setting the reader into an actual world also attend carefully to pictorial techniques of perspective. In "Bivouac on a Mountain Side," the poet reviews a scene from the war as if it were a painting. Like the cicerone in "Pictures," he directs our attention to the details of the canvas, leading us across the background—valley first, then mountains—before advancing to foreground details that "loom large" on the imaginary canvas, though small in actual relation to the fields and rocks beyond. "By the Bivouac's Fitful Flame" involves also a sense of atmospheric perspective, objects becoming more obscure as they recede from the foreground. Likewise in "Cavalry Crossing a Ford," we are brought forward from the coarse texture of "line" and "serpentine course" to the sharp focus of brown faces and guidon flags. We hear once again the admonitions of the cicerone:

> Hark to the musical clank;
> Behold the silvery river
> [. . .]
> Behold the brown-faced men—each group, each person,
>   a picture.

This unobtrusive voice guides us through the painting, bidding us study its details as pictures within a larger picture, as though we were viewing some monumental canvas by Thomas Cole or Frederick Church.[5]

Perhaps those "thumb-nail sketches" owe some of their clarity and power to their origin in Whitman's imagination rather than in his direct experience. Certainly, Whitman had occasionally visited the army in Virginia; but most of the poems seem to have originated with experiences recounted for him by wounded soldiers. His great empathic sense transformed their words into his images, which he set within his own landscapes and rendered in language through a set of poetic and pictorial conventions. Like some early photographs, they are composites, and their dramatic clarity may result from their being staged in the theater of Whitman's brain-gallery. However, these poems do not betray their artifice. Sustaining his attention to his subjects, Whitman effaces his own imaginative presence, taking rather the role of witness and recorder.

❖

In their conventional pictorialism, then, the great visualist poems of *Drum-Taps* support Whitman's new bid for public acceptance. Although the wound-dresser poet acknowledged Satan by standing apart from the triumphs and the generals, he merged his voice with the Good Gray Poet in adopting a poetic much closer to what his contemporaries would have recognized as traditional in its intent. The Satan-poet of 1855 had annihilated those intermediating forms

---

5. See Novak, *Nature and Culture*, 25–26.

and institutions that buffered the soul from naked contact with all of his experience (while trafficking quietly with political rhetoric and genre art). The postwar Whitman bargained more openly with his old enemies. He stilled the bardic voice and narrowed the panoramic scope of his earlier poetry, in favor of a quiet attentiveness to the commonplace heroism of bivouacs and hospital wards. As the Civil War gave steadying purpose to his personal life, so it resolved (for these poems, though not for all of *Drum-Taps*) the shuttling between objective and subjective, I and Not-Me, that had so agitated the first three editions of *Leaves of Grass*. These poems bespeak a commonsensical realism about dumb real things.

And the specifically pictorial quality of their visualism reveals something more. Whitman did not just mean for his readers to "see" the war, but to see it *as pictures*. Through these poems, the reader would be taken into the war's interior, there to see—as if at first hand—events that had proved invisible to the official historians and to the journalists of victory. Whitman would join him there, on the path between a recognizable world of visual experience and a mutual civic belief in the importance of the war's most commonplace events. The reader was also to recognize in these poems the strategies through which he was customarily shown pictorial images of his world, at second hand, and offered interpretations of their meaning. Whitman's pen-portraits of the war draw upon familiar artistic and poetic devices, and meet the reader also on the ground of the conventions of picture-viewing—conventions that the poet, in a note to himself, was warning himself against: "Poet! beware lest your poems are made in the spirit that comes from the study of pictures of things—and not from the spirit that comes from the contact with real things the[m]selves" (*N*, IV, 1569).[6]

Whitman's pictures of commonplace soldier life were part of a process in which the public learned to visualize the war. Readers today might relate Whitman's "thumbnail sketches" to paintings by Winslow Homer, such as *Prisoners from the Front,* or to the photographs attributed to Mathew Brady. Homer and Brady were indeed successful in capturing the "unofficial" side of soldier life; and oil painting and those cameras with their great depth-of-field could pro-

---

6. Edward Grier dates this note from the 1860s, just as Whitman's poetry was becoming more conventionally pictorial. Before revision (Whitman revised even his memoranda), the note was more directly self-critical: "Are your poems not made in the spirit that comes from the study of pictures? . . ."

vide a sense of depth and context comparable to that found in Whitman's poems. However, such comparisons are not altogether apt. Neither oils nor watercolors nor photographs were media through which the public could come to see the actual look of war. There was as yet no technology for wide distribution of their images. It had just become possible to replicate photographic images at all—let alone translate them into forms that could be reproduced en masse.[7] For such, Whitman's age relied on the lithograph and on engravings in metal or wood.

Lithographs were made to display, and so their subjects had to be compatible with tastes in painting. Many of those made during the Civil War represent the "official" war: portraits of its leaders, patriotic symbols like the flag, or sentimental scenes of farewell or return. Those concerned directly with military life usually purport to depict specific battles and are indebted not to genre illustration but to historical painting. Hurried into print while news of the battle was still current, they sacrificed the lithograph's potential for detail and depth, in favor of a quick press. The armies are represented by long ranks of identical hats or bayonets, and the landscape is usually obscured in smoke. What details they offer—a few soldiers, some of them wounded; a dismounted cannon; a general issuing commands—are confined to a shallow foreground plane. Whitman alluded to the lithographic Civil War in "I Saw Old General at Bay" (quoted in Chapter 3). English grammar expects a personal name to be set into the line after "General": "I saw old General _____ at bay." The effect of this omission, in leaving the officer and the occasion unspecified, suggests the lithographers' practice of preparing a stone in advance: they would model a standard commander in a standard heroic posture, leaving the figure faceless so that the features could be worked in later, from a portrait, when the occasion arose.[8]

Steel engraving, which might have rendered well the effects of an oil by Homer or Edwin Forbes, was a slow and expensive process little seen in renderings of camp and battlefield. The mass medium for Civil War illustration was the wood engraving, only recently de-

7. *Gardner's Photographic Sketch Book of the Civil War,* published in 1866, cost $150 (Sweet, *Poetry, Photography,* 120); a craftsman's daily wage at that time was around $2.50.
8. See, for example, the Currier and Ives print, *The Storming of Fort Donelson* (Fig. 2), in which Grant's features have been forced into an oval blank left between the hat and collar of a mounted officer (Rawls, ed., *The Great Book of Currier and Ives' America,* 308).

Pictorialism

Fig. 3 Winslow Homer, *Bivouac Fire on the Potomac* (wood engraving, 1861)

Courtesy The Metropolitan Museum of Art, Harris Brisbane Dick Fund, 1929. [29.88.1 (6)]. All rights reserved, The Metropolitan Museum of Art.

veloped for illustrated magazines like *Harper's* and *Leslie's*. Inexpensive and quickly made, they enlivened the pages of those weeklies not only with the stock heroic postures that sold papers, but also with unpretentious images of the commonplaces of warfare.[9] Homer and Forbes were two of the best-remembered of the "special artists" who drew for the illustrated magazines. Although Homer produced a few spirited, and fictional, views of cavalry charges and infantry in close combat, most of his illustrations—like his oils from that period—depict soldiers in bivouac, smoking, pitching horseshoes, feigning illness, or drawing and spending their pay (Fig. 3). Like the wartime lithographs, however, these illustrations are often shallow

---

9. Hermann Warner Williams, Jr., *The Civil War: The Artists' Record* (Washington, D.C., 1961), 17–20. Williams quotes a William J. Hoppins, who in 1863 complained: "It is true that the illustrated newspapers are full of sketches purporting to be pictures of important scenes; but the testimony of parties engaged shows that these representations are, when they are not taken from photographs, not always reliable. The desire of producing striking effects sometimes overcomes all other considerations, and the truth is now and then sacrificed to the demand for dramatic action or a pleasing play of light and shadow" (24).

in composition, both because the medium itself presented technical obstacles to treating a recession through several planes of depth and because the pressures of publication encouraged both the artist and the engraver to skimp or omit details that were not in the foreground.

Whitman's pen-sketches, then, referred to a stock of images that his readers had already encountered in the illustrated weeklies. To that extent, they resemble the pictorial passages in "Song of Myself" and "Salut au Monde!" that draw upon a repository of common images of America. Technically, though, the *Drum-Taps* poems differ from his earlier work in concentrating on single experiences and rendering each experience in depth rather than concentrating on just a foregrounded figure or action, as he had in "Song of Myself." The difference between

> None obeyed the command to kneel,
> Some made a mad and helpless rush .... some stood
>   stark and straight,
> A few fell at once, shot in the temple or heart .... the
>   living and dead lay together,
> The maimed and mangled dug in the dirt .... the new-
>   comers saw them there;
> Some half-killed attempted to crawl away,
> These were dispatched with bayonets or battered with
>   the blunts of muskets.
>
> (§34, *V*, I, 54–55)

and

> Entering but for a minute, I see a sight beyond all the
>   pictures and poems ever made:
> Shadows of deepest, deepest black, just lit by moving
>   candles and lamps,
> And by one great pitchy torch, stationary, with wild red
>   flame, and clouds of smoke;
> By these, crowds, groups of forms, vaguely I see, on the
>   floor, some in the pews laid down;
> At my feet more distinctly, a soldier, a mere lad, in
>   danger of bleeding to death, (he is shot in the
>   abdomen;)
>
> (*V*, II, 494)

is not just the difference between innocence and experience. It is the difference between a rapid-fire series of imaginary tableaux, each restricted to a dramatic foreground, and an entry into a space that is perceived as an actual space, occupied by forms at differing focal points and with differing illumination.

In "Song of the Broad-Axe" and "Bivouac on a Mountain Side" alike, depth is context, both physical and emotional. And so Whitman brought to his "minor scenes and interiors" a sense of depth, which the woodcut (and journalism itself) could not provide, when he glanced about the field hospital, or discovered the three shrouded stretchers in the midst of an awakening camp, or caught the cavalrymen splashing through the ford. The traveler on the Acropolis may see nothing he has not previously encountered in illustrations; but now the Parthenon occupies a place on its hill, in the midst of Athens, in Attica, at the end of the traveler's geographical and spiritual journey. So Whitman opens a space, in his poem, in which the infantryman stands with McClellan's retreating army behind him and a hemorrhaging youth at his feet; and the reader stands there too.

In his Lincoln elegy, Whitman asked, "What shall the pictures be that I hang on the walls?" (§11, V, II, 533). The great achievement of the wound-dresser poet was to offer for the American public images of the war more truly suitable than those they would have chosen to hang on their walls: poems largely or exclusively pictorial in design, which redeemed the magazine woodcut from a lack of "depth" and which lavished on the commonplaces of camp and hospital the sense of intimacy and the sense of typicality that were the province of lithograph or genre painting. But the pictorialism of *Drum-Taps* did not just invoke popular art to establish a mediating context between Whitman and his desired readership. It also reaffiliated him with a literary tradition. In becoming a Civil War poet, he began to become as well a landscape poet, for it was through establishing a more thoroughly realized physical context for his foreground figures that he rescued them from entrapment in the poet's personal consciousness and assured his readers that these were the actual men whose marches up and down Virginia and Tennessee had reshaped the American republic.

Thus the postwar Whitman became in yet another way a more conventional poet than the democratic bard of 1855. Ceasing altogether to question whether appearances—colors, densities, and forms—might be merely apparitional and whether his words could ever match the splendor of his inward vision, he adopted a descriptive style that accepted the senses' account of the world and sought in words to duplicate that account. The techniques of that style had been developed in England nearly two hundred years before, at a time when words were (like etched steel or, later, inked stone) a medium for conveying visual information.[10] In picturesque description, visual experience is treated as a glass or canvas, a surface that lies immobile while attention passes over it, assimilating the arrangement of its details from a fixed point of view. The writer employs the sequential nature of his medium, language, to scan his subject systematically, arriving finally at the most significant point in the scene. Whitman began to do this in "Bivouac on a Mountain Side."

Probably this style of writing arose from the "prospect" poems that followed John Denham's *Coopers Hill* (1642). A common issue for such poems is the relationship of language, which conveys meaning by passing through time, to landscape, which endures time with little change. Denham's poem observed an English countryside in relationship to the history of England as it was suggested by several features of the landscape: Windsor, Runnymede, London, and the Thames.[11] James Thomson, whose *The Seasons* (1726–1730) was long a popular and influential work, arranged the poem not only as a diurnal sequence but also as a series of accounts of rapid changes in the landscape's appearance caused by shifts of weather and light or by the spectator's motion through the scene.[12] Most notably, however, Thomson used the temporal quality of his medium to direct the reader/viewer's attention through the elements of his tableaux, indicating the spatial relationships among them:

> At length the finish'd Garden to the View
> Its Vistas opens, and its Alleys green.
> Snatch'd thro' the verdant Maze, the hurried Eye

---

10. The pictorial poem and its relationship to the visual arts have been carefully studied in recent years by Jean Hagstrum, Karl Kroeber, Ronald Paulson, James A. W. Heffernan, Donald Ringe, and John H. Johnston—to name only the writers whose work I have found most helpful.

11. Karl Kroeber, *Romantic Landscape Vision: Constable and Wordsworth* (Madison, Wis., 1975), 91–92; John H. Johnston, *The Poet and the City: A Study in Urban Perspectives* (Athens, Ga., 1984), 28–32.

12. Kroeber, *Romantic Landscape Vision,* 100; Heffernan, *The Re-Creation of Landscape,* 10.

Pictorialism

> Distracted wanders; now the bowery Walk
> Of Covert close, where scarce a Speck of Day
> Falls on the lengthen'd Gloom, protracted, sweeps;
> Now meets the bending Sky, the River now,
> Dimpling along, the breezy-ruffled Lake,
> The Forest darkening round, the glittering Spire,
> Th' etherial Mountain, and the distant Main.[13]

Now . . . now . . . now: in another passage the terms may be *here, there, o'er, beyond*. Guided by the picturesque painters like Poussin and Claude Lorraine, with their delight in leading the viewer's eye into the depths of their landscapes, Thomson and his inheritors would paint on their reader's inward eye a succession of details that coalesced into a landscape that rose before them as it receded away from them, and whose substantive, four-dimensional presence one could no more question than one can question the walls, posts, and wagons of a painting by Constable.

Byron's *Childe Harold* had taught a century of tourists how to assemble picturesque landscapes:

> Dusky and huge, enlarging on the sight,
> Nature's volcanic amphitheatre,
> Chimæra's alps extend from left to right:
> Beneath, a living valley seems to stir;
> Flocks play, trees wave, streams flow, the mountain-fir
> Nodding above . . .
>
> (2.51)

Wordsworth, though he repudiated the tyranny of the eye over poetry, could still lead *The Prelude* to a climax in which the view from Mount Snowdon unfolds in a succession of foci that are both farther and higher, the visual field becoming a symbol of the soul:

> . . . At my feet
> Rested a silent sea of hoary mist.
> A hundred hills their dusky backs upheaved
> All over this still ocean; and beyond,
> Far, far beyond, the solid vapours stretched,
> In headlands, tongues, and promontory shapes,

---

13. James Thomson, "Spring," in *The Seasons,* ed. James Sambrook (Oxford, 1981), 26.

> Into the main Atlantic, that appeared
> To dwindle, and give up his majesty,
> Usurped upon far as the sight could reach.
> Not so the ethereal vault; encroachment none
> Was there, nor loss; only the inferior stars
> Had disappeared, or shed a fainter light
> In the clear presence of the full-orbed Moon,
> Who, from her sovereign elevation, gazed
> Upon the billowy ocean.
>
> (14.41–55)

During his days as a newspaperman, Whitman had reviewed an American edition of *The Seasons* and quoted *Childe Harold* in his articles.[14] It may seem unlikely that a journalist, harried by deadlines, would have absorbed these conventions about landscape from his quick perusal of two of its most illustrious practitioners. But during the Civil War—even as *Drum-Taps* was aborning—Whitman had in his hands a collection of poems by Gray, Collins, Young, and others, which he read "at the Army Hospitals, or waiting for the boats bringing loads of wounded."[15] Also, by Whitman's time these had become standard mechanisms for arranging descriptive passages: he would have seen them in the practice of countless inheritors of the Age of Thomson. So Longfellow begins *Evangeline* (1847):

> In the Acadian land, on the shores of the Basin of
>   Minas,
> Distant, secluded, still, the little village of Grand-Pré
> Lay in the fruitful valley. Vast meadows stretched to the
>   eastward,
> Giving the village its name, and pasture to flocks
>   without number.

14. Whitman, *The Gathering of the Forces,* I, 300–301. Although the notice is short and superficial, Whitman knew what Thomson was doing: "Among nature's truest worshippers and most graphic painters has for a hundred years been considered the poet, Thomson. His 'Seasons' is not surpassed by any book with which we are acquainted, in its happy limning of the scenes it professes to represent, in its faculty of bringing before the reader the clear sight of everything in its scope." Whitman devotes the rest of the review to the printers' use of an electrotype process that allowed the integration of text and illustration. For the use of Byron, see Stovall, *The Foreground of "Leaves of Grass,"* 242. Thomas comments briefly on Wordsworth, Whitman, and the picturesque (*Lunar Light,* 126–29).

15. Whitman's words quoted in Horace Traubel, *With Walt Whitman in Camden,* ed. Gertrude Traubel and William White (Carbondale, Ill., 1982), VI, 254–55.

. . . .
West and south there were fields of flax, and orchards and
   cornfields
Spreading afar and unfenced o'er the plain; and away to
   the northward
Blomidon rose, and the forests old, and aloft on the
   mountains
Sea-fogs pitched their tents.[16]

And Whittier, in a Wordsworthian matching of memory and sight:

Here is the place; right over the hill
   Runs the path I took;
You can see the gap in the old wall still,
   And the stepping-stones in the shallow brook.

There is the house, with the gate red-barred,
   And the poplars tall;
And the barn's brown length, and the cattle-yard,
   And the white horns tossing above the wall.[17]

And William Cullen Bryant, too, in poems like "Summer Wind" and "Monument Mountain," chooses his viewstand, sets up his camera lucida, and systematically discloses what it shows.

These are the poets whom Whitman believed to be America's greatest, among whom he thought to take a place or even to supplant: he had studied them enviously.[18] And he had seen their imitators in the papers. The same methods of description had passed over into prose as well. In the novels of Scott and Cooper, which he had read since childhood, narrative is routinely preceded by a general pictorial passage that commences with the most general features of a landscape, fills in its details plane by plane, and eventually delivers the reader into the foreground, in the presence of the novel's characters.

   16. *The Complete Poetical Works of Henry Wadsworth Longfellow* (Boston, 1902), 87. In about ninety lines, Longfellow will describe his way down to the door of Benedict Bellefontaine, Evangeline's father. Whitman reviewed *Evangeline* in 1847 (Stovall, *The Foreground of "Leaves of Grass,"* 121).
   17. "Telling the Bees," in *The Poetical Works of John Greenleaf Whittier* (Boston, 1872), II, 321.
   18. Walt Whitman, *Rivulets of Prose* (New York, 1928), 101–103; Stovall, *The Foreground of "Leaves of Grass,"* 232.

In the hands of a Wordsworth or a Shelley, these techniques create analogues, in physical sensation, for the passage to spiritual vision. The prospect from Mount Snowdon and the imaginary ascent up the Valley of the Arve to Mont Blanc penetrate the surface of the visible and look upon a sublimity in the heart of things. In the more pedestrian excursions of Thomson or Cowper, or even Whittier, it can be argued that the outward seeing is an index of inward, aesthetic, or spiritual discovery.[19] But for derivative and conventional imaginations—like Bryant and Longfellow, like the poet Whitman was becoming in 1865—the two visions no longer join as one; there is no longer any depth, or mystery, in the eyesight. Here is the "world," there is the soul: not an apparitional world of dots and specks, but just the world; not the soul of an élève or an intimate companion in the night, but of such a reader as had bought *Evangeline*. Between them stands the poet as a kind of optic nerve, with his words turning the big world of things into the little world of images inside the reader's head. Having filled that canvas, he may speak further to offer an interpretation of what he sees. Poems painted pictures, pretty ones; and there were comfortable formulas according to which the painting was done and then explained. Desperate to encounter his nation, if only on that nation's own artistic terms, Whitman as Good Gray Poet would turn himself into a camera lucida. Almost all the poems in *Drum-Taps* adhere to conventions of pictorial description that his readers would have accepted effortlessly.

❖

After the war, most of the poems added to *Leaves of Grass* are reminiscences, reflections on public events, brief proclamations or perceptions—the poems of the mind, which had been the staple of Whitman's poetry since 1855. The others are pictorial illustrations, serenely transmitting a stable physical world seen in depth, such a world as his readers knew from the media of popular illustration in their time, rendered according to the conventions for literary descriptions:

19. See Patricia Meyer Spacks, *The Poetry of Vision* (Cambridge, Mass., 1967), 13–65, 165–206.

Pictorialism 127

> After the Sea-Ship—after the whistling winds;
> After the white-gray sails, taut to their spars and ropes,
> Below, a myriad, myriad waves, hastening, lifting up their necks,
> Tending in ceaseless flow toward the track of the ship:
> Waves of the ocean, bubbling and gurgling, blithely prying,
> Waves, undulating waves—liquid, uneven, emulous waves,
> Toward that whirling current, laughing and buoyant, with curves,
> Where the great Vessel, sailing and tacking, displaced the surface;
> Larger and smaller waves, in the spread of the ocean, yearnfully flowing;
> The wake of the Sea-Ship, after she passes—flashing and frolicsome, under the sun,
> A motley procession, with many a fleck of foam, and many fragments,
> Following the stately and rapid Ship—in the wake following.
>
> ("After the Sea-Ship," *V*, III, 673)

This 1874 poem divides its attention between ship and ocean, moving systematically through the time of the ship's and the poem's passage. However, its unconventional syntactical form, a series of dependent phrases lacking a governing statement, mirrors the vacuousness of the image it depicts. This ship is—a ship; and the waves, waves. The poem says nothing more about them. There are, of course, unacknowledged containers for these moiling details. One is "Behold" or "I see": the lines appear to be flotsam from some unwritten larger poem, as "A Paumanok Picture" was from "Salut au Monde!" But here the subject does not begin to act for itself. Those boats separated and rowed off, the nets were drawn in, the fishermen lounged or stood. The vestigial "I see" fell away. But here the ship, the sails, and the waves still lack the throb of independent life. They remain merely phenomena perceived by an unacknowledged I. The other implicit context for these lines is popular illustration: they invoke one of the most common subjects for lithograph and folk art, a ship at sea. The image endorses both the ship's aesthetic beauty and its instrumentality in America's identity as a commercial nation. What shall the pictures be that I hang on the walls?—those that public taste has already ratified.

It was in *Drum-Taps* that these inert sketches first appeared, not as pen-pictures of the war but as the miscellanea of the Good Gray Poet. Although not syntactically incomplete, they lack the power of discovery common to the war poems and instead seem to claim status as poems because of their reference to some of the common themes of popular art. The following are complete poems:

> I see the sleeping babe, nestling the breast of its mother;
> The sleeping mother and babe—hush'd, I study them
>   long and long.
>
>   ("Mother and Babe," *V*, II, 491)

> On my northwest coast in the midst of the night, a
>   fishermen's group stands watching;
> Out on the lake, expanding before them, others are
>   spearing salmon;
> The canoe, a dim and shadowy thing, moves across the
>   black water,
> Bearing a Torch a-blaze at the prow.
>
>   ("The Torch," *V*, II, 503)

> Through the ample open door of the peaceful country
>   barn,
> A sun-lit pasture field, with cattle and horses feeding.[20]
>
>   ("A Farm Picture," *V*, II, 497)

Each of these poems fills out the bottom of a page given to a longer poem, suggesting that Whitman, ever the newspaperman, may have begun to use scraps to fill empty space. Unlike the brief "Thoughts"

---

20. In 1871 Whitman added another line to this third poem, so that it read:

> Through the ample open door of the peaceful country barn,
> A sunlit pasture field with cattle and horses feeding,
> And haze and vista, and the far horizon fading away.

This amendment completed the movement from a foreground "frame," to a highlighted pastoral subject, to a background lost in atmospheric perspective.

Pictorialism

and "Says," which he had introduced in the 1860 edition, these make no "statement" but just record an experience of vision. In each case, the vision is not only commonplace, but the kind of commonplace that would lend itself to popular illustration: a domestic theme, a bucolic, a dramatically illuminated "regional." Other late poems—on a running athlete, two mating eagles, a dandelion, views from Montauk Point, a prairie sunset—likewise record a picture without comment; for the pictures (except for the notorious eagles) drew their significance from the nation's store of publicly certified subjects for art.

However, there are other poems from those years in which Whitman, aware of the New Englanders with their tradition of parabolic imagery, would trace a "literal" image and then match it with a figural meaning:

> A noiseless patient spider,
> I mark'd, where, on a little promontory, it stood,
>   isolated;
> Mark'd how, to explore the vacant, vast surrounding,
> It launch'd forth filament, filament, filament, out of
>   itself;
> Ever unreeling them—ever tirelessly speeding them.
>
>
> And you, O my soul, where you stand,
> Surrounded, surrounded, in measureless oceans of
>   space,
> Ceaselessly musing, venturing, throwing,—seeking the
>   spheres, to connect them;
> Till the bridge you will need, be form'd—till the ductile
>   anchor hold;
> Till the gossamer thread you fling, catch somewhere, O
>   my Soul.
>   ("A Noiseless Patient Spider," V, III, 585)

The first stanza announces a text from nature; the second proclaims the application, reviewing the physical details in a new, figural light. (In the first draft, the spider was only a simile in a poem about "the Soul.") In the reissues of *Leaves of Grass* that followed the first appearance of *Drum-Taps,* Whitman produced a number of poems that followed such conventional paths from the object to the soul.

"Aboard at a Ship's Helm" (1867) first pictures a ship escaping from shipwreck and then explains that this is the "ship of the soul." "On the Beach at Night" (1871) depicts a child and her father watching storm clouds obscure the constellations; the middle stanza promises the child that the stars are not gone forever; and the final stanza offers a spiritual immortality "longer even than lustrous Jupiter" (*V*, III, 589). The poem makes a visual scan, up from the beach to the horizon and on to the zenith, and then a spiritual retracing of the same path.

But among these mechanical poems there are some flashes of the young man for whom the visual world was a prodigy almost too much for words. In "To a Locomotive in Winter," despite his metaphors and anthropomorphisms, Whitman's interest is in the locomotive, not in his attempt to "render" it in words. When in the middle of the poem he refocuses his gaze typologically ("Type of the modern! emblem of motion and power!"), he briefly becomes self-conscious, asking the locomotive to "come serve the Muse, and merge in verse"—and it at once disappears, leaving a trail of sounds from its bell, cylinders, and whistle:

> Thy trills of shrieks by rocks and hills return'd,
> Launch'd o'er the prairies wide—across the lakes,
> To the free skies, unpent, and glad, and strong.
>
> (*V*, III, 666–67)

Probably the most remarkable of Whitman's late visualist poems is "Sparkles from the Wheel."

> Where the city's ceaseless crowd moves on, the livelong day,
> Withdrawn, I join a group of children watching—I pause aside with them.
>
> By the curb, toward the edge of the flagging,
> A knife-grinder works at his wheel, sharpening a great knife;
> Bending over, he carefully holds it to the stone—by foot and knee,
> With measur'd tread, he turns rapidly—As he presses with light but firm hand,

Pictorialism

131

> Forth issue, then, in copious golden jets,
> Sparkles from the wheel.
>
> (*V*, III, 602)

How like the young Whitman, the *flâneur* with an eye for the genre scene in a city street! Once again he is both in and out of the game. "Withdrawn" from the crowd, he empathizes with the attentive children; he is a spectator like them, yet he feels the touch of the knife upon the stone. It could be a passage from "A Song for Occupations." But the poem continues:

> The scene, and all its belongings—how they seize and
>   affect me!
> The sad, sharp-chinn'd old man, with worn clothes, and
>   broad shoulder-band of leather;
> Myself, effusing and fluid—a phantom curiously
>   floating—now here absorb'd and arrested;
> The group, (an unminded point, set in a vast
>   surrounding;)
> The attentive, quiet children—the loud, proud, restive
>   base of the streets;
> The low, hoarse purr of the whirling stone—the light-
>   press'd blade,
> Diffusing, dropping, sideways-darting, in tiny showers
>   of gold,
> Sparkles from the wheel.

This section speaks for the older poet. Now the experience becomes a "scene," its features embellished with adjectives, the knife-grinder in particular (*sharp-chinn'd old man*). The painter-poet ranges back from his foregrounded figures to establish their setting in the "vast surrounding" of the city streets.[21] By restating the scene's details, as in "A Noiseless Patient Spider," Whitman encourages the reader to discover a symbolic significance implicit in the phrase "sparkles

---

21. In 1870 Eastman Johnson painted a scissors-grinder surrounded by children: a high-art (and rather more mellow) extension of the engraved illustrations in *Harper's* and *Leslie's,* in the decade after the Civil War, that depicted scenes from the streets. (See Kouwenhoven, *The Columbia Historical Portrait of New York,* 316–49). During the same decade, in England, Oscar Rejlander was making a vogue for his sentimental photographs of Dickensian street people. (More about Rejlander in Chapter 7.) There is, however, nothing sentimental about Whitman's scene.

from the wheel" and in his emphasis on the mobility and evanescence of both the scene and the crowd.

But what he discovers subverts the bargain that the older poet had made with his readers. We are again thrust into the apparitional world of the Calamus poems, the intestinal warfare of Self and World that Whitman had brought to a truce in *Drum-Taps*. Once more the poet succumbs to the city-experience of destabilization, of men and women turning into dots and dreams, flashes and specks—sparkles from the wheel. And this time the poet himself has become a "phantom," disembodied and unreal.

This poem catches up the fundamental division in Whitman's pictorial sense. "Inside" the scene, it is substantial enough: sharp-chinned old man, leather shoulder-band, measured foot on the treadle, play of knife against wheel, showering sparks and quiet children, all real as can be. This is the world, make no mistake. This is the world, and the poet's Self finds its place there, on the curb, out of the traffic, taking it in, setting it down, passing the sketch along. "Outside" the scene, all becomes phantasmal: whirling stone and dropping sparks; I effusing, Not-Me diffusing, the Self devouring its experience and then itself dissolving in Heraclitean fire. The first section of the poem is Holmes or Whittier; the second is Baudelaire.[22]

Contemporary with "Sparkles from the Wheel" is *Democratic Vistas* (1871), the book in which Whitman's Satan was permitted to speak for the first time since "Chanting the Square Deific." Besides its well-known animadversions against the actual state of American Democracy, it contains passages that cast renewed doubt on the substantiality of "Nature" and on the pictorial impulse in art: "The shows and forms presented by Nature, the sensuous luxuriance, the beautiful in living men and women ... —out of these, and seizing what is in them, the poet, the esthetic worker in any field, by the divine magic of his genius, projects them, their analogies, by curious removes, indirections, in literature and art. (No useless attempt to repeat the material creation, by daguerreotyping the exact likeness by mortal mental means.)" (*Democratic Vistas, PW*, II, 419). So Whitman returns, sixteen years older, to the theme of the Preface of his first *Leaves of Grass*: the American poet "absorbs" the "shows" of

22. Thomas catches the dividedness in this poem: "what emerges from the poetry is not a visionary version of the contemporary city, but a visionary alternative to it, hauntingly centered on a 'sad' old craftsman" (*Lunar Light,* 174).

Nature and "projects" them, through "indirection," in his art. In his major poems, from "Song of Myself" (1855) to "Song of the Redwood-Tree" (1876), Whitman wrote a poetry of consciousness, recording the events and objects of American life as the undiscriminated thoughts of the American Soul or as the phenomena of the American Ideal. The world was in the mind.

Kerry Larson has shown how Whitman created a poetry that both addresses and creates its audience, a plural and national "you," so as to move "from isolated individuality ('the simple, separate person') to affirmed unanimity ('the word Democratic, the word En-Masse')."[23] In the late 1850s and early 1860s, as America splintered north from south, town from country, tree from machine, and as Whitman's own Self delaminated through a succession of masks, he appealed again to "You," his reader—no longer such a paragon as he had thought to create through his first three editions of *Leaves of Grass,* but the actual reader as he supposed him, someone with an uncritical faith in the stability of things and in the reliability of both primary perception and perception mediated through art. For such a reader he began, in *Drum-Taps,* to write of an objective world that contained the mind, a world in which the eye could take up a viewstand and render a scene in depth, through words, as surely as lithograph or daguerreotype could.

In the "sketches" of *Drum-Taps,* this approach created some of Whitman's most memorable poems, the poems that today we regard as typical of that volume. There his empathic powers, sharpened by his experience as a wound-dresser, meshed with his belief in the symbolic amplitude of democracy. This was a war on behalf of democracy, whose true heroes were commoners, anonymous foot soldiers and cavalrymen; in their commonest deeds, their bivouacs and marches, the Matter of America took the full measure of the Matter of Troy or of Rome. "Let the age and wars of other nations be chanted and their eras and characters be illustrated and that finish the verse," he had written in the 1855 Preface. "Here the theme is creative and has vista" (*CRE,* 712).

The great *Drum-Taps* poems do literally have vista. In them he abandoned the poetry of consciousness, with its rapid play of foregrounded images "corroborated" by their reference to genre work in lithograph and engraving. In occasional passages in that poetry,

---

23. Larson, *Whitman's Drama of Consensus,* 6.

the mind's play had been suspended for a moment when Whitman's imagination paused on some object long enough for it to become a subject—autonomous, perhaps enigmatic, having its own depth of being and occupying space in a world other than the poet's brain-gallery or the rhetoric of the poem. In his pen-pictures of the war, Whitman confines himself within that moment of suspension, quietly attentive in the presence of a subject that extends beyond him, in space and time, into the geography and the history of the Republic. To render that sense of "vista," Whitman returned to techniques of the picturesque that had been developed by British poets a century and more before him, and adopted by those elder American poets whom the American people had already affectionately absorbed. From *The Seasons* and *Childe Harold,* he distilled a Good Gray pictorial poetry untroubled by those satanic doubts about whether sense, word, and self were real enough to communicate.

But with the passing of the war, there passed too the empowering urgency of this mode, which he himself had rendered obsolete in the catalogs of *Song of Myself.* Whitman's later excursions into the pictorial were seldom more than the "poems distilled from other poems" for which, in the 1855 Preface, he had predicted an inevitable demise. The World was in the Self; or the Self was in the World. To the stricken and exhausted Whitman who survived the 1860s, it did not matter which. Writing "A Backward Glance O'er Travel'd Roads" in 1888, as his last preface to an edition of *Leaves of Grass,* he voiced again his enduring expectation that his work would at last be accepted as the only possible poetry for a democratic America. And without the *Drum-Taps* years and experiences, he said, "*Leaves of Grass* would not now be existing." He continues: "Although I had made a start before, only from the occurrence of the Secession War, and what it show'd me as by flashes of lightning, with the emotional depths it sounded and arous'd (of course, I don't mean in my own heart only, I saw it just as plainly in others, in millions)—that only from the strong flare and provocation of that war's sights and scenes the final reasons-for-being of an autochthonic and passionate song definitely came forth" (*PW,* II, 724).

It was again to the metaphor and the reality of eyesight that Whitman turned to declare how the war had helped him find a bond between the emotions of his own heart and the feelings of the American millions. And it was to a conventionalized poetry of the visual and the pictorial that he had turned in order to create the poems that were his bid to escape from his role as Satan, the outsider, and to become one with the gray-bearded American sages. On those terms, it seems, the American people might at last absorb and accept him.

PART II

The Citizen of Manhattan

Thrive, cities! Bring your freight, bring your shows, ample
 and sufficient rivers!
—"Crossing Brooklyn Ferry," §9

[5]

Panoramas

In 1867, a year after the sequel to *Drum-Taps*, Whitman brought out a new edition of *Leaves of Grass*. This poem was its opening inscription:

> Small is the theme of the following Chant, yet the greatest—namely, one's-self—that wondrous thing, a simple, separate person. That, for the use of the New World, I sing.
> Man's physiology complete, from top to toe, I sing. Not physiognomy alone, nor brain alone, is worthy for the muse;—I say the Form complete is worthier far. The female equally with the male, I sing.
> Nor cease at the theme of One's-Self. I speak the word of the modern, the word en-masse.
> My Days I sing, and the Lands—with interstice I knew of hapless War.
> O friend, whoe'er you are, at last arriving hither to commence, I feel through every leaf the pressure of your hand, which I return. And thus upon our journey link'd together let us go.
> ("Small the Theme of My Chant," *V*, II, 557)

Its epic formulas—"I sing," the homage to the muse, and the hint of Homeric wars and journeyings—measure another stage in that surrender to poetic decorums that had begun with the pictorial effects in *Drum-Taps*. But the poem is still a clear-sighted anatomy of the original *Leaves of Grass*. It itemizes the Matter of America: heroic individualism; democratic egalitarianism, not just as social practice but as an inclusive habit of thought; the landscape; the commonplace works and days of a small, simple anyman. Capital letters advertise the two antithetical principles of his poetry: first his devotion to the Self and to the uncompromised integrity of the separate, personal consciousness; and second, his ambition to absorb America en masse and *as* mass. The 1855 "Song of Myself" had announced that the "word of the modern" was "a word en masse" (§23, *V*, I, 30), and eventually Whitman would revise this 1867 Inscription to affirm that "En-Masse" was also "the word Democratic" ("One's-Self I Sing," *V*, II, 558). In a modern, democratic society, as Tocqueville had said, no intermediate allegiances stand between the individual citizen and the entire body politic. The Self is indeed separate, isolated; it has renounced party and creed and local custom, all mediating bodies that provide a system of preference or exclusion.

"Song of Myself" demonstrated the exhilaration of a Self standing face-to-face with the All. But it also hinted at its loneliness and the solipsism of its vision. Consciousness incessantly reverses form and field, from World-in-Mind to Mind-in-World. On what basis can the solitary Self corroborate its vision of the universe? On what basis can it address another as "You"? Where could Whitman find the ground of mutual faith that would bind him together with dumb real objects, common folk, and his poetic language? He had first represented that conflict as it struck the innocent sensibility of the child who, in the first edition of *Leaves of Grass,* went forth from the pastoral world into the destabilized experience of the city:

> [. . .] The sense of what is real .... the thought if after
>   all it should prove unreal,
> The doubts of daytime and the doubts of nighttime ...
>   the curious whether and how,
> Whether that which appears so is so .... Or is it all
>   flashes and specks?
> Men and women crowding fast in the streets .. if they
>   are not flashes and specks what are they?
>   ("There was a Child Went Forth," *V*, I, 151)

In the city streets, amid "phantoms" and "shows" and "facades," Whitman's poetry first confronted the dissolution of a world conceived as I and Not-Me. The transitory crowds of men and women in the streets, the encounter with artifice and illusion, at once exhilarated Whitman and alienated him. These antithetical emotions he reconciled by adopting the pose of the spectator, both in and out of the game—one whose aesthetic visual detachment might neutralize his intense tactile and auditory attraction. In some of the city poems, Whitman may appear most completely isolated in his own subjectivity. The objects of consciousness fade into flashes and specks, dreams or dots; the spectatorial Self, recognizing its own bad faith, recedes through an infinity of masks. However, at some points in these poems consciousness itself may recede, delivering us into the presence of an injured fireman, a gang of bricklayers, or a woman awaiting her lover. Whitman's cosmos endlessly turns itself inside out.

In the first three editions of *Leaves of Grass,* Whitman sought to stabilize this reversal by appealing to a You in the form of an ideal readership whom he addressed through an expansive political rhetoric and through the conventions of popular illustration. In the Calamus poems and in the Satan poems of *Drum-Taps,* he retreated from public poetry into cozy intimacy with the camerado-reader whom he could touch through the pages of his book. In *Drum-Taps,* he capitulated to America's actual readers, donning the mask of the Good Gray Poet, affecting first a patriot's and then a mourner's sentiments about the war, and employing recognized conventions about pictorial poetry. But in truth he most successfully consolidated the role of the citizen poet—bard, America, reader; I, Not-Me, You—in two poems of city experience that germinated together from a few lines jotted in a notebook (*N*, I, 142–43): "There was a Child Went Forth" (1855) and "Crossing Brooklyn Ferry" (1856). It is through the city itself, in these poems, that he finds a bridge between reality and the soul, between You and I. And he finds it through the mystery of the eyesight.

❖

These poems draw upon the conventions of pictorial art, like much of Whitman's poetry. They expand upon those moments of dilation in which Whitman was able to relinquish his urge to absorb his subject into the syntax of his own utterance: here men and women, streets, and ships enact the rhythms of their own being. At the same time, they enact the rhythms of visual perception, as does "A March in the Ranks." And "Crossing Brooklyn Ferry" achieves, finally, an enactment of corporate identity, encompassing Whitman, New York, and the reader within a *civitas* that resolves the daytime and nighttime doubts that so often undermined his efforts to take on the role of citizen poet.

Extolling the American bard in his 1855 Preface, Whitman said that in assimilating "the essences of the real things" (there followed a catalog of such things), the poet's expression would be "indirect and not direct or descriptive or epic. Its quality goes through these to much more. Let the age and wars of other nations be chanted and their eras and characters be illustrated and that finish the verse. Not so the great psalm of the republic. Here the theme is creative and has vista" (*CRE,* 712). Here Whitman does not renounce the characteristics of Old World national poetry. Theirs was chanted; America's is a psalm: their eras and characters were illustrated; ours have vista. Neither the auditory nor the visual is rejected, but both become more than they had been in elder hands. The poet passes through the styles and genres of traditional literature to become, indirectly, much more. Poetic high diction, picked up through his forays into Homer and Shakespeare, appears everywhere in *Leaves of Grass;* but Whitman uses it without regard for the sense of decorum that formerly had proportioned language to occasion. Sometimes it is solemn enough for Milton: "There in the fragrant pines, and the cedars dusk and dim" ("When Lilacs Last in the Dooryard Bloom'd," §16, *V,* II, 539). Sometimes it shares a sentence with colloquial American phrasing: "I guess it must be the flag of my disposition, out of hopeful green stuff woven" ("Song of Myself," §6, *V,* I, 6). And sometimes it is reduced to quite humble services: "The resurrection of the wheat appears with pale visage out of its graves" ("This Compost," §2, *V,* I, 212). Shorn of its justifying context, it supplies the high tones in Whitman's "barbaric yawp." Likewise, poetic mimesis—"direct" narrative and description—becomes in his hands not the reproduction of an illustration, but a process in which reader and poet jointly create a "vista." And this can be done, as he tells us here, only indirectly.

As in *Drum-Taps,* he drew on the tradition of landscape poetry, so these two poems refer, "indirectly," to other Romantic genres. "There was a Child Went Forth" begins as narrative, a story about a Wordsworthian child who advances from innocence to experience, questions sense and outward things, attains perhaps a philosophic mind, and becomes the father of the man who tells his story. Along the way, though, the narrative pools into descriptions of fish and fieldsprouts and parents, shifting from pastoral to georgic to urban and finally to maritime. It reaches its resolution—if at all—only in the extended description of the harbor sunset. Although the reader feels that the story has then been completed, the crisis in midpoem ("the thought if after all it should prove unreal") is not explicitly addressed either through the child's experience or through the narrator's reflections. First invoking a familiar literary pattern, "There was a Child Went Forth" then disappoints the expectations created by that pattern, yet ultimately satisfies them "indirectly" through oblique, unorthodox means. What those means are will be explained in the following chapter.

Likewise, "Crossing Brooklyn Ferry" can properly be regarded as an American variant of that genre defined by Meyer Abrams as the Greater Romantic Lyric.[1] So to classify it may seem odd or reductive, like calling a moose a variant of the English deer; or—given the tenuousness of Whitman's acquaintance with the British Romantic poets and the scarcity of such lyrics in the work of earlier American poets whom he may have known—a comparison founded only on coincidental analogies. However, recognizing its kinship with poems like "Tintern Abbey" and Coleridge's Dejection Ode is essential as a first stage in describing Whitman's most successful effort to unite poet, subject, and reader through his words.

Abrams characterized this genre:

> They present a determinate speaker in a particularized, and usually a localized, outdoor setting, whom we overhear as he carries on, in a fluent vernacular which rises easily to a more formal speech, a sustained colloquy, sometimes with himself or with the outer scene, but more frequently with a silent human auditor, present or absent. The speaker begins with a description of the landscape; an aspect or change of aspect in the landscape evokes a varied but integral process of memory, thought, anticipation, and feeling which remains closely intervolved with the outer scene. In the course of this meditation the lyric speaker achieves an insight, faces up to a tragic loss, comes to a moral decision, or resolves an emotional problem. Often the poem rounds upon itself to end where it began, at the outer scene, but with an

---

1. Abrams, "Structure and Style in the Greater Romantic Lyric," in *From Sensibility to Romanticism,* ed. Frederick W. Hilles and Harold Bloom (New York, 1965), 527–60, hereinafter cited as "Greater Romantic Lyric." Abrams himself links Whitman's poem with this genre, without elaborating.

altered mood and deepened understanding which is the result of the intervening meditation.[2]

"Crossing Brooklyn Ferry" is a carefully structured poem. It is quite different from "Song of Myself," where all structure seems problematic, and from such poems as "Salut au Monde!," "Our Old Feuillage," "By Blue Ontario's Shore," "This Compost," "A Song of the Rolling Earth," and the other bardic declamations whose lines so often seem unsequenced and even interchangeable from one poem to another. "Crossing Brooklyn Ferry" has a dramatic structure comparable to that of "Frost at Midnight" and "Tintern Abbey," in which an inward crisis is introduced and resolved. Typically the crisis, according to Abrams, is that separation between subject and object, or poet and world, that the Romantics termed "dejection"; and it is through a meditation on the landscape that this division is overcome. "When the Romantic poet confronted a landscape, the distinction between self and not-self tended to dissolve."[3]

The dominant mood of "Crossing Brooklyn Ferry" is exaltation, not dejection; but readers who come to it along the route from "Song of Myself" through "There was a Child Went Forth" will realize that its joy, like that of Emerson's "Self-Reliance," is a hard-won triumph over dejection. Near the poem's midpoint, Whitman confronts his adversary directly:

> I too felt the curious abrupt questionings stir within me,
> In the day, among crowds of people, sometimes they
>   came upon me,
> In my walks home late at night, or as I lay in my bed,
>   they came upon me.
> [. . .]
> The best I had done seemed to me blank and suspicious,
> My great thoughts, as I supposed them, were they not
>   in reality meagre?
>
> (§§5, 6, *V,* I, 221)

These "abrupt questionings" are like the doubts of daytime and of nighttime that put an end to the child's innocence. These now chill the poet's confidence in the power of his language to mediate between reality and experience, and between private experience and

---

2. *Ibid.*, 527–28.
3. *Ibid.*, 553, 551.

shared meaning.[4] In such a moment, the Romantic ego—having thought it had subjected the world to the laws of its consciousness—looks back and discovers how small and weak the capital was from which these conquests were launched.[5]

Here are its first five lines as published in 1856:

> Flood-tide of the river, flow on! I watch you, face to
>   face,
> Clouds of the west! sun half an hour high! I see you also
>   face to face.
>
>
> Crowds of men and women attired in the usual
>   costumes, how curious you are to me!
> On the ferry-boats the hundreds and hundreds that cross
>   are more curious to me than you suppose,
> And you that shall cross from shore to shore years
>   hence, are more to me, and more in my meditations,
>   than you might suppose.
>
> (§1, *V*, I, 217)

You river; you clouds and sun; you men and women; you reader remote in space and time, whoever you are: the poet begins with an intuitive sense of communion with all that he sees. There is no question of I and Not-Me. Sight instantly has delivered us into a world of presences, face to face, *You*. It resembles that ecstatic union of self and soul, one transparent summer morning, to which Whitman had borne witness in "Song of Myself":

> Swiftly arose and spread around me the peace and joy
>   and knowledge that pass all the art and argument of
>   the earth;
> And I know that the hand of God is the elderhand of my
>   own,

---

[4]. Erkkila identifies this mood "of fracture, anomie, and doubt" as "the catalyst for the poem" (*Whitman the Political Poet*, 141). More boldly than she, M. Wynn Thomas discovers in "Crossing Brooklyn Ferry" Whitman's confrontation with "the alienating signs of his society's passion for wealth," an attitude discernible in his journalism but invisible in this poem (*Lunar Light*, 104–109).

[5]. "You see my wretched *I*—I will confess to you, it is empty, and whatever I do in myself, as a result of experiencing and using, does not fathom its emptiness" (Buber, *I and Thou*, 71).

> And I know that the spirit of God is the eldest brother
> of my own,
> And that all the men ever born are also my brothers ....
> and the women my sisters and lovers,
> And that a kelson of the creation is love.
>
> (§5, *V*, I, 6)

But that had been a solitary and idyllic vision, extended to other creatures only as a consequence. On Brooklyn ferry, the vision begins with men and women, in the thick of a crowd and with the actual light of sunset transforming their faces—a commonplace miracle in an utterly commonplace setting, tired people journeying home from work. For a moment, the poet's alienation from his subject and his audience dissolves: "I am with you."

All the rest of the poem seeks out the ground of that miracle, the ground on which he could address these "curious" strangers as You.[6] First Whitman adverts to his customary poetic posture, the egoistic consciousness delighting in its own powers to absorb or be absorbed:

> The impalpable sustenance of me from all things at all
> hours of the day,
> The simple, compact, well-joined scheme—myself
> disintegrated, every one disintegrated, yet part of the
> scheme,
> The similitudes of the past and those of the future,
> The glories strung like beads on my smallest sights and
> hearings—on the walk in the street, and the passage
> over the river,

---

6. Carlisle points out the threefold ground: in the actual crossing of the river; in the interhuman community; and in spiritual experience (*The Uncertain Self*, 61–63). Larson shows that the subject of "Crossing Brooklyn Ferry" is creating terms and conditions of address with a "you" who is both listener and reader: it is "not . . . a cunningly deployed pattern of significances, a shrewdly arranged narrative, nor even . . . a 'field of action'; it is, before all these, a gesture, summons, or petition" (*Whitman's Drama of Consensus*, 8–13). William Chapman Sharpe writes: "Whitman situates the reader as part of a specific urban landscape, the poet's own. As it develops, their bond will depend increasingly on their common experience of the scene they share, each inseparable from the harbor and its sights" (*Unreal Cities*, 93). Sharpe is one of the few readers of "Crossing Brooklyn Ferry" who has recognized its fusion of physical and urban experience, though his emphasis is on a sexual fusion of poet, city, and reader.

> The current rushing so swiftly, and swimming with me
> far away [. . .].
>
> (§2, *V*, I, 217–18)

Here is life en masse, without structure. Each citizen stands disintegrated and alone in the inclusive schema of America, drawing spiritual sustenance from a world reduced to "experience." Memories and ideas swarm in the consciousness, each with its own particular glory but without organic connection, unified only by the sequence in which the mind adverts to them or by the similitudes that allow the mind to pass from one to another. Whitman might be describing here both the poet and the poetics of "Song of Myself."[7]

But for the experience recreated in this poem, there are other less centripetal schemes. Whitman has sited himself in a specific place and time, using the conventions of the topographical poem and of the Greater Romantic Lyric to organize his meditation and to give it anchorage and substance. Elsewhere in the 1856 edition, Whitman interrupts poems like "Song of the Broad-Axe" and "Salut au Monde!" with dilations in which his willful manipulation of statement and image gives way to an attentive rendering of the rhythm of some human activity like fishing or carpentry. Here the entire poem is shaped by the passage of Fulton ferry between Manhattan and Brooklyn, and by its passengers' perception of the harborscape through which they move. From the sharp particularity of those sundown faces, Whitman passes through a myriad of other details—the water, the sky, the harbor traffic, the other passengers—while his mind grows more and more dense with imaginary life, the "others" who will share the same sense experiences, directly ("Fifty years hence others will see them as they cross, the sun half an hour high") or, when Fulton ferry sails no more, through the mediation of this poem ("The men and women I saw were all near to me, / Others the same—others who look back on me, because I looked forward to them") (§2, 4, *V*, I, 218, 220).

So, by extending and multiplying points of view, eventually

---

7. Tenney Nathanson says, "Moving objects into a fluid, centripetal space and transmuting individual actions into varieties of an eternal, undulating process, Whitman's catalogue also effaces the difference between the things it renders and the subject who names them" ("Whitman's Tropes," 125). Although this is true of the opening sequences of the poem, Nathanson—following Anderson—does not speak for the total effect of "Crossing Brooklyn Ferry."

Whitman passes over to a vision that is always in the present tense, a viewpoint from which his own present moment of 1855 can be seen as simply historical:

> I loved well those cities,
> I loved well the stately and rapid river,
> The men and women I saw were all near to me,
> Others the same—others who look back on me, because I looked forward to them,
> The time will come, though I stop here today and tonight.
>
> What is it, then, between us? What is the count of the scores or hundreds of years between us?
> Whatever it is, it avails not—distance avails not, and place avails not.
>
> I too lived,
> I too walked the streets of Manhattan Island, and bathed in the waters around it;
> I too felt the curious abrupt questionings stir within me,
> In the day, among crowds of people, sometimes they came upon me,
> In my walks home late at night, or as I lay in my bed, they came upon me.
>
> (§4–5, *V*, I, 220–21)

These "curious abrupt questionings" now appear not as temptations to skepticism and solipsism, but as the tuitions of a romantic Platonism, stirrings of dissatisfaction with a merely phenomenal world. The very phrase recalls, from the Intimations Ode, Wordsworth's

> . . . obstinate questionings
> Of sense and outward things,
> Fallings from us, vanishings;
> Blank misgivings of a Creature
> Moving about in worlds not realised.

Wordsworth's misgivings soon delivered him from noisy years, listlessness, and mad endeavor into the presence of the timeless Universal:

> Though inland far we be,
> Our Souls have sight of that immortal sea
> Which brought us hither,
> Can in a moment travel thither,
> And see the Children sport upon the shore,
> And hear the mighty waters rolling evermore.
> (ll. 141–45, 163–68)

Emerson too, in the later pages of *Nature,* burst through the illusions of time and place: "Thought tends to relax [the] despotism of the senses which binds us to nature as if we were a part of it, and shows us nature aloof and, as it were, afloat"; it reduces the world to "one vast picture which God paints on the instant eternity for the contemplation of the soul."[8] Perhaps influenced by Emerson's characteristic hydraulic metaphors for Spirit and Idea, certainly attuned to the element on which he floats, Whitman renders this transcendental scheme in the image of a supersaturated solution[9]:

> I too had been struck from the float forever held in
>   solution,
> I too had received identity by my body,
> That I was, I knew was of my body, and what I should
>   be, I knew I should be of my body.
> (§5, *V,* I, 221)

Now on the farther shore of his meditation, Whitman attains a vision of reincarnation, according to which each personal soul is a temporal precipitate from the eternal Soul.[10] His affinity with his fellow travelers, he discovers, really follows from their communal membership in that Oversoul; it is toward that principle in one another that we yearn. And it is through that immortal principle that he is bound

---

8. *Nature,* Chap. 6 (*Emerson,* 43, 48).

9. Owing to the nonacademic nature of Whitman's education, it is difficult to trace the origins of his scientific and pseudoscientific lore; much of it apparently came from his attendance at public lectures and demonstrations, where inducing precipitation from a solution by striking the container would make a fine piece of showmanship. See Joseph Beaver, *Walt Whitman—Poet of Science* (Morningside Heights, N.Y., 1951), 128.

10. This may seem to have neoplatonic origins, but in a notebook from the same year, Whitman speaks of "the Egyptian idea of the return of the soul after a certain period of time" (*N,* I, 198)—another fruit of his visits to Henry Abbott's Egyptian Museum on Broadway.

with readers "a hundred years hence, or ever so many hundred years hence" (§2, *V*, I, 218).

> Who knows but I am as good as looking at you now, for
> all you cannot see me?
>
> It is not you alone, nor I alone,
> Not a few races, not a few generations, not a few
> centuries,
> It is that each came, or comes, or shall come, from its
> due emission, without fail, either now, or then, or
> henceforth.
>
> (§7, *V*, I, 222)

Thus Whitman is able to address his reader as You, not only because both may have passed through the same harborscape and not only because the reader holds this book in his lap and hears, in the mind's ear, its words, but also because both are vessels of an indivisible spiritual energy:

> [. . .]what is more subtle than this which ties me to the
> woman or man that looks in my face,
> Which fuses me into you now, and pours my meaning
> into you.
>
> (§8, *V*, I, 223)

Whitman, though, is not a transcendentalist like Emerson. (Or like the elder poet of "Passage to India.") This "float" is not some utterly immaterial ectoplasm. Reality for Whitman is material and specifically carnal. "Crossing Brooklyn Ferry" never deserts the physical ground of its vision. In "Song of Myself," he used the "float" image to speak of the physical beginnings of life:

> If I and you and the worlds and all beneath or upon their
> surfaces, and all the palpable life, were this moment
> reduced back to a pallid float, it would not avail in the
> long run.
>
> (§45, *V*, I, 74)

And in another 1855 poem, "I Sing the Body Electric," referring to the origin of matter itself, he writes that "matter has cohered together from its diffused float" (§6, *V*, I, 128). For Whitman, it seems, spirit and matter are together the eternal "float" from which emerge the temporal souls and mortal bodies that surround him on the ferry. In a preliminary sketch of "Crossing Brooklyn Ferry," Whitman was even more explicit:

> That I am is of my body, and what I am is of my body
> What identity I am, I owe to my body .... what soul I
>   owe to my body,
> What belongs to me .... that it does not yet spread in the
>   spread of the universe, I owe to my body
> Of all that I have had, I have had nothing except through
>   my body,
> Of the make of my body was not my mortal experience
>   only,
> My body makes my immortal experience.
>   (N, I, 230)

In developing the poem, Whitman excised most of these clumsy assertions (the passage that survives is gawky enough), transferring their spirit to the way that the poem returns faithfully to the material and corporeal world. Whereas Emerson's visions, and those of latter-day Whitmans like Hart Crane and Allen Ginsberg, trail away into the impalpable and ineffable, Whitman's—like the ferry itself—swing back to recognize and to celebrate the tangible world from which his meditation first departed:

> Flow on, river! Flow with the flood-tide, and ebb with
>   the ebb-tide!
> Frolic on, crested and scallop-edged waves!
> [. . .]
> Cross from shore to shore, countless crowds of
>   passengers!
> Stand up, tall masts of Manahatta!—stand up, beautiful
>   hills of Brooklyn!

"We realize the soul only by you," he says, "you faithful solids and fluids" (§9, V, I, 223–25). At its end, Whitman's poem, like the British Romantics', turns once more to the landscape that first called him to meditation. But unlike them, it has recovered the ecstatic unity with which he began, addressing directly the presences around him, You and You and You.

Early in the crossing, as he surveyed the East River and its shores,

Whitman stood at its center, validating the scene as its presiding consciousness:

> I too many and many a time crossed the river, the sun
>   half an hour high,
> I watched the December sea-gulls, I saw them high in
>   the air floating with motionless wings oscillating
>   their bodies,
> I saw how the glistening yellow lit up parts of their
>   bodies, and left the rest in strong shadow,
> I saw the slow-wheeling circles and the gradual edging
>   toward the south.
>
> (§3, V, I, 219)

I saw . . . I looked . . . I watched: the empowering verbs were functions of Whitman's visual consciousness, and the objects of that consciousness piled up in nouns (*circles*), phrases (*floating with motionless wings, oscillating their bodies*), and a few subordinate clauses (*how the yellow lit their bodies*). Glories strung like beads, they hung inert in Whitman's brain-gallery. But now at the poem's end, when they are recognized both as "solids and fluids" and as "beautiful ministers," the verbs shift from perception to action:

> Fly on, sea-birds! fly sideways, or wheel in large circles
>   high in the air!
> Receive the summer-sky, you water! faithfully hold it till
>   all downcast eyes have time to take it from you!
> Diverge, fine spokes of light, from the shape of my
>   head, or any one's head, in the sun-lit water!
> Come on, ships, from the lower bay! pass up or down,
>   white-sailed schooners, sloops, lighters!
>
> (§9, V, I, 224)

With this shift in verbs and a corresponding noun shift from objects to subjects, Whitman acknowledges the substantial, autonomous reality of the passengers, the ferry, the river, and the harbor.

But he does not simply relinquish them into their own declarative constructions, as he did the bricklayers in "Song of the Broad-Axe," and as later he would the cavalrymen and the mossbonker fishermen. Rather, with the imperative mood, he unites *their* action with *his* authorial self; the energy flows through both at once. Fusing his will with their acts, he authorizes them to be themselves; he partakes in them. Whereas in "Mannahatta" the actual city would dissolve into a "word," here the substantive beings of the city, going about their own business, define the word-sayer and confirm his presence to them:

> Thrive, cities! Bring your freight, bring your shows,
>   ample and sufficient rivers!
> Expand, being than which none else is perhaps more
>   spiritual!
> Keep your places, objects than which none else is more
>   lasting!
>
> We descend upon you and all things, we arrest you all,
> We realize the soul only by you, you faithful solids and
>   fluids,
> Through you color, form, location, sublimity, ideality,
> Through you every proof, comparison, and all the
>   suggestions and determinations of ourselves.
>
> (§9, *V*, I, 224–25)

Whitman's crossover to a metaphysical vision has led him back surely to the physical experiences from which he began. But the light falling on faces and warehouses now comes not just from the setting sun but from the "soul" he has discovered within them. Whitman addresses them as "dumb beautiful ministers" (§9, *V*, I, 225). For what they offer is *mute* testimony, delivered from the solipsism and bad faith that can unmoor the web of words that a poet may spin out of himself. It was just such a crossover and return that he hoped for when, in the 1855 Preface, he described the duty of a democratic poet: "folks expect of the poet to indicate more than the beauty and dignity which always attach to dumb real objects .... they expect him to indicate the path between reality and their souls" (*CRE*, 714). In "Crossing Brooklyn Ferry," the path is a trackless waterway, flowing not between matter and spirit but between the soul and reality. Reality is both matter and spirit; and the beauty and dignity of those objects spring from their testimony of the soul, to the soul.

Because "Crossing Brooklyn Ferry" is a search for a structure for experience, it is appropriate that it should be a structured poem and that its literary form should be traditional and appropriate for the subject. But though it resembles the Greater Romantic Lyric, it is peculiarly American in its confident return to experience—in its faith that the material object and the corporeal eye are not tyrants but ministers. Further, this poem does not end just with "meanings . . . brought to [the scene] by the private mind which perceives it," as Abrams said of the British poems.[11] As E. Fred Carlisle said, Whitman does not reduce the persons and things he sees to simple projections of his own subjectivity, but "insists on their independent, other reality," a reality discovered through his dialogic relation with them.[12] In the cityscape, there is a "scheme" through which meaning might again be made public. So the identification of a literary model is not enough to account for this poem.[13] The reader must look beyond the poem to find its significance—in the rhythm of visual perception playing upon the texture of manmade and natural forms that make up the city.

❖

In visualizing this passage between two cities, Whitman has discovered identity: the way in which personal "identity" originates in the incarnation of soul in body; the sense of spiritual identicalness that binds passenger to passenger and reader to writer; the "similitude" between what Whitman has seen and what the reader has imagined, responding to his words. These are the "identities of the spiritual world" to which we may be admitted through "the curious mystery of the eyesight" (*CRE*, 714).

Abrams notes that the British Romantics "manifested wariness, almost terror, at the threat of the corporeal eye and material object to tyrannize over the mind and imagination," and so they structured their poems as meditations, using the visual report mainly as the occasion of the poem. Compared with them, Whitman keeps his eye much more steadily on his subject. His devotion to seen things and his fascination with the process of seeing suggest both his heartier

   11. Abrams, "Greater Romantic Lyric," 556.
   12. Carlisle, *The Uncertain Self*, 65.
   13. As Larson has said of "Crossing Brooklyn Ferry," "It desires to affirm an unparalleled intimacy with its auditor that suggests him to be absolutely intrinsic to the poem's development at the same time it is moved to stipulate that those ties which bind listener to author are absolutely extrinsic to interpretive reflection" (*Whitman's Drama of Consensus,* 12). Larson sees the relation between these two desires as discrepant; the following discussion will present them as sequent or, in Whitman's terms, as direct and indirect.

appetite for the sensuous and physical, and perhaps also that Ruskin (1819–1900) and the first generation of photographers were more nearly his chronological neighbors than Wordsworth and Coleridge. "There was a Child Went Forth" and "Crossing Brooklyn Ferry" show that the truth must be seen not only *through* the eye but also *with* and *in* the eye. Speaking of Paul Valéry's consciousness of his own visual perception, Geoffrey Hartman makes a distinction that opens the space separating Whitman from the British Romantics: "The desire for a perception pure of all percepts need not in the modern poet involve a denial of the necessity of sense experience or of the reality of sense objects. It is unmistakably perception desired and experienced as the plenary manifestation of a creative presence.... Perhaps we have only begun to understand the creative power of the senses, the extent to which they are enabled to give immediate, real interpretations."[14] The principal subject of "Crossing Brooklyn Ferry" is not transcendental meditation, but the creative power of the senses. A creative visual imagination delivers Whitman into the presence of his fellow passengers and citizens, and through the same power we too are recreated as fellow passengers and citizens.

In his *Biographia Literaria,* Coleridge complained of some protracted descriptive passages in Wordsworth's *The Excursion*:

> It must be some strong motive . . . which could induce me to describe in a number of verses what a draughtsman could present to the eye with incomparably greater satisfaction by half a dozen strokes of his pencil, or the painter with as many touches of his brush. Such descriptions too often occasion in the mind of a reader, who is determined to understand his author, a feeling of labour, not very dissimilar to that, with which he would construct a diagram, line by line, for a long geometrical proposition. It seems to be like taking the pieces of a dissected map out of its box. We first look at one part, and then at another, then join and dove-tail them; and when the successive acts of attention have been completed, there is a retrogressive

14. Abrams, "Greater Romantic Lyric," 528; Hartman, *The Unmediated Vision,* 153–54. Hartman's other comments on Valéry, however, are applicable mainly to the self-reflexive pole of "Song of Myself," as he writes: "[Valéry] has accepted with rare consistency that all knowledge is of one's body; between person and person there is simply visibility" (152). In "Crossing Brooklyn Ferry," as we will see, visibility is not "simple," nor does it exclude interpersonal relationships.

effort of mind to behold it as a whole. The poet should paint to the imagination, not to the fancy.[15]

Coleridge refers here to the conflict, well known from Lessing's discussion of it, between the time-bound disclosures of language and the instantaneous revelations of pictorial art. Directing the reader "here" and "there," "beyond" and "below," the poet hands him "the pieces of a dissected map": the image existed in the poet's mind before, and in the reader's mind after; but the process of reading the poem, the actual experience, is a tedious bother. So it had been with the landscape poets who preceded Wordsworth, and so it would be with Whitman in the *Drum-Taps* poems. But, as we will see, this is not the case with "Crossing Brooklyn Ferry." The poem's subjects move through time as its words do; and the question that it answers "without mentioning it" (§8, *V*, I, 223) is not, How can we escape from time? but, What endures?

Obviously, Whitman did not share Coleridge's weariness with descriptive poetry. Living in the middle of the great age of travel writing, he absorbed its trust in the power of words to evoke, in the mind's eye, a reliable image of prairies, savannahs, forests, and sierras to which draughtsmen and painters made their way less frequently than they did to Windermere. As a journalist, he had composed such descriptions himself—not of the continent's remote interiors, but of harborscapes that became exotic because they were so familiar: "Many books have been written," he said in a newspaper article in 1849, "to describe journeys between the Old and New World, and what was done or seen therein, and afterward. But we know of no work . . . describing a voyage across the Fulton Ferry." He then supplied one:

> Who has crossed the East River and not looked with admiration on the beautiful view afforded from the middle of the stream! The forests of the New York shipping, lining the shores as far as one can see them—the tall spire of Trinity looming far up over all the other objects—various other spires—the tops of the trees on the Battery and in the Parks—these we have left behind us. In front stands Brooklyn—Brooklyn the beautiful! The Heights stretch

---

15. *Samuel Taylor Coleridge,* ed. H. J. Jackson (Oxford, Eng., 1985), 392 [Chap. 22].

along in front, lined now with dwellings for nearly the whole extent; but with space still left for a Public Promenade, if it be applied to that purpose *soon*. To the left of the Heights, the open mouth of Fulton street, the great entrance to the city—up whose vista you can see many of the principal Brooklyn buildings, particularly the square squatty tower of St. Ann's Church. Away to the left lies the Navy Yard, and the great Dry Dock, now nearly finished. Then Williamsburgh, another place of beauty. She too, has her high banks, and they show admirably from the river.

On the other side our eyes behold a still more varied scene. Governor's Island, in shape like a well proportioned wart, looks green even at this season of the year; and those straight, regularly planted poplars are in perfect accordance with the military character of the place. Far to the distance is Staten Island, and the Jersey shore. The Battery Point is hidden by the masts of the shipping.

A moving panorama is upon all parts of the waters. Sail craft and steamboats are in every direction.[16]

The scene here is depicted according to those conventions of sequence familiar from the pictorial poems reviewed in the previous chapter: *In front . . . to the left . . . vista . . . away to the left . . . On the other side . . . Far to the distance . . . panorama*. The reader is invited to compose imaginatively an encompassing view of New York harbor, arranging its features in accord with innumerable other "views," in engraving and lithograph, that depicted it crowded with commercial life and surrounded by shores on which were traced the signs of public and private development. (See Fig. 4. In the middle ground, Fulton Ferry departs for Brooklyn.) New York harbor was for Whitman a culturally mediated image like those he had invoked for his quick, epithetic pictures in "Song of Myself" and those that he had modified into the "sketches" of *Drum-Taps*. In the 1860 *Leaves of Grass,* he would employ another of the conventions for rendering such scenes, the balloon view:

16. Walt Whitman, "Letters from a Travelling Bachelor" (New York *Dispatch,* December 23, 1849), in Joseph Jay Rubin, *The Historic Whitman* (University Park, Pa., 1973), 347–50.

Fig. 4 Detail from Edwin Whitefield, with David Moody, *View of Brooklyn, L.I. from U.S. Hotel* (tinted lithograph with additional coloring, 1846)

Courtesy the I. N. Phelps Stokes Collection, Miriam and Ira D. Wallach Division of Art, Prints and Photographs, The New York Public Library; Astor, Lenox and Tilden Foundations

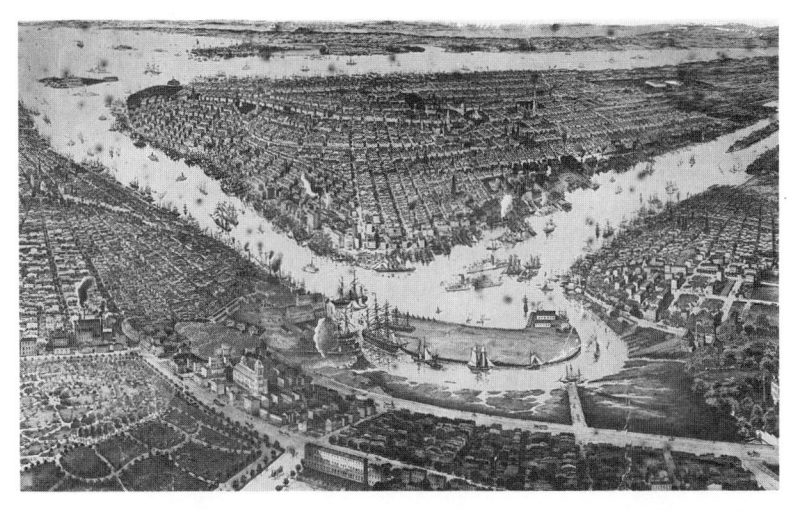

Fig. 5 Detail from J. Bachmann, *Bird's Eye View of the City of New York* (colored lithograph, 1859)

Courtesy the Eno Collection, Miriam and Ira D. Wallach Division of Art, Prints and Photographs, The New York Public Library; Astor, Lenox and Tilden Foundations

> Rich, hemmed thick all around with sailships and steamships—an island sixteen miles long, solid-founded,
> Numberless crowded streets—high growths of iron, slender, strong, light, splendidly uprising toward clear skies;
> Tides swift and ample, well-loved by me, toward sundown,
> The flowing sea-currents, the little islands, the larger adjoining islands, the heights, the villas.
> ("Mannahatta," *V*, II, 419)

From this aerial viewpoint, Whitman takes in the entire scene at once, presenting the island's coarsest topographical features before looking in greater detail at its houses, traffic, and citizens. By 1850, overhead views had become a common way to advertise the metropolis, either through illustrations or through a scale model of the city that was displayed in New York in 1845–1846 (Fig. 5).[17] This viewpoint was well suited to promotion because it rendered the city's

---

17. Kouwenhoven, *The Columbia Historical Portrait of New York*, 189–94.

imposing extent better than any earthbound vantage point could, while allowing the artist to represent at least the principal buildings and landscape features scenographically, giving the view far greater imaginative legibility than an abstract map could offer.[18]

The pictorial effects of "Crossing Brooklyn Ferry," however, begin from more old-fashioned techniques. As he had in the *Dispatch* article, Whitman places the viewer on water level and systematically assembles the scene before him:

> [I] looked on the haze on the hills southward and southwestward,
> Looked on the vapor as it flew in fleeces tinged with violet,
> Looked toward the lower bay to notice the arriving ships,
> Saw their approach, saw aboard those that were near me,
> Saw the white sails of schooners and sloops, saw the ships at anchor,
> The sailors at work in the rigging or out astride the spars,
> The round masts, the swinging motion of the hulls, the slender serpentine pennants,
> The large and small steamers in motion, the pilots in their pilot-houses,
> The white wake left by the passage, the quick tremulous whirl of the wheels.
>
> (§3, *V,* I, 219–20)

Directing his reader's eye from background to middle ground and filling the middle ground with vivid and energetic detail, Whitman elaborates such a harborscape as his readers knew from illustrations, if they did not know it in direct experience. To assist in the appropriation of that scene, occasionally he uses conventional epithets, as he does in his expansionist poems like "Mannahatta," "A Broadway Pageant," and "Salut au Monde!": the sails are white, the wake is white, the masts are round.

---

18. Since the Renaissance, the overhead perspective has been the viewpoint of political and economic hegemony. In the 1850s and 1860s, Baron Haussmann, aided by an aerial survey map, was rebuilding Paris as a symbol of imperial power. See James Dougherty, "The Triumph of the Map," in *The Fivesquare City,* 54–86.

More noteworthy, though, are the violations of such conventions, when Whitman reports exactly what his eyes see:

> I watched the December sea-gulls, I saw them high in
>   the air floating with motionless wings oscillating
>   their bodies,
> I saw how the glistening yellow lit up parts of their
>   bodies, and left the rest in strong shadow,
> [. . .]
> Looked on the vapor as it flew in fleeces tinged with
>   violet,
> [. . .]
> On the river the shadowy group, the big steam-tug
>   closely flanked on each side by the barges—the hay-
>   boat, the belated lighter,
> On the neighboring shore the fires from the foundry
>   chimneys burning high and glaringly into the night,
> Casting their flicker of black, contrasted with wild red
>   and yellow light, over the tops of houses, and down
>   into the clefts of streets.
>
> (§3, V, I, 219–20)

In passages such as this, Whitman's attention to the apparent color of objects and to atmospheric effects on the qualities of sight suggests an approach to perception that can be found in the Romantic poets or in Ruskin's *Modern Painters*.[19]

The painterly quality of such moments (as well as in "There was a Child Went Forth") has led many interpreters of this poem to compare it to various kinds of painting and to infer from this comparison that "Crossing Brooklyn Ferry" is a romantic attempt to preserve a single privileged moment of time.[20] One of them writes:

> In the first two lines of Whitman's "Crossing Brooklyn
> Ferry," a surprising movement to painterly conventions

---

19. Heffernan, *The Re-Creation of Landscape*, 137–69.
20. Matthiessen to the plein-airists (*American Renaissance*, 599, 615); Barton St. Armand to the Impressionists and the Luminists ("Transcendence Through Technique: Whitman's 'Crossing Brooklyn Ferry' and Impressionist Painting," in *The Arts and Their Interrelations*, ed. Harry R. Garvin and James M. Heath [Lewisburg, Pa., 1978], 62–72); Thomas to the Luminists also (*Lunar Light*, 94–96); Stephen Adams once more to the Luminists ("The Luminist Walt Whitman," *American Poetry*, II [Winter, 1985], 2–16); and S. Betsky-Zweig to Turner ("An Uncommon Language: Crossing with Whitman," *Dutch Quarterly Review of Anglo-American Letters*, X [1979], 262).

occurs. A poet who works mostly with the oral devices of chant, recitation, repetition, the long breath, Whitman here focusses his eye on a canvas rather than his ear on a cataloguing song. Spaces, perspective, colour, working through a central metaphor, are his materials. . . . Space is manipulated by the poet's eye. It sees each phenomenon where it belongs. Using his own eye as point of view he remains centred in the canvas while his vision encompasses and records the disparate pieces.[21]

Likewise, many readers of "Crossing Brooklyn Ferry" have felt that the city into which it opened was not Manhattan or any secular city, but a city of the mind. M. Wynn Thomas, though he acknowledges the "full glory of . . . materiality" expressed in this poem, nevertheless notes how Whitman transforms "the limited, changeful prospect of the historical present . . . into an ideal, timeless conspectus."[22] James L. Machor, in *Pastoral Cities*, observes that Whitman can ignore the problems of industrialization because "he is not writing about social actualities but is composing a poetic world . . . a mythical urban middle landscape existing outside time and space by dint of the poet's power as time melder."[23] Quentin Anderson, in *The Imperial Self*, treats this poem with great respect, but he links it with his general (and accurate) view of Whitman's egotistical sublime. Although "Crossing Brooklyn Ferry" is free of "the bullying persona of the poet" and his "all-inclusive consciousness," which were at the center of other poems like "Song of Myself," Anderson writes, nevertheless, that unitary consciousness is at work here too: "What the poem dissolves into the plenum of consciousness is not only the apprehended world, but the conventional epistemology, the way the world is beheld when it is conceived as the scene of drama and change. . . . In 'Crossing Brooklyn Ferry,' he deprived himself and all the rest of us of generational place and put everything into the eternal moment of the sunset, ferries, gulls, and radiating images in the water."[24]

21. Betsky-Zweig, "An Uncommon Language," 261.
22. Thomas, *Lunar Light*, 115, 103.
23. James L. Machor, *Pastoral Cities: Urban Ideals and the Symbolic Landscape of America* (Madison, Wis., 1987), 182–83.
24. Anderson, *The Imperial Self*, 121, 95. See also James W. Gargano, "Technique in 'Crossing Brooklyn Ferry': The Everlasting Moment," *JEGP*, LXII (1963), 262–69; and R. W. B. Lewis, *The American Adam* (Chicago, 1955), 52–53.

Doing all this was indeed Whitman's ordinary poetic business. But "Crossing Brooklyn Ferry" is Whitman's extraordinary poem. Although it is possible to find lines and details in which he wavers back toward his usual division between the absorbing I and an inert Not-Me, this poem uses pictorial materials and techniques to overcome that division. And in overcoming it, he reveals a cityscape in which time has the same substantial presence as the sunset, the hills, and his fellow passengers.[25] As Paul Bové has written of Whitman: "Poetry must have an essentially temporal structure, which is marked by 'vista.' . . . The poet not only testifies to man's being present in the world, but 'he places himself where the future becomes present,' at the point where 'sight' and 'eyes' are retrieved from metaphysics and coercion."[26]

One of the visual techniques used freshly here is the catalog. In other poems, it is the instrument of an imperial national consciousness that assimilates everything through sheer rhetorical power and holds it all in simultaneous vision. The catalogs of "Our Old Feuillage" and "Song of the Broad-Axe" are successive only because words cannot say everything at once. But here the catalog is used much more sensitively, and its every detail must be attended to. Stanley K. Coffman has drawn attention to the care with which Whitman here uses catalogs to effect changes in tone as the poem unfolds.[27] The catalogs are constructed not to document a flat canvas caught in a timeless moment, but to trace the physical movement of Walt Whitman through a familiar daily passage, and the way in which his attention to that familiar scene establishes not a painting but a world.

❖

The viewstand is important. Whitman does not rise above his subject and dominate it as he would in "Mannahatta" and as he had in the

---

25. Carlisle says well that in "Crossing Brooklyn Ferry" "meaning arises only in the lived moment. . . . Whitman dramatizes *living*—not life nor some fixed, eternal state." The "moment" then is not timeless, but is instead the point at which "the continuity of life from the past into the future" is experienced in the human community (*The Uncertain Self*, 65, 68).

26. Bové, *Destructive Poetics*, 146–47.

27. Stanley K. Coffman, "'Crossing Brooklyn Ferry': A Note on the Catalogue Technique in Whitman's Poetry," *Modern Philology*, LI (1954), 225–32.

nationalistic poems of the first two editions. He is in the midst of the city. The eye cannot see everything at once when it is in a human face, in a living body, in a specific place. Seeing is not instantaneous, but rather a process. It has duration. Whitman recognized this in the newspaper article when he brought his reader down Fulton Street toward the ferry, commenting on the street's crookedness ("We like to come upon new shows—to turn a bend, and behold something fresh"[28]) and retailing anecdotes of the buildings along the way. Once aboard the ferry, Manhattan is "behind us" (though we still see its shipping and spires and treetops) while Brooklyn and the bay lie "in front" and "on the other side." Surrounded by the scene, we lose some of our aesthetic distance from it. We cannot confine and compose it as we could a two-dimensional painting. In the newspaper article, Whitman identifies by name what he is creating in the poem. He calls it a panorama.

The 1850s knew two or three distinct kinds of panoramas. One was a misnomer for the diorama, which we will consider later. Another was a long strip of canvas that scrolled before the viewer, representing a serial view of its subject, usually a river: Banvard's panorama of the Mississippi was the best known of these.[29] The other, the first to be developed, was a stationary scene that surrounded the viewer and created an illusion of three-dimensional experience.

Whitman uses "panorama" frequently in his poetry. One of the more significant early occasions is in the passage in "Song of Myself" that calls into question the relation of artifact to reality:

> My words are words of a questioning, and to indicate reality:
> This printed and bound book .... but the printer and the printing-office boy?
> The marriage estate and settlement .... but the body and mind of the bridegroom? also those of the bride?
> The panorama of the sea .... but the sea itself?

---

28. Rubin, *The Historic Whitman*, 348.

29. In *Kavanagh*, Longfellow sketches comically a literary nationalist who announces: "We want a national literature commensurate with our mountains and rivers.... We want a national epic that shall correspond to the size of the country; that shall be to all other epics what Banvard's Panorama of the Mississippi is to all other paintings" (115). Temperaments like Longfellow's often find their caricatures coming true.

> The well-taken photographs .... but your wife or friend
> close and solid in your arms?
>
> (§42, *V*, I, 67–68)

In each of these lines, the point is not that the artifact is inferior to the reality, but rather that the artifact, in its recognized artificiality, delivers us into the presence of the reality for which it is a metonym. Testing the ground of its claim to "tally" with the reality, we discover the path between reality and the soul that the poet undertakes to indicate for us. The panorama and the photograph, two midcentury marvels, opened a new path by making sight self-conscious.

Although there is no record of Whitman's viewing any of the panoramas displayed in New York City, it is most probable that this frequenter of museums, theaters, and daguerreotype galleries would have seen many of them. Charles Zarobila has collected the passages of prose and poetry in which Whitman uses the term *panorama* to show that he was acquainted with the specific qualities of this popular form of entertainment.[30] The passages quoted suggest that most often Whitman was thinking of the moving panorama that unreeled before its viewers: a journey up the Hudson, for example, he described as a "constantly changing but ever beautiful panorama on both sides of the river" (*PW*, I, 167).[31] The "panorama of the sea" in "Song of Myself," however, would be most plausibly the stationary panorama painted on the wall of a circular or semicircular chamber.[32] So too the "panorama of visions" in "When Lilacs Last in the Dooryard Bloom'd," for the circular form was used often to represent battles:

> I saw the vision of armies;
> And I saw, as in noiseless dreams, hundreds of battle-
>   flags;
> Borne through the smoke of the battles, and pierc'd
>   with missiles, I saw them,
> And carried hither and yon through the smoke [. . . .]
>
> (§15, *V*, II, 538)

30. Charles Zarobila, "Walt Whitman and the Panorama," *WWR*, XXV (June, 1979), 51–59.

31. Miles Orvell has linked the scroll panorama and its "new sense of American space" with Whitman's "synoptic effects" and wide-ranging shifts of scene ("Reproducing Walt Whitman," 338).

32. One can imagine Mark Twain's Duke and King offering the habitans of Bricksville a moving panorama of the Indian Ocean. But for only two nights.

In 1871 he revised the first line: "I saw askant the armies"—that is, sidelong, at the edge of one's vision. The circular panorama always presents the viewer with more than he can see, a frameless or boundless view in which he is deprived of the "edge" reference that allows one to distinguish a conventional painting from its background. Robert Altick has described the means by which the circular panorama achieved the illusion of depth that so overwhelmed its first viewers: "The building was so designed that two of the forces which militate against perfect illusion in a gallery painting—the limiting frame and standards of size and distance external to the picture itself—were eliminated in the panorama. . . . The intrusive elements of the spectators' surroundings being blocked out, the world in which they were enwrapped consisted exclusively of the landscape or cityscape depicted on the canvas suspended thirty feet away."[33] (This effect would have been unavailable to the scroll panorama, unless one were seated very close to it: a London *Times* review, quoted by Altick, complained that in the moving panorama a "bending or collapsing" of the canvas "occurs to destroy the pictorial illusion and discover the artificial effects."[34] To create a sensation of depth, some viewers of the immense "panoramic" paintings of Church, Moran, and Bierstadt looked at them through opera glasses, thus screening out the frame and the gallery setting.[35])

In *The Prelude,* Wordsworth attested to the power of the illusion he experienced in one of the early London panoramas:

> At leisure, then, I viewed . . .
> those sights that ape
> The absolute presence of reality,
> Expressing, as in mirror, sea and land,
> And what earth is, and what she has to show.
> I do not here allude to subtlest craft,
> By means refined attaining purest ends,
> But imitations, fondly made in plain
> Confession of man's weakness and his loves.
> Whether the Painter, whose ambitious skill
> Submits to nothing less than taking in

---

33. Robert Altick, *The Shows of London* (Cambridge, Mass., 1978), 133.

34. Review in London *Times,* December 25, 1848, quoted in Altick, *The Shows of London,* 160.

35. Novak, *Nature and Culture,* 27.

> A whole horizon's circuit, do with power,
> Like that of angels or commissioned spirits,
> Fix us upon some lofty pinnacle,
> Or in a ship on waters, with a world
> Of life, and life-like mockery beneath,
> Above, behind, far stretching and before.[36]
>
> (7.229–47)

To Wordsworth, the panorama is the quintessential illusion at the heart of phantasmagoric London; at the same time that he acknowledges its power, his phrasing compares it to Satan's temptation of Christ atop the Temple (Matt. 4:5–7). Its deceptiveness is one with the exploitation and immorality that Wordsworth found everywhere in London. But for Whitman, more fond of city "shows," the illusion was not to be feared but to be emulated. "The panorama of the sea" leads us, across an ellipsis, to "the sea itself."

In "Crossing Brooklyn Ferry," the catalogs of description enwrap the reader in a whole horizon's circuit. To conceive the harborscape as "static" or "timeless" is to overlook how Whitman directs our attention around the scene—not as the cicerone in the brain-gallery, leading his viewer to the climactic detail, but as one on the deck of the moving ferryboat might look to various points during the crossing. The long catalog in section 3 is unique in *Leaves of Grass* for its attention to specifics of direction and orientation: the gulls edge toward the south; the hills stand up to southward and southwestward; ships arrive from the lower bay; the "stretch afar"—apparently up the East River—grows dimmer; there are storehouses near the docks, and on the neighboring shore a foundry. At the outset of the crossing, we are looking down the bay toward Staten Island and the Narrows; as the ferry nears Brooklyn, that view is closed off and the vista up the East River enlarges. In this poem, the catalogs are not random collections of impressions, nor are they harmonized merely by theme.[37] Rather, like the view of the bricklayers in "Song of the Broad-Axe," these catalogs follow the rhythms of an action contextualized in its own time and space rather than in the mind of the poet. They render the actual, sequential process of looking out

---

36. The passage continues, balancing the "whether" with an "or" concerning the other form of trompe-l'oeil, the scaled miniature.

37. For Malcolm Andrews, the catalogs are random ("Whitman and the American City," 183, 194); for Coffman, they are thematically unified.

from the deck of a ferry moving between two cities, watching some objects come into view while others are screened out, shifting attention from one shore to the other.

The pictorialism of the *Drum-Taps* poems requires a privileged viewstand that puts the entire scene at the viewer's disposal and secures his aesthetic detachment from it. The circular panorama relaxes this control, choosing a place but not an orientation. The viewer must turn his head and move about the platform to absorb the entire picture and to participate in the illusion of reality. The panorama then becomes a kinetic experience, even though the picture itself does not move: the viewer apprehends it not all at once, but rather in a sequence extended through time as his attention shifts from one part of the scene to another.[38] Just as the canvas has no dimensional "edge," so the experience of viewing it moves not toward simultaneity but toward extension; the temporal "edge" also becomes less determinate. The panorama *takes time*; and the passage of time is part of its magic. It is not just the eye that is fooled.

The midnineteenth century also applied the term *panorama* to another form of illusionist spectacle in which the passing of time was even more immediately involved. This was the show more accurately called the diorama. By shifting from frontlighting to backlighting or by introducing different colors of artificial light, a scene painted on fabric could be made to change appearance: Canterbury Cathedral passed from sunlight to shadow; a daylit scene gave way to dusk and then to night; an avalanche engulfed an Alpine village.[39] As in the panorama, the illusion was enhanced by setting the canvas at the end of a darkened tunnel, thereby excluding the sense of edge and preventing the viewer from making a judgment of comparative size. Several dioramas, at first castoffs from London and Paris, were on display in New York in the 1840s. In 1856 John Greenleaf Whittier imagined a specifically American diorama for his poem "The Panorama." In it, a "Showman" exhibits first the panorama of a primeval New World scene. Then he transforms it, first into a pastoral landscape—

> Slowly the curtain rose from off a land
> Fair as God's garden. Broad on either hand

---

38. See Eugene McNamara, "'Crossing Brooklyn Ferry': The Shaping Imagination," *Walt Whitman Quarterly Review*, II (1984), 34.

39. Altick, *The Shows of London*, 165–72.

> The golden wheat-fields glimmered in the sun,
> And the tall maize its yellow tassels spun

—thanks to "the homely old-time virtues of the North." Then it is changed to a scene of lassitude, decay, and violence:

> "Look," said the Showman, sternly, as he rolled
> His curtain upward; "Fate's reverse behold!"
> . . . .
> Look once again! The moving canvas shows
> A slave plantation's slovenly repose.
> Where, in rude cabins rotting midst their weeds,
> The human chattel eats, and sleeps, and breeds.[40]

Grasping the essentially temporal character of the diorama, Whittier adapts it as a stage for Abolitionist eschatology, rendering alternative political futures through dioramic shifts in the American landscape. The legibility of this polemical poem depends on his audience's understanding of America as a panoramic "scene"—the approach Whitman had also taken a year earlier in his Preface to the first edition of *Leaves of Grass*—and on their understanding of the diorama as a temporal and historical medium rather than one that invited their detached contemplation of a timeless aesthetic moment.

The panoramas of "Crossing Brooklyn Ferry" are similarly timebound and dioramic in nature. Again, the sequence of the catalogs is not random. Whitman's crossing that begins with "the sun half an hour high" passes through a series of changes in lighting:

> the glistening yellow lit up parts of their bodies [. . .]
> the shimmering track of beams [. . .]
> fine centrifugal spokes of light [. . .]
> scallop-edged waves in the twilight [. . .]
> The stretch afar growing dimmer and dimmer [. . .]
> On the river the shadowy group [. . .]
> the fires from the foundry chimneys burning high and
>   glaringly into the night
>   (§3, *V*, I, 219–20)

---

40. Whittier, *The Poetical Works*, II, 181ff. Although Whittier speaks of the "moving canvas," as though this were a scroll panorama, its effects are those of the diorama: curtain, lighting, sudden shifts in the appearance of a single scene.

So passed the day in many a diorama. But whereas in the show, time was accelerated, Whitman has retarded time so that the passage across the East River, which actually took less than ten minutes, is made to occupy more than an hour, from the half-hour sun over Newark to a dusk deep enough to contrast with the flaring chimneys around Corlear's Hook.[41] Rather than attempting to freeze time, Whitman has exaggerated its duration.[42]

Surrounding his reader with visual details and blurring the pictorial "moment" by dramatizing the passage of time, Whitman in "Crossing Brooklyn Ferry" is not aiming for a two-dimensional pictorial effect of the sort he was to use in *Drum-Taps*. Rather, he seeks to inveigle the reader into a more participatory experience, like the panoramic and dioramic "shows" that entertained the city crowds of the nineteenth century. In those lines from *The Prelude* quoted above, Wordsworth anxiously insisted that the panorama was not true art, because its aim was not aesthetic detachment:

> I do not here allude to subtlest craft,
> By means refined attaining purest ends,
> But imitations, fondly made in plain
> Confession of man's weakness and his loves.

John Constable thought the same of the diorama—"it is without the pale of Art because its object is deception."[43] But the standards of these two countrymen were different from those of Whitman and the urban crowds, British or American, who thronged to the panorama and diorama and who knew perfectly well that they were not standing on the dome of Saint Paul's Cathedral, or on the parterres of Versailles, or floating down the Mississippi. If they were deceived, that was just what they had paid for; and they complained only when the illusion was so faultily executed that they could not cooperate

---

41. [Henry Evelyn Pierrepont], *Historical Sketch of the Fulton Ferry, and Its Associated Ferries, By a Director* (Brooklyn, 1879), 69, 99n.

42. One unaccountable violation of this progression, capitalized on by Anderson (*The Imperial Self*, 156), is the shift from "December" or "Twelfth-month" seagulls to the "summer" sky in a space of four lines. These adjectives were not present in Whitman's original notes for the poem, so they must represent some considered intention, possibly an effort to extend a manifestly summer scene into its opposite, just as he extended it into nighttime. Thomas suggests that "Whitman is adding material from memory of previous summer and winter crossings" (*Lunar Light*, 103). See the next chapter for another interpretation.

43. Quoted in Altick, *The Shows of London*, 166.

with its intended effect. They were out for something that catered to their weakness and their loves, their desire to participate, through imagination, in making the unreal real.

James A. W. Heffernan says that "the English romantic poets and painters draw the beholder into their landscapes and thus seek to dissolve the opposition between the outer world and the inner one." The means for doing this, he says, was a "language of transformation" that turned prospect into perception—"a language of power, a language that turns a known and familiar landscape into something extraordinary."[44] He concludes: "Ultimately, I believe, the synoptic study of romantic poetry and painting allows us to see romanticism as the representation of temporalized space. We commonly associate romantic literature with relentless temporality—with process, development, and becoming rather than being, with the fear of stasis that paradoxically accompanies and complicates the desire for timelessness. But the correspondences between romantic poetry and painting force us to recognize that romantic temporality is wedded to space."[45] For Heffernan's British poets and painters, this temporality is primarily inward—the process by which "a verbally pictured landscape [gives] us the picture of a poet's mind."[46] In "Crossing Brooklyn Ferry," the sensory perception of space moves outward to admit us to a time-bound urban world that is, finally, the one we share with Whitman and he with us.

44. Heffernan, *The Re-Creation of Landscape,* 120–21, 154.
45. Ibid., 226.
46. Ibid., 47.

[6]

The Mystery of the Eyesight

Impure arts that catered to man's weaknesses and loves, the diorama and panorama extended two-dimensional scenography into time, enticing the spectators by softening the boundary between art-experience and life-experience. Joseph Frank has shown how, in both painting and literature, the alternatives are two dimensions or four: a "flat" art that seeks the timeless and transcendent; or an art that expresses its acceptance of time and its sense of being at home in the world through its evocation of "depth." "Depth," he writes, "the projection of three-dimensional space, gives objects a time-value because it places them in the real world in which events occur."[1] In "There was a Child Went Forth" and "Crossing Brooklyn Ferry," Whitman sought to illuminate space in such a way that we would apprehend his harbor cities not as two-dimensional paintings but as four-dimensional reality, objects bound together, perceivers delivered from their individual self-containedness through encounter with a world seen in time and in depth.

Whitman's city poetry uses a vocabulary of illusory spectacle—pageants, panoramas, "shows" (again and again, "shows")—and, as we have seen in an earlier chapter, "phantoms." In "There was a Child Went Forth," it was the city that awakened Whitman to the illusoriness of solipsistic "experience," dissolving into "flashes and specks" those objects that, in the country, had seemed essences: *sow, mare, cow; mother, father*. At the poem's end, Whitman had turned

---

1. Joseph Frank, *The Widening Gyre: Crisis and Mastery in Modern Literature* (New Brunswick, N.J., 1963), 56. Frank quotes Wilhelm Worringer from *Abstraktion und Einfühlung*: "Space . . . linking things together and destroying their individual closedness, gives things their temporal value and draws them into the cosmic interplay of phenomena."

back from these doubts to the evocation of New York harbor at sunset:

> The streets themselves, and the facades of houses .... the goods in the windows,
> Vehicles .. teams .. the tiered wharves, and the huge crossing at the ferries;
> The village on the highland seen from afar at sunset .... the river between,
> Shadows .. aureola and mist .. light falling on roofs and gables of white or brown, three miles off,
> The schooner near by sleepily dropping down the tide .. the little boat slacktowed astern,
> The hurrying tumbling waves and quickbroken crests and slapping;
> The strata of colored clouds .... the long bar of maroontint away solitary by itself .... the spread of purity it lies motionless in,
> The horizon's edge, the flying seacrow, the fragrance of saltmarsh and shoremud;
> These became part of that child who went forth every day, and who now goes and will always go forth every day,
> And these become of him or her that peruses them now.
> (*V*, I, 151–52)

Certainly, this seems to read like the descriptions in "Bivouac on a Mountain Side" and "On the Beach at Night." It can be understood why critics would compare this scene or the comparable scenes in "Crossing Brooklyn Ferry" to the pictorial achievements of the Luminist painters: there are the same genre harborscape, the tranquillity, the clarity of perception, the preoccupation with the quality of light, that are found in Heade and Kensett and Lane.[2] But simple pictorial effects will not resolve the crisis of solipsistic isolation—"the curious whether and how, / Whether that which appears so is so .... Or is it all flashes and specks?" Such a harborscape then would be just another sketch by that connoisseur of experience whose

---

2. See Adams, "The Luminist Walt Whitman," 2–16; Thomas, *Lunar Light*, 94–103; St. Armand, "Transcendence Through Technique," 72; and Sharpe, *Unreal Cities*, 94.

works adorned the brain-gallery of "Pictures."[3] A different approach to light and to visual experience is required if this passage is to serve as an adequate resolution to the "doubts of daytime and the doubts of nighttime ... the curious whether and how" (*V*, I, 151).

As E. H. Gombrich and William Ivins have pointed out, how we conceive of sight affects our representation of what we see, and representation reciprocally affects our concept of sight.[4] Interest in the process of seeing and in artful manipulation of it seems to have been a particular and popular concern of the nineteenth century. From philosophers like John Stuart Mill, to aestheticians like John Ruskin, to Broadway impresarios, Whitman's time was thinking about vision. It is most unlikely that Whitman knew about the studies of perspective and of optics that had gone forward in Europe since the invention of lenses; but he lived in a culture and in a city where those studies were continually being adapted into technologies of popular entertainment. The panorama and the diorama were scaled for crowds, but there were other shows that worked in more intimate and individualized settings. The perfecter and first entrepreneur of the diorama was L. J. M. Daguerre, who also was developing another form of trompe l'oeil, a method of photography.[5]

Like the diorama and the panorama, the photographic camera disturbed profoundly the way that people regarded the once-naïve process of seeing. Matters that had once been the domain of philosophers and physiologists came into public view. Among these was the perception of depth. The reports of those who first saw the photographic image are like those of people newly delivered from blindness. The writers—Samuel F. B. Morse and Edgar Allan Poe, for example—drew attention to the daguerreotype's undiscriminating

---

3. Arguing in the other direction, St. Armand points out that "without the overarching spiritual bond, the 'ties' between human soul and human soul, Whitman's art would be, in his own view, only phenomena, only surface, only externality. Objects themselves and the sensations they produce are meaningless unless they become the medium of what Whitman . . . calls the 'fluid and attaching character.' Otherwise . . . reality would be 'all flashes and specks'" ("Transcendence Through Technique," 68). My concern here, though, is that Whitman begins and ends not with the "float forever held in solution" as a basis of human unity, but with the visual experience. "Of the make of my body was not my mortal experience only. My body makes my immortal experience" (*N*, I, 230).

4. Gombrich, *Art and Illusion*, 314; William Ivins, *Prints and Visual Communication* (Cambridge, Mass., 1953), 138.

5. Graham Clarke has noted some connections between Whitman's poetic seeing and the visual technologies of the nineteenth century ("'To emanate a look,'" 92–94).

fineness of detail, even in the backgrounds: "The exquisite minuteness of the delineation cannot be conceived. No painting or engraving ever approached it. For example: In a view up the street, a distant sign would be perceived, and the eye could just discern that there were lines of letters upon it, but so minute as not to be read with the naked eye. By the assistance of a powerful lens . . . every letter was clearly and distinctly legible, and so also were the minutest breaks and lines in the walls of the buildings; and the pavements of the streets."[6]

The early photographs seemed to reproduce the visible world with the clarity and detail of sight itself, a precision that no painter could match. And yet the photographs were unlike sight, for with their infinite depth of field they put objects at all distances in sharp focus—as painting could, but the human eye cannot. The eye moves selectively through its field, continually shifting its limited power of close attention, discriminating those objects that it has learned are worth attending to. The photographic camera seemed to make no discriminations. And so it was the emblematic instrument of the first era of democracy.[7] Not only could its secrets be mastered by any clever youth; not only did it afford a portrait to every navvy and housemaid; but the technique itself was inclusive, undiscriminating, antihierarchical. When Hawthorne made Holgrave, in *The House of the Seven Gables,* both a daguerreotypist and an apostle of democratic leveling; when Melville in *Moby-Dick* spoke of an "ethereal light" of equality "shining in the arm that wields a pick or drives a spike"; and when Whitman, in the 1855 Preface, announced that the American poet "judges not as the judge judges but as the sun falling around a helpless thing" (*CRE,* 713), they heralded a new art of the indiscriminate, not only in subjects but in principles of composition—or rather anticomposition—for the pictorial representation of vision was to become more fragmentary, less formally composed, more discontinuous in its sense of space. The revolutionary discomposing of vision in the canvases of Monet and Degas lay more than a decade in the future; but this revolution had already begun, late in the eighteenth century, alike in high art and in popular culture, influ-

---

6. Samuel F. B. Morse, quoted in Robert Taft, *Photography and the American Scene* (New York, 1938), 11–12; Edgar Allan Poe, quoted in *Classic Essays on Photography,* ed. Alan Trachtenberg (New Haven, Conn., 1980), 38.

7. Ed Folsom develops this connection in "Whitman and the Visual Democracy of Photography," *Mickle Street Review,* X (1988), 56–57.

enced first by the widespread use of the camera obscura and camera lucida, and later by technological entertainments like the diorama and the photographic camera.[8]

By the time this revolution began in painting, Whitman was retreating to the poetic equivalent of the old, formal, and dramatic way of painting: the pictorialism of "Bivouac on a Mountain Side" and "The Torch," which surveys its subject as though it were a painting, culminating at the scene's most important detail. For the wider audience he was seeking in *Drum-Taps,* this was the way that "art" should work. In the 1855 *Leaves of Grass,* however, the poem "Faces" suggests that Whitman had learned the cameralike trick of adverting to his field of vision, seeing "flat" whatever it contained:

> Sauntering the pavement or riding the country byroad
>   here then are faces,
> Faces of friendship, precision, caution, suavity, ideality,
> The spiritual prescient face, the always welcome
>   common benevolent face,
> The face of the singing of music, the grand faces of
>   natural lawyers and judges broad at the backtop,
> The faces of hunters and fishers, bulged at the brows ....
> [. . .]
> Sauntering the pavement or crossing the ceaseless ferry,
>   here then are faces;
> I see them and complain not and am content with all.
>
> (§1, *V,* I, 132–33)

The *perpetuum mobile* of images dancing on the retina complemented the ceaseless, undiscriminating flow of images through Whitman's consciousness, in poems like "Song of Myself" and "Song of the Open Road." In the twentieth century, recording the visual field would become a characteristic device of William Carlos Williams. It was a *flâneur*'s trick, a connoisseurship apt for the novelties of the urban show. It enhanced that spectatorial sense, I and Not-Me, which so divided Whitman's mind, especially when he considered his city experience. This self-consciousness about the process of sight, however, led to far different approaches to the city in "There was a Child Went Forth" and "Crossing Brooklyn Ferry."

---

8. Peter Galassi expounds these connections in *Before Photography: Painting and the Invention of Photography* (New York, 1981).

The "flat" camera image could reproduce exactly the positions that an array of objects occupied in a monocular field of vision. Shift the focal point ever so slightly—less than three inches—and some of those positions would be altered, as they are in binocular vision. Soon, in the 1850s and 1860s, stereoscopic photography brought to these flat images the illusion of depth. Oliver Wendell Holmes, writing in the *Atlantic Monthly* in 1859, discussed depth perception along with other once-arcane questions such as the apparent size of visual images. Explaining that "everything is seen only as a superficial extension, until the other senses have taught the eye to recognize *depth,* or the third dimension, which gives solidity," Holmes expounded the principle of stereoptic vision through an analogy with touch:

> If we look at a square piece of ivory with one eye alone, we cannot tell whether it is a scale of veneer, or the side of a cube, or the base of a pyramid, or the end of a prism. But if we now open the other eye, we shall see one or more of its sides, if it have any, and then know it to be a solid, and what kind of a solid. . . . By means of these two different views of an object, the mind, as it were, *feels round it* and gets an idea of its solidity. We clasp an object with our eyes, as with our arms, or with our hands, or with our thumb and finger, and then we know it to be something more than a surface.

Convinced that the stereograph's illusion was perfect, Holmes argued that the viewer entered into its image in the same tactile way: "the mind feels its way into the very depths of the picture."[9] Depth, perceived by sight but corroborated by the tactile and kinetic senses, transforms an array of surfaces into a world of presences, each occupying its own space and having its own network of relationships with the others around it.

Implicit in Holmes's words is the question of how it is that visible objects "touch" the optic nerves, an ancient question that had lost none of its urgency to midnineteenth-century philosophers and physiologists such as Mill and Johannes Müller.[10] Long before this,

---

9. Oliver Wendell Holmes, "The Stereoscope and the Stereograph," in *Photography: Essays and Images,* ed. Beaumont Newhall (New York, 1980), 56–57. Holmes's italics.

10. Holmes refers to Müller's *Elements of Physiology* (1838): for Müller, what we see is images on the retina; touch instructs us on how to correlate these with a physically extended world (Pastore, *Theories of Visual Perception,* 131).

George Berkeley had distinguished "immediate" visual objects from "mediate"—that is, those at a distance, which we know purely by sight, opposed to those near at hand, in which our sense of touch "mediates" the visual phenomena, helping us to interpret size, shape, and position.[11] Sherman Paul has shown that Emerson's metaphors of sight usually draw on distant vision, which "enspheres" nature (whereas close vision "atomizes" and seeks to possess it): distant vision is the symbol of intuitive Reason, the "transparent eyeball" that apprehends nature all at once, in pure and detached ecstasy.[12] With Holmes's metaphor, sight loses some of its seeming immediacy, spirituality, and detachment from its physical object and its physiological organ. "Feeling round" the object, sight becomes a more bodily and time-bound process, like that of a tired man at sundown moving slowly athwart the East River tide, his gaze drifting over familiar landmarks.

And yet this corporeal and thoroughly "mediate" seeing is not debarred from transcendental vision: the body, Whitman said, makes both his mortal and his immortal experience. As Geoffrey Hartman wrote, apropos of Valéry, true knowledge depends on an account of perception that is based not just on a "mechanical" contact between sense and object, but on the acknowledgment of "the body in the exercise of a continuous primary act of knowledge, that of perception." "The immediate interpretation given by the senses to physical event can only be understood by analogy to the act of original creation."[13] Celebrating the miracle of eyesight in the 1855 Preface, Whitman spoke first of its immediacy, its being "removed from any proof but its own" and so "forerun[ning] the identities of the spiritual world." Then, with a homely metaphor alluding to its physical organ, the eyeball occupying "the space of a peachpit," he gloried in the power of the eye to give audience to far and near and to the sunset and have all things enter with electric swiftness (*CRE,* 714). It lays hold of all things, far and near, spiritual and sensual, present and future. The power that mediates them is, from one side of this crossing, the "spiritual world" of identities accomplished by the Oversoul; from the other side, it is an intensely physical encounter with a fully realized and specifically urban space.

11. Berkeley, "An Essay Towards a New Theory of Vision," 39–42, 45–46 (§45–51, 59–60).
12. Sherman Paul, *Emerson's Angle of Vision* (Cambridge, Mass, 1952), 72–74.
13. Hartman, *The Unmediated Vision,* 151–54.

Ruskin's *Modern Painters* (1843) displays the same self-consciousness about the physiological process of seeing and the same recognition that the perception of depth lured the viewer into a more participatory relationship to the painting. He gives much of his time to distinguishing what we see from what we know we are seeing.[14] He praises J. M. W. Turner and other modern landscapists for rendering not the supposed essences of things (as the old masters had, as the picturesque poets had), but rather their appearance in the viewer's eye. And the eye is not a passively "transparent" aperture, but a muscular, shifting organ. In the chapter "Truth of Space," Ruskin reminds his readers of the physical readjustment of focus needed when the eye moves from foreground to middle and background: "The eye, like any other lens, must have its focus altered, in order to convey a distinct image of objects at different distances; so that it is totally impossible to see distinctly, at the same moment, two objects, one of which is much farther off than another. . . . Objects at unequal distances cannot be seen together, not from the intervention of air or mist, but from the impossibility of the rays proceeding from both, converging to the same focus." He condemns the classic painters for presenting all planes of their compositions in focus, providing only the "aerial perspective" of diminishing detail. Turner, he says, "sinks" the foreground into an out-of-focus blur so as to direct the viewer's attention into the middle and background. The effect of this is to "compel" the viewer into the painting, as Holmes felt the stereographic camera thrust the viewer actively into the midst of its scenes: "It was possible to express immediate proximity to the spectator, without giving anything like completeness to the forms of the near objects. . . . The spectator was compelled to go forward into the waste of hills—there, where the sun broke wide upon the moor, he must walk and wander—he could not stumble and hesitate over the near rocks, nor stop to botanize on the first inches of his path."[15]

---

14. John Ruskin had seen dioramas in London in the early 1830s and referred to them and to the daguerreotype in *Modern Painters* (New York, 1847). He speaks of the diorama as affording a "noble pleasure," but that of nature rather than that of art (I, 20 [1.1.4.7]). He seems also to have regarded the daguerreotype just as a "mechanical" and loveless means of verifying accuracy of detail (I, 76 [2.1.7.5]; I, 110 [2.1.7.30]; I, 325 [2.5.1.5]).

15. Ruskin, *Modern Painters*, I, 182–87 [2.2.4]. In a note, Ruskin acknowledges that he may have claimed too much for Turner. But this reservation does not mitigate the self-consciousness about vision, which he invokes throughout *Modern Painters*. Ruskin's description of a sunset and of the play of light on distant objects, in "Of

Whitman reviewed Ruskin's book—albeit cursorily—in the Brooklyn *Daily Eagle* in 1847. In a review of paintings by W. S. Mount and Walter Libbey, which he published in the New York *Evening Post* in 1851, Whitman notes, Ruskin-like, that in one of Libbey's paintings depicting a flute player, "in the scene of the background, and in all the accessories, there is a delicious melting in, so to speak, of object with object; an effect that is frequent enough in nature, though painters seem to disdain following it, even where it is demanded."[16] In speaking of "melting" in the background, Whitman could be referring to atmospheric perspective, the painterly simulation of how glare or haze causes a loss of detail in distant objects. He employs atmospheric perspective as part of his evocation of depth in both "There was a Child Went Forth" and "Crossing Brooklyn Ferry":

> Shadows .. aureola and mist .. light falling on roofs and
>   gables of white or brown, three miles off

> [I] looked on the haze on the hills southward and
>   southwestward
> [. . .]
> The stretch afar growing dimmer and dimmer [. . .]
> On the river the shadowy group, the big steam-tug
>   closely flanked on each side by the barges—the hay-
>   boat, the belated lighter.
>   (*V*, I, 152; §3, 219–20)

But elsewhere in the review, he describes the background as "clear and sunny," and atmospheric perspective was hardly a "disdained" technique among the painters of his time. Also, atmospheric "melting" would not apply to the "accessories"—the flute player's basket and the wayside bank he sits on. It seems that Whitman is thinking of the blurring caused by objects' being out of focus or not in the field of attention—an effect uncommon in painting, though late-nineteenth-century photographers like Peter Emerson would es-

---

Truth of Colour" and "Of Truth of Chiaroscuro" respectively, might have been a guide to Whitman in composing the sunset harborscape that concludes "There was a Child Went Forth."

   16. Holloway, ed., *The Uncollected Poetry and Prose of Walt Whitman*, I, 238.

pouse the use of a shallow depth of field to simulate more exactly the experience of sight.[17] It was, of course, common enough in "nature"—if one has become self-conscious about the physiology of seeing.

Let us return to that limpid scene that culminates "There was a Child Went Forth":

> The streets themselves, and the facades of houses .... the goods in the windows,
> Vehicles .. teams .. the tiered wharves, and the huge crossing at the ferries;
> The village on the highland seen from afar at sunset .... the river between,
> Shadows .. aureola and mist .. light falling on roofs and gables of white or brown, three miles off,
> The schooner near by sleepily dropping down the tide .. the little boat slacktowed astern,
> The hurrying tumbling waves and quickbroken crests and slapping;
> The strata of colored clouds .... the long bar of maroontint away solitary by itself .... the spread of purity it lies motionless in,
> The horizon's edge, the flying seacrow, the fragrance of saltmarsh and shoremud.
>
> (V, I, 151–52)

These eight lines are all that stands between the poem's crisis—his confession of doubt—and the serene reassertion of a substantial, continuous, and mutual world in the final two lines. Of course, this description might be simply an assertion that things are as real as doubt, like Samuel Johnson kicking the rock.[18] And James Perrin Warren, in a linguistic analysis of this passage, has found in its play of "stative" nouns and dynamic participles a subtle assertion of "or-

17. Peter Henry Emerson, *Naturalistic Photography for Students of the Art* (1889; rpr. New York, 1973), 132–33.
18. Edwin Haviland Miller thought it a "leap" from despair to affirmation: "perhaps rationally unconvincing, but emotionally there is satisfaction in Whitman's expression of the personal and cultural hunger for an edenic state" (["There was a Child Went Forth"], in *Critical Essays on Walt Whitman,* ed. James Woodress [Boston, 1983], 274). The drama here is neither rational nor emotional, nor does the poem return to the eden of rural childhood.

derly, progressive temporal movement" underwriting the constancy of identity and the reliability of language.[19]

But there is more. Working "indirectly," these eight lines resolve the child's doubt through the very sequence of its descriptives. These rapid, random shifts in attention, darting among objects at many different ranges, reveal a world that is more than subjective impression. From a viewstand on the water's edge, the eye takes in the traffic on the river, then lifts to the horizon, flickers back to the river, studies the sky, drops again to the river, focuses on the nearby waves (with an auditory corroboration: they slap). Then the darting sequence begins again, horizon-sky-river, ending near at hand with the further corroboration of odors from marsh and mud.

This is not a depiction of pictorialized objects, Not-Me, but rather a mimesis of the very process of perception, the practiced intimacy of the senses with their surroundings. This is the way we see: not all at once, in a simultaneous "picture"; not by systematically scanning the scene before us as though it were a page of print; not in a dramatic sequence culminating at the viewscape's most significant feature.[20] Rather, attention skips haphazardly about the visual field, picking out details, blurring past others, referring moving objects to the more stable elements in view.[21] The linguistic tension of statives and dynamics, which Warren detects in this passage, thus replicates the process of seeing that it depicts. From "flashes and specks," raw optical data, the imagination builds a world that conserves itself. The eye, moving through time, discovers and remembers the "village" in the play of shadows, aureola, and mist, and light falling across roofs and gables; it conserves the "schooner" through the several glances that establish its slow (not stationary) movement through the waves; it reports both the seemingly motionless clouds and the soaring seacrow. Furthermore, the entire scene coheres as the experience given

19. Warren, *Walt Whitman's Language Experiment*, 60.
20. James J. Gibson: "The remarkable fact about visual scanning is that awareness of the succession of temporary retinal impressions is completely absent from the perceptual experience. There is awareness of the simultaneous existence of all the objects in the world, or all the parts of a picture, despite the fact that the objects, or parts, are fixated one after another—at least with our kind of vision. The whole physical array seems to coexist phenomenally although it has been looked at sequentially" (*The Senses Considered as Perceptual Systems* [Boston, 1966], 252).
21. Ulric Neisser, *Cognition and Reality* (San Francisco, 1976), 124. These random shifts in focus and attention are called "saccadic" movements. Through them the eye compensates for its inability to see more than a small area in detail. See also James J. Gibson, *The Perception of the Visual World* (Boston, 1950), 29.

in a particularized place and moment, with relatively fine detail and sensory variety in its foreground (*quickbroken crests and slapping . . . fragrance of saltmarsh and shoremud*) falling back to larger, plainer surfaces, visual phenomena only (*bar of maroontint . . . spread of purity . . . horizon's edge*). The scene thus is presented "in depth," and the reader is inveigled into the process of so perceiving it.[22]

"In a little house pictures I keep," Whitman had written in "Pictures" (*CRE,* 642). This poem and "Song of Myself," "Salut au Monde!" and the other poems with a bent for the pictorial treat the objects of sight as commodities that the poet can keep, hoarded in his mind's treasure-house. The poetic process is essentially an enactment of memory, capturing the picture, then displaying it and tracing out its details. So to objectify the visual image is to set it firmly in the Not-Me and, as we have seen, ultimately to question its "objective" reality. That process is at work in the first part of "There was a Child Went Forth," as Whitman draws forth childhood's pictures from the brazen book of memory. But in the concluding passage, sight becomes a dynamic interaction, at once physiological and imaginative, with the landscape; language serves as a mode of address rather than an instrument of capture. Poet, reader, and world are placed in each other's presence, all autonomous beings, as in one of those moments of dilation in "Song of the Broad-Axe."

The reiterated visual passages in "Crossing Brooklyn Ferry" use the same "indirect" way to introduce the reader to a realizable world. So the poem begins: "Flood-tide of the river, flow on! I watch you, face to face, / Clouds of the west! sun half an hour high! I see you also face to face" (§1, *V,* I, 217). This shift will become the poem's most habitual gesture: from water to sky, or from sky to water, or sometimes from water to the sky reflected in it.[23] So long as the poem's eye is looking outward—in its first three sections and its final two—it ranges fluently and variously among several depths of focus or attention: the faces near at hand, the "bright flow" around the

---

22. John Dolis traces in Nathaniel Hawthorne a similar tension between a two-dimensional "daguerrean" subject and a descriptive method that implicates the reader in the process of seeing—and touching—the object "in depth" ("Hawthorne's Tactile Gaze: The Phenomenon of Depth," *MLQ,* XLIV [1983], 267–84).

23. Ruskin again: "Now the fact is, that there is hardly a road-side pond or pool which has not as much landscape *in* it as above it. . . . Down in that, if you will look deep enough, you may see the dark, serious blue of far-off sky, and the passing of pure clouds. . . . Now, this far-seeing is just the difference between the great and the vulgar painter" (*Modern Painters,* I, 322 [2.5.1.4, "Of Truth of Water"]).

ferry, the shipping near and far, the mast-hemmed shore, the horizon, and the sky. Seeing dominates the poem's consciousness, though the setting obviously would have provided crowd noise, hooting steamboats, and the mew of gulls, as well as the touch of the wind, the press of passengers, the roll of the ferry, and a seaport's pungent odors. "Crossing Brooklyn Ferry" thus does not offer those corroborations between the senses that appeared in "There was a Child Went Forth," but it does orchestrate carefully the decreasing acuity of sight as the eye moves from "fine centrifugal spokes of light round the shape of my head in the sun-lit water," to "pilots in their pilot-houses," and finally to the hazy and indeterminate hills around the Narrows. As the ferry moves across the East River, objects at different distances shift their relative positions: the "lower bay" disappears from sight behind Red Hook, while the prospect of the Hudson expands, revealing the big steam-tug with its barges. And as twilight falls, the intricate patterning of light and shadow upon the water becomes visible, while "the stretch afar grow[s] dimmer and dimmer" (§3, *V*, I, 219–20).

"Keep your places, objects than which none else is more lasting!" (§9, *V*, I, 225): working "indirectly" and "without mentioning it," Whitman reveals a world of substantial beings, each occupying its own four-dimensional niche, its own set of relationships with the other beings around it: they "keep their places." First and most fully realized in the poem's third section, this revelation of "depth" confers through description the same autonomy to river, cities, ships, and passengers that the final movement conveys by shifting its verbs into the imperative mood. Delivered from the prison of the poet's ego, they are found to be real; and the poet in turn is delivered from the task of sustaining his world.

The diorama, blurring the boundary between art-experience and life-experience, brought together a city crowd whose enjoyment lay in appreciating how close looking at the illusion came to looking at reality.[24] By analyzing sight into pure optical phenomena, "flashes and specks," Whitman invites his reader to reconstitute the actual experience of crossing the ferry to Brooklyn. The sequence of ob-

24. Barbara Novak discusses the "simultaneously intimate and distant" effect of panoramic paintings like those of Frederic Church and Albert Bierstadt: "His awareness of the communal or popular nature of such an experience led [James Jackson] Jarves, one of the period's most vocal exponents of an ideal, elitist art, to reject any claims on the part of the large landscapes to being high art" (*Nature and Culture*, 27).

jects and actions in this poem is not dictated by the poet's imperious will, as it was in "Song of Myself," nor is it an imitation of memory, conned from earlier pictorialist poets. It recreates the very play of sight, the instinctive or intuitive process by which eye and mind discern a network of substances beyond the dance of unconnected impressions.[25] In "There was a Child Went Forth," Whitman spoke of "the curious whether and how," the doubts that city experience awakened in him. These two city poems show that the answer to *whether* is *how:* collaborating with the flow of light and darting through every plane of the field of vision, they establish the viewer's presence within an actual, four-dimensional world. From one consciousness to another the phenomena are transmitted, and so they are conserved—not as a list of nouns, but as a many-stranded verb.

When he changed the title from "Sun-Down Poem" to "Crossing Brooklyn Ferry," Whitman recognized that this poem achieves its understanding with the reader not by naming objects but by reminding him of a familiar process, the haphazard but dependable way that we descend stairways, negotiate streets, eat food, and recognize our friends. This process is not "retrogressive," as Coleridge described the pictorialists, but rather continuous, the reader half-discovering and half-creating the scene in cooperation with the poet. Coleridge, who had dismissed descriptive poetry because it was mechanically directed by the "fancy," might have recognized in these passages from Whitman the play of that "living power and prime agent of all human perception" that he called the primary imagination—not "flashed at once upon the eye," as he thought, but endlessly constructed and reconstructed by perception feeling around its world.[26]

❖

Thus far we have concentrated on the two great set-piece descriptions, the concluding lines of "There was a Child Went Forth," and the third section of "Crossing Brooklyn Ferry." But in the latter

25. St. Armand writes: "Whitman . . . creates a personal depth that the Impressionists could not achieve through boldness of color, the cunning use of silhouette, or a radically oblique perspective. Monet cannot coax a viewer into one of his canvases in the same way that Whitman can incorporate a reader into his poem, exercising a psychic control based on the phenomena of shared sensation" ("Transcendence Through Technique," 71).

26. Samuel Taylor Coleridge, *Biographia Literaria,* Chap. 13 (*Coleridge,* 313). See also Hartman, *The Unmediated Vision,* 153.

poem there is more than just the setting up of a dioramic space; and the invocation of the eyesight goes beyond the division between "immediate" seeing and vision mediated by touch and the other senses, which the nineteenth century had inherited from Berkeley. In "Crossing Brooklyn Ferry" the elements of the scene are rehearsed over and over. Again and again they furnish their parts toward the soul. A concluding summary of motifs may be characteristic of the Greater Romantic Lyric:

> these steep woods and lofty cliffs,
> And this green pastoral landscape, were to me
> More dear, both for themselves and for thy sake!
> ("Tintern Abbey," 157–59)

But in Whitman's poem we hear many times about the crowd, the waves, the foundry chimneys, and the setting sun. These repetitions are his response to the question, What endures?; and they make "Crossing Brooklyn Ferry" one of the great poems of urban life.

For all the richness of the finale in "There was a Child Went Forth" and for all its skillful realization of depth and presence, it remains a single moment of perception, from a single viewstand and a single consciousness. It is a unique visual field, like "Cavalry Crossing a Ford" or "Bivouac on a Mountain Side," or like the quickly sketched figures in "Song of Myself." Like the diorama, there is something irresolvably illusory about it:

> May-be they only seem to me what they are, (as doubtless they indeed but seem,) as from my present point of view—And might prove, (as of course they would,) naught of what they appear, or naught any how, from entirely changed points of view.
> ("Of the Terrible Doubt of Appearances," V, II, 377)

The city over the river might yet prove a mirage, owing to the isolation of the viewer and of the moment, if these were confined to the "present point of view." "There was a Child Went Forth" conveys the sense of a substantial world, but it does so as did the stereopticon, from the viewpoint of a single individual. At the poem's end, Whitman makes the Not-Me a path by which to escape his isolation and become one with You. As he completes the sunset catalog, he announces:

> These became part of that child who went forth every
> day, and who now goes and will always go forth
> every day,
> And these become of him or her that peruses them now.
>
> (V, I, 152)

To the reader now, as well as to Whitman, the converging objects of his universe flow, but only by taking the poet's place at the stereopticon. Like many optical illusions, it achieves a sense of depth and solidity only for the solitary viewer standing at one determined point.[27] "There was a Child Went Forth" does not create a communal topology, based on shared culture or belief, through which the experience of this sundown harbor can be understood as the corroborated experience of many people.

Demolishing provincial topologies was part of Whitman's democratically inclusive program: "The American bard shall delineate no class of persons nor one or two out of the strata of interests nor love most nor truth most nor the soul most nor the body most .... and not be for the eastern states more than the western or the northern states more than the southern" (CRE, 718). However, as this demolition opened a world of new poetic possibilities, it also closed off many of the bases of communal discourse, isolating the individual consciousness even as it enfranchised it, and calling into question the reality of those "dumb objects" upon which the poet was to construct the path between his own soul and the souls of his readers. "There was a Child Went Forth," through its mimesis of the process of visual perception, reestablishes their reality, as they stand in a landscape with which Whitman was most intimate, New York harbor and its cities. "Crossing Brooklyn Ferry" enlarges the same visual experience into a basis for communal life by setting it in motion and by emphasizing its specifically urban quality.

The achievement of "There was a Child Went Forth" is its recreation of the experience of a *visual field,* that is, what registers on the eye in a single "present" place and time. James J. Gibson, a twentieth-century authority on seeing (who debated Gombrich's views on artistic "illusion"), described the visual field in *The Perception of the Visual World*. It is bounded, perspectivist, limited in its

---

27. The "Ames" chair, for example, of which Gombrich makes so much, is an assemblage of cardboard and sticks, which, through a peephole, appears to be a chair (*Art and Illusion,* 248).

register of depth, and subject to deformation and displacement as the viewer moves. We can advert to it only by an introspective, analytical examination of the phenomena of sight, fixing the gaze and overriding its faculty of selective attention. "Descriptively, the visual field always seems a little illusory."[28] This illusoriness was something the nineteenth century discovered and cherished. Ruskin expounded its mysteries in *Modern Painters*. Emerson in *Nature* made it a portal into Idealism. Recreating the visual field was the mission of the Impressionist painters, and it lent to the cityscapes of Dickens and Dostoevsky their plausible unreality.[29] In popular entertainment, it provided the appeal of the stereopticon, the panorama, and the diorama.

The great physiologist of the midnineteenth century, Hermann von Helmholtz, used the stereopticon as a laboratory tool to disprove the claims of "intuitionist" theories of perception that argued that the ability to locate objects in space is innate. No, he said; it depends on experience, and that experience may begin with touch, but it extends beyond touch. The potentially illusory visual field is corrected by motion—that of the object and that of the perceiver: "The correspondence between the external world and the perceptions of sight rests . . . upon the same foundation as all our knowledge of the actual world—on experience, with constant verification of its accuracy by experiments which we perform with every movement of our body."[30]

In actual perceiving life, then, the visual field disappears from consciousness, absorbed in the larger and more communicable context that Gibson terms the *visual world*. This is "the familiar, ordinary scene of daily life, in which solid objects look solid, square objects look square, horizontal surfaces look horizontal, and the book across the room looks as big as the book lying in front of you." It offers "an array of familiar objects at definite locations and distances," "every part of it . . . fixed relative to every other part."[31] It is continuous, centerless, four-dimensional, and stable. From one perceiver to another, it varies relatively little. This is the world that danced before Whitman's eyes every day, though at the touch of a word it might dissolve into surface and appearance. This world is what Whitman aimed to recover in "Crossing Brooklyn Ferry," as the key

28. Gibson, *The Perception of the Visual World*, 42.
29. Donald Fanger, *Dostoevsky and Romantic Realism* (Chicago, 1965), 66, 202.
30. Helmholtz, "Recent Progress in the Theory of Vision," 222.
31. Gibson, *The Perception of the Visual World*, 26.

of his address to You. And the qualities of urban life helped him to capture it, indirectly, in that poem.

Gibson's studies begin by noting how one visual field dissolves into another, as the eye's attention shifts, the head turns, or the body moves. Detecting several constancies in these transformations, Gibson argues that it is through movement that we correct any illusions or misreadings offered by the single visual field and concludes that the reliability of sight derives from "an adjacent order of things":

> Let us first define the physical environment in which a man lives as the one in which he gets about. . . . At any given physical point in such an environment there is one and only one ocular image which a standard human eye will produce when it is pointed in a given direction. This image is unique . . . and the 360° panorama of images is a unique collection. . . . An eye can explore the flux of light at a given position like a blind man feeling an object on different sides in succession, and the panoramic image is just as immovable as a fixed object. . . .
>
> If now we suppose that the eye moves from one point to another in the environment (as its possessor goes about his business) the image becomes a continuous serial transformation which, as a series, is unique to the path travelled. . . . Assume next that the panoramic series and the locomotor series are combined, as they must be if an observer both scans his environment and moves about. The combination yields a range of images in two dimensions which corresponds to the whole of a three-dimensional environment, independent of any given point of view. It will not only be stable, panoramic, and unbounded, but it will approximate the range of images possessed by another man who lives in that environment in the degree to which they have been in the same places. It will be something very much like objective space.[32]

Whitman (like Helmholtz, a professed physiologist) reflected on the curious mystery of the eyesight and drew very comparable conclu-

---

32. *Ibid.*, 161. Gombrich likewise notes that trompe l'oeil works only from a single point and is undone by the spectator's movement (*Art and Illusion*, 274–75).

sions.[33] Recent studies of the physical in Whitman's poetry have gone wrong insofar as they have attended only to sexual and specifically genital physicality. His poems express—often "indirectly"—an exquisite sense of the workings of the body, from the play of an ankle to the darting of the eye, and of the body's movements through space and time. In "Crossing Brooklyn Ferry," "panoramic series" and "locomotor series" are combined, as Whitman scans the harbor scene while the ferry moves from Manhattan to Brooklyn. The succession of words provides not a pictorialist analysis of a picture (*i.e.*, a visual field), but rather the fluid experience of a man going about his business in a three- (and four-) dimensional environment, a visual world. The transformations of that world are continuous: like the circular panorama, it has no "edge." Yet it is stable. Whitman can anticipate places and events that he cannot yet see. He knows where he is bound: at the end of his walk he will be "home." He knows that the sun is half an hour high and the tide at flood. Gibson comments on this stability: "'Being oriented' . . . requires, over and above the visual world, a frame of reference or a topographical schema. The individual must perceive the space which surrounds him on all sides . . . and must also apprehend the world beyond the visible scene—the layout of the building, of the city and its streets, of the region, and of the country with its highways and cities." Gibson continues, "orientation is inseparable from locomotion, for, only because an observer gets a different visual field at every different standpoint, does he perceive a single integrated world."[34] It is important then that the standpoint of "Crossing Brooklyn Ferry" is in motion, as it was not in "There was a Child Went Forth."

And, moreover, it is important that this motion is periodic and routine, a passage that Whitman made several times a day and that the people around him also made daily, going and coming from work. To celebrate individual consciousness, a poem might spin forth images of incessant novelty: the "perpetual journey" of "Song of Myself"; the open road; the streets through which Whitman the *flâneur* passes "watching and wondering" at the display of his visual field. But in "Crossing Brooklyn Ferry," Whitman is striving to invoke a stable ground for experience, one that does not depend solely

---

33. Emerson's preoccupation with the visual field and its seemingly im-mediate clarity supports his intuitionist theory of knowledge and his emphasis on the singularity of each person's insight.

34. Gibson, *The Perception of the Visual World*, 230.

on his own vision or even on his poem alone. What he proclaimed "directly" in his transcendental revelation of the float of universal being he also calls forth "indirectly" through the poem's reiterated descriptive passages. They are indexed to a topographical schema that is not unique to Whitman or to the singular moment of his crossing, but lies in the grasp of all who cross on the Fulton Ferry. It is the map of their city—not a static overhead map, like the balloon view of "Mannahatta," but a "cognitive map," as Ulric Neisser describes it in *Cognition and Reality*—an orienting structure for perception that alternately explores the present environment and modifies itself to accommodate new information.[35]

Following the urban theorist Kevin Lynch, Neisser describes the cognitive map of a city:

> Such cognitive maps typically include certain characteristic features. *Landmarks* such as towers, unusual buildings, or monuments, play an important role because they can be easily spotted from a distance. *Paths* are travelable routes—most often streets—by which the city dweller gets about, and *nodes* are salient points where several paths meet. *Districts* are regions of the city characterized by some easily recognized cultural or geographical property. Finally, *Edges* are the visibly defined boundaries of districts or other areas: rivers, expressways, and the like. It is these features that define a city's structure as that structure is understood and used by its inhabitants.[36]

The details of this map are not like the urban imagery of "Song of Myself," in which the selection and order of images seem dictated entirely by the presiding ego, nor like the systematic disclosure of "Sparkles from the Wheel." Those were the rhythms of individual consciousness and of pictorial observation. As the "housebuilding" passage in "Song of the Broad-Axe" shifted the rhythm out from subjective to objective—the sequence of practiced skill discerned by a knowledgeable onlooker—so "There was a Child Went Forth"

---

35. Neisser, *Cognition and Reality*, 111–13.
36. *Ibid.*, 123. Neisser says further that landmarks and edges especially are the features to which the eye returns, for they "offer the kind of continuous information that is essential for the development of a schema." So it is the hills of Brooklyn and the masts and chimneys of Manhattan, the shorelines and waterways of New York harbor, to which "Crossing Brooklyn Ferry" repeatedly returns us.

moves into the rhythm of perception itself; and "Crossing Brooklyn Ferry" extends the rhythms of perception from private to public, showing how a city's inhabitants make their ways through familiar space, guided by landmarks, following paths, crossing edges. These are the rhythms of inhabitation. The poem is a map of the city where he dwells. Although it may open with Whitman's own visionary encounter, "face to face," with the presences all around him, the poem instantly falls back into the quotidian ("the impalpable sustenance of me from all things at all hours of the day"): when he first addresses the others who are to be his neighbors, the "tie" between him and them is not ecstasy but the "certainty" of the daily round:[37]

> Others will enter the gates of the ferry, and cross from shore to shore,
> Others will watch the run of the flood-tide,
> Others will see the shipping of Manhattan north and west, and the heights of Brooklyn to the south and east,
> Others will see the islands large and small.
> (§2, *V*, I, 218)

In the original version of the poem, he explicitly named his local citizenship as one of the grounds for his claim of union "with you": "I was a Manhattanese"; and in 1860 he inserted, twenty lines earlier, "I was of old Brooklyn." "I am with you," he says to his fellow dwellers in Brooklyn and Manhattan, "and know how it is" (§6, 5, 3, *V*, I, 221, 218).

Whitman's account of his city, then, while always in dynamic readjustment, is at the same time constant. It sums up his crossings by day and by night, on all the days between December and summer. It approximates the experience of the other men and women who stand and lean on the rail yet hurry with the swift current. The map that Whitman creates approximates also the experience of those others, fifty years hence, who will cross from shore to shore, and those, many generations hence, who follow the sequence of Whitman's poem as it "feels round" the cityscape, confirming its solid reality and discovering how such a visual world conserves itself, from one

---

37. Erkkila writes: "The redemption he imagines is achieved not through personal immortality but through the collectivity—through participation in the rituals of ordinariness that radiate outward from the daily action of the ferry carrying crowds of people across the East River" (*Whitman the Political Poet*, 143–44).

The Mystery of the Eyesight

viewer to the next and one time to the next, and so constitutes a ground of address between I and You. All seeing then is mediate, whether through the senses of touch and kinesis or through its reference to the communal map shared and continuously created by all the citizens of Whitman's New York.[38]

One of the effects of reiterating the descriptive passages in "Crossing Brooklyn Ferry" is to confer upon the reader an analogous sense of citizenship. This poem defines a range of images in its first section, fills in more detail in the second and third, and expands it in the sixth; it then returns to the same images, with slightly varied phraseology, in eight and nine. The long roll of imperatives in section nine offers a map of the poem itself, drawing its imagery from almost every part of it. The descriptives that were brilliantly inventive when first heard—

> I watched the December sea-gulls, I saw them high in the air floating with motionless wings oscillating their bodies,
> [. . .]
> I saw the slow-wheeling circles and the gradual edging toward the south.
>
> (§3, *V*, I, 219)

—these return, toward the poem's end, as epithets generated from the poem itself:

> Now I am curious what sight can ever be more stately and admirable to me than my mast-hemm'd Manhatta, my river and sun-set, and my scallop-edged waves of flood-tide, the sea-gulls oscillating their bodies, the hay-boat in the twilight, and the belated lighter.
> [. . .]
> Fly on, sea-birds! fly sideways, or wheel in large circles high in the air!
>
> (§8, 9, *V*, I, 223–24)

---

38. Jon Rosenblatt describes Whitman's poetry as "a mediating agency that converts poetic language into a body and that understands the human body as a language. This equivalence between body and language is central to Whitman's poetry and provides it with a tremendous energy" ("Whitman's Body, Whitman's Language," in *Walt Whitman Here and Now*, ed. Krieg, 103–104).

The imagery is familiar. We have walked through it many times, following different routes. We are at home; this is the city where we live.

The poem thus creates a topology of images, from within itself, at the same time that it retraces this topology in the environs of New York harbor. Some readers have said that the "New York" of this poem is a "city of the mind" because it is timeless, or apolitical, or lacking in closeup realism. Rather, it is more accurate to say that it recreates the mentality of the city, of the way that city dwellers formulate a map that gives their habitation a shape and a significance. Through this ground of reiterated images—quotidian landmarks, paths, and edges—Whitman establishes a basis, at once material and immaterial, on which he can say You to his fellow passengers, then and now. Later in his book, Gibson explains that it is through sharing such a map that human beings take their place in a mutual world: "The conception of an objective world, independent of the standpoint of any observer, rests upon . . . orientation. The ability to take the position of another person, to see from his point of view, depends on being oriented in space."[39] It is just such a topographical schema that Whitman creates in this poem, moving through a cityscape and establishing through visual experience its objective reality as a basis of orientation and of sympathy—a ground in the Not-Me through which I can address You. True vision depends on the imaginative incorporation of sight. In "There was a Child Went Forth," sight was physiologically incorporated; in "Crossing Brooklyn Ferry" it is incorporated both physiologically and communally.

In section 3, Whitman "looked at the fine centrifugal spokes of light round the shape of my head in the sun-lit water." In section 9, this has become: "Diverge, fine spokes of light, from the shape of my head, or any one's head, in the sun-lit water!" (*V*, I, 219, 224). In these lines, and in the lines quoted just above, the objects and their names are still there; but they have been put into a new syntax. The landmarks of the poem, as of the city, are constant; but the standpoint from which they are seen and the particular context of meaning into which they are set can change, and change again, without undoing their reality. As Neisser says, "Such a schema can be detached from its original function and used as an independent source of information. One can imagine one's city as well as explore it."[40]

39. Gibson, *The Perception of the Visual World*, 230.
40. Neisser, *Cognition and Reality*, 125.

The Mystery of the Eyesight

To his question, What endures?, this poem has discovered a further answer: the city endures, as that topographical schema of which Gibson and Neisser speak; and this schema makes it possible that the glory around Whitman's head might appear around anyone's.[41]

Therefore, few of the things Whitman sees are as private and as fleeting as that glory. Instead, what he sees are the features of the city that all the passengers might hold in common—the cognitive maps that make possible their common discourse: the two rivers and their confluence in the bay; the two great islands, Manhattan and Long Island; the human path between them running athwart the path of the rushing flood tide; the gates of the ferry that define the limits of the poet's journey; the city streets with their human encounters—where he feels the gaze of men and women, hears the voices of young men, and experiences both glories and questionings; the emerging distinction in function between mast-hemmed Manhattan, with its storehouses and foundries, and Brooklyn, whose "beautiful hills" above the river were filling with residences; and, almost all around, the hills that form for this world not only a visual horizon but also a sense of corporate limit. This was the space he shared with his fellow passengers on the ferry; the *civitas* that, through the dynamics of his visual encounters with it, he sought to share as well with his fellow wayfarers in his poem. At the crossways of such a world, as he had said in "Song of Myself," one might find the handkerchief of the Lord. The mystery of the eyesight, opening to far and near, might reveal the identities of the spiritual world, and the glories strung like beads on his own sights and hearings might be laid open to every citizen.[42]

---

41. A few pages earlier in the 1856 edition, Whitman had announced, "I paint myraids of heads, but paint no head without its nimbus of gold-colored light" ("To You," [*V*, I, 215]). M. Wynn Thomas remarks, apropos of these lines: "Genuinely egalitarian democracy entails, for Whitman, the organizing of society in accordance with the perception that its center is everywhere, and its circumference nowhere" (*Lunar Light*, 99).

42. This articulation of the possibilities of mutual urban space is indebted to Kevin Lynch (*The Image of the City* and *What Time Is This Place?*), Ulric Neisser (*Cognition and Reality*), and Christian Norberg-Schulz (*Existence, Space, and Architecture*). Such a space is defined by such qualities as *landmarks, paths, nodes, termini, domains,* and *limits*. See especially Norberg-Schulz, 17–36. Norberg-Schulz refers extensively to Heidegger's essay "Building Dwelling Thinking" ["Bauen Wohnen Denken," in *Vorträge und Aufsätze*, 1954]. In one useful sentence, Heidegger writes: "To say that mortals *are* is to say that *in dwelling* they persist through spaces by virtue of their stay among things and locations" (*Basic Writings*, ed. David Farrell Krell [New York, 1977], 334).

"Crossing Brooklyn Ferry" asserts "directly" Whitman's claim that he is united with his fellow citizens and readers through the neoplatonic "float forever held in solution" (*V*, I, 221). He makes this assertion at the furthest limit of his metaphysical exploration, in section 5, at almost the linear center of the poem. But throughout its length the poem has been asserting indirectly his bondings through the landscape, the physiology of seeing, and the power of the primary imagination to create a cognitive map of the city. So near the end Whitman can say:

> We understand, then, do we not?
> What I promised without mentioning it, have you not
>   accepted?
> What the study could not teach—what the preaching
>   could not accomplish is accomplished, is it not?
>
>   (§8, *V*, I, 223)

And it is.

Whitman understood clearly enough the schematic understructure of city experience. And though he does not "preach" it anywhere in the poem, he does "mention" at the outset a "simple, compact, well-joined scheme" that might account for "the similitudes of the past and those of the future" and the ties uniting him, with "certainty," to "the others that are to follow." It may figure in his metaphor of the "knitted . . . knot of contrariety" that binds him in a self-interfering pattern with his fellow citizens as doers of evil and practicers of deception. Certainly, he is thinking of the city's cognitive map in the ensuing stanza and in the finale, when he introduces the metaphor of a play:

> [I] lived the same life with the rest, the same old
>   laughing, gnawing, sleeping,
> Played the part that still looks back on the actor or
>   actress,
> The same old role, the role that is what we make it, as
>   great as we like, or as small as we like, or both great
>   and small.
>
>   (§6, *V*, I, 222)

Like the script for a play, the city provides roles, scenes, and backdrops; these remain, durable, while the cast, incessantly changing, works its changes on the relationship of these elements and on their relative prominence. This deep sense of space prevents men and women from disintegrating into dots and specks, and allows Whitman, or any other citizen, to advance from the catalog of perceptions in section 3 to the litany of presences in sections 8 and 9—from that which appears to that which is. "Appearances, now or henceforth," he says near the end, "indicate what you are!" And as appearances become presences, Whitman must address them as beings to respect and trust, rather than as consumable commodities. "We fathom you not," he says;"—we love you." Finally, this shared space provides for continuity through time. "Expand," he says—and it is the city, with both its "scheme" and its "shows," that he is addressing: "Expand, being than which none else is perhaps more spiritual! / Keep your places, objects than which none else is more lasting!" (§9, *V,* I, 225–26).

"What is it, then, between us?" Whitman asks (§5, *V,* I, 220). If it is space, it "avails not" to separate us; for the moving panorama of New York harbor, with its subtly shifting perspectives, has compelled us to feel our way into the actual experience of crossing on the Fulton Ferry, near sundown, in the midst of the crowd, with the cities and their shipping all about us. If it is time, it avails not; for it is time actually that unites us with him, a sense of time that penetrates down from "scores or hundreds of years" between the writing of the poem and its reading, to the temporal matrix of perception, the process through which Whitman, and we, inhabit our common experience. In time, the ferry moves and the scene shifts around; in time, Whitman recreates the sum of many crossings; in time, our senses create an experiential world, and verify it, and share it with one another.

It is within the schema of the city that Whitman might have most successfully fulfilled his ambition to be the public poet, drawing for his fellow citizens a path between their souls and the "dumb real objects" of America. "I am a habitan of St. Petersburgh," he announced in "Salut au Monde!" (§9, *V,* I, 170). But he was not. In essaying to be the citizen of the world, he became instead the prisoner of his own consciousness. But he was truly an inhabitant of New York (and later of Washington, and finally of Camden). His sense of indwelling in New York enriched "Crossing Brooklyn Ferry" and "There was a Child Went Forth," as well as great passages in "Song of Myself," "The Sleepers," and "To Think of Time," and also his prose and his journalism.[43] Within the bounds of his city he became at times truly the bard, discovering through his powerful visual sense a mutual space in which he could join his readers (whoever you are) in a common corporation. Within that space he encountered real presences: blacksmiths, shopgirls, bricklayers, and carpenters; crowds, parades, and omnibuses; and, along the limits of the metropolis, beaches where men fished for mossbonkers and where, at night, one might hear the song of a mockingbird, a visitor up from the south. These beings he portrayed not as the flotsam of consciousness but with an empathetic sense of the rhythms of their own autonomous being.[44]

Whitman's program as an American poet, of course, did not allow him to remain within the limit of his native city. His sense of geographical synecdoche was not so intense as that of Thoreau, the poet who dug himself deep into the ground of Concord. Or perhaps he better understood the diversity of his nation and so felt obliged to venture out into an America he knew only through the instruments of his culture. What he then invoked for his readers was their common membership in a less directly experiential world, one mediated not by the physiology of eyesight but by the political rhetoric of his age or by its taste in popular graphics: its "brain" he called it in "Small the Theme of My Chant" (*V*, II, 557). He knew Manhattan and Brooklyn in his body, as one knows the number of steps and the headroom in a familiar stair. He knew what it was to be a dweller in a city and how that city might serve as identity-giver and buffer against the isolation of individual consciousness. When that incar-

---

43. In his journalism, however, the indweller's vision is often clouded by the mannerisms of the press: "By four or five o'clock the feminine promenaders gradually disappear, and the successive waves of the morning tide now begin to roll backward in an inverse order—merchants, brokers, lawyers, first; clerks next; shopgirls and laborers last; all tired, and all hastening to whatever of comfort boarding-house, hotel, or hired home can give, of dinner, rest, and sleep. Gradually the sidewalk is emptied, for an hour or two the street is left to the stragglers of the mighty army, to the hideous women of the night, who now come forth to their miserable patrol, and to the scattered policemen" (*New York Dissected* [New York, 1936], 121–22).

44. M. Wynn Thomas writes: "Although such observations are rooted in the particular social, and indeed, political, experiences of Whitman's youth and early manhood, they grow here into a spiritual vision that values people not for conventional reasons but for that precious singularity of life each one possesses. The city is for Whitman the place in which this natural equality of men in their 'abundance of diversity' most torrentially and therefore irresistibly displays itself" (*Lunar Light*, 151).

nate knowledge or that space failed him, he stood alone in the void that Tocqueville had said surrounded the democratic individual after the collapse of traditional communal associations.[45]

And even as Whitman was compelling his vision out onto the unfamiliar roads of national and imperial utterance, New York was moving beyond the limits of imaginability, not only because of its growth but also because it was taking on those characteristics of a mass society that Whitman proclaimed and enacted in his poetry, characteristics that would render citizenship abstract and the citizen anonymous.

❖

In *The Confidence Man,* someone (it sounds like Melville himself) remarks about theatergoers that "though they want novelty, they want nature, too; but nature unfettered, exhilarated, in effect transformed. . . . It is with fiction as with religion: it should present another world, and yet one to which we feel the tie."[46] The crowds that thronged the dioramas and panoramas of the 1850s, and those like Holmes who peered through stereopticon lenses, knew well enough that they were not truly standing atop Saint Paul's Cathedral, or witnessing the battle of Waterloo, or walking in the churchyard of Alloway Kirk. They came seeking novelty, and yet nature—another world, and yet one to which they felt bonded by their own experience. Exhilarated by the illusion, they might see the reality in a new light. Not only might they see its beauty, through the illusion's stimulation of that aesthetic pleasure that Wordsworth and Constable thought could come only from legitimate art; but also they might attain a further discovery that Whitman would probably have called religious, for it was the discovery of identity: "The land and sea, the animals fishes and birds, the sky of heaven and the orbs, the forests mountains and rivers, are not small themes ... but folks expect of the poet to indicate more than the beauty and dignity which always attach to dumb real objects .... they expect him to indicate the path between reality and their souls" (*CRE,* 714). At this critical point in the Preface, when the reader expects to learn of the path to the soul, Whitman seems to divagate into a description of "outdoor people,"

45. Tocqueville, *Democracy in America,* II, 98–99.
46. Herman Melville, *The Confidence Man: His Masquerade,* ed. Hershel Parker (New York, 1971), 158 [Chap. 33].

the characteristics of the perfect poem, and his counsels for spiritual perfection. However, when he returns to the topic, he assimilates these wanderings into it: "The fruition of beauty is no chance of hit or miss ... it is inevitable as life .... it is exact and plumb as gravitation. From the eyesight proceeds another eyesight and from the hearing proceeds another hearing and from the voice proceeds another voice eternally curious of the harmony of things with man" (*CRE*, 715).

The path then is the discovery of correspondence and harmony in which poetic "rhymes" reveal cosmic rhyme and individual persons and objects are bound by their kinship. Beyond the illusory play of words, Whitman seeks to discover and display an enduring analogical world, at once material and spiritual. Wordsworth, Ruskin, and Constable were right: this is not art, for at a certain point the questions encountered are no longer art-questions but life-questions. The proper response to Whitman's city, finally, is not detached aesthetic scrutiny, but (as he says near the end of "Crossing Brooklyn Ferry") love. And to that world he entrusts himself.

In an age straying toward infidelity, for which everything is becoming private "experience," the poet then is the man of faith: "As he sees the farthest he has the most faith. His thoughts are the hymns of the praise of things. In the talk on the soul and eternity and God off of his equal plane he is silent. He sees eternity less like a play with a prologue and denouement .... he sees eternity in men and women ... he does not see men and women as dreams or dots. Faith is the antiseptic of the soul ... it pervades the common people and preserves them ... they never give up believing and expecting and trusting" (*CRE*, 713). M. Wynn Thomas says acutely of "Crossing Brooklyn Ferry" that at its end Whitman has "successfully reconstructed and thus reconsecrated a profane world. The restoration of faith is primarily marked by a restoration of trust in the sheer physical process of existence."[47] The reconsecrated world is still secular; the poet is silent about matters off his plane. But compactly knotted in that secular "float" are flesh and spirit, time present and time imagined, reality and the soul, restlessly gazing passengers and enduring urban schemata. And so Whitman has named this encounter rightly when he calls it faith. As Buber put it: "Only he who believes in the world is given power to enter into dealings with it, and if he

---

47. Thomas, *Lunar Light*, 114.

gives himself to this he cannot remain godless. . . . He who truly goes out to meet the world goes out also to God."[48] The final stanza of "Crossing Brooklyn Ferry" addresses corporately all the manifold of beings he has just named, calling them You, and acknowledging their material reality at the same time that he recognizes their spirituality:

> You have waited, you always wait, you dumb beautiful
>   ministers! You novices!
> [. . .]
> We fathom you not—we love you—there is perfection
>   in you also,
> You furnish your parts toward eternity,
> Great or small, you furnish your parts toward the soul.
>   (§9, *V*, I, 225)

"There was a Child Went Forth" and "Crossing Brooklyn Ferry" are fraternal twins. Born from one journal entry, they were nourished by Whitman's decades of life as a dweller in Brooklyn and Manhattan. In them, as almost nowhere else in his poetry, he found an answer to the dilemma of individualist consciousness, with its lust to engulf the world or be engulfed by it. Attending closely to the physiology of the eyesight, he created in these poems the illusion of depth—not the third dimension only, but the fourth. And through time and movement we are delivered from the solipsism of the man in the crowd. ("Only through time," said a later poet who also knew well how it was to drift among a city's phantasmagoria, "time is conquered."[49]) Whitman in these poems enacted the ways in which a city dweller discovers the Form of his city, at once its physical landmarks and its enduring schemata, and through this form he found a structure incorporating him with his fellow passengers, a trustworthy basis on which to say *You* to the men and women with whom he was in passage.

48. Buber, *I and Thou*, 94–95.
49. T. S. Eliot, "Burnt Norton," *CPE*, 178.

PART III

Surface and Depth

> Paris . . . hung before him this morning, the vast bright Babylon, like some huge iridescent object, a jewel brilliant and hard, in which parts were not to be discriminated nor differences comfortably marked. It twinkled and trembled and melted together, and what seemed all surface one moment seemed all depth the next.
> —Henry James, *The Ambassadors*

[7]

Artful Juxtapositions: Jacob Riis and John Sloan

Whitman had taught himself how to see the city—and the nation of which it was for him a miniature—as an endless sequence of surfaces, visual fields assembled within the gallery of the mind or unreeling before him along a street. In one extraordinary poem, "Crossing Brooklyn Ferry," he had found his way into full membership in the city by recreating it "in depth" as a series of visual encounters with its existential space, both physically present and contained in the communal imagination of its inhabitants. Surface and depth—in the generations of writers and artists to follow Whitman, these alternatives would determine the quality of their citizenship, their way of mediating the I with the Not-Me. James's metaphor for Paris, quoted above, anticipates not only the later scene in which Strether's visual composition of "boaters" is transformed when he recognizes the persons within it, but also how the city would appear in twentieth-century literature and art—now an object observed by a detached consciousness, now a liminal place where recognition passes between two human persons; a wilderness of walls unexpectedly opening into an angel's mouth.

In some of Whitman's poems dramatizing the flow of consciousness, there are sequences recounting how the poet ambles through his city:

> Shop-windows, coffins in the sexton's ware-room, fruit
>   on the fruitstand—beef in the butcher's stall, the
>   slaughter-house of the butcher, the butcher in his
>   killing-clothes,
> The area of pens of live pork, the killing-hammer, the

> hog-hook, the scalder's tub, gutting, the cutter's
> cleaver, the packer's maul, and the plenteous winter-
> work of pork-packing,
> Flour-works, grinding of wheat, rye, maize, rice—the
> barrels and the half and quarter barrels, the loaded
> barges, the high piles on wharves and levees,
> Bread and cakes in the bakery, the milliner's ribbons, the
> dressmaker's patterns, the tea-table, the home-made
> sweetmeats.
>
> ("A Song for Occupations," §5, *V*, I, 95–96)

These variegated catalogs proclaim the diversity of American life and the capacity of the American bard and his poem. When confined to a single setting, as in the passage above, they celebrate also the rich unpredictability of city life that Whitman embraced in "Give Me the Splendid Silent Sun": "Let me see new ones every day! [. . .] Give me such shows! give me the streets of Manhattan! [. . .] O an intense life! O full to repletion, and varied!" (§2, *V*, II, 499). Rural life conformed to the decorums of an agrarian ideal; city life forever contradicted and surpassed one's expectations, show replacing sight, spectacle replacing show, feeding and renewing the *flâneur*'s appetite for novelty and incongruity.

Incongruity, life violating decorum, has long been a convention of writings about city life. Insofar as cities always have been conceived as the earthly or material embodiment of the ideals of those who founded them, ruled them, or lived in them, they lay claim to a single soul, a unifying identity. Insofar as cities are points of cultural and economic interchange, they are theaters of the unexpected: different trades, distinct classes, various nationalities and languages, changing fashions. The bard walking through his city's streets must deal simultaneously with his knowledge of its ideals and with his immediate experience of life that is at odds with those ideals. So Jeremiah roves the squares of Jerusalem looking for an upright man following the law of the Lord (Jer. 5:1–17), and Ezekiel finds idolatry even in the courts of the Temple (Ezek. 8). So Juvenal's friend Umbricius upbraids Rome's moral and social anarchy while standing at the Capena gate, where a grove sacred to the city's ancient deities has become a gaudy showplace haunted by foreign beggars (Satires 1.3.1–20). So London enriched Jonathan Swift's verse by impugning his principles.

One connoisseur of the paradoxes of urban life in the nineteenth century was Charles Dickens, who constantly juxtaposed the political power and wealth of London with the most wretched of its poor.[1] Sometimes the effect was satire; more often it was taken for pathos. In *Bleak House,* the street-boy Jo, wolfing down some scraps of food, looks up at the dome of Saint Paul's: "And there he sits, munching and gnawing, and looking up at the great Cross on the summit of St. Paul's Cathedral, glittering above a red and violet-tinted cloud of smoke. From the boy's face one might suppose that sacred emblem to be, in his eyes, the crowning confusion of the great, confused city; so golden, so high up, so far out of his reach" (Chap. 19). This is a tactic of urban irony, matching a symbol of the city's values against the spectacle of its moral failures and the victims of those failures. One adjustment of the eye, redirecting the reader from foreground to background, juxtaposes the almost invisible beggar boy with the city's most imposing monument to its highest ideal.[2] A confusion, the description calls it; a contradiction: if the citizen of London orients himself upon that cross and dome, what is he to make of Jo and his crust of bread? Dickens' genteel readership defused such ironies by reducing characters like Jo to objects of pathos, figures providing a reflector for private feelings like self-pity or fear of failure. At their best, Dickens' ironies created a civic context within which the reader was bound to feel complicit in the deprivation and outcast lot of his characters. When sentimentalized—sometimes with his assistance—the characters are deprived of that context, and the emotion experienced by the reader is a purely aesthetic one. The contextual background, which might morally envelop the reader, drops out of sight. The city where Jo lives becomes some other place, its fatal workings not the same as those of the city that sustains those who read his story. A private and delicious pity is enough to give him.

Dickens' contemporary Walt Whitman wrote a few early poems in the ironic style: "A Boston Ballad" describes Revolutionary Boston as an ironic backdrop for officials enforcing the Fugitive Slave Law upon Anthony Burns (*V,* I, 146–47). But in his mature poetry,

1. Fanger, *Dostoevsky and Romantic Realism,* 65–100.
2. Marshall McLuhan wrote, in "The Aesthetic Moment in Landscape Poetry": "Those who re-established discontinuity as an artistic principle in the eighteenth century did so in the name of democracy. The art of Fielding, like that of Scott and Dickens, is strictly 'picturesque' in achieving social inclusiveness by means of discontinuous perspectives" (in *English Institute Essays, 1951,* ed. Alan S. Downer [New York, 1952], 171).

Whitman did away with irony, for irony involves the recognition of a violated decorum and implies a preference for norms and those who set them. To represent visually his egalitarianism, as we have seen, he catalogs images indiscriminately, as though the eye had not learned in infancy to focus, to select, and to interpret; as though it refused to accept society's tutelage about what things were worth seeing and what were not. As some of his poems were influenced by the panorama and the self-consciousness that it brought to vision, others seem to suggest the kind of "seeing" accomplished by the photographic camera, which juxtaposed the mean and the glorious as a matter of course, seemingly without reference to any standard of aesthetic decorum according to which objects were to be recognized or excluded.

When Whitman inspected the daguerreotypes in Plumbe's studio, the faces he saw there each invited its own personal response.[3] But in the streets, encountering faces en masse, he can no longer go forth to them as individuals, but shifts his attention to their momentary appearance as images passing across his visual field. In "Faces," his attention focuses not on what he sees but on the act of seeing. A little more, and they become "Men and women crowding fast in the streets [. . .] flashes and specks" (*V*, I, 149–52). In "There was a Child Went Forth" Whitman recoiled from the flatness of this vision to recreate in depth the harborscape before him. But what his visualist poems usually render is the experience of images rendered flat, as the details in photographs appeared to Oliver Wendell Holmes when, defeating the illusion of depth, he inspected a stereograph picture beneath a magnifying glass.

Holmes, like many of those who wrote down their reactions to the first age of photography, was struck with the infinite detail of its image as well as with its apparent fidelity to the actual experience of seeing.[4] In 1859 he wrote: "The first effect of looking at a good photograph . . . is a surprise such as no painting ever produced. . . .

---

3. Whitman, "Visit to Plumbe's Gallery" [July 2, 1846]: "An electric chain seems to vibrate, as it were, between our brain and him or her preserved there so well by the limner's cunning. Time, space, both are annihilated, and we identify the semblance with the reality" (*The Gathering of the Forces*, II, 17).

4. Ed Folsom writes: "[T]he first photographs stunned people with their clutter—every detail of a scene insisted on equal emphasis, and nothing was ignored. Nothing was left out because it was considered irrelevant or unaesthetic or inessential. The photographic field, then, was purely democratic territory" ("Whitman and the Visual Democracy of Photography," 56).

There is such a frightful amount of detail, that we have the same sense of infinite complexity which Nature gives us. A painter shows us masses; the stereoscopic figure spares us nothing,—all must be there, every stick, straw, scratch, as faithfully as the dome of St. Peter's, or the summit of Mont Blanc. . . . The sun is no respecter of persons or of things."[5] That is, no *dis*respecter: the sun's pencil on the camera plate finds nothing unworthy of its attention. "The very things which an artist would leave out, or render imperfectly, the photograph takes infinite care with, and so makes its illusions perfect," Holmes continued.

Although these two contrasts are made at the expense of the painter or artist, it is clear that Holmes did not regard the photograph as art. Also, it is not clear whether he realized that it was not just the artist who blurs and omits for the sake of his pictorial composition, but that human faculty which Coleridge called the "primary imagination," the power that moment by moment composes and construes raw optical data. The imagination has learned how to do this not only through cultural training as to the relative importance of various objects, but also through its experience of how each momentary visual field relates to the continuous realities of a visual world. It overlooks because it already knows.[6] Holmes's words are an early instance of that embarrassment or even guilt to which our primary imaginations succumb when confronted with a photograph. The photographic image seems so much like seeing that it is taken as a standard of what the human eye ought to see. The eye, like Holmes's artist, has failed its responsibilities.

"Form is henceforth divorced from matter," Holmes wrote; meaning, partly, that the camera had leaped Plato's line, from the physical and changeable to the enduring idea. But what he also meant by "form" was shape. In the future, men would learn to know things by their visual "skins"—their photographable surfaces—rather than by their material substance. In his concluding paragraph, he restated this distinction more explicitly, and more ominously, calling it a "divorce of form and substance."[7] This shift in terminology enacts Holmes's final prediction, that the visual imagination was about to enter a new epoch.

And so it was. Documentary and travelogue stereographs devel-

---

5. Holmes, "The Stereoscope and the Stereograph," 58–59.
6. See Gibson, *The Perception of the Visual World*.
7. Holmes, "The Stereoscope and the Stereograph," 60–61.

oped into a medium of art whose aesthetics were based on its uncomposed and inclusive character. As Peter Galassi put it: "Many early photographers sought to emulate the look and meaning of traditional [painterly] compositions, but the medium often defeated them. The photographs obstinately described with equal precision (or imprecision) the major and minor features of a scene, or showed it from the wrong point of view, or included too little or too much.... The description was seamless, but only in two dimensions. The photographer ignored this fact at his peril, risking obstructions and discontinuities, fortuitous juxtapositions, and unexpected densities and gaps in spatial logic."[8]

Nineteenth-century photographers learned how to manipulate artfully their supposedly unsophisticated medium; painters learned from photography how to break the formality of composition and framing, to select the unexpected point of view, to compress depth, to open a painterly eye to the clutter that fills the world. Photography's claims to the status of art, however, were not based on purely aesthetic achievements. As Galassi also observes: "If photography had an impact on painting (and it certainly did), it is because the new medium was born to an artistic environment that increasingly valued the mundane, the fragmentary, the seemingly uncomposed—that found in the contingent qualities of perception a standard of artistic, and moral, authenticity."[9] To link moral "authenticity" with the documentary authenticity of the mundane and uncomposed would make city life, in the nineteenth century, the natural object for the camera. For a culture convinced of the innocence of rural folk, the city was both a theater for moral crisis and the object of reform-minded moral concern. Earlier photographers had spent several decades experimenting with imitations of pastoral painting and with formal views of urban monuments.[10] Then they realized that the city was the ideal place in which to exploit the camera's aptitude for an indecorous art that mounted the unnoticeable detail flat alongside the subject of recognition. And so they began to descend from the studio to the street.

By the end of the nineteenth century, the photographer could capture, as a two-dimensional juxtaposition of surfaces, those ruptures

  8. Galassi, *Before Photography,* 28–29.
  9. *Ibid.,* 28.
  10. Peter B. Hales, *Silver Cities: The Photography of American Urbanization, 1839–1915* (Philadelphia, 1984), 11–65.

Artful Juxtapositions 211

in context and decorum that had delighted Dickens—and such Americans as Walt Whitman, a connoisseur of city life. Dixon Scott, a British photographer, reflected on recent developments when he wrote in 1906 that "the native concern of the camera" must be with events that are "transient and irrecoverable," "full of vital complexities," and structured upon "elements of bulk and contour"—Holmes's "skins." He concluded, "It is to the town's prodigality of incident and unsurpassable fluidity, that the Photographer of the Future will turn most frequently. The constant flux of her protean roadways, the intricacies of her disordered buildings, her passion for surprises—these are all characteristics which commend her to the camera."[11]

By 1906, photographers had already turned to the city to exploit the camera's aptitude for juxtaposing "elements of bulk and contour" to create effects born of transience and complexity. In England, in the 1870s, John Thomson had documented the life of London with photographs in which the poor stand unposturing in their streets and markets—unposturing, though the bulk of his camera, and his slow shutter speed, dictated that the subjects be posed, rather than "snapped" or "taken."[12] The French photographer Eugène Atget, burdened with a similar camera, concentrated on the city's inanimate containers: gardens, courtyards, cul-de-sacs, shopwindows. Stricken with a sense that even these apparently solid surfaces would soon crumble, he chose the unpeopled hours of early morning and protracted exposures to filter out the ephemeral passage of human beings. Some of his most memorable work records the miscellany and clutter of shopwindows. Withdrawn from the dynamics of trade—peering shoppers, clerks removing or rearranging merchandise—the window becomes a collage juxtaposing merchandise, mannequins, and reflections of the street; while the eye slides from object to object, texture to texture, savoring the surprise.[13]

In the 1880s, dry-plate photography and hand-held cameras made possible the dynamic urban photography described by Scott. So-called "detective" cameras, carried like a small case, allowed the pho-

11. Dixon Scott, "The Function of the Camera," in *Photography: Essays and Images,* ed. Beaumont Newhall (New York, 1980), 202–203.
12. John Thomson and Adolphe Smith, *Street Life in London* (1878; rpr. New York, 1969); see Alan Thomas, *Time in a Frame: Photography and the Nineteenth-Century Mind* (New York, 1977), 146–47.
13. John Szarkowski and Maria Morris Hambourg, *The Work of Atget* (New York, 1981).

tographer to shift his vantage point easily and often to take his picture unnoticed or at least without forewarning. Some critics of photography have seen in this the rupture of relation between subject and artist—the aestheticizing of the subject and the investment of power in the photographer.[14] The photograph is "taken," not requested, from a person whose unpreparedness is a condition of the picture's claim to authenticity. And that person is thereby reduced to an object, an "other" over whom the photographer has asserted his priority. Indeed, the medium can be exploited this way. But the camera need not always assert the photographer's power and the subject's dehumanization. What happens in the photograph often depends, as in Dickens' fiction, on the relationship of foreground and background, surface and depth. It depends on the relationship of subject and artist to a context that is both interpersonal and public. It depends on a quality of mutual citizenship.

A good example of this citizenship is found in the work of Jacob Riis. Riis took his photographs simply to support his crusade to improve housing conditions on the Lower East Side, a crusade he carried on first through newspaper articles and lectures illustrated with lantern slides, and then through such books as *How the Other Half Lives*.[15] Since the 1950s, his photographs have been treated as works of art. It is clear how some of the more simply documentary might be so aestheticized. As the immediate issue of building codes dissolved, his studies of rear porches, air shafts, and fire escapes reformed as treatments of architectural geometry and texture; his alleyways and cellars became renderings of photographic perspective. Well acquainted with the camera's curious juxtapositions, we may respond aesthetically to a hallway by Riis as we would a shopwindow by Atget. We may read it, today, as "art."

We can do so, however, only by refusing his photographs' invitation to common citizenship. Theodore Roosevelt, who was then president of New York's police board, described Riis as "New York's most valuable citizen."[16] His engagement with his subject, as a citizen, endows his work with a tension of motives. The camera does

---

14. See, for example, Susan Sontag, *On Photography* (New York, 1977); and Carol Shloss, *In Visible Light: Photography and the American Writer, 1840–1940* (New York, 1987).

15. Jacob Riis, *How the Other Half Lives: Studies Among the Tenements of New York* (1890; rpr. New York, 1980).

16. Jacob Riis, *How the Other Half Lives* (New York, 1971), vi.

serve to objectify the conditions of tenement life and to fix an image of the "other half" who dwells there. At the same time, it is a medium of address to his fellow citizens that acknowledges the alienation of the poor and seeks to mend the division between "halves" and "others." Many times his prose reinforces that division, through its patronizing tone or its resort to ethnic and racial stereotypes. Of the Italians in the Lower East Side he writes: "Like the Chinese, the Italian is a born gambler. His soul is in the game from the moment the cards are on the table, and very frequently his knife is in it too before the game is ended."[17] In these words we hear the tone of the policeman or housing inspector, one of the professionals for whom poor Jo, or hot-blooded Antonio, replicated a thousand times, has become little more than one instance of an overwhelming problem. En masse, in his or her strangeness, the tenement dweller becomes the other.

Some of his photographs reflect this otherness in their very occasion. To record conditions that the tenants themselves had reason to conceal, Riis sometimes took his camera into darkened tenement rooms or shadowy dives that were illuminated only momentarily by his flash powder. He scarcely knew whom he had photographed, and against what backdrop, until the slide was developed. The discovered postures, groups, and settings might correspond to the designs of art. If such a photograph resembles a composition by Degas, it is—like many photos—a kind of art trouvé. The viewer looks ambivalently into these intrusive glimpses of squalor and chaos.[18] It is stare and glare. Our schemes for civic improvement have cost these people some of their rest and some of their dignity, and may soon deprive them of the places where, illegally overcrowded, they could afford to sleep. They do not thank us for our concern. Riis's photograph, unplanned in its taking, unintentionally confronts and challenges the viewer. These men and women are a stumbling block to our—and Riis's—good intentions.

At his most acute, however, Riis can write with Dickensian irony.

17. Riis, *How the Other Half Lives* (1890), 52–53.
18. Carol Shloss, for example, reads Riis's photos as intrusory violations of the poor and identifies the photographer as one allied with power (*In Visible Light*, 127–28). Indeed, some of the original shock of the photographs may have come from their impromptu violation of moments of privacy, especially sleep; but this in turn forces the middle-class viewer to recognize that the poor have few means to maintain their privacy. Riis remarked that there were few lockable doors in the slums (*How the Other Half Lives* [1890], 159).

"I went up the dark stairs in one of those tenements," he once wrote, "and there I trod upon a baby." He continued, "It is the regular means of introduction to a tenement house baby . . . but I never was able to get used to it."[19] Such artful juxtapositions of feeling, often achieved with the cooperation of his subjects, are the hallmark of most of his photographs. In them, depth works against surface to produce a collision of emotions at once sentimental and ironic. The subject of recognition, in the fore- or middle ground, is a baby, a group of children, or a family setting. As Peter Hales has pointed out, Riis "successfully manipulated the principal symbols of the Victorian age to his purposes: the child, womanhood, motherhood, the home, privacy, separation of the sexes, and the virtues of work."[20] Frequently, Riis invoked these values by capturing poses that referred to the artistic tradition through which they had often been set forth. Hales observes, as an example, that his image of an Italian mother and child resembles a Renaissance painting of Virgin and Child (Fig. 6).[21] Likewise, his photographs of "Street Arabs"—homeless boys sleeping in doorways and alleys—catch them in the pose of that favorite topic of nineteenth-century popular art, The Babes in the Woods, with its invitation to shelter the defenseless sleeping children (Fig. 7). Gatherings of the homeless around stoves in police-station shelters invoke the strong familial sense of Dutch interiors and more immediately the New World sociability depicted in the widely circulated paintings of William Sidney Mount. So Riis seeks to overcome the otherness of the "other half" by inviting his viewers to identify appropriate (that is, decorous) emotions and situations among them.

But the evocation of familiar sentiments would not, by itself, accomplish Riis's purpose. There was a genre of popular art, with its own conventions and sense of decorum, devoted to sentimentalizing the poor or to depicting them as a strange, ineradicable tribe. In Henry Mayhew's *London Labour and the London Poor*, they appear, classified by trade, as picturesque souvenirs of bygone, provincial, or foreign ways of life. John Thomson portrayed them as he had the exotics of China and Siam. In the lithographs, they are the cheerful, sturdy figures of low comedy, cousins of the Artful Dodger. For

19. From Riis's *The Peril and the Preservation of the House*, quoted in Alexander Alland, Sr., *Jacob A. Riis: Photographer and Citizen* (Millerton, N.Y., 1974), 120.
20. Hales, *Silver Cities*, 203.
21. Ibid., 191. See also Thomas, *Time in a Frame*, 150.

Artful Juxtapositions 215

Fig. 6 Jacob Riis, *Home of an Italian Ragpicker*
Courtesy the Museum of the City of New York; The Jacob A. Riis Collection, no. 157

Oscar Rejlander, a Swedish photographer living in Victorian England, they were figures of pathos. Alan Thomas describes one of his most famous: "It is a view of a boy huddled on a doorstep, his white limbs showing through rents in his trousers, his body crouched in an attitude of despair. The photograph, taken up by the public, was dubbed Poor Jo, after the street-sweeper of Dickens's *Bleak House*."[22] Rejlander worked in a studio, posing costumed models among a few props. In his photograph of "Jo," the great Cross on the summit of Saint Paul's Cathedral does not appear in the background. Dickens' readers decontextualized his ironies, the better to savor the pathos of sentimentalized characters. The visual form of this screening-out was the suppression of background. The engraved illustrations in Dickens' novels, by the nature of their medium, offered mostly characters without setting. When the illustrations in Mayhew were con-

22. Thomas continues: "[T]he idea of the photograph expressed in the boy's pose is not taken directly from life we have evident reason to believe, but from images established by popular literature and entertainment" (*Time in a Frame*, 143).

Fig. 7 Jacob Riis, *Street Arabs in the Area of Mulberry Street, ca. 1889*
Courtesy the Museum of the City of New York; The Jacob A. Riis Collection, no. 123

verted from daguerreotype to engraving, the backgrounds disappeared. The American photographer Sigmund Krausz, for his Thomson-like *Street Types of Great American Cities* (1896), posed his subjects before a neutral studio backdrop. Viewers beheld a quaint or pathetic human figure about whom it was easy to formulate an appropriate response—whether pity, or sorrow, or amusement—because nothing in the composition complicated that response. There was no cross, no dome, whose significance must be correlated with the pitiable Jo.

But with Riis's photographs it is otherwise. He once observed, "New world poverty is not often picturesque. . . . It lacks the leisurely setting, the historic background."[23] His words imply that "old world" poverty is poverty as portrayed in paintings, colorfully clad and set decorously in a Neopolitan street scene. His statement then refers not to comparative economic or housing conditions, but to

23. Quoted, from an 1896 article in *Century*, by Ferenc M. Szasz and Ralph F. Bogardus, in "The Camera and the American Social Conscience: The Documentary Photography of Jacob A. Riis," *New York History*, LX (1974), 436.

Artful Juxtapositions 217

art—to his own indecorous way of using a camera, his refusal to restrict his depth of field or otherwise assume the role of a primary imagination, selecting and unifying his subject. The human figures, whatever their poses, are caught in the midst of the clutter and flux of their untidy lives. And the lens aperture, stopped down against the flare of magnesium powder, sets every detail in focus.

The kitchen has a homey look, with tall cabinets and windows overlooking a court. Around the table, six children cluster with their mother, who has a baby on her lap. They are making artificial flowers: the children are pieceworkers. . . . Between a hallway sink and the roped-up balusters of a stair, a baby in a long dress leans against a wall. The wainscoting, scarred and loose, rises from the recesses of the hallway, backgrounds the baby, and fills the right-hand third of the photo. She is sucking her thumb. . . . In a police lodging-room stands a filthy and exhausted old woman. Beside her—behind her—against a water-stained wall, leans her sleeping-board. It looks like the lid of a coffin. From the edge of the picture a hand gestures at her head. *Ecce mulier!*

Peter Conrad has read these photographs as Oliver Wendell Holmes had his stereographs, finding in them an art that subverts art: "Objects which to the painter are images are to Riis evidence: an ash barrel on a sidewalk, dingy bedding draped on a fire escape, punctured sacks of refuse in Bottle Alley. These things . . . have not been pictorially composed, and their very randomness—by which the momentary art of photography is unperturbed—impugns the tidiness of painting."[24] The viewer who might sentimentalize the ragpicker's wife must deal at the same moment with the litter on the floor, the hat on a hook, the smudgy tubs of galvanized iron. Were this an illustration from Dickens, one might focus on the appealing, sentimental figure alone, reducing the rest to out-of-focus, "leisurely" background. But Riis's camera puts it all in focus at once: everything is figure, everything is field. The eye ranging over such a photograph finds its aesthetic expectations defeated and must engage the "evidence" with a new act of imagination.[25] Writing of Atget,

24. Peter Conrad, *The Art of the City: Views and Versions of New York* (New York, 1984), 68.
25. Peter Hales writes: "The unerring specificity and literalness of the camera are here used by Riis to save the picture from the threat of sentimentality and keep it true to its subject. . . . The popular illustration of his time was bent on imposing sentimental models on the poor or converting them into picturesque 'types.' Riis emphasized the photographic qualities of the medium: its specificity, its almost overwhelm-

Walter Benjamin spoke of how photographs strip away the "aura" from pictures, just as bourgeois ownership and exploitation have stripped the aura from reality.[26] The American Riis would have served him as a more complete witness than Atget could.

The shock of these juxtapositions reaches the viewer today much less impeded than it could in 1890. The original edition contained about fifteen photographs, in murky halftones that submerged much of their detail. The other twenty-two illustrations were all engraved line drawings, most of them based on photographs, but very different in effect. Their draftsmanship is of high quality, and some of them reproduce the camera's way of presenting perspective. But the tone is lighter; the pictures are mostly white paper. The backgrounds have been suppressed, the litter cleaned from the floors, the mounds of street soil hauled away. The composition fades artistically at its edges. In the ragpicker's home, the walls' coarse textures and the stained floor have been effaced, so the room feels less confining (Fig. 8). The tubs at the right no longer bulge (too close to us for comfort) into the drawing's geometrics. And this madonna seems to sit before, rather than among, the soiled refuse of her husband's trade. Even the halftones, through cropping and lost detail, undergo a comparable simplification. Where the Street Arabs sleep, the grating has softened into a few parallel lines, and above their heads the downspout and the rubbish cans have disappeared: the Arabs have become the Babes, huddled against a seemingly rustic wall (Fig. 9).[27] Imposing their well-learned sense of artistic and social decorum, the illustrators overcame the challenging flatness of Riis's actual photographs, in which the sentimental and the intolerable are so powerfully joined in a single plane. By reducing the slum to a muted backdrop, they subverted the irony of violated decorum. What they rendered was, once again, and unquestionably, art.

What the illustrators suppressed was nothing so overtly ironic as a cross and dome. Riis does not set his figures against structures

---

ing attention to detail, the casual directness of the edges it drew around things, its ability to arrest the flux at moments packed with implication, its tendency to suggest relationships between things one might ordinarily consider unrelated, and its capacity to transform the mundane object into icon or symbol without divesting it of its reality" (*Silver Cities*, 191–92).

26. Walter Benjamin, "A Short History of Photography," in *Classic Essays on Photography*, ed. Alan Trachtenberg (New Haven, 1980), 208–10.

27. Riis, *How the Other Half Lives* (1890), 202.

Fig. 8 Kenyon Cox, after Jacob Riis, *In the Home of an Italian Ragpicker* (wood engraving, 1889)

From Jacob A. Riis, How the Other Half Lives: Studies Among the Tenements of New York *(1890)*

affirming the city's values. Rather, he presents them in the midst of their quotidian circumstances. Yet it is through these circumstances that Riis, like Dickens, reveals to his viewer-audience their common citizenship with the dispossessed. He aims to subvert not just the viewer's aesthetic sense, but his moral certainties as well. Dickens' ironies are themselves sentimentalizable: one can savor them without essential discomfort. Even Juvenal and Hogarth invite us to share their righteous indignation, for the context established by their city backgrounds affirms good sense and good citizenship. But in Riis's photographs the enveloping context for his figures prompts more unsettling feelings—repugnance, fear, anger, an urge to intervene.

Riis took these photographs to use as lantern slides for lectures addressed to his fellow citizens of New York—members of the other "other half" who shared at least a little of his care for their city. Those who first beheld these images were members of civic organizations and religious mission groups concerned with the problems of the poor. At about the same time in Chicago, Jane Addams was addressing similar groups, trying to lure suburban ladies to come

Fig. 9 Jacob Riis, *Street Arabs in Sleeping Quarters*
(engraving, 1890)

From Jacob A. Riis, How the Other Half Lives: Studies Among the Tenements of New York *(1890)*

down to Hull House and see for themselves—to enter the space of the poor.[28] Riis brought their poverty and oppression uptown. No disrespecter of any person or thing, his camera presented with infinite care the very things an artist would leave out or render imperfectly. Viewers trained to aestheticize and sentimentalize the poor were inveigled into Riis's pictures by the touching figures of mothers, children, and families, or accosted by the stares of young toughs; once inside, their pictorial sensibilities were assaulted by a welter of unsubordinated detail. There are no white spaces, no fading at the edges. Litter, paraphernalia, activity, and human presence crowd every corner of the picture—all wedged indecorously into a single plane of focus.

Viewers trained to assimilate the iconic detail of a Dutch interior must have felt intensely the conflict between those human figures

28. Jane Addams, *Twenty Years at Hull-House* (New York, 1912), 342–70. It is fashionable now to dismiss reformers like Addams and Riis as relatively privileged outsiders who brought into the slums a program based on their own values rather than on the actual situation of the poor. Although liberal intellectuals would always prefer that the masses put forth their own champions, reforms and revolutions are usually brought about by people with a base in the world of power as well as in the world of the oppressed.

Artful Juxtapositions

and the overpowering clutter that Riis's camera did not subordinate. To encounter these crowded photographs is to experience some of the sensory confusion and shock that one experiences in an utterly foreign setting: the inability to sort, select, and arrange one's experience; a failure of the primary imagination. The overcrowded picture plane matched, in its feeling, the overcrowded tenements and streets that were the object of Riis's crusades; the indecorous composition spoke of lives short on "decencies" (as his audience would have called them). And the random objects, unassimilable to any "artistic" purpose, again spoke accusingly to the primary imagination. But now the accusation is not just aesthetic, as it had been to Holmes. It is moral. *This is what you should have seen. If you had been there. If you had not been blind from birth.* The "problem" of poverty is reversed: it is not the poor who are "other," but rather the well-intentioned viewer, now put in a state of disequilibrium for which there is no adequate aesthetic remedy.[29]

At times, that disequilibrium is reinforced by the faces and postures of Riis's subjects. In concluding that what he is looking into is something like real space, rather than the artificially composed volume of a painting, the viewer of a Riis photograph encounters human presences occupying that space—not mirrors of his own emotion, but other persons, having selves of their own, to which he must respond on their terms as well as on his own. In such photographs, citizenship becomes, as it should be, a matter of negotiation. One of the most dramatic examples of this is the well-known *Bandit's Roost*. It uses a street perspective from Renaissance theater design to afford his bourgeois viewer with a glance down an alley lined with watchful forms leaning out of windows or lounging on stoops, with a pair of elegant toughs posed at its entrance and overtopped by a glare of sunlight aimed right in the viewer's eye. Perspective invites the imagination to enter; but the imagination also forewarns that viewer: *accosted . . . beaten . . . robbed*. Riis understood perfectly well that the reforms he sought would be motivated as much by fear as by compassion. His photographs demand that even those who "sympa-

---

29. In *Unreal Cities*, William Chapman Sharpe makes a similar evaluation of the "blind beggar" episode in book 7 of Wordsworth's *Prelude*. Citing Walter Benjamin's distinction between *Erlebnis* (in which shocking sights are transmuted into something familiar) and *Erfahrung* (in which the sight remains enduringly traumatic), Sharpe writes that "the blind beggar insists on the autonomy of the unknowable Other, the frightening independence of each member of the urban community" (21, 31).

thize" with the poor examine the complexity of their own sense of citizenship.

By violating pictorial conventions about foregrounding and decorum, Riis's photographs opened up a world that required of its viewers a moral response. His camera seemed to efface its own intervening, interpretive role and to set the viewers in the presence of tenement families and sweatshop children. Those who heard Riis's dramatic speeches and saw his pictures shuddered, wept, or talked back to the images they saw.[30] (Projected, they would have appeared life size.) It was not an aesthetic experience. The poor who confronted them were not picturesque, but wretched. And they appeared *real*. Riis's photographs, by the discord of responses they suggested, defeated the mechanisms by which viewers could keep these human beings at any comfortable distance.[31] The ironies they contained were not to be aesthetically savored, but politically contested. Reforms followed: slum clearance, building codes, sanitary requirements.

Peter Galassi observed, in a passage quoted above, that photography "found in the contingent qualities of perception a standard of artistic, and moral, authenticity."[32] Riis's photographs had an almost unprecedented moral relationship to their viewers. "What shall the pictures be that I hang on the walls?" Whitman had asked in his elegy for Lincoln (§11, *V*, II, 533); and the answer was, pictures that affirm the values—largely pastoral—of the American Republic. Art was to hang on the walls, as a Currier and Ives allegory of virtue, or to repose in a volume on the parlor table, like Krausz or Rejlander. It affirmed the moral values of those who purchased it and displayed it. But the faces and rooms that one encountered in Riis's work left no room for comfort. Even today, it is hard to imagine a domestic decor that could accommodate his sweated children, his exhausted women, his truculent men. They are, as Gertrude Stein once said of one of Hemingway's stories, *inaccrochable*. Today Riis can be recognized as an artist—but only if "art" can encompass such a process of imaginative displacement in which sentiment is set against docu-

---

30. Szasz and Bogardus, "The Camera and the American Social Conscience," 431; Hales, *Silver Cities*, 193.

31. "My words are words of a questioning, and to indicate reality," Walt Whitman had written in 1855; "the well-taken photographs. . . . but your wife or friend close and solid in your arms?" ("Song of Myself," §42, *V*, I, 68).

32. Galassi, *Before Photography*, 28.

mentation, aesthetic motives against moral ones, beneficent intentions against the recognition of complicity.

The stereographs and dioramas of the midnineteenth century had sought in the physiology of vision a way to simulate the experience of depth. In "Crossing Brooklyn Ferry," Whitman had found that by manipulating his range of focus and by reiterating the pattern of images he could cross over from Not-Me to You, and then to We. Riis's photographs, effacing physical depth while encouraging his viewers to recognize the complexity of their own relationship to poverty, found a way to compel his viewers out of the comfort of their presumed otherness and to set them in the presence of the victimized: "This is how our fellow citizens live. . . . This is how *we* live."

❖

After the Civil War, the city became "visible" for American artists. First it was the city of those who bought the paintings. John Singer Sargent painted the urbane amusements of the American international set; Childe Hassam, the atmosphere of parks and boulevards. The later decades around the turn of the twentieth century have been remembered as the Progressivist era and the time of the "discovery of the poor."[33] Writers like Frank Norris (*The Pit*, 1903) and Upton Sinclair (*The Jungle*, 1906) or a painter like John Sloan could consider themselves citizens and dedicate their art to civic reform. "Renaissance" movements in Chicago and New York encouraged artists to identify with their cities and to find their subjects in urban life.[34] The New York Realists—John Sloan, George Luks, Everett Shinn, William Glackens, and George Bellows—frequently painted the life of the Other Half: street scenes, immigrant festivals, the demimonde of theater and saloon. Most of them had learned their trade as illustrators for magazines and newspapers, mediating images of common life to the public just before the coming of techniques to reproduce photographs directly in print. Appropriately or necessarily, they were also readers of Walt Whitman. Robert Henri, their mentor, frequently invoked Whitman not only as an artist unabashed by aca-

---

33. The title of Robert Bremner's *From the Depths: The Discovery of Poverty in the United States* (New York, 1956).

34. Shloss, *In Visible Light*, 112; Arthur Frank Wertheim, *The New York Little Renaissance* (New York, 1976).

demic standards or popular disapproval, but as one whose passion for life had found expression in the personal and the commonplace.[35]

At first they did meet disapproval. They were called "the Black Gang" by some of the genteel academic painters, among them Kenyon Cox, one of the illustrators who tidied up Riis's pictures for the first edition of *How the Other Half Lives*.[36] Later they were called the "Ashcan" school, impudent painters of ugliness. Today these paintings appear not as impudence but as an extension of the American tradition of Inness, Homer, and Eakins, informed by the photographically influenced work of Degas and Manet. Vigorous, attractive (and altogether *accrochable*), they assimilated hitherto invisible reaches of the American city into the vocabulary of twentieth-century painting. From the glamorous theaters and concert halls of Everett Shinn to George Luks's vivid portrayals of immigrant children and of Hester Street, these painters followed the doctrine of Emerson and Whitman that they had heard from Henri—that the Matter of America required only an eye that could see it, a democratic eye judging not as the judge judges but as the sun falling around a helpless thing. "Whitman's descriptive catalogues of life . . . helped to interest me in the details of life around me," Sloan said later.[37]

At times they saw New York with Whitman's *flâneur*'s eye, recording surfaces; but at their greatest, these artists convey a sense of familiar, inhabited space. An apt name for them would be the Clothesline School. As an example of those objects that a painter would leave out, while the photograph impartially recorded them, Oliver Wendell Holmes had chosen the clothesline: "Among the accidents of life, as delineated in the stereograph, there is one that rarely fails in any extended view which shows us the details of streets and buildings. . . . Clothes-drying, or a place to dry clothes on, the stereoscopic photograph insists on finding, wherever it gives us a group of houses. This is the city of Berne. How it brings the people who sleep under that roof before us to see their sheets drying on that fence!"[38] In Riis's photographs, pathetic festoons of laundry drape

---

35. Robert Henri, *The Art-Spirit: Notes, Articles, Fragments of Letters and Talks . . .*, comp. Margery Ryerson (1923; rpr. Philadelphia, 1960), 85, 142, 147; see also Joseph J. Kwiat, "Robert Henri and the Emerson-Whitman Tradition," *PMLA*, LXXI (1956), 617–36.
36. Bennard B. Perlman, *The Immortal Eight* (New York, 1962), 171, 158.
37. In a 1948 interview with Joseph Kwiat cited in Kwiat, "Henri," 620n.
38. Holmes, "The Stereoscope and the Stereograph," 59.

Artful Juxtapositions 225

many a tottering balcony or fire escape; above the ominous alley in *Bandit's Roost* hang ironic rows of shirts and chemises. The Realists discovered the clothesline both as an artistic opportunity—a catenary of rectangular and sinuous forms—and (like Holmes) as an image evoking the common folk who dwelt below the rooftops, inside the fire escapes, above the cluttered areaways. The clothesline painters asserted (without the polemical ironies of Riis) that these too are citizens of New York, laughing, gnawing, sleeping, living the same life with the rest. On them too shines the bright light of Monet; they too come and go through streets suffused in the atmospherics of Inness or Degas.

None of the Realists felt his citizenship more intensely than Sloan, a transplanted Philadelphian. He kept a diary of those years around 1910 when Henri's group was most intensely engaged with city life; excerpts from it have been published as *John Sloan's New York Scene*.[39] They are the pages of a very literate painter, who read a good deal and who wrote fluently about his own quotidian life and the life he observed around his studio on west 23rd Street. His empathy for all of that life led him out onto the streets and roofs of lower Manhattan, and it led him into Socialist politics. Each of these engagements produced its own form of art.

During those years, Sloan relied for income mainly on commissioned work for mass-circulation publications, including illustrations for stories in the *Saturday Evening Post, Collier's,* and other popular magazines. His paintings reflect his successful grasp on the conventions of those popular art forms. Some resemble journalistic "human interest" or "feature" art—representative scenes of city life or renderings of particular places. Others emulate the photographer who captures the humor of some momentary conjunction of people or circumstances. Others imply a narrative. Distrustful of the camera and even the sketchbook, Sloan walked his city as did Whitman, now a self-conscious see-er, now bound by empathy to what he saw.[40]

Sloan shared Riis's interest in the "invisible" and indecorous in urban life, but his techniques had little to do with massing conflicting detail on a single plane of attention. Nor, through most of his urban phase, did he make moral demands upon his viewers. At first

39. Bruce St. John, ed., *John Sloan's New York Scene* (New York, 1965).
40. *Ibid.*, 242. See also Lloyd Goodrich, *John Sloan* (New York, 1952), 20–22; and Van Wyck Brooks, *John Sloan: A Painter's Life* (New York, 1955), 57–70.

he was the observer, in and out of the game and watching and wondering at it. His first essay into depicting the New York scene was a series of etchings, influenced by Daumier, whom he admired not for his furious satire but for his rendering of "the homely things."[41] He drew what he saw on the streets and in the tenements of the city, often with a humorous irony about displays of wealth and fashion.[42] Ladies in a carriage on Fifth Avenue inspect the couture and equipage of another *grande dame*. Preadolescent girls giggle over the display in a corsetmaker's showcase while past them strolls a plump woman whose figure also advertises the corsetmaker's wares.

At times the irony shifts from the subjects to forces out of sight, and the humor softens into sympathy. In *Women's Page,* a woman sits in the single room she shares with her young son: she is wearing only a chemise; her hair is unkempt; the room is strewn with laundry she hasn't finished scrubbing in the tub beside the dresser. She is reading the fashion pages of her newspaper. In later years, Sloan commented twice on this etching, in 1949 saying "It's the irony of that I was putting over," and in 1945 insisting it was "done with sympathy but no 'social consciousness.'"[43] Both statements are true: Sloan sympathizes with the woman's situation—the impossibility of ever "catching up," the pleasure of fantasy. His irony is directed toward the image of womanhood offered by the newspaper; but there is no "social consciousness," that is, none of the reformist anger of Jacob Riis, no dramatized incongruity between planes or areas within the etching itself. The most Riis-like of the series, *Roofs, Summer Night,* depicts a tenement rooftop to which the residents have fled to escape the heat of their rooms. The roof is covered with sleepers, adults and children. The intimacy of their repose contrasts with the crowding, the lack of privacy, and the uncleanliness of the roof. The irony, again, is gentler than that of Riis. Sloan has come not to make an example of their housing conditions, but to share their restless slumbers.

Summarizing his credo as an artist, Sloan late in his life wrote: "The best creative inspiration and stimulation you can get is the tempting impossibility of expressing by signs the third-dimensional realization of Things. . . . Keep your mind on such homely things, such deep-seated truths of reality, that there is no room for the su-

---

41. John Sloan, *The Gist of Art* (New York, 1939), 41.
42. Peter Morse, ed., *John Sloan's Prints* (New Haven, Conn., 1969), 134–49.
43. *Ibid.*, 141.

perficial. . . . Don't be afraid to be human. Draw with human kindness, with appreciation for the marvel of existence."[44] Drawing with human kindness, while attempting to realize the three-dimensional being of homely things, was Sloan's approach to rendering city life. A painter in the perspectivist tradition, Sloan opens up volumes of space—rooms, areaways, squares, streets—that are inhabited by his fellow humans. "Use the background as a container for the people," he told his students. "Make it solid. Get the textures of the buildings and ground and sky. Find something to say about the quality of the place, the real atmosphere, the feeling of light and color. . . . Go out in the street and see how simply the [human] figures exist as textures upon the surroundings."[45]

In his book on Sloan, written for the 1952 Whitney Museum retrospective, Lloyd Goodrich wrote: "The chief motivating force of Sloan's art was his interest in human beings—not humanity as a vague abstraction but actual men and women, his many friends, and beyond them, the city's millions. . . . He liked the places and occasions when people got together for sociability and enjoyment—restaurants, barrooms, dance halls, parks, and that new phenomenon, the five-cent movie. He enjoyed character, in people and in places, and the humor of daily life. . . . With all his naturalistic gusto for truth, his viewpoint was fundamentally affirmative."[46] This description identifies Sloan's affinity with Whitman (and also a profound difference between them, as we will see presently). "Read some of Whitman's 'Song of Myself,'" Sloan wrote in late May of 1909; "Then out for a walk in the sunshine." A year later he writes "I walked across Brooklyn Bridge for the first time. I enjoyed it immensely. . . . I walked a little in Brooklyn which was the town Whitman knew so well, and on the bridge I thought of Whitman's Brooklyn Ferry."[47] The titles and subjects of Sloan's paintings in those years read like a catalog from "Song of Myself," linking two visualist temperaments seeking the path between commonplace things and the soul:

44. Sloan, *The Gist of Art*, 41.
45. Ibid., 78–79.
46. Goodrich, *John Sloan*, 22.
47. St. John, ed., *Sloan's New York Scene*, 314, 428. Both of these Maytime readings of Whitman may be connected with the poet's birthday (May 31); on the evening of this walk to Brooklyn, Sloan and his wife attended the Whitman Fellowship Dinner and talked with their friend Horace Traubel, one of Whitman's confidants and literary executors.

> On a rooftop, a woman is hanging out laundry .... it is
> sunset ... the apartment building yonder looms
> against the bright clouds ... trolleys glimmer in the
> street below;
> A dust storm is whirling across Fifth Avenue ... the
> children scurry for doorways ... ladies in white
> dresses cling to their hats and their skirts;
> It is a gray morning on the ferry .... she stands alone at
> the after railing ... there is nothing for her to see;
> On the roof-top two friends have opened their coops ....
> white and black, the pigeons whirl in the evening
> sky;
> It is Election Night .... under the El the crowds are
> rejoicing .... with horns, with masks, with fists of
> confetti, gangs of them dance about the bonfires or
> press against the lighted shopwindows;
> In the tavern's back room the old man sits by a window
> .... his mug of ale rests on the table .... he is
> recollecting his many friends.

In many of the paintings from those years, there is an implied narrative, as there had been in the genre paintings of Mount and Bingham and as there often was in the entries in the catalogs of Whitman's poems, especially at those points where the flow of consciousness was temporarily arrested by a flow of empathy from Whitman into the life-space of the other person. Sloan's paintings often choose a moment when the pose and situation of his people seem representative. He is a genre painter whose subjects—like those in Mayhew, Riis, and the other early pictorial sociologists—typify groups or common activities among city people. What gives life to these subjects, though, is Sloan's recognition of how the depicted moment represents the quality and history of their individual lives. In *Chinese Restaurant* (Fig. 10), a young couple sits at a table: the man, crude-featured, still wearing his hat, eats vigorously from a bowl just a few inches below his mouth; across from him a young woman sits, "elegantly dressed" (according to Sloan's diary), the scarlet plume in her hat dulling the red of the woodwork that frames her.[48] From her small dish she is tossing bits of food to an attentive gray-and-white cat. At another table, behind her, two well-dressed

---

48. *Ibid.*, 292.

Fig. 10 John Sloan, *Chinese Restaurant* (oil painting, 1909)
Courtesy the Memorial Art Gallery of the University of Rochester; Marion Stratton Gould Fund

men take in the scene with amusement—perhaps with interest. Years later, Sloan amplified the story: "The girl is feeding her boy friend before taking him home."[49] With little appetite of her own, she is poised at the center of a web of appetite; her byplay with the cat occupies a moment of deferral and perhaps extends it. Something better may come along.

Although some of this narrative element may follow from his work as a story illustrator, it also stems from his impulse to draw "with human kindness," an impulse of fellow-feeling for his subjects that is comparable to Whitman's. While capturing a moment of visual recognition, the painting "goes with" its subject, as Whitman would say, acknowledging the rhythm of his or her life, imagining the other's share in the life of their city. Sloan frequently channeled that sense of empathy through the women whom he depicted. A painting's leitmotif is often determined by the implied situation or

49. Sloan, *The Gist of Art*, 221.

story of the woman or women who appear in it. Conventions of pictorial sentiment seldom dictate their poses, nor does his art reduce them to objects to be desired or protected. But it is some aspect of their femininity, as Sloan felt it, responding to the urban space they occupy, that composes his painting.

Sloan's encounter with the city has an erotic element like Whitman's.[50] He had difficulty exhibiting his *New York Life* series in shows or galleries and was unable to sell the ten as a set, because several of them were thought vulgar or indecent. In the "corsetmaker" etching, one girl's hand is comparing her own undeveloped breast with the corpulent bosom of the mannequin. Other etchings acknowledge the sexual life of the poor. In *Man, Wife, and Child,* a young man and woman are embracing: his suspenders are unfastened; she is tugging at the collar of his shirt. Their happiness with each other shows also in the face of their little daughter, who is watching them.[51] In *Turning Out the Light,* a woman kneels on her bed to extinguish the gaslight, turning her head to smile invitingly at the man who shares the bed.

Sloan's sensuality usually involves *seeing*—not just the artist and his friend the viewer, but also onlookers in the picture. In *Chinese Restaurant*, the men at the other table brings into the painting the viewer's grasp of the situation. In his many drawings and paintings of parks, the men watch the women and the women show off for them. In a later etching, *Night Windows,* a woman hangs out laundry from a window, while on the roof just above, her husband is watching a woman undress in her flat across the areaway. With Sloan we watch all three. "Psychologists say we all have a little peeper instinct," he remarked on these etchings later.[52] Against that instinct, which his art required, Sloan set his deep affection for the people he portrayed.

Like Whitman, he follows his subjects off the streets, through a window, into the intimate spaces of their dwellings. His notes and diaries repeatedly identify the source of a drawing or painting as something he saw in the apartments behind his studio or on the

50. Peter Conrad writes: "Sloan's initial predecessor is the confessional Whitman. . . . [His] New York is lovingly stripped of the defenses in which it's clad and shown to be a body, warmly comforting and carnally needy" (*The Art of the City,* 90).

51. Sloan later remarked, piously, "The conjugal status given by this title always has, I hope, prevented any improper interpretation being placed on this scene" (Morse, ed., *John Sloan's Prints,* 145).

52. Ibid., 141.

Artful Juxtapositions   231

nearby rooftops.[53] When the window shows in the picture, as in *Night Windows,* the voyeurism is often subject to Sloan's humorous irony; in the oil painting *Hairdresser's Window,* a group of seven or eight people watch from the sidewalk (the men gaping, the women laughing) as the hairdresser, in a second-story window, prepares to bleach the hair of a woman who is sitting with her back to the window. At other times, the window is a passageway between subject and viewer, and the painting's emotional tone is governed by the passage between two volumes of space, public and private. In *A Window on the Street,* a young woman (who looks rather like those pre-Raphaelite women Sloan had once drawn for newspapers) leans pensively on the sill of an open window, chin in hand, elbow on a cushion, her gaze directed obliquely down the street. Masonry and window frame define a plane of focus that contains almost every object in the painting. The woman's pose, however, invites interpretation. A penny for her thoughts. We would like to see further into her mood. Sloan himself was moved to conjecture, saying later that his subject in this painting was "the sullen wistfulness of the woman whose housekeeping was limited to one room."[54] In the dimly lit room behind her can be seen a chair, a bed, a bowl atop a dresser. She yearns outward from it, while we viewers peer in, discerning only a few vague shapes, attempting to match the background with the mood of the foreground figure. The space she occupies, we see, is not just a single furnished room, but the defining and confining framework of a way of life. Yet the painting respects that space, adumbrating it as background to her presence at the window but not presuming to anatomize it. In a pen-and-crayon drawing of the same subject a year later, the woman's surroundings are more clearly visible and more squalid. This visual flatness makes it a far less evocative work. The rendition of depth is essential to the emotional transference that the painting achieves.

In other paintings, the window passage is only implied: in *Three A.M.* (Fig. 11), a young woman in her nightgown, smoking a cigarette, turns meat in a skillet while another girl, fully dressed, talks to her. This painting too came from what he saw through his windows, but here we are brought up close. The canvas has become the window. We are brought close psychologically as well. Sloan's paint-

53. St. John, ed., *Sloan's New York Scene, passim;* also see Brooks, *John Sloan,* 61–63.
54. Sloan, *The Gist of Art,* 230.

Fig. 11 John Sloan, *Three A.M.* (oil painting, 1909)
Courtesy The Philadelphia Museum of Art; given by Mrs. Cyrus McCormick

ing does not reduce them to Not-Me, nor does it assert over them the voyeur's power to see and remain detached because he is himself unseen. It serves as an aperture through which the viewer enters their presence. We are inside their kitchen, sharing their intimacy, sharing the story she is telling over her cup of tea. We share as well their time: the overlapping of two circadian rhythms in the deep hour of night is so essential to the implied narrative that Sloan provides it as a title. Sloan brings us to them on equal terms—as he does the men tending their pigeons, the three women drying their hair in the sun, the families sleeping on the hot rooftop, the table of literati at Petit-pas' pension, and all the other subjects whom he catches in moments of intimacy. Generously, out of their own confidence and vitality, they accept us within the private spaces they have created. Of *Three*

Artful Juxtapositions 233

A.M. he later said, "This picture is redolent with the atmosphere of a poor, back, gaslit room. It has beauty, I'll not deny it; it must be that human life is beautiful."[55]

When Goodrich spoke of Sloan's enjoyment of "character in people and in places," he named a quality rarely seen in Whitman's poetry. Only in "Crossing Brooklyn Ferry" did Whitman dramatize an engagement with the existential spaces of Manhattan and Brooklyn that allowed him to cross over from I to We. His intimate familiarity with New York, evident in his prose and journalism, had no place in most of his poetry, where experiences are generalized in order to make them more universal. Sloan, whose daily walks and whose sociability made him as much the habitan of lower Manhattan as Whitman had been, specified the names of his scenes and painted their likenesses: "Fifth Avenue"; "Sixth Avenue and Thirtieth Street" (a lithograph and an oil both bore this title); "Sixth Avenue Elevated at Third Street"; ". . . Herald Square"; ". . . Madison Square"; ". . . Union Square"; "Renganeschi's"; "Petitpas'"; "McSorley's"; "The Haymarket"; "Jefferson Market, Sixth Avenue." He caught them in particular atmospheres, at particular moments: at sunset, in falling snow, at rush hour. By rendering the individuating textures and quality of a place, he established a ground for common citizenship for his subjects and his viewers. Keeping his mind and his eye on homely, local things, he found (as he put it) the deep-seated truths of reality.[56]

Whitman, a simple separate person, experienced the city en masse. To his globalizing consciousness, the particulars that distinguished Madison Square from Washington Square would have been less important than the difference between I and Not-Me. His radical democratic temperament (and perhaps his strain of transcendentalism) rejected intermediate, interpreting structures between the Self and the All. Sloan, however, was not a simple separate person, but rather one who affiliated himself with his adopted city not only through a wide network of private friendships but also through public associations of artists, such as the committees that arranged the 1910 Exhibition of Independent Artists and other shows, and the Society of Independent Artists, whose presidency he held for twenty-six years. And in the heyday of his engagement with New York, he entered directly into political life as well.

55. *Ibid.*, 220.
56. *Ibid.*, 41, quoted above.

In May, 1909—the same month when he was reading "Song of Myself" and walking in the sunshine—he was reading *The Conservator,* the Socialist magazine published by Whitman's literary executor, Horace Traubel.[57] He also read Eugene Debs's platform for the Socialist party and began meeting with the leaders of the Socialists in New York. One night he walked down to Jefferson Market night court and watched the magistrate sentencing prostitutes and women vagrants and drunks—the women Riis had been photographing twenty years earlier. On entering, Sloan accidentally sat down "on the women's side of the room," and though the bailiffs soon ordered him to move, his sense that these voteless women were being treated without justice or humanity put him firmly on their side.[58] (In "Song of Myself" he would have read, "Not a mutineer walks handcuff'd to jail but I am handcuff'd to him and walk by his side, / [. . .] / Not a youngster is taken for larceny but I go up too and am tried and sentenced" [§37, *V,* I, 59].) Before the end of 1909, he and his wife had joined the Socialist party, and during the next two years they were fiercely involved in the meetings and causes of that party: he drew cartoons for their magazines, and in 1910 he ran for the New York state assembly on the Socialist ticket.

In 1912, as he began to disengage from active politics, he joined Max Eastman in reorganizing a journal, *The Masses,* which was socialist in concern and tone but not doctrinaire in editorial policy. Sloan served as art editor and provided many cartoons and illustrations.[59] Although his preoccupation with the city as a subject for oils began to wane around the same time (his palette changed, he began to summer in Gloucester, and New York was being rebuilt in a vertical and commercial form less congenial to his eye), his graphics continued to depict the city, and from a political viewpoint that grew from the sense of comradeship implicit in his paintings of city dwellers.

Some of these drawings are fiercely polemical and make use of a foreshortened picture plane to thrust incongruous images upon the reader. Most of them, though, draw upon the varying blends of sympathy, humor, and irony on which he had grounded his urban painting: shopgirls coming home from work; a young nursemaid on

---

57. Joseph J. Kwiat, "John Sloan: An American Artist as Social Critic, 1900–1917," *Arizona Quarterly,* X (Spring, 1954), 54.
58. St. John, ed., *Sloan's New York Scene,* 314.
59. David W. Scott, *John Sloan* (New York, 1975), 110–14.

a park swing, enjoying a brief return to the joy of the playground; Isadora Duncan dancing; stylishly dressed women and men gawking at Indians wearing tribal attire on Broadway; a bedraggled but unpathetic street woman cursing some tormentor—who stands just where the reader is. These are neither the Dickensian humble poor nor the oppressed masses of Socialist propaganda. Confident and unreflecting democrats, they occupy fully the space and time of their lives. To publish their images, rather than the fashionable lay-figures seen in the mass-circulation magazines, was a political declaration of faith in a cooperative commonwealth, like the one Whitman had made in "Song of the Broad-Axe." But it did not seem so to the other editors of *The Masses,* who wanted more ideologically explicit material; and in 1916 Sloan gave up his editorship and withdrew from party activity, though not from the beliefs and sympathies that had first led him to the Socialist cause.

He withdrew as well from the city, summering in New England and in the Southwest and painting the landscapes there. His urban interiors became backdrops for studies of the female nude, as he privatized both the sensuality of the earlier work and his concern with the volume and texture of city spaces. The man had changed; and so had his city and the kind of art it fostered.

[8]

Fierce Momentary Tension: T. S. Eliot and William Carlos Williams

T. S. Eliot was writing the "Preludes" in Boston around 1910, during the heyday of the New York Realists. His first Prelude seems almost to refer to Everett Shinn or John Sloan:

> And now a gusty shower wraps
> The grimy scraps
> Of withered leaves about your feet
> And newspapers from vacant lots;
> The showers beat
> On broken blinds and chimney-pots,
> And at the corner of the street
> A lonely cab-horse steams and stamps.
>
> (*CPE*, 13)

And the fourth Prelude draws its concluding simile from the world that Jacob Riis had made visible: "The worlds revolve like ancient women / Gathering fuel in vacant lots"[1] (*CPE*, 15). The women, though, are present only as a metaphor of hopelessness; for between the cab-horse and the women falls an introspective process revealing that Eliot is recounting a tour through his own brain-gallery rather than a walk in the streets:

> You dozed, and watched the night revealing
> The thousand sordid images
> Of which your soul was constituted;

---

1. Hales's *Silver Cities* includes a newspaper photograph from 1903, depicting a consequence of the coal shortage: "Women [in an empty city lot] Picking up Wood for Fuel" (271).

> They flickered against the ceiling,
> And when all the world came back
> And the light crept up between the shutters
> And you heard the sparrows in the gutters,
> You had such a vision of the street
> As the street hardly understands.
>
> (CPE, 14)

"I am moved," he writes near the end, "by fancies that are curled / Around these images." This is just the modern man whom Buber described. His *I* contains the world, explicitly reduced to "images"; and yet there is nothing to the *I* except its hoard of images and fancies.

This poem, and several other urban nocturnes like "Rhapsody on a Windy Night," play on the unpredictable variety of consciousness, just as Whitman's "The Sleepers" had done. Eliot's poetry is often portrayed as the antithesis of Whitman's, but his first three books dramatize the same state of mind that Whitman confronted in the "dark" passages and poems written between 1855 and 1860—a self-awareness poised to implode into solipsism. Eliot's major poems from those books struggle between total subjectivity and total objectivity, between I and Not-Me. This struggle can be measured by the kind of irony with which Eliot juxtaposes images of an urban world.

"The Love Song of J. Alfred Prufrock" is the meditation of a reclusive man for whom the world has become a panorama of images—"as if a magic lantern threw the nerves in patterns on a screen" (*CPE*, 6). Will he attend this afternoon's tea, or not? To do so entails a passage through the streets. Obediently projecting a series of "experiences" for the route and for his destination, the mind revels in indecorous juxtapositions:

> Let us go then, you and I,
> When the evening is spread out against the sky
> Like a patient etherised upon a table;
> . . . .
> Would it have been worth while,
> After the sunsets and the dooryards and the sprinkled
>   streets,
> After the novels, after the teacups, after the skirts that
>   trail along the floor—

. . . .
> Shall I say, I have gone at dusk through narrow streets
> And watched the smoke that rises from the pipes
> Of lonely men in shirt-sleeves, leaning out of win-
>   dows? . . .
>
> (CPE, 3, 6, 5)

Prufrock takes a connoisseur's pleasure in the discord of these subjective images and ultimately chooses to stay at home with them. Like the images in "Preludes," these are not altogether fantastic. They match with a visual world and can be situated within a city's existential space. There is the home-space where Prufrock stands, featureless within, but surrounded by a yellow fog that isolates and insulates it. Outside are the streets and finally the goal-space—the rooms of tea and porcelain, of music and artistic chatter, which Prufrock knows intimately. The streets are much like those of Sloan, full of apertures into other lives—the doors of cheap hotels and oyster bars, the windows where lonely smokers sit. The lives within them are forbiddingly "low" and unapproachable. The party, too, is a matter of entrances into rooms where he will be scrutinized, into conversation where he might ask, or answer, some "overwhelming question." Compared with his seamless gallery of two-dimensional images, these are terrifying spaces indeed. Imagining them, he can be wry about their superficiality. But thinking further, projecting into them his own actual presence, they open into four-dimensional passages where any response might tumble him into another life, an unforeseen avowal. By tracing Prufrock's imaginary journeys, Eliot's poem charts the abyss that he is avoiding.

There is a norm, then, against which Eliot's ironies are measured as Juvenal's were against ancestral Rome—the *civitas* of social, personal, and sexual commitments. But Eliot cannot invoke this world directly. Sharing Prufrock's reticence, his poem hints at values it cannot directly invoke. So the poem presents directly only the aesthetic incongruities detected by Prufrock, while reducing to innuendo Eliot's ironic criticism of the privatized subjectivity from which Prufrock projects the images of which his soul is constituted.

The Waste Land abounds with ironic juxtapositions of language, setting, and historical moment. At once the handbook of disjunctive "modernist" literary techniques, a poem simulating the associations and dissociations of consciousness, and the indispensable literary text on the modern city, *The Waste Land* is founded on discontinuity and incongruity. It dismisses itself as "a heap of broken images" and "fragments." Although readers today are possessed of many guides to the ruins, Eliot's poem must always be understood as a mosaic of unrelated surfaces. In this city poem one might encounter anything, at almost any place. Its intersections are clogged with interfering traffic. One of its notes refers us to a pair of lines from Charles Baudelaire: "*Fourmillante cité, cité pleine de rêves, / Où le spectre, en plein jour, raccroche le passant!*"[2] ("Swarming city, city filled with dreams, / Where ghosts in broad daylight accost the passerby!"). In an essay, Eliot mentions these lines as the epitome of his experience growing up in an industrial city in America.[3] Eliot's city, like Whitman's, is a teeming nation of nations, a state of mind intermixing not only different levels of society, but different kinds of reality. Crowds of people crossing London Bridge are twinned with the legions of the spiritually irresolute whom Dante saw drifting about the gateway to Hell. Later in the poem, the word "horns" hinges between a Renaissance poem about a staghunt and Eliot's description of noisy motorcars in a modern red-light district. Such juxtapositions should be incongruous, but are they? If incongruous, they could be ironic, but are they? There appears no basis for establishing preferments or making discriminations. Yet they seem unlike Whitman's egalitarian shifts from bride to opium-eater, from prostitute to president. They seem to imply judgments, but despair of a judge's authority. Eliot's city is best understood not as egalitarian, but as profane. The spiritual values by which ironies might be accurately discerned have been effaced. His prophet, unlike Isaiah, has found no godly vision in the Temple; his satirist, though still keen-scented as Juvenal in ferreting out corruption, confronts it with impotent sadness rather than with fury. Everywhere in *The Waste Land* there is irony; but it is equivocal, detached, self-deprecating, and self-protecting.

The prophet's measuring-rod is still near the poem, but only by reference: an end-note invites a diligent reader to consult the book

2. Charles Baudelaire, "Les Sept Vieillards," in *Les Fleurs du Mal*, ed. M. Mathews and J. Mathews (New York, 1953), 331.

3. "From Baudelaire I learned first, a precedent for the poetical possibilities, never developed by any poet writing in my own language, of the more sordid aspects of the modern metropolis, of the possibility of fusion between the sordidly realistic and the phantasmagoric, the possibility of the juxtaposition of the matter-of-fact and the fantastic" (T. S. Eliot, "What Dante Means to Me," *To Criticize the Critic and Other Writings* [London, 1965], 126–27).

of Ezekiel. The fury of Swift and Johnson is close at hand, but only in the subtext to be found in the poem's original typescript, where among discarded pages one may read a heavy and unequivocal apostrophe to London and its "swarming life" that knows "neither how to think, nor how to feel."[4] What were subjective "images" in the "Preludes" now are objectified in Eliot's jeremiad on the physical and spiritual oppression of the Londoners. In these canceled pages, prophetic voices invoke the ideal cities of Plato and of Saint John, urging the citizen-reader to recoil from the City of Mammon and to do penance. But none of this is actually in *The Waste Land*. It has settled into the poem's underground, like some Roman temple beneath a city bank.

Ghosts from this underworld do occasionally accost the passerby. Although the poem presents a sequence of disparate "experiences" bathed in a neutralizing irony, though Eliot was temporarily fascinated by Ezra Pound's modernist doctrine of the autonomous text, though he was bound by a powerful sense of scruple and shame to "depersonalize" his writing, there are interstices in its panoply of image and allusion through which the reader is implored to make a decision: "HURRY UP PLEASE ITS TIME" says a voice that is not just the pub-keeper's, and it speaks from the poem's inaccessible depths. But *The Waste Land* is very nearly an equivocation. Should the reader be angry with this London? or moved to pity for its infinite suffering? Or does it call for an aesthete's detachment from rights and wrongs, a cameralike eye that detects, composes, and savors from a spectator's distance the extraordinary surface collisions of city life? How is the poet to inhabit his city?

❖

Later in life, Eliot found a schema that would structure his life as a citizen of London and also undergird his plays and *Four Quartets*. But the poise between fascination and alienation, in his first address to the city, was also the dilemma that the city offered to a man who saw himself as Eliot's antagonist, William Carlos Williams. Eliot's deliverance as man and poet followed from his commitment to what he termed a culture, a structure of mediating associations that set

---

4. T. S. Eliot, *The Waste Land: A Facsimile and Transcript of the Original Drafts Including the Annotations of Ezra Pound,* ed. Valerie Eliot (New York, 1974), 43.

him within a shared four-dimensional world. Thus he escaped from the void that Whitman had found between the I and the Not-Me, between devouring the world and being reduced to one of its objects.[5] Williams, who stayed in America, knew he could not simply evade Whitman's individualist legacy in national and urban consciousness. He wrote, early in his career, "We cannot advance until we have grasped Whitman and then built upon him."[6] The advances within Williams' career obliged him again and again to grapple with the protean Whitman, whom he could follow only by not imitating him. But their mutual concern with the public role of poetry would lead both men to encounters with the city's manifest surfaces and unfathomable depths.

Williams served as a physician for the people of Rutherford, New Jersey, and the surrounding cities of an industrial precinct a few miles west of the Hudson River. His aspirations as a poet led him to a dilemma that Whitman also had faced. Was he to be the bard and wound-dresser, or would he write of Self and of the Modern Man as a separate and private person, immured in the magic prison of consciousness, the doors of libraries closed to him? For Williams, the decision was never final nor the choices always irreconcilable; but by 1923, influenced by the modernist painters and photographers in his acquaintance, he had espoused a modernist poetics of fragments and of surfaces, and with it the latter role.

This choice was reluctant but inevitable, given his individualist nurture and postwar America's indifference to art.[7] But he began as a citizen poet. He was still claiming a public role for poetry in his 1925 prose work, *In the American Grain,* and in an essay, "The American Background" (1934). "Unless everything that is, proclaim a

---

5. Eliot's few remarks about Whitman are directed toward his metrics and his use of languages. Perhaps his distaste for the techniques kept him from reading carefully those poems in which Whitman confesses to states of mind that Prufrock and Sweeney also knew. *Mon semblable, mon frère!*

6. William Carlos Williams, "America, Whitman, and the Art of Poetry," *Poetry Journal,* VIII (November, 1917), 31. Of the countless studies of this relationship, the three most profound are James E. Breslin, "William Carlos Williams and the Whitman Tradition," in *Literary Criticism and Historical Understanding,* ed. Phillip Damon (New York, 1967), 151–79, and "Whitman and the Early Development of William Carlos Williams," *PMLA,* LXXXII (1967), 613–21; and Stephen Tapscott, *American Beauty: William Carlos Williams and the Modernist Whitman* (New York, 1984).

7. See David Frail, *The Early Politics and Poetics of William Carlos Williams* (Ann Arbor, Mich., 1987). Jeffrey Walker agrees, though he places the responsibility on the poet's rhetorical choices rather than on a philistine audience (*Bardic Ethos,* 154–202).

ground on which it stand, it has no worth," he wrote; but though "what has been morally, aesthetically worth while in America has rested upon peculiar and discoverable ground," Americans from the beginning have been unable to discover it: "we recognize no ground our own."[8] Our economic life lays waste to nature and humans, and intellectual and artistic culture acknowledges only what is European. As a consequence, Americans are utterly demoralized:

> [A culture] has to be where it arises, or everything related to the life there ceases. It isn't a thing: it's an act. If it stands still, it is dead. It is the realization of the qualities of a place in relation to the life which occupies it; embracing everything involved, climate, geographic position, relative size, history, other cultures—as well as the character of its sands, flowers, minerals and the condition of knowledge within its borders. It is the act of lifting these things into an ordered and utilized whole which is culture. It isn't something left over afterward. That is the record only. The act is the thing. It can't be escaped or avoided if life is to go on.[9]

Williams thought that the people themselves must heal this demoralization, summoning into view that American "ground" rendered invisible by our colonial and utilitarian frame of mind, finding the words that enact the process of "lifting things into an ordered and utilized whole." Their artists cannot do it for them, though they can abet and record this recovery. (Whitman affirmed the same priority, when he said in the 1855 Preface that the common people of America "have probably the fullest poetical nature," perceiving for themselves "the beauty and dignity which always attach to dumb real objects." Of the poet they ask only articulation: "they expect him to indicate the path between reality and their souls" [*CRE,* 709, 714].[10])

It is appropriate for a democratic poet so to trust the innate genius

---

8. William Carlos Williams, *In the American Grain* (New York, 1956), 109.

9. William Carlos Williams, "The American Background: America and Alfred Stieglitz," in *Selected Essays* (New York, 1969), 157.

10. This relation between people and artist suggests the distinction that Coleridge had made between the primary imagination, the process of construing our experience into meaning, in which all human beings are forever engaged, and the secondary imagination, through which artists record and recreate that process.

of his people; but when the tastes and tendencies of the people confound the poet's own aesthetic and political sense, a rift opens between the unacknowledged legislator and his constituency. This befell Williams as it had Whitman. Williams did not suppose that people "expect" their poets to do anything: he is more the Whitman of the 1856 letter to Emerson or of *Democratic Vistas*. Modern America is possessed by what he called a "secondary culture"—that is, one bought secondhand from Europe by our plutocracy. The people feel little need for a primary culture or for artists to instigate and record its development. As he said in his poem "To Elsie," the "pure products of America" reveal our lack of a supporting culture. Our "imaginations . . . have no / peasant traditions to give them / character," no language to "express" what has befallen us (*CPW*, I, 217). Could a poet instruct these imaginations? Could he provide a new language? Or should he withdraw into a poetry of private feelings, as Whitman had in the 1860 *Leaves?* Or was there an intermediate position?

For both Whitman and Williams, the democratic poet had to be an urban poet, encountering people in the mass as they struggled with economic and social modernity. For Williams, the denizen of Rutherford, cities like New York posed an enormous challenge. In his mind, they were the seats of that secondary culture founded on personal wealth alone, a "culture of purchase." They had supplanted America's smaller communities and their primary "culture of immediate references."[11] Whitman in "There was a Child Went Forth" acknowledged that in the city, once society's traditional contexts had been lost, "men and women crowding fast in the streets" dissolved into "flashes and specks," mere optical phenomena. Likewise, Williams' treatment of the city reflects incoherence and discontinuity. "It is only in isolate flecks that / something / is given off," he concluded in "To Elsie." For both Whitman and Williams, the task was to find a new context, aesthetic or social, in which flashes and specks, isolate flecks, could be resolved into a true democratic culture.

Al Que Quiere! (1917), Williams' first book of mature poetry, sought such a context, a place where imaginations might still be open to instruction. In it he addressed his hometown of Rutherford,

---

11. Williams, "The American Background," 147.

one of those decaying small communities where democracy had begun and where he thought the qualities of the place might still be realized as the ground of a primary culture. *Al Que Quiere!* was to have been subtitled *The Pleasures of Democracy* (*CPW,* I, 480). Calling repeatedly on "my townspeople," Williams dedicates himself to "realizing" the life lived there by the "nonentities"—those who were both poetically and politically invisible. Sometimes he presumes to instruct his townspeople about traditions and public rituals, such as funerals, as he does in "Tract," confident that they "have the ground sense necessary" to enact his advice (*CPW,* I, 72). Sometimes he is content just to record what he sees, as though he were a street photographer. In a poem called "Pastoral," he describes the dignified tread of a street cleaner; another poem with the same title depicts the poet "walk[ing] back streets / admiring the houses / of the very poor" (*CPW,* I, 42, 64–65).

Why urban poems might be "pastoral" he made clear in a Whitmanian address to his townspeople near the end of *Al Que Quiere!:* "Waken! my people, to the boughs green / With ripening fruit within you! / Waken to the myriad cinquefoil / In the waving grass of your minds!" ("Abroad," *CPW,* I, 113). Healthy city life could pulse with the same generative energy conventionally associated with the country. But if the imagination—longing for "deer / going by fields of goldenrod," as he put it in "To Elsie" (*CPW,* I, 218)—tramples the present underfoot, then life in the industrial precincts of northern New Jersey (which was built by just such a nostalgic imagination) will seem dull and dead. So the artist's task is to search out those places and persons where that vital energy still flourishes—where the imagination of common people continues to engage the qualities of the place in which they live.

Sometimes, then, the artist is more than an aesthetically detached photographer. Seeing might lead his townspeople to recognition. A powerful visual image, like those in Whitman's catalogs, may open a door of empathy between subject and object:

> —what a blessing it is
> to see you in the street again,
> powerful woman,
> coming with swinging haunches,
> breasts straight forward,

supple shoulders, full arms
and strong, soft hands (I've felt them)
carrying the heavy basket.
>   ("Woman Walking," *CPW,* I, 66)

This approach would become one of Williams' most successful addresses to urban life. Although some of these early poems suggest the detachment of Whitman the *flâneur,* Williams usually found the means to deliver us into the presence of creative energy. The means was both linguistic and visual, reproducing through words the quality of visual encounter. The spirit of such poems as these are the ground of Williams' kinship with painters like Sloan. This poet might describe his métier as did the painter: "Keep your mind on such homely things, such deep-seated truths of reality, that there is no room for the superficial. . . . Don't be afraid to be human. Draw with human kindness."[12]

In a later poem, the comradely "Fine Work with Pitch and Copper," Williams captures a group of workmen in characteristic action, as Whitman's imagination once dilated upon the bricklayers in "Song of the Broad-Axe," moving with the rhythm of their work:

Now they are resting
in the fleckless light
separately in unison

like the sacks
of sifted stone stacked
regularly by twos

about the flat roof
ready after lunch
to be opened and strewn

The copper in eight
foot strips has been
beaten lengthwise

---

12. Sloan, *The Gist of Art,* 41.

> down the center at right
> angles and lies ready
> to edge the coping
>
> One still chewing
> picks up a copper strip
> and runs his eye along it
>
> (*CPW,* I, 405–406)

Williams puts his lines at the service of the visual imagination, arresting a moment of representative action in the genre tradition that goes back to William Sidney Mount and extends through Sloan and George Bellows to photographers like Paul Strand and Lewis Hine. The poem's lines (three foot lengths mostly) measure out its information according to its own system, sometimes bending the reader's pace of apprehension to meet its own requirements; but at the end, its rhythms run true to those of the workman and his unresting attention to his trade. As Mike Weaver said, the best analogy in painting for the poems of *Al Que Quiere!* is the "Ashcan" school of New York Realists.[13]

The analogy with Sloan is well taken. One of the delights of Williams' poetry is his recreation of immediate visual encounters, recognitions at those interstices of urban living when the expedient blindness of our customs falls away and the subject is discovered occupying his or her own space, a space created by an act of imagination—not imagination as defined by a secondhand culture or as the production of works of art, but as an act of realization.[14] In these poems, Williams' "secondary" imagination, his poem, recognizes not an "isolate fleck" merely, but the gestures of his townspeople's primary imaginations as they take the measure of the realities that surround them. The poet's own act of primary imagination, his em-

---

13. Mike Weaver, *William Carlos Williams: The American Background* (Cambridge, Eng., 1971), 39. There were, however, few actual contacts between the "Ashcan" painters and the modernist writers associated with Stieglitz and the Arensbergs.

14. Although such poems are found mainly in the first half of his career, in the late 1930s Williams wrote "The Forgotten City," narrating how he once got lost, coming back to Rutherford from Connecticut, and discovered entire cities, quite near his own, that he had never seen before. He comically describes "avenues / with unrecognized names" and "people with completely / foreign manners"—"a strange commonplace"—and wonders "How did they get / cut off this way . . . ?" (*CPW,* II, 86–87).

pathetic seeing, places him between the poem and these stubborn men and women as both a fellow townsman and an artist.

❖

Of course, the catalogs of "Song of Myself" or "Crossing Brooklyn Ferry" would have engorged whole volumes of Williams' recognitions. Whitman's poems contextualize their images within his ground sense of national or metropolitan citizenship. Williams specifically rejected Whitman's poetic structure; and he increasingly felt displaced in Rutherford, in Manhattan, and in the United States.[15] But he was not content with a poetry of isolate flecks; nor was he fully in sympathy with the disengagement practiced by Red Eric and Daniel Boone, his heroes from *In the American Grain*. His urban poetry searched for an inclusive space—if not a "primary" culture, then an extended poetic form—within which the poet too might realize the qualities of a place in relation to the life that occupies it.

In *Al Que Quiere!* he made two preliminary overtures toward an inclusive urban space. "The Wanderer" is a narrative poem of about 350 lines—old-fashioned, more or less decasyllabic lines in a highfalutin poetic diction that Williams had nearly put behind him:

> . . . One day, crossing the ferry
> With the great towers of Manhattan before me,
> Out at the prow with the sea wind blowing,
> I had been wearying many questions
> Which she had put on to try me:
> How shall I be a mirror to this modernity?
>
> (*CPW*, I, 108–17)

"She" is the Muse for whom he searches the industrial hinterlands of New York, as he attempts to answer the questions put in the last line: how to encounter modern life (with the primary imagination); how to record the encounter (with the secondary). Despite his Whitmanian opening, with its inclusive rhetoric and panoramic point of view, the Wanderer finds these cities antipoetic, as the Realists' paintings had been found ugly. He meets crowds "hasting nowhere" with expressionless faces; ugly immigrants brutalized by their work; labor

---

15. Williams, "America, Whitman, and the Art of Poetry," 30–31; Frail, *The Early Politics and Poetics,* 123–44.

violence; slums, hunger, filth. Much has been made of the poem's ending, in which the muse bathes the poet in "the Passaic, that filthy river," and the poet's self dissolves and flows away with the river. If it does represent the dissolution of the authorial ego and his submission to the being of the things about which he writes, as J. Hillis Miller said, then the poet has placed himself at the mercy of his townspeople. It is up to them to "act"; he will "record"—"afterward." But if the people forsake their ground sense to embrace a secondhand mass culture, then the "modern" city cannot be "mirrored"—certainly not by the outmoded poetics of "The Wanderer." To discover or design a compact, well-joined scheme, the citizen poet will have to redefine his task and his means.

The other long poem in *Al Que Quiere!* is cast in a modernist form. "January Morning" is a series of fifteen brief visual images:

>   —and the sun, dipping into the avenues
>   streaking the tops of
>   the irregular red houselets,
>   and
>   the gay shadows dropping and dropping.
>   (*CPW*, I, 100–104)

The poem's Whitmanesque montage of disparate visual fields is drawn together only by its final address to Williams' muse/mother: "All this— / was for you, old woman. / I wanted to write a poem / that you would understand." He addresses her as one whom he must meet on a common ground. But in urging her "you got to try hard," the poet recognizes that she may not understand. And "what good is it to me / if you can't understand it?" Balked by the incoherence and intractability of the modernity around him and by the indifference or incomprehension of his townspeople, Williams has found that the spaces he can create do not overlap those inhabited by the common folks of Rutherford and Paterson.

Al Que Quiere! was followed by a book of prose improvisations titled *Kora in Hell*—experimental writing not designed for old women to understand or to teach his townspeople how to occupy their city. Its prologue acknowledges his doubt about whether immediate experience can serve as a common ground between poet and reader, as it did in *Al Que Quiere!* Confessing "the virtual impossibility of lifting to the imagination those things which lie under the direct scrutiny of the senses," Williams blames this on the senses' failure to free themselves from "the so-called natural or scientific array"—what Gibson called the visual world. Rather than attempt to mirror modernity, the imagination must assert itself against the fixity of the natural array, moving freely from one isolate fleck to another, as Whitman had in "Song of Myself," setting them in fictive rather than natural arrangements.[16]

Although some poems in *Spring and All* (1923) renewed the communitarian gestures of *Al Que Quiere!*, Williams' emphasis had clearly shifted from the recovery of a democratic culture to the creation of an autonomous art-world. And with the shift, he had redefined "the imagination." At the end of the book, he acknowledges that he has spoken of the imagination sometimes as a power, sometimes as a place: "It is immaterial which" (*CPW*, I, 235). But from the perspective of the democratic bard of *Al Que Quiere!*, it is *not* immaterial which. If the imagination is a power, then it might be turned either on the immediate world or on the world of art—as Coleridge's distinction between primary and secondary imagination suggests. Whitman's great achievement in "Crossing Brooklyn Ferry" was to cross over from the second power to the first, and back. Williams' ambition, in *Al Que Quiere!* and in *In the American Grain*, was to rehabilitate the imagination as a common human power, a power to set human beings in relation to the qualities of their geographical place. It would be available to the common folk of America in the creation of a culture, and available to the artist in recording the processes of that culture.

But Williams now treats "the imagination" as an autonomous place of its own, a separate world where the writer "would find himself released from observing things for the purpose of writing them down later" (*CPW*, I, 207); that is, released from the duties within a democratic culture that he had tried to assume in *Al Que Quiere!* In a passage that seems to have been dictated by Wallace Stevens, he writes that "the only world of reality that men know . . . [is] the world of the imagination, wholly our own. From this world alone does the work gain power, its soil the only one whose chemistry is perfect to the purpose" (*CPW*, I, 215). Now it is not within a shared

---

16. "A poem is tough by no quality it borrows from a logical recital of events nor from the events themselves but solely from that attenuated power [of the imagination] which draws perhaps many broken things into a dance giving them thus a full being" (William Carlos Williams, *Imaginations,* ed. Webster Schott [New York, 1970], 14, 16–17).

existential space, a *civitas,* that "men" are joined in the creation of a culture, but rather within the more flexible world of the imagination. There the poet encounters not only no division between I and Not-Me, but also none between I and You. "To whom then am I addressed?" he asks at the very outset. "To the imagination." Not to his townspeople. "In the imagination, we are from henceforth (so long as you read) locked in a fraternal embrace, the classic caress of author and reader. We are one" (*CPW,* I, 178). So Williams takes up Whitman's struggle to cross over from I to You, and on the same terms that Whitman had eventually accepted, when he wrote: "This is no book, / Who touches this, touches a man" ("So Long!" *V,* II, 452). A comradeship that cannot be confirmed in the social world is consummated on the provisional ground of the poem.

To argue for this transposition of reality, *Spring and All* turns to modernist painting. This reflects Williams' enthusiasm for the artists whose work he had seen at the Armory Show and those whom he had encountered in the Arensbergs' salon, among them Marcel Duchamp and Marsden Hartley, and others of the avant-garde like Alfred Stieglitz and Charles Demuth.[17] Williams dismisses illusionist painting (like Sloan's) in favor of "the modern trend" represented, in *Spring and All,* by Juan Gris. This trend "escapes plagiarism after nature" by "separat[ing] things of the imagination from life" (*CPW,* I, 198, 194).[18] The imagination, he insists, "affirms reality most powerfully and therefore, since reality needs no personal support but exists free from human action . . . it creates a new object, a play, a

17. There has been extensive commentary on Williams' relationship with modern art. See Dickran Tashjian, *Skyscraper Primitives: Dada and the American Avant-Garde, 1910–1925* (Middletown, Conn., 1975), and *William Carlos Williams and the American Scene, 1920–1940* (New York, 1978); William Marling, *William Carlos Williams and the Painters* (Athens, Ohio, 1982); F. Richard Thomas, *Literary Admirers of Alfred Stieglitz* (Carbondale, Ill., 1983); Christopher J. MacGowan, *William Carlos Williams's Early Poetry: The Visual Arts Background* (Ann Arbor, Mich., 1984); and Peter Schmidt, *William Carlos Williams, the Arts, and Literary Tradition* (Baton Rouge, 1988).

18. Even now he appeals to Whitman: "Whitman's proposals are of the same piece with the modern trend toward imaginative understanding of life. The largeness which he interprets as his identity with the least and the greatest about him, his 'democracy' represents the vigor of his imaginative life" (*CPW,* I, 199). Although this image of the "democratic" and empathetic Whitman recalls the program of *Al Que Quiere!,* it is yet the aesthete Whitman, at once in and out of the game, to whom he refers. This self-consciousness and sense of the resistance of things to words had often locked Whitman in the magic prison of individual selfhood and deprived him of any ground on which to fulfill the role of civic poet. Williams, however, feels that he can have it both ways.

dance which is not a mirror up to nature" (*CPW,* I, 234–35). The poem, then, is not a mirror for modernity, nor an illusionist window through which vision passes, nor a door admitting the reader into a common space. It is, rather, an "object" thought of as an opaque space upon which representations of objects can be placed in juxtaposition. Although some of the poems in *Spring and All,* like "To Elsie," do prolong the spirit of *Al Que Quiere!,* Williams at that time forsook his addresses to his townspeople and identified himself with an artistic movement preoccupied with the problems of self-conscious and skeptical modernity.

In doing so, he put behind him the bardic Whitman, but exposed his poetry to the dilemma that Whitman had faced as the poet of consciousness. Was the world contained within the mind, or did the world contain the mind, as one more object in its array? In his middle career, Williams preferred the latter, in old age the former. Because he continued to dwell and to practice medicine in Rutherford, and to cross the Hudson for contact with artists and writers, his writing would always encounter city life and face the challenges of form that the city set for him.

One way to meet the challenge was to differentiate the role of genres. In *Spring and All,* he distinguished the possibilities of prose from those of poetry, identifying poetry with "the imagination," but prose with communication and with "the exposition of facts." He began to write short stories about "life along the Passaic River," as he eventually titled a collection of them—mimetic prose, realistic in form, colloquial in style, about the people among whom he moved as a doctor. Like Whitman's prose about wartime Washington, the short story was open to the recreation of specific incidents and details. In it people talk and talk and talk, exchanging ideas and opinions, effortlessly sharing the space of their city:

> The young men, in their twenties or early thirties, when they have a hard job on their hands often use shirts with the sleeves ripped out at the shoulders to give themselves more arm room. Swell looking muscles. What for? What good are they to a man when someone lands a slug of lead between his ribs? And you don't get to be a Delegate lifting quarter-ton bales onto a truck all day long either. You might as well take and trim the rim off an old soft hat the way they do sometimes, to keep their hair slicked

down while working, that is, if you don't travel. Then you can run a scollop around the edge and cut the top full of airholes, stars, circles, and all that. And good luck to you.[19]

This prose, though driven by the same energies that fueled his poetry, evidently has secured an exemption from Williams' skepticism about the relationship between words and things, and between his citizenship and his art.

The poems, on the other hand, responded to the dilemma of consciousness by setting the poet altogether within his world as a participant rather than as an interpreter, and by incorporating the poem as an act among all the other actions. "Objectivism," as his friend Louis Zukovsky called it, was such a poetry of immersion as Williams had foreseen in "The Wanderer." (Whitman, too, had been an Objectivist, in "Bivouac on a Mountain Side" and "Cavalry Crossing a Ford.") In their speech rhythms and in their typographical arrangement, Williams' poems absorb the life-rhythm of their objects and translate that rhythm to the reader's mind. Although far more visualist than the short stories, the poems coordinate seeing with feeling. In "Young Sycamore," the poem's lines coincide with lines of growth as our gaze moves systematically upward:

> I must tell you
> this young tree
> whose round and firm trunk
> between the wet
>
> pavement and the gutter
> (where water
> is trickling) rises
> bodily
>
> into the air with
> one undulant
> thrust half its height [.]
>
> (*CPW*, I, 266)

19. William Carlos Williams, *Life Along the Passaic River* (Norfolk, Conn., 1938), 11.

Fierce Momentary Tension

While describing the tree visually, Williams' words and syntax translate its tactile and kinetic reality into mental equivalents. We feel the sycamore's place, there between the gutter and the pavement. Earlier he had asked his townspeople to awaken to the waving grass of their minds; his mature "pastoral" instinct often flowered empathetically through the weeds and brush—Queen Anne's lace, mullein, bushes, and vines—that burst through the sidewalks and flourished in the vacant lots and fields of his North Jersey cities. Unlike the Alfred Stieglitz photograph to which it is thought to refer, the poem does not contextualize its visual field within any larger schema.[20] Whitman placed the cavalrymen in a campaign; Stieglitz rhymed his tree with its architectural and human surroundings. For Williams, the tree is; the poem is; and that is enough.

"View of a Lake" is more purely visual:

> Where a
> waste of cinders
> slopes down to
>
> the railroad and
> the lake
> stand three children
>
> beside the weed-grown
> chassis
> of a wrecked car
>
> (*CPW*, I, 380)

Again the poem scans its object, setting its incongruous parts into pictorial relationship. It continues for thirty-six lines more, filling in details. The juxtaposition of the children with the cinders and junk is not ironic; it does not even glance toward a vanished irony, as in Eliot. It is just what the eye sees while inspecting a lake near a highway. The poet does not presume to add anything to the visual array as he finds it. Even more absolutely photographic:

---

20. Stieglitz' *Spring Showers* (1900) matches the black tree's upward thrust with the gray shafts of tall buildings, muted by the rain, behind it to left and right. And its slight undulation is duplicated in the white-clad body of a street cleaner a few yards behind the tree.

BETWEEN WALLS

the back wings
of the

hospital where
nothing

will grow lie
cinders

in which shine
the broken

pieces of a green
bottle

(*CPW,* I, 453)

The poem occurs at a chance intersection between the sun, the eye, and a shard of glass. Dixon Scott had described such as the moment for photography—"intimate, unanimous, organic,—every item within vision contributing to the fierce momentary tension."[21] Isolate flecks, Williams had called them in "To Elsie." They issue from a poetic based on the visual field, at the verge of disintegrating into flashes and specks, pure uninterpreted optical phenomena. Williams draws back from that verge. The poet has at least a minimal role in organizing and interpreting. Like a photographer, he can "witness / and adjust." He can draw unlikely objects into common focus. He can direct the reader's view: "something / is given off"; "I must tell you"; "so much depends on." The imagination—more place than power—is the glass on which the photographer composes the luminous figure he has found; the flat canvas where Gris fastens his overlapping images; it is Atget's shopwindow, within which unlikely objects appear side by side.

In a number of medium-length poems he wrote in the 1930s, Williams sought ways to bond urban images together, to realize the qualities of a place in relation to the life that occupies it. In "Perpetuum Mobile: The City," Williams addressed not his own city but rather the metropolis rising prodigiously across the Hudson. This

21. Scott, "The Function of the Camera," 202.

poem is organized as a narrative about a provincial couple's response to this "miracle." The poem first depicts their yearning toward the city,

> a dream
> we dreamed
> [. . .]
> of love
>   and of
> desire—
> [. . .]
>   A dream
> a little false.
>
> (*CPW*, I, 430–35)

At last they "break / through / and go there—"; and the poem passes into a montage of disconnected city images, like those in "January Morning," but emphasizing the sensational (a bank robbery), the grotesque (the coiffure of a black transsexual), the wasteful (the garbage from a banquet). The city is treated as a congeries of disparate experiences. It can be unified teleologically, as Saint Augustine had, by realizing that all these things are done "for love, for love!"; or it can be unified as events observed by a bewildered visitor from beyond the Hudson. Aesthetically, though, it epitomizes Williams' remark in the prologue to *Kora in Hell:* "Given many things of nearly totally divergent natures but possessing one-thousandth part of a quality in common, provided that be new, distinguished, these things belong in an imaginative category and not in a gross natural array."[22]

Translated to the imagination, these city events spin about forever, like the perpetual motion machine mentioned in the title. Chance intersections are neither humorous (as in Sloan) nor ironic (as in Eliot), but simply phenomenal. They suggest the city's inexhaustible variety and possibility, which Whitman had celebrated, but they do not imply a perspective from which the poet can discern a word, "specific and perfect" comprehending the city's meaning, as Whitman had in "Mannahatta" (*V*, II, 419–20). As Henry M. Sayre remarks more generally about Williams, "the city—New York or Paterson—does not resolve the conflicts it embodies; it simply de-

---

22. Williams, *Imaginations*, 14.

fines a space in which its conflicting parts compete."[23] The poem and the poet enter the space and submit to its motion, one more fact in a maelstrom of facts. At the end of "Perpetuum Mobile: The City," the Jersey couple simply step off the ride, looking back at the city "dwindling / in a wall of / rain—" and bid it farewell. Disengaged from the imagination, the reader's ride is over too.

Two poems stay home in Rutherford, drawing on locales that Williams knew as a doctor. "Morning" is set in an Italian neighborhood where the poet wanders about observing how a transplanted tradition struggles to root itself in unfriendly soil. As in his fiction, Williams is unsentimental about what he sees. It's ugly; the people are unsanitary, devious, strange. And before long they too will be pure products of America, absorbed into its secondary culture and as demoralized as Elsie. His report is pictorial, recalling George Bellows' urban landscapes or Ernest Lawson's views of the city's fringes:

>   Down-hill
> in the small, separate gardens (Keep out
> you) bare fruit trees and among tangled
> cords of unpruned grapevines low houses
> showered by unobstructed light.
>
>   Pulley lines
> to poles, on one a blue
> and white tablecloth bellying easily.
> Feather beds from windows and swathed in
> old linoleum and burlap, fig trees. Barrels
> over shrubs.

Gardens, clotheslines, and old linoleum—the eye reports it all, amassing details unselectively. Weeds, ashes, junk, obscenities on fences. Image after image. The poem's techniques resemble those of "Perpetuum Mobile: The City." But the details that Williams sees and hears this morning have an objective coherence. They occur along "a broken fringe of wooden and brick fronts / above the city, fading out": what Kevin Lynch would call an edge, a seam, a line of exchange.[24] Italian peasant life meets American industrial.

23. Henry M. Sayre, *The Visual Text of William Carlos Williams* (Urbana, Ill., 1983), 56.
24. Lynch, *The Image of the City*, 100.

> And a church spire sketched on the sky,
> of sheet-metal and open beams, to resemble
> a church spire—
>
> *(CPW, I, 459–62)*

Further, the sights are the consecutive experience of a walking man. Like Whitman in "There was a Child Went Forth," Williams recounts the darting passage of his attention through the scene, from the houses to the sky, to the streets and gardens, then to the people walking along the streets. Not at all flashes and specks, they are heard speaking to each other, giving orders, shouting at a stray dog. The poem seems to lead nowhere, ending (like Eliot's "Preludes") with the image of an old woman poking about in an empty lot. But Williams' image is not restricted to his immediate visual experience; he then imagines her going to church to pray for a son who died of tuberculosis twenty years before. She has a story. The poem's sequence emerges from the interaction between a landscape, a culture, and an experiencing consciousness.

Before the poem ends, Williams discovers what he has been seeking:

> Spirit of place rise from these ashes
> repeating secretly an obscure refrain:
>
> This is my house and here I live.
> Here I was born and this is my office—

Recognizing the hallmarks of a culture, if a foreign one, Williams realizes that the foundation of an American culture depends on an "obscure refrain" about existential space, invoking a place in which one can recognize edges, domains, passages—ultimately, a dwelling place. The poem recreates an in-depth encounter with such a space and with those who dwell in it, including (Williams discovers) himself.

In "The Catholic Bells," Williams encounters another imported culture—from northern Europe this time—whose domain is marked out by the sound of church bells. Again Williams immediately disclaims actual membership in their community and then recreates that membership in imagination:

> Tho' I'm no Catholic
> I listen hard when the bells

> in the yellow-brick tower
> of their new church
>
> ring down the leaves
> ring in the frost upon them
> and the death of the flowers
> ring out the grackle
>
> toward the south, the sky
> darkened by them, ring in
> the new baby of Mr. and Mrs.
> Krantz.
>
> (*CPW*, I, 397–98)

The bells ring for Sunday morning and for old age, for the day's churchgoers and for the families in the parish. Williams comprehends this "pastoral" community whose membership is defined not only by locality but also by ways of marking time that are diurnal, seasonal, and generational. It is a four-dimensional world defined through sound more than sight, and the poem ends affirming that sound:

> the beginning and the end
> of the ringing! Ring ring
> ring ring ring ring ring!
> Catholic bells—!

Throughout the 1930s, Williams tried to launch a major poem that would achieve the cultural goals set forth in "The American Background," a poem for indigenous America embracing climate, geographic position, history, and the condition of knowledge within its borders. *Paterson,* named for the city near Rutherford, had been on his mind since the late 1920s, when studies and fragments for a long poem began to appear in his books. ("Morning" was such a fragment.[25]) In 1926 he had written the first of those studies, under the immediate inspiration of Joyce's *Ulysses.*[26]

Probably, *Paterson* would have been most successful as a middle-length poem. During his career, Williams wrote several masterpieces

---

25. Paul Mariani, *William Carlos Williams: A New World Naked* (New York, 1982), 415.
26. *Ibid.*, 263.

of one or two hundred lines: "Perpetuum Mobile," "Rain," "The Clouds," and "Burning the Christmas Greens." Their length is the longest span practicable for that verbal mobile of rhythms and images for which Williams had a gift. But he was driven to write a longer work, by his place in a chain of emulation. The example of Joyce's great city-imagining had led Eliot into *The Waste Land*. Ezra Pound, compelled by the success of his protégés Joyce and Eliot, had launched after them an unnamed poem whose Cantos accumulated for decades. Envious of the fame his coevals had won with these works—each the product of a culture, each urban in setting and form—Williams, like Hart Crane, felt compelled to strike up a New World composition on the same premise, on the same scale. For the Americanist poets, it was not a propitious enterprise.

Paterson, New Jersey, was an ideal locale for Williams' search for the spirit of place. Near Rutherford, it was not Rutherford.[27] Paterson was rooted deep in American history, having arisen around one of the manufacturing enterprises of Alexander Hamilton. Furthermore, it had an intelligible landscape, half encircled by the Passaic River, focused on a dramatic fall in that river, overseen by Garret Mountain. However, "The Wanderer" had visited Paterson during a textile strike in 1913, there realizing how little the modern city offered the poet.

In *American Beauty: William Carlos Williams and the Modernist Whitman*, Stephen Tapscott shows how Williams adapted John Dewey's axiom "the local is the only universal" so that "the words of the poem, the 'local material' of the poem-city Paterson, become 'things' in a new world."[28] In the late 1920s, he published a poem, "Paterson," which is the germ cell of the later, longer poem (*CPW*, I, 263–66). It begins with details, grass and trees and houses, and lifts to comprehend spires, office towers, surrounding fields, and the river "crash[ing] from the edge of the gorge." But, although this poem insists four times, "no ideas but in things," Williams must distance himself from the visual array and translate these things into the imagination. He introduces a presiding consciousness whose name is Paterson—a writer and perhaps a doctor. Before the poem is a dozen lines old, the elements of the envisioned landscape have

---

27. Robert Frost wrote his great pastoral *New Hampshire*, he said, while living in Vermont.

28. Tapscott, *American Beauty*, 93–104. In Tapscott's reading, "local" often seems to mean "American," as opposed to the internationalism of Pound and Eliot.

become "the ideas . . . of Paterson, that great philosopher." Among his ideas are the townspeople: "Inside the bus one sees / his thoughts sitting and standing. His thoughts / alight and scatter." Like Whitman's Mannahatta, Williams' Paterson is actualized within the poet's consciousness—his imagination. Again the poet devours his world.

Each time Williams insists on the interiority of his city, he refers to his earlier struggles to be the bardic poet, to record the creation of a culture, to pierce the natural array of things, to lift something from fact to word.

> Who are these people (how complex
> this mathematic) among whom I see myself
> in the regularly ordered plateglass of
> his thoughts, glimmering before shoes and bicycles—?
> They walk incommunicado, the
> equation is beyond solution, yet
> its sense is clear—that they may live
> his thought is listed in the Telephone
> Directory—

Williams' fellow citizens were oblivious of the failure of their language; they revelled in a culture of the secondhand and the ersatz. They ignored him and his poetry, as did the prevailing critics and academics. *Paterson,* though he sometimes thought of it as a proletarian epic, eventually became what his friend Wallace Stevens called a poem of the mind, the thoughts of a man enduring an internal exile.[29] In most of the criticism written about him these past thirty years, the mentalization of Paterson has been taken as the right course, a vindication of this or that critical method.[30] But it is a retreat from the bardic ambitions of *Al Que Quiere!, In the American Grain,* and even some of its own early projects—a retreat for which

---

29. "Of Modern Poetry," in *The Collected Poems of Wallace Stevens* (New York, 1954), 239.

30. There are exceptions to this critical unanimity. John H. Johnston criticizes the abstractness of *Paterson,* writing in *The Poet and the City:* "Though the reader sees or visits various localities around the city . . . he is never really 'in' Paterson in the sense that he is aware of the community as a place of streets and structures. But the reader is very much 'in' Williams's mind and he is very much subject to its distinctive flow and content" (221). Robert Coles, on the other hand, simply denies that *Paterson* is not "about" Paterson. In *William Carlos Williams: The Knack of Survival in America* (New Brunswick, N.J., 1975), he argues that the texture of *Paterson* is the texture of Williams' experience of North Jersey people. Coles is right when he says this of Williams' prose, but the long poem seems much more Parnassian.

he found comfort in the theory and practice of the modernist painters among whom he moved.

Paterson, however, is not a pictorial poem. Although there are passages of visual description, especially in the first book and the opening of the second book, it does not extend directly from the montage techniques of "January Morning" or "Perpetuum Mobile: The City." The visuals in *Paterson* are like those moments of dilation in Whitman's poems, intervals when the imagination is diverted from preoccupation with its own activity. And when Williams is not recording Dr. Paterson's interior monologue, he is listening to his fellow citizens rather than watching them. Among his preliminary studies, Williams published several renditions of the speech he heard from, or among, his patients. He must have seen how Joyce had reconstituted Dublin out of the speech of its citizens. Perhaps not realizing what wealth in spoken language and in existential space the Irishman could draw on, Williams made *Paterson* one of his most oral poems, incorporating in it street evangelism, fragments of conversations, extended dialogues. As Whitman collected faces, it seems at times that Williams collected the rhythms of the common speech he heard around him.

>   That was your little dog bit me last year.
>   Yeah, and you had him killed on me.
>
>   (the eyes)
>
>   I didn't know he'd been killed.
>
>   You reported him and
>   they come and took him. He never hurt
>   anybody.
>   He bit me three times.
>   They come and
>   took him and killed him.[31]

As Joyce had shown and as Williams had discovered in "The Catholic Bells," a culture's existential space can be defined by sound as well as by sight.

It was not *Ulysses* that undid Williams' good intentions for *Pater-*

---

31. William Carlos Williams, *Paterson* (New York, 1963), 157.

son, but rather Ezra Pound's *Cantos.* Williams' lifelong daimon, his "worst friend," Pound had said that an epic was a poem including history. Throughout *Paterson,* Williams imitates the trick of historical "rhyme," the poetic echo between a profane present and a sacred past, which Pound had discovered in *Homage to Sextus Propertius* and Joyce in *Ulysses,* and which Eliot had mastered so well for *The Waste Land.* Williams, however, seems to have attended only to the leaden echo of the middle Cantos. *Paterson* is littered with documents—fragments of histories, letters, newspapers, economic tracts. The city of immediate experience, sight or sound, disappears under a layer of texts.[32] What we see, in effect, is what Dr. Paterson reads; the space that we inhabit in Paterson is the library. The rhythms of the poem are the rhythms of his own thinking, not those of the voices he hears, or of the things he sees, or of daily and diurnal time.

Paterson was to have ended with a scene in which a swimmer comes ashore from the sea, naps, dresses, eats a plum, and heads inland. The rhyming figure might seem to be Ulysses, but the name that Williams gave to this swimmer, and later removed, was that of Walt Whitman.[33] Through this image, Williams must have wanted to claim his rank as a major poet, misunderstood and ignored in his own time, who had nevertheless uttered the word Democratic, the word En-Masse. The Whitman whom he claimed most directly, though, was the poet of heroic consciousness. In "Russia," first published in 1946, the same year as the first four books of *Paterson,* Williams contrasted the threat of renewed war with the "dream" of the imagination, inviting the Russians

> [. . .] Come with me into
> my dream [. . .]
> [. . .] Come with me
> in the spirit of Walt Whitman's earliest
> poem.
>
> (*CPW,* II, 145)

Probably, he meant the first poem (following the inscriptions) in the standard 1891–92 version of *Leaves of Grass,* "Starting from Paumanok." There Whitman announces that it is "in my poems" that one

---

32. To Tapscott this is a virtue, a way of moving from the timeless moment of the short imagistic poems to the accreting history of a poem-as-city, without resorting to "the illusion of sequential, experiential time" (*American Beauty,* 146).

33. Ibid., 188–89.

finds the wigwam and the backwoods village, the mechanics and plowmen, steam presses and locomotives, and the cities solid and vast. In the poems, not in actual America. At the end of his career, in *Paterson* and *The Desert Music,* Williams was still writing his own song of his Self. The poem he had sought to write, from *Al Que Quiere!* till then, was "Crossing Brooklyn Ferry." But that vision of existential space—solid, time-bound, mutual—perpetually dissolved into surfaces, resolved into thoughts in a doctor's mind. Perhaps that kind of space was harder to find in the metropolitan twentieth century—if ever this were easy. Certainly, his modernist poetic, reinforced by his alliance with modernist painters and photographers, did not help him discover or create that kind of space, even in the poems.

[9]

Surface and Depth: Alfred Stieglitz, Charles Sheeler, Berenice Abbott

The painters and photographers confronted the same tension between observed surface and imagined depth. In 1922, at a time when landscapes and nudes had begun to preoccupy his eye, John Sloan turned back to the cityscape once more. Since he had encountered the work of Cézanne and the modernists at the Armory Show, he had been rethinking his treatment of space, especially of perspective. In preparing for this painting, he did several pencil sketches—a deliberation that had not always been his style. He called the painting *The City from Greenwich Village* (Fig. 12). Later he reflected on it in *The Gist of Art:*

> Looking south over lower Sixth Avenue from the roof of my Washington Place studio, on a winter evening. . . . Although painted from memory it seems thoroughly convincing in its handling of light and space. The spot on which the spectator stands is now an imaginary point since all the buildings as far as the turn in the elevated have been removed, and Sixth Avenue has been extended straight down to the business district. The picture makes a record of the beauty of the older city which is giving way to the chopped-out towers of the modern New York. Pencil sketch provided details.[1]

What in fact the pencil sketches provided was a record of how Sloan gradually elevated the point of view, from a "rooftop" study to a bird's-eye view of the El, while at the same time pushing back the

1. Sloan, *The Gist of Art,* 267.

Surface and Depth 265

Fig. 12 John Sloan, *The City from Greenwich Village* (oil painting, 1922)
Courtesy the National Gallery of Art, Washington, D.C.; gift of Helen Farr Sloan

horizon.[2] The finished painting looks down almost vertically upon the bands of light along Sixth Avenue, along which the El moves as a strip of darkness punctuated by its glowing windows and by the pavement light shining up through the tracks. (Formerly, Sloan had painted this world from street level, with the El high above.) The curving line of the El leads the eye up and back to a pool of radiance at Carmine Street, and then—it requires a refocusing, a distinct readjustment of seeing and of reading perspective—away to the horizon in the upper left corner of the painting, where the Singer Building and the Woolworth Building shine in a light that has already disappeared from the streets of Greenwich Village.[3]

The painting testifies to the eclipse of Sloan's urban village of ma-

2. David W. Scott and E. John Bullard, eds., *John Sloan 1871–1951* (Boston, 1976), 168–69.
3. Commenting on the development of Sloan's approach to pictorial structure after 1916, David Scott observes: "To achieve firmer structure he employed such devices as the repressing of the foreground planes and tilting up of the background, stressing the principal geometric lines of the composition" ("John Sloan: His Life and Paintings," *ibid.*, 23).

sonry dwellings, restaurants, and shops, and the rise—the painting says "apotheosis"—of a massive commercial city. Also, it marks a departure from Sloan's customary techniques. The painting interprets the city as an array of geometrical forms. Distance, dusk, and rain conspire to minimize detail. Were it not for the tiny parallelograms of colored light that represent windows, the painting might be almost an objectivist study of opaque surfaces. There are no apertures into the city's interior life; no implied narrative or genre motif; indeed, scarcely any human presence at all.[4] *The City from Greenwich Village* is a panoramic painting in the spirit not of Sloan's earlier work, but rather of an alternative strain of urban art, that of Alfred Stieglitz and his school of Precisionist painters and Objectivist poets (among them William Carlos Williams). For them, as for Williams, the city was not depth, but juxtaposed surfaces, a visual array of "flashes and specks."

The career of Stieglitz is an epitome of how American art has approached the city in the past century. Beginning as a disciple of Peter Emerson and as a champion of photography as one of the fine arts, his early photographs invoked the European and rural values of late-nineteenth-century painting. Among them are a portrait of a waif in Venice, in the sentimental-picturesque style of Rejlander, and studies of the street people of New York, in the genre of Henry Mayhew. Some depict the "other half" photographed by Riis just three or four years earlier. But Stieglitz, as Carol Shloss has pointed out, was interested not in defining a social context for his images, but in recontextualizing the photograph among the fine arts.[5] The backgrounds are obscured or out of focus. The most indecorous juxtaposition is that of a tree beside the Flatiron Building. The camera does not arrange confrontations between the viewer and its subjects, but distances and aestheticizes them, somewhat as the paintings of George Luks would a decade or so later.

However, Stieglitz took several urban photos of a more evocative sort. Most of these catch a city scene under some atmospheric con-

---

4. Of Sloan's cityscapes in the 1920s, Lloyd Goodrich says they were "concerned less with the life of the masses than his earlier paintings, more with the city as a spectacle. . . . His people were now seen less as individuals than as parts of the whole spectacle—. . . the glamor and excitement of the city. He was painting cityscapes from a poetic viewpoint like that of the landscapist" (*John Sloan,* 53). See also Robert L. McGrath's Introduction to *John Sloan: Paintings, Prints, Drawings* (Hanover, N.H., 1981), 19.

5. Shloss, *In Visible Light,* 97.

Surface and Depth 267

dition that limits or diffuses the light. The earliest of these is *The Terminal* (Fig. 13), a view of a horse-car driver watering his teams on a cold winter morning. On the right are pails, crates, a broom—the paraphernalia of the terminal; on the left is the car itself and the horses. Steam is rising from their backs. A pedestrian hurries away. The snow underfoot is trodden and fouled. At the center, the darkest objects in the photo, are the bundled-up driver and his near horse. His back conceals what he is doing for the horse. The clearly recorded details of toil, chill, and discomfort, to left and right, channel attention to the concealed ministry that the driver is performing. That the animals are tired and cold is sharply manifest; but the step from pity to action requires the viewer to enter the obscure: to step imaginatively into the invisible space between the driver and the horse; to take the unseen bucket in his own gloved hands.

Another wintry, atmospheric cityscape is *Winter, Fifth Avenue,* a view of a horse-drawn omnibus working its way up the avenue, snow falling and slush thick in the street. Setting the omnibus well

Fig. 13 Detail from Alfred Stieglitz, *The Terminal* (photograph, 1892)
Courtesy The Philadelphia Museum of Art; The Alfred Stieglitz Collection, permission of the Georgia O'Keeffe Foundation

back, in the photo's middle ground, Stieglitz catches the background buildings dimming in the snow and fills the photo's lower third with an expanse of slush crisscrossed with wheel tracks, with a pair of timbers or girders lying in the gutter. A lithographer would have minimized such a foreground, moving the omnibus close to the lower edge of his composition. But that nearly featureless snow is the long bridge over which the eye trudges as the viewer enters the mood of the photograph. It must have been these photos that William Carlos Williams was thinking of when, near the end of "The American Background," he turned to praise Stieglitz for using his camera to recover attention for "the immediate and the actual."[6]

By the time Stieglitz came into his heyday as a photographer, technological solutions had been found to the problem of mass-reproducing photographs—the problems that had at first restricted Riis to wood engravings and a few bland halftones. Photogravure, coming soon after Eastman's simplification of the picture-taking process, completed the democratization of visual art by instructing a mass audience in the seemingly artless standards for photographic "seeing."

In the early 1900s, Stieglitz published in *Camera Work* a series of his own photographs of New York, his closest approach to a Whitmanian celebration of the metropolis. Shot under clear skies, sometimes with sun-riddled clouds overhead, they reflect the city's technological exuberance. In one, a steam shovel loads earth in a horse-drawn wagon; several depict the steam, soot, and steel of a railroad switching yard. Like Whitman, Stieglitz seems to have been most attracted to Manhattan's encircling waters: there are several pictures of crowds aboard a ferry, one of the liner *Mauretania,* several of the Manhattan skyline viewed from across one of the rivers, with shipping in the middle ground and, sometimes, the pilings and white-painted bollards of a pier in the foreground. Human beings, though present, are not the subject of these photos. Rather, it is the masses and the tones of the structures and machines that humans have made. Stieglitz said that he always photographed what was within himself; and—despite a few deprecatory titles like "The Hand of Man" and "The City of Ambition"—what he photographed was an excitement felt in the presence of great power. Although humans are dwarfed by the setting they have created, the

---

6. Williams, "The American Background," 160.

photographs are no more ironic or critical than were the descriptions of Whitman in "Give Me the Splendid Silent Sun." It is, after all, their city; it is their power.[7]

One photo of this period, though, proved to be prophetic. Called *Old and New New York* (Fig. 14), it depicts a street of four- and five-story buildings, straw-hatted passersby, an electric tram. In the foreground is a clipped hedge defining the corner of a residential lawn. The camera lens aperture has been opened so as to catch the texture of shades in the dark buildings, the soberly dressed pedestrians, and the shadowy hedge. But down the street, filling what would have been the background sky, is the pale steel framework of a skyscraper that has already risen twenty stories into glaring sunlight. The camera's f-stop, it would seem, was not prepared for this bright apparition in the sky; nor was the eye that had been nurtured on the more modest scale and more subtle texture of the older streetscape. The aesthetic of juxtaposition works here not through the shutter's capture of intersecting movement, but through the plate's limited sensitivity to light.

What figures as an intruding force in this photograph would come to direct Stieglitz' later perspective of the city. The 1900–1910 photographs mainly are records of New York as seen by a man on its streets, a *flâneur* such as Whitman had been, such as Sloan was even in those same years. The camera looks up at the buildings, across the East River toward the skyline, down at the crowds on the ferry, from a common point of view. It offers its experience, as Whitman did in "Song of Myself," as the experience that any might have; it is an eye in the crowd, watching the excavators, waiting for the horsecar; it claims no privilege. After 1910, however, Stieglitz adopts the skyscraper's point of view, taking in the city first from his fifth-floor studio at 291 Fifth Avenue, later from the American Place gallery on the seventeenth floor of 509 Madison Avenue and from his thirtieth-

---

7. Perhaps Paul Rosenfeld was the first to link Stieglitz with Whitman. In the article that anticipated his tribute to the photographer in *Port of New York* (1924), Rosenfeld wrote: "Save for Whitman, there has been amongst us no native-born artist equal to this photographer" ("Alfred Stieglitz," in *Photography: Essays and Images,* ed. Newhall, 215). More recently, Susan Sontag made use of the connection to dismiss both poet and photographer. Describing *Camera Work* and "291" as "the most ambitious forum of Whitmanesque judgments" about the beauty and vitality of every kind of American experience, she argues that "American photography has moved from affirmation to erosion to, finally, a parody of Whitman's program" (*On Photography,* 29).

Fig. 14 Alfred Stieglitz, *Old and New New York*
(photograph, 1910)
Courtesy The Philadelphia Museum of Art; Collection of Dorothy Norman

story apartment in the Shelton Hotel. As the angle of vision rises above the street, the city becomes more and more an array of opaque surfaces, as it does in Sloan's *The City from Greenwich Village*.

At first this change is not evident. Some of the views from *291* have the intimate quality of back-window paintings by Sloan. The best of them is a nocturne, a bulk of darkened flats in the middle ground, fully lighted commercial towers above and behind them. The dark mass is pierced by a few bright windows; from one of them, a festoon of laundry sweeps out into the night. The windows disclose nothing of Sloan's human comedy, but they imply a domes-

Surface and Depth

ticity that the viewer can project, imaginatively, as Whitman discovered stories in the faces on the street.

The other views from *291*, however, reveal that Stieglitz' eye was reading a composition of forms and shades rather than seeking human presence in the buildings around him. The daytime photographs are studies of rectilinear, vertical forms textured by the steel, masonry, and glass of their composition. Except for a few sprays of foliage in the foreground, it is a man-made environment, but there are no human figures. A new skyscraper rises in the midst of the towers, dynamic in its incompleteness and in the diagonals of its exposed girders; but no one appears to be working on it. The nearby rooftops also are empty of the human occupations that Sloan seemed always to discover there. Sloan's window was a passage for curiosity and sympathy; *291*'s is a screen on which the sun projects an array of opaque surfaces. Although Stieglitz and the New York Realists were active in New York at the same time, there seems to have been little contact and very little sympathy between them.[8]

In the years around 1910, as he studied the work of Cézanne and Matisse and listened to the theorizing of Marius de Zayas, Stieglitz absorbed the modernist doctrine of form and surface that was soon corroborated by the Armory Show (1913) and by the practice of the American modernists in his circle: John Marin, Marsden Hartley, Charles Sheeler, and Georgia O'Keeffe. As Sarah Greenough has pointed out, their influence is evident in the formalism of most of the *291* photographs.[9]

Additionally, Stieglitz' romance with O'Keeffe led him into a bifurcated artistic world. Inside the studio was the realm of intimacy. (The gallery after "291" was called The Intimate Gallery.) At times it was his home. Always it was the salon of that circle of artists and writers for whom he was the paterfamilias. And it was the setting for most of the portraits of O'Keeffe, the photographs that celebrated the spiritual and erotic intensity of their union. Outside the

---

8. Dorothy Norman quotes Stieglitz on the New York Realists: "I could not see anything truly revolutionary or searching in their paintings. Their line, form and color seemed mediocre. Certainly they lacked freshness or a sense of touch. I could not feel committed to what was mere literature, just because it was labeled social realism" (*Alfred Stieglitz: An American Seer* [New York, 1973], 77). See also Perlman, *The Immortal Eight*, 203–205.

9. Sarah Greenough, "Alfred Stieglitz and 'The Idea Photography,'" in *Alfred Stieglitz: Photographs and Writings*, ed. Sarah Greenough and Juan Hamilton (Washington, D.C., 1983), 19–20.

studio there was the sky and the city that he now depicted almost entirely as it appeared in the windows of the studio or of his apartment.

(There was, as well, the mediate pastoral world of Lake George, New York, scene of his photographs of landscape and rural architecture, as well as background for portraits of many of those in his company of relatives and friends.)

Inside was the personal and private; outside, an "objective" world of forms presented not as other beings, presences, but as figures for Stieglitz' own feelings and ideas. He called the cloud studies "Equivalents," that is, external equivalents of "my most profound life experience, my basic philosophy of life."[10] So, it seems, were his cityscapes, for which the vantage point gradually moved higher and higher, looking out and down on the metropolis from perches that, in *Old and New New York,* had been lost in a glaring sky. Too distant for their windows to suggest any indwelling human presence, his buildings stand as gnomons for the passing sun, staffs against which to chart the rise of other empty buildings. It is an almost geological image of New York, more intensely lifeless than the boneyard deserts of O'Keeffe's Southwest. Stieglitz seems to have found in the outer world no human *civitas,* but only a range of blank windows and swirling natural forces, intensifying the preciousness of the personal world inside.

Stieglitz in his tower represents the isolated modern man whom Buber depicted in *I and Thou:*

> Taking his stand in the shelter of the primary word of separation, which holds off the *I* and the *It* from one another, he has divided his life with his fellow-men into two tidily circled-off provinces, one of institutions and the other of feelings—the province of *It* and the province of *I.* Institutions are "outside"; . . . they are the tolerably well-ordered and to some extent harmonious structure, in which, with the manifold help of men's brains and hands, the process of affairs is fulfilled. Feelings are "within," where life is lived and man recovers from institutions. Here the spectrum of the emotions dances before the interested glance. . . . Neither of them has access to

10. Quoted in Dorothy Norman's Introduction to *Alfred Stieglitz* (New York, 1976), 12.

real life. Institutions yield no public life, and feelings no personal life.[11]

This isolation, in Buber's view, stems from the failure of communitarian relationship: "The true community does not arise through people's having feelings for one another (though indeed not without it), but through, first, their taking their stand in living mutual relation with a living Centre, and, second, their being in living mutual relation with one another."[12] The first modern nation, America ventured into the atomized individualism celebrated by Walt Whitman, in which "living mutual relation" was not essential. The career of William Carlos Williams witnesses how unimaginable the modern city becomes when it affords no mediating, contextualizing patterns of human relationship.

Stieglitz' desolate cityscapes reflect as well the antisocial quality of intensive land use and high-rise architecture, to which Sloan's *The City from Greenwich Village* also testifies. After the First World War, much of Manhattan was rebuilt on a scale that afforded no existential space for human indwelling. And finally, the emptiness of Stieglitz' city follows from a modernist aesthetic that—embracing the Whitmanian egotism that divides the world into I and Not-Me—finds no way of discovering and representing common human interests; an aesthetic for which art becomes skeptically "objective," or intensely private—or both.

❖

So it is with Charles Sheeler also. A painter of shapes and surfaces, he seems to offer an "objective" vision of the American landscape, rural and urban. And yet in its very austerity, his work reveals in barns and factories the "equivalents" of a profoundly subjective and private vision. Like Stieglitz, Sheeler found some of his most communicative images in the pastoral world. In his renderings of Pennsylvania farm buildings, techniques honed by cubism unite with realist perspectivism to convey the undoubtable substance of these massive works of folk art in wood and stone. His country interiors, especially the staircases, are at one and the same time studies in plane geometry and (like stairways themselves) invitations to pass imagi-

11. Buber, *I and Thou*, 43–44.
12. Ibid., 45.

natively into the volumes of space that they imply.[13] Shaker chairs and stoves, on his canvases, offer not only refined aesthetic form but also promises of domestic comfort. In painting the buildings of the Shakers and other communal sects, he captured both the diaphanous spirituality that called these groups into being and the obstinately physical agriculture and handicraft that sustained them. In Sheeler's rural paintings there is a reciprocity between the artist and his subjects that acknowledges both their independent being and the existence of a cultural context, American agrarianism, which both artist and subject occupy.

The pastoral world offered Sheeler both exterior masses and interior volumes, the exteriors measured against their natural surroundings and the interiors implying the aesthetic and practical ideals of inhabitation. On the other hand, the city presented only an impenetrable array of surfaces to which his modernist sensibility responded with an art of depthless juxtaposition. His painting *City Interior,* for example, depicts the exterior of an industrial plant, a passageway for rail and foot traffic beneath a web of gantries and conveyors. Although it does make pictorialist sense, it appears rather an assemblage of mechanical forms whose patterning follows from technological function rather than from any sense of indwelling presence. Sheeler, who often both photographed and painted the same subject, once said "with the lens . . . everything within the plane of focus is in equal definition at the same time, but the eye is roving, and includes at one time only a very small area that is sharply defined."[14] The camera seems to have taught his brush how to see. In either medium, everything is in focus; the objects displayed tend toward a single plane. The title, "City Interior," puzzles the reader. This is not like an interior by Sloan, *Three A.M.,* for instance; and

---

13. Theodore E. Stebbins, Jr., has shown how Sheeler's photographs of his Doylestown house, individually, constitute a series of nearly abstract patterns of form, light, and shade, while as a group they map a domestic space around such iconic forms as stove, door, and stairwell (*Charles Sheeler: The Photographs* [Boston, 1987], 10). Patrick L. Stevens notes the same quality in some of Sheeler's paintings of interiors: "One gets the intriguing visual effect of slipping back and forth between objective reality and abstract relation" ("Charles Sheeler, William Carlos Williams, and Precisionism: A Redefinition," *Arts Magazine,* LVIII [November, 1983], 105).

14. Quoted in Constance Rourke, *Charles Sheeler: Artist in the American Tradition* (New York, 1938), 120–21. Sheeler continued: "The total vision of a landscape, for instance, is really a mosaic of small fragments separately seen." Here he adverts to the "saccadic" motion of the eyes, mentioned in Chapter 6, apropos of Whitman's darting gaze in "There was a Child Went Forth" and "Crossing Brooklyn Ferry."

while the walls and overheads do form a sort of concavity, Sheeler has foreshortened it and deprived it of any suggestion of enclosure. Unlike the farmhouse stairwells, this painting offers no sense of depth and no invitation to enter. Could the title be ironic? No.

Sheeler's work with the urban scene began around 1920, while he was living in New York and in touch with both Stieglitz' circle and the Arensberg salon, where he met William Carlos Williams. His immediate stimulus, however, involved Walt Whitman. Sheeler and the photographer Paul Strand produced a short experimental film, *Manhatta*, which juxtaposed motion-picture images of New York with lines from several of Whitman's poems about the city.[15] Whitman-like in its transitionless leaps from one image to the next, the film is organized like Williams' "Perpetuum Mobile," as a day in Manhattan. It begins with the skyline and with crowds pouring ashore from a ferry. After a few scenes of street crowds taken from a second-story vantage point, it shifts to long shots of buildings and machines. It ends with a panoramic view of the harbor at sunset and with Whitman's closing address to the cityscape in "Crossing Brooklyn Ferry": "Gorgeous clouds of the sunset! drench with your splendor me, or the men and women generations after me!" (§9, *V*, I, 223).

The film delights in motion: the flow of crowds, jets of smoke and steam, tugs, locomotives and trolleys passing by. The camera pans up or down the facades of skyscrapers, zooms toward or away from its subject. Jump-cuts splice together scenes of varying length, interspersed with the intertitles from Whitman's poetry. Many of the images resemble those of Stieglitz' pre-1910 studies of the city, both in subject and in composition: the ferry, the ocean liner, the excavators, the railyard, all seen by that mechanized *flâneur,* the Debrie motion picture camera. But Strand and Sheeler also anticipate Stieglitz' later work, for their camera is soon seduced by the long-range views provided by tall buildings, sometimes taking in a prospect of the harbor, more often peering steeply down into the crevasses between buildings. The Debrie does not track; it cannot move through the streets collecting faces, as Whitman would have. But its rapid-fire cutting gives this account of Manhattan the commanding inclusiveness of a catalog from "Song of Myself," while its fixed, superior

---

15. Affinities between Whitman's poesis and cinematography have been noted by both Reese Alexander Bond ("Whitman's Visual Imagination") and by Graham Clarke ("'To emanate a look,'" 92–97). Neither, however, refers to Sheeler's *Manhatta*.

point of view modernizes the balloon views and panoramic perspectives of Whitman's later poems. At longer range, the city begins to lose its particularity and texture, becoming light and shade, plane and void; at some extremely steep downward angles, both horizon and perpendicular disappear, and the city's surfaces become almost abstract.

From the experiments with composition and viewpoint in *Manhatta,* Sheeler developed a cubistic approach to painting New York.[16] *Skyscrapers* (1922) (Fig. 15) is based on a photograph of a building scanned in one of the sequences in the film. The viewpoint looks down on the Park Row Building, a cluster of narrow shafts twenty-five or thirty stories tall. The paint, applied as impersonally as a photographic emulsion, directs attention to a precise vision of the Not-Me. Sheeler has removed the textures of brick and stone, and the ephemera of smoke and the shadows of smoke that had been so important to the dynamics of *Manhatta.* The walls and the voids between them compose a row of rectilinear bands of brown ranging from near-black to tan, their values deepened in places by the shadow of another building. Three of the columns are featured with windows that seem like bits of paper glued upon their surface. At the picture's bottom, helping us read the composition, is an abstract version of some rooftops in the middle ground. The painting, however, eliminates the photograph's sense of perspective: the shapes here have closed ranks, so that the imagination plays across them but cannot enter. Similarly, *Church Street El* (1920) looks down vertiginously on the tracks, a train, and the surrounding buildings, all reduced to plane surfaces in several hues: brown, yellow, gray, pink. The painting seems to read equally well as a cityscape or as a diverging spray of angular shapes composed on a plane surface.

Faced with so objective a treatment of so rigorously depersonalized a subject, viewers sometimes infer a critical or even satiric tone to Sheeler's work: the windowless walls must convey an urban claustrophobia; the depopulated factories must protest the dehumanization of work; titles like "City Interior" and "American Landscape" (the River Rouge Ford plant) must be ironic. Such inferences are attempts to find another way to "enter" the paintings by treating them as communications of shared value. We would take Sheeler to

---

16. As an immediate model for Strand's and Sheeler's visualization of the city, Stebbins identifies not the European painters (whom of course they knew), but the British photographer A. L. Coburn (*Charles Sheeler: The Photographs,* 10, 19).

Fig. 15 Charles Sheeler, *Skyscrapers* (oil painting, 1922)
© *The Phillips Collection, Washington, D.C.*

be our fellow citizen, sharing our discourse about urban life. We would take his artworks as a passage for that discourse.

William Carlos Williams struggled with this question in an essay he wrote about Sheeler in 1939. The essay, and the revisions it underwent, tell as much about Williams as about Sheeler.[17] Aware, as a canceled passage admits, that Sheeler's art may seem "inhuman,"

---

17. Bram Dijkstra has printed the essay with its canceled passages and variations in *A Recognizable Image: William Carlos Williams on Art and Artists* (New York, 1978), 140–45.

Williams asserts that the painter is "a citizen of the arts" whose cameralike acuity of vision illuminates the everyday world "for anyone . . . whose eyes might be blurred by the general fog that he might, if he cared to, see again."[18] Williams stresses that Sheeler's art deals with familiar American realities: "[T]his world of the artist is not of gauze but steel and plaster. It is the same men meet and talk and go to war in. . . . Any picture worth hanging, is of this world—under our noses often—which amazes us, into which we can walk upon real grass." And we can walk into it, Williams says, because artists like Sheeler have cut away false associations so as to "give us such a world, of elements we can believe in, things for our associations long familiar or which we have always thought familiar."[19]

This essay assigns to Sheeler the role of the citizen artist that Williams had described in *In the American Grain* and "The American Background." We can walk "into" his paintings, into a new world freed from the "impost" of a secondary culture. Yet the Williams who writes it is not the democratic citizen of *Al Que Quiere!*, but rather the advocate of detached modernism found in *Kora in Hell* and *Spring and All*. The drafts of the essay record a battle between these two personae: Williams was trying to have it both ways. Deleted sentences distinguish sharply between the world of inhabitation and the world of art, a world that the painter "makes up for us in detail . . . with paint on a piece of stretched cloth."[20] "The best pictures take us most wholly into another world," the world of the "imagination" where the local is released into the universal. Williams as the resident of *Paterson* gives the better account of Sheeler, for his paintings are in fact landscapes of the imagination, that inward country where Whitman found the generalized, unbackgrounded images of his catalogs, to which Williams pledged allegiance in *Spring and All*.

Of the composition in *Church Street El*, Sheeler wrote: "I used an intentional reverse of perspective . . . placing the point of greatest concern close to the position of the spectator, well down in front, rather than at some distant point on the horizon. In a way the picture includes the spectator, makes him a point of focal attraction, gives him importance."[21] The spectator, then, is truly the painting's focal point. The city is not a city, but the visual field of the artist—or of

18. Williams, "Introduction," *Selected Essays*, 234.
19. *Ibid.*, 232.
20. Dijkstra, ed., *A Recognizable Image*, 142.
21. Quoted in Rourke, *Charles Sheeler*, 90.

the viewer, who is afforded the same privilege of overseeing and containing his experience. As is often the case in Whitman, what appears to be purely objective, Not-Me, is actually the subjective possession of a single consciousness. Sheeler's cityscapes must be seen as private experiences, visual arrangements that really reveal not the city but the power of aesthetic consciousness to discern and display its underlying forms.[22] Hence the "City Interior." Sheeler flattens his compositions not to reveal an irony by juxtaposition, as did Riis and Sloan, but rather as Atget did, to produce a collage of adjacent surfaces harmonious in shape and color and corresponding to an interior harmony.

Martin Friedman said of Sheeler, "Neither metaphysics, social comment, nor irony accurately describes Sheeler's particular response to technology. He treated the industrial theme with reverence."[23] Artist joins engineer, recognizing the affinity of their interests in design and economy and their common faith in the deep structure of matter. The city paintings, like Sheeler's studies of industrial power, resemble Whitman's celebration of American technical prowess. In Whitman's poems, catalog gives way to brag, brag to catalog; the achievements of the States, turned inside-out, are the conquests of consciousness. There is no overt "brag" in Sheeler's work, no drawing attention to the I through technique or composition. Nevertheless, his illustrated catalog of American design, in its very lack of corroborating or responding human presence, must be read like a catalog of Whitman's, as the record of a search for spiritual correspondences between experience and consciousness. Beneath the row of pictures is written: "One and all."

❖

If Sheeler seldom painted the human form, minimized his own role in painting, and rarely implied an irony in his juxtapositions, then we should not be surprised that his self-portrait is ironical. *Self-*

---

22. Sheeler said: "All nature *has* an underlying abstract structure and it is within the province of the artist to search for it and to select and rearrange the forms for the enhancement of his design" (Archives of American Art, NSh-1, frame 8; quoted in Karen Tsujimoto, *Images of America: Precisionist Painting and Modern Photography* [Seattle, 1982], 80).

23. Martin Friedman, *Charles Sheeler* (New York, 1975), 65. In *Skyscraper Primitives,* Dickran Tashjian wrote that "the technology that stimulated [Joseph] Stella's emotions provoked Sheeler's sense of rational harmony in the universe" (220).

Portrait (1923) shows an upright telephone on a table before a closed window; on the windowpane a dim reflection gives us Sheeler's image, from waist to chin. Looking at an object before or behind a sheet of glass, the human eye usually dismisses interfering images on the glass and scrutinizes the object. The camera adverts undiscriminatingly to both object and reflection.[24] Atget's photographs of Parisian shopwindows often encompassed not only the goods inside the showcase but also the street and the buildings opposite, reflected in the glass. The American photographer Berenice Abbott, a friend of Atget's, used the camera's power of indiscrimination in some of her most powerful urban photographs.

After Atget's death, Abbott acquired his photographic inventory of nineteenth-century Paris. She campaigned long for the recognition of Atget's artistry and in some ways emulated his work, though her best photographs go well beyond it. When she returned to America at the end of the 1920s, she began recording New York as Atget had Paris, under the auspices of two civic institutions, the New York Public Library and the Museum of the City of New York. Later she worked with the Federal Art Project. Seeing her adopted city with the acuity of a postexpatriate, she worked in the spirit of Atget, as a citizen and an antiquarian preserving the ephemera of (as she titled her collection) *Changing New York*.[25] Statues in Times Square, gravestones in Trinity churchyard, advertising signs, architectural details. Shopwindows. Jacob Heymann has filled the two big plate glass windows of his butcher shop with placards listing cuts of meat and prices per pound. The A & P window shows canned and packaged goods below, placards above: "Kate Smith invites you to try Bokar Coffee . . . vigorous and winey." Her titles, like Sloan's, keep a firm grasp on circumstances. Meticulously placed and dated, her photos tell you that a pound of Bokar cost twenty-three cents on Third Avenue on March 16, 1936, a pound of butter thirty-seven cents. Walt Whitman would have loved her *Hardware Store,* where the goods in the windows have spilled out—birdcages, sun lamps, and hammers—halfway across the sidewalk; or her *Newsstand,* with

24. Later in his career, Sheeler began to exploit this doubleness, painting on glass or Plexiglas, or floating two compositions on one canvas.

25. The Berenice Abbott photographs cited in these pages are found in *Changing New York* (1939; rpr. as *New York in the Thirties* [New York, 1973]); and in *Berenice Abbott: Photographs* (New York, 1970).

its yards of movie and romance magazines, its *Racing Form* and Baby Ruth candy bars.[26]

Her work, like Stieglitz' high-rise photographs and Sloan's *The City from Greenwich Village,* testifies to the rapid remaking of the city in the postwar decade. In the 1890s, Riis had campaigned for "model tenements" built with uniform standards for hygiene and safety; in the 1920s, Abbott preserves one, *Model Early Tenement, east 70's,* as a historical curiosity. (Seen from a rear courtyard, the six-story buildings appear sketchily through the laundry hanging from dozens of clotheslines: Oliver Wendell Holmes is vindicated again.)

Abbott did not confine herself to images of the past. She used the juxtaposing power of great depth of field to set the old city and the new together in one frame, as Stieglitz had in *Old and New New York*. Lower Manhattan's skyscrapers fill the rigging of a four-masted schooner moored at Pier 11. In *West Street,* a truck follows a horse-drawn wagon while a roadster, blurring its image, passes another wagon. Behind the traffic, a row of walk-up buildings, with fire escapes and leaded windows, faces the afternoon sun. Behind—or rather atop them—rise the steel office buildings of lower Manhattan. In *Washington Street* stands a single tenement building, literally overshadowed by the massive structures around it. Its balconies still are cluttered, and two lines of laundry remain aloft; but—in accord with the commercial form of slum clearance—its space must soon be preempted by a loftier structure, where no one will live.

Much of Abbott's work on New York makes no such sentimental judgments, but compresses the dynamic shapes of the city into abstract compositions, often adopting dramatic perspectives, from above or below, like those Strand and Sheeler had used in *Manhatta*. In photo after photo, the city plunges beneath our feet, down to streets where small white rectangles betoken cabs and buses. In *The Financial District,* faceless buildings soar overhead at crazy angles, threatening to collapse (as the district had, in 1929). What is perpendicular in reality slants diagonal in the print; bright facades, shade and shadow radiate from a small triangle of sky. Seen from below,

---

26. Graham Clarke has noted the parallel between Whitman's poetic intentions and Abbott's professed desire to "reveal and celebrate reality." See "'To emanate a look,'" 82.

fire escapes cover a six-story facade with an arabesquerie of iron; next door an immense neon rooster says, in plain English, POULTRY. Ironwork fascinated Abbott with its unpaintable intricacies of light and shade: she took great photographs of the elevated, of Pennsylvania Station, of the bridges, the railyards, and the piers. Emulating Atget, she photographed shop fronts. In Christopher Street, a pushcart stands like a midget hearse in front of a darkened jeweler's shop; a clock in the window says that it is 10:39 on some everlasting sabbath morning.

On other days, however, Abbott's city is not untenanted or swarmed by faceless crowds beneath the steel buildings. Although many of her cityscapes are, like Sheeler's, images of facades and surfaces, she often saw through the surface, discovering—as had Sloan—in a face or a situation the aperture into human presence. During her years in Paris, she had been a portrait photographer, the creator of some of our most familiar images of James Joyce as well as of other cultural celebrities of early modernism. In New York, she photographed John Sloan, Edward Hopper, and Huddie Ledbetter. She had the portraitist's empathetic knack for eliciting the spontaneous gesture that conveys character. Her best American portrait is of an anonymous individual. *East Side Portrait* portrays a bearded man, about forty, dark-suited, wearing a hat; he sits at a white table, some playing cards in his large, stained hands, other cards spread for solitaire before him. Close behind him is a wall of flowered wallpaper; above his shoulder an electric receptacle—a documentary touch recalling Riis's East Side studies forty years earlier. However, this man has not been photographed to typify some social problem. "I asked if I could take his picture," Abbott recalled; "he agreed."[27] Erect and serene, he occupies his space with dignity, gazing just to the right of the camera. His pose invites no sentimental response from the viewer. He is playing his own game. He says, *I*. Abbott's portrait conveys and maintains his integrity: it says, *You*.

More typically, her human subjects are unposed. Cameras had grown smaller and faster since the time of Riis; she carried hers into the streets and the subways. Although many of her photographs seem carefully composed, in others she responds to a contingent opportunity: she is that "Photographer of the Future" whom Dixon Scott had foreseen in 1906, alert for those transient and irrecoverable

---

27. Hank O'Neal, *Berenice Abbott: American Photographer* (New York, 1982), 180.

Surface and Depth 283

intersections that the city, with its passion for surprises, sends her: a vendor of roast corn, a peddler pulling a cart, a vagrant asleep in the rectangularly dappled shade of the El, a young black man dancing to maracas in a Macdougal Street club. The variety and inclusiveness suggest once again the images unfolding in Whitman's galleries in "Song of Myself." But the sharply detailed backgrounds are important as they were not in Whitman's poem. Contextualizing their subjects in place and time, the backgrounds direct our responses to the photographs. Two men and a woman warm themselves at a stove in the IRT station at Columbus Avenue; it is February in the seventh winter of the Depression. At the Lyric Theatre vagrants can sleep all day for a dime. A solitary, overcoated man is buying a ticket to the Chaplin movie: he too, it seems, is a tramp. In these it appears that Abbott was attracted by the setting, not its occupants. But the interposed human figures, with their implied stories, transform a documentary photograph into an evocation of urban displacement and loneliness.

While some of her shopwindows are closed at the back, others frame the faces of those who work inside. The Blossom Restaurant on Fulton Street offers Tripe a la Creole for fifteen cents, while downstairs Jimmy the Barber will cut your hair for twenty; but up the steps comes a man wearing a white jacket over his vest and trousers (waiter? barber?), fortuitously walking into the space of Abbott's camera. He glares at her: certainly *his* permission had not been granted for this intrusion into his domain. Meanwhile, behind the barber pole, a white-jacketed boy gazes off into an unphotographable distance. Although the building's interiors are unseen, their integral reality is affirmed by these two occupants, whom the camera cannot seduce or capture.

One of Abbott's most appealing images, again coincidental in its composition, is another shopwindow. A. Zito's Sanitary Bakery on Bleeker Street spreads an array of long and round loaves below two placards—"5¢ A Loaf" (Fig. 16). (The caption says that Zito's bread is baked the old-fashioned way, on its own bottom rather than in a tin.) Below the window are some large wicker baskets. It was to record this facade that Abbott set about her photographic business on the sidewalk. The printed image, though, gives us more. In reflection, we see a delivery truck in the street and the tall brick front of a furniture and storage company across the street, their surfaces mottled with the stacks of five-cent loaves behind the glass. And still

Fig. 16 Berenice Abbott, *A. Zito's Bakery, New York, 1937*
(photograph, 1937)
Courtesy Berenice Abbott/Commerce Graphics Ltd., Inc.

there is more; deeper in the store, a woman in a dark jacket and white blouse is looking out to see what Abbott is doing. On her face there are both curiosity and suspicion (Will she try to sell us her picture?), but there is also security. It is her shop, and she is inside it, selling bread baked the old-fashioned way. Looking out, she sees the photographer, beyond her the bakery's truck, across the street the furniture store. While Abbott's lens is focused on the window display, accidents of light and circumstance have juxtaposed on its surface images from other planes behind the photographer and beyond the glass, giving the five-cent bread a context that is both economic and personal. To read her photograph, we must disentangle these planes and interpret their relationship, taking our own stand on Bleeker Street on February 3, 1937. Elsewhere in Abbott's New York, men and women are crowding fast in the streets and dissolving into photochemical flashes and specks. But in this photograph, as in "There was a Child Went Forth," we encounter a person situated in an actual, dimensioned world in which we are invited to take part.

❖

It is this same quality, incidentally, that distinguishes Edward Hopper's *Nighthawks* from much of his work. Often Hopper rivals Sheeler in purging human presence from his urban paintings. *Approaching a City* is more a collage of angular shapes than a representation of a railway entering a tunnel; *The City* is one more aerial view of brownstones, tall buildings, and an almost empty park; *Early Sunday Morning* is a facade of shopfronts, among them a barbershop, all utterly deserted. But Hopper's visual experience does not dissolve into dots and specks or resolve into shapes. It is instead the entry to a substantial and shareable world. Although he is sometimes taken as a painter of urban alienation, actually he shares with Sloan and with Abbott—and with the Whitman of "Crossing Brooklyn Ferry"—a faith in the implicit mutuality of our encounter with human presence in a fully dimensioned urban world.

In some of his city paintings there is an implication of narrative, as there was in Sloan's. *Sunlight in a Cafeteria* might be compared with Sloan's *Chinese Restaurant*. A woman sits alone at a table, fronting the viewer, her hands and forearms relaxed on the table. She has a cup of coffee. At an adjacent table a man turns in her direction, lifts his hand as though to gesture. Hopper's palette is lighter than Sloan's, and his detailing much simpler. A blank wall towers behind them, lit from a huge plate glass window. The street and the building opposite appear lifeless. There is no food in evidence. Rather than Sloan's complex interplay between woman, "boy friend," cat, and other male diners, here there is only an unintelligible gesture, a not-quite-averted glance. At the same time, the painting offers a not-quite-aborted gesture of human kindness on Hopper's part. Among great angular urban masses of gray, cream, and khaki, stories are intersecting—or at least a refusal of story, the sort of unrealized narrative that shimmers through *The Waste Land* and the chapters of

Dubliners. Hopper's painting engages sympathetically the mystery of human loneliness.

Although Hopper disclaimed any direct reliance on the camera, photography had an influence on his composition, perhaps through Degas.[28] Objects are cut off at the edges of his canvas, as they would be by a camera; telephone poles lean awkwardly across the fronts of buildings, just as they intrude on our own family photos. Incongruous objects consort together on the plane of focus: a mansarded house and a railroad embankment, a nude woman and a rank of brownstones.[29] Humans are frozen in awkward, contingent poses. Two hundred years ago, the movement of the man in "Sunlight in a Cafeteria" would surely have been a gesture, selected by the painter from a repertoire; but in the age of the snapshot we cannot be sure. There is a cigarette in his hand; perhaps the painter has merely arrested the motion of smoking. In this painting, Hopper typically compresses depth, as though looking through a lens. Background—the plain surfaces, the empty volumes—is made foreground, part of the interest. In Hopper, however, this flattening is not done to create an abstract composition, as in Sheeler, but rather, as in a Riis photograph, to provide emotional counterpoint for the human action it surrounds. The austere cafeteria setting intensifies the unarticulated, incomplete relation between the two figures.

It is this narrative and sympathetic possibility that has made *Nighthawks* Hopper's most popular painting. The painting's viewpoint, like Whitman's, is both in and out of the game.[30] We begin outside. The diner thrusts its sharp corner between the viewer and the background row of shops. Looking into its depths, compressed as if in a photograph, we pass from dim exterior to bright interior to a dark exterior—and even, reading the shadows, into another window across a foreshortened street. Against that darkness the three customers and the counterman are posed, occupying the only lighted space in the painting. Each seems to have a private share of

---

28. Brian O'Doherty, "Portrait: Edward Hopper," *Art in America,* LII (December, 1964), 77.

29. See J. A. Ward, *American Silences: The Realism of James Agee, Walker Evans, and Edward Hopper* (Baton Rouge, 1985), 177–78.

30. Brian O'Doherty speaks of "the reversals that his pictures provoke: switching emptiness into fullness, isolation into spiritual richness, lack of emotion into feeling.... This extraordinary traffic through opposites leads one into their apparent source—the separation and fusion of object and subject" ("Portrait: Edward Hopper," 76).

Surface and Depth

that space (unlike the two young women in *Three A.M.*!). They are the nighthawks, excluded from the customary rhythms of human eating, sleeping, and socializing. The huge glass window puts them on display, as though their loneliness were bread in a Bleeker Street shop. Watching from outside, we become the fifth nighthawk, excluded even from their common solitude.

At the same time, Hopper's windows, like Sloan's, are passageways. (In many paintings a wind blows through them.) Usually they are preternaturally transparent and free of reflection, as the diner's window is. While we watch, the painting reverses field and figure; we are brought inside, into a human context. This is a painting we can hang on the walls; it says, *We*. Currents of contact or refusal eddy through the diner, inviting our recognition and curiosity. There are stories here, as in *Chinese Restaurant,* though they have been cooled down—just as Hopper's palette is cooler than Sloan's. The woman seems to be in the company of the man to her right; but her gesture (she appears to be reading a matchbook cover) is not for him, though it may be for him to interpret. The solitary man can see this pair and hear them, too, if they are saying anything. He must have some interpretation of their presence; if not, there's a story in that, too. The counterman, bending over, has looked up. At whom is he gazing? Who has spoken to him? Why, in this clean well-lighted place, is there a water glass on the empty stretch of counter? Is it ours?

[10]

Angels' Mouths and Existential Space

Seize the Day is one of the most Whitmanesque of Saul Bellow's fictions. Its hero, Tommy Wilhelm, is a resident of New York City. He has discarded all other identifiers, all the affiliations that once mediated between his Self and the enormous metropolitan All. Jewish in ancestry, he changed his name, Wilhelm Adler, to the more "American" Tommy Wilhelm when, as a young man, he went to Hollywood to become an actor. Failing at that, he returned to New York and worked as a salesman. As the book begins, he has separated from his wife and children and has resigned from his job. He has a room in a retirement hotel on the upper West Side where his father, a retired physician, also lives. Dr. Adler rebuffs his feckless forty-two-year-old child, declining to lend him money or to ratify his excuses and complaints. In an eloquent, often-quoted soliloquy, Tommy pins responsibility for his misery on the quality of urban life in the midtwentieth century. His is the Song of Myself in a minor key:

> There was no easy way to tell the sane from the mad . . . in any big city and especially in New York—the end of the world, with its complexity and machinery, bricks and tubes, wires and stones, holes and heights. And was everybody crazy here? What sort of people did you see? Every other man spoke a language entirely his own, which he had figured out by private thinking; he had his own ideas and peculiar ways. If you wanted to talk about a glass of water, you had to start back with God creating the heavens and earth; the apple; Abraham; Moses and Jesus; Rome; the Middle Ages; gunpowder; the Revolution; back to Newton; up to Einstein; then war and Lenin

and Hitler. After reviewing this and getting it all straight again you could proceed to talk about a glass of water. "I'm fainting, please get me a little water." You were lucky even then to make yourself understood. And this happened over and over and over with everyone you met. You had to translate and translate, explain and explain, back and forth, and it was the punishment of hell itself not to understand or be understood, not to know the crazy from the sane, the wise from the fools, the young from the old or the sick from the well. The fathers were no fathers and the sons no sons. You had to talk with yourself in the daytime and reason with yourself at night. Who else was there to talk to in a city like New York?[1]

This was the outcome of American democracy as Tocqueville had anatomized it—a great undifferentiated mass in which the separate individual soul thirsted for a word and a glass of water. Between them, as mediator or translator, was nothing. A hundred years earlier, while pioneering in the egotistical sublime, Walt Whitman had discovered its severe limitations for a poet who intended to be heard not just as a solitary singer but as a citizen. *Leaves of Grass* was Whitman's "language experiment," figured out by private thinking. In it he claimed to renounce historical and social mediation, to go back to first principles—actually to become God creating the heavens and the earth. Enacting a world whose images danced according to a grammar entirely his own, Whitman twinned his personal consciousness with a universalizing principle that he often called "America." In the contredanse of Whitman's consciousness, I becomes America, America I. But this unmediated vision is also an uncorroborated vision. Of what use is it to a thirsty man? How does this language respond to common needs like the thirsts of Riis's tenement people, or Williams' Rutherford plebeians—"common" not only because they are commonplace but also because they are communal?

The ensuing paragraph in Bellow's novel is far less frequently quoted, perhaps because in it Tommy's thoughts (unfashionably, for post-Nietzschean readers) begin to turn toward solutions to his own thirst for reaffiliation and the renewal of a common language:

1. Saul Bellow, *Seize the Day* (New York, 1987), 83–84.

> He went several degrees further—when you are like this, dreaming that everybody is outcast, you realize that this must be one of the small matters. There is a larger body, and from this you cannot be separated. The glass of water fades out. You do not go from simple *a* and simple *b* to the great *x* and *y*, nor does it matter whether you agree about the glass but, far beneath such details, what Tamkin [one of Tommy's advisers, untrustworthy and yet truthful] would call the real soul says plain and understandable things to everyone. There sons and fathers are themselves, and a glass of water is only an ornament; it makes a hoop of brightness on the cloth; it is an angel's mouth. There truth for everybody may be found, and confusion is only—only temporary.[2]

How does one reach the real soul? rejoin the larger body? find truth for everybody? Tommy muses on an experience he had in a Times Square subway corridor a week before. In its stench and squalor, among its freakish denizens, "unsought, a general love for all these imperfect and lurid-looking people burst out in Wilhelm's breast. He loved them. . . . As he walked he began to say, 'Oh my brothers—my brothers and my sisters,' blessing them all as well as himself. So what did it matter how many languages there were, or how hard it was to describe a glass of water?"[3]

This is the pulse of sympathy that Whitman's poems forever recount and dramatize. But in itself it may be only the gape of consciousness, I engulfing Not-Me. However, it is also the experience from which "Crossing Brooklyn Ferry" began its search for the larger body, the ground from which it is possible actually to say "You" to sisters and brothers. In that poem, the crossing-over is accomplished through Whitman's discovery of a mediating existential space that he shares not only with his fellow passengers but also, through the poem's reenactment of the "miracle of the eyesight," with reader-citizens fifty years hence, or a hundred years.[4]

This existential space was a city, though perhaps not the kind of city that New York—or any megalopolis—became in the hundred years that separate Tommy Wilhelm from Walt Whitman. Modern

---

2. *Ibid.*, 84.
3. *Ibid.*, 84–85.
4. "Crossing Brooklyn Ferry" (1856); Bellow, *Seize the Day* (1956).

urban life destroys such common spaces; modern thought repudiates both the common language and the common body in which language and spatial sense are both incorporated. *Seize the Day*, however, depicts many entries to this space, past which Tommy walks unheeding. His chosen example, the glass of water, locks into a net of descriptions that are woven into his story. Bellow's narrative moves in and out of Tommy's consciousness, now reporting his thoughts, now interpreting his behavior and observing the surroundings that he is too preoccupied to see. The novel is studded with brief, seemingly superfluous envisionings of city life. The Hotel Ansonia "looked like the image of itself reflected in deep water, white and cumulous above, with cavernous distortions underneath." There is unnoticed traffic in the air: "Light as a locust, a helicopter bringing mail from Newark Airport to La Guardia sprang over the city in a long leap." That morning, Tommy had sat at breakfast with his father in the dining room of his hotel. This is what he could have seen: "The old man was sprinkling sugar on his strawberries. Small hoops of brilliance were cast by the water glasses on the white tablecloth, despite a faint murkiness in the sunshine. It was early summer, and the long window was turned inward; a moth was on the pane; the putty was broken and the white enamel on the frames was streaming with wrinkles."[5]

Tommy, like Whitman, moves among glories strung like beads on his smallest sights and hearings. But, like Elsie and the other Americans to whom William Carlos Williams addressed his early poems, he moves impercipient, his imagination self-destructively fixed either on his many troubles or on his desired escape to some pastoral world. ("I miss the country," he says.) Tamkin, who claims to be a psychologist, advises him: "You have to pick out something that's in the actual, immediate present moment. . . . Don't let your mind wander. 'Here and now I see a man in a brown suit. Here and now I see a corduroy shirt.' You have to narrow it down, one item at a time, and not let your imagination shoot ahead. Be in the present."[6] Tamkin's motives for this advice are corrupt, for he is planning to cheat Tommy out of his share in an investment in commodities futures. Nevertheless, his counsel could heal the distracted, self-tormenting Tommy. "Seize the day," he tells him.

5. Bellow, *Seize the Day*, 5, 74, 31.
6. Ibid., 89–90.

Through the novel's brief but extravagant descriptions, Bellow is negotiating that point of exchange between the aesthetic and the spiritual that Whitman had sought—the bridge between beauty and the soul. The water glass first enters the novel's narration as Tommy Wilhelm and his father play a cautious game of chess, the son pressing for sympathy and help, the father (wisely? selfishly?) retreating and demurring. The father is no father, the son no son; a moth is on the pane, and putty wrinkles under its broken enamel. But there stands the glass, spreading its hoop of brightness on the cloth. It is, as Bellow says, an angel's mouth.

Readers of Bellow have sometimes noted his affinity with the visionary tradition of Hasidic Judaism; Robert Kegan's *The Sweeter Welcome* draws frequently on Buber's writings as keys to the psychological and spiritual depths of Bellow's work.[7] Although Kegan bases his argument mainly on plot movement and on statements by the characters, it is clear that in *Seize the Day* the visual descriptions are important entrances to the novel's meaning. And in turn, the mundane objects described are apertures through which Tommy might recognize the meaning of his life. Hasidism, as Buber interprets it, is not unworldly. It makes no discrimination between the profane and the sacred. The everyday world is holy: "Man's existence in the world becomes fraught with meaning because the things and beings of the world have been given to him in their sacramental potentiality. . . . The chassidic world is the concrete world as it is in this moment of a person's life; it is a world ready to be a sacrament, ready to carry a real act of redemption."[8] At every moment, the commonplace stands ready to bring meaning into the void and to serve as the bond between one human and another. The recurrent Hasidic image for this potentiality is "sparks," light—in Bellow's words, a hoop of brightness. Seize the moment; plunge through the hoop.

It was toward this truth that Whitman aimed when, in the 1855 Preface, he said that "facts are showered over with light" (*CRE*, 721). It was at this truth he had arrived, in his passage over Brooklyn ferry, when he addressed sunset, flags, waves, ships, and passengers as "dumb beautiful ministers":

---

7. Robert Kegan, *The Sweeter Welcome: Voices for a Vision of Affirmation: Bellow, Malamud and Martin Buber* (Needham Heights, Mass., 1977).

8. Martin Buber, *Mamre: Essays in Religion,* trans. Greta Hort (Westport, Conn., 1970), 106. This quotation is found in Kegan.

> Expand, being than which none else is perhaps more
>   spiritual!
> Keep your places, objects than which none else is more
>   lasting!
>
> We descend upon you and all things, we arrest you all,
> We realize the soul only by you, you faithful solids and
>   fluids,
> [. . .]
> We fathom you not—we love you—there is perfection
>   in you also,
> You furnish your parts toward eternity,
> Great or small, you furnish your parts toward the soul.
>   (§9, V, I, 224–25)

In the communal "soul" to which Whitman for once penetrated, objects retain their existential selfhood. They can be loved, but not fathomed; recognized as real presences, but not enrolled on the inventories of the self. This is the "larger body" that Tommy Wilhelm glimpsed in the nightmarish subway corridor. Near the novel's end, he enters into its presence when, stripped of everything by Tamkin's misdealings, he emerges from the hotel into such a street as Whitman had known:

> On Broadway it was still bright afternoon and the gassy air was almost motionless under the leaden spokes of sunlight, and sawdust footprints lay about the doorways of butcher shops and fruit stores. And the great, great crowd, the inexhaustible current of millions of every race and kind pouring out, pressing round, of every age, of every genius, possessors of every human secret, antique and future, in every face the refinement of one particular motive or essence—*I labor, I spend, I strive, I design, I love, I cling, I uphold, I give way, I envy, I long, I scorn, I die, I hide, I want*. Faster, much faster than any man could make the tally. The sidewalks were wider than any causeway; the street itself was immense, and it quaked and gleamed and it seemed to Wilhelm to throb at the last limit of endurance.[9]

---

9. Bellow, *Seize the Day*, 115.

The crowd on this causeway carries Tommy into a mortuary, where he comes to stand before a dead man, and he begins to weep, recognizing in his extremity how he is bonded with his father, his estranged wife, Tamkin, and all the rest: "He . . . sank deeper than sorrow, through torn sobs and cries toward the consummation of his heart's ultimate need."[10]

This conclusion has seemed to some readers only to show Tommy giving way to complete self-pity legitimized by the mortuary setting and the surrogatory dead man. However, when Bellow reprised this scene in the far more acidic *Mr. Sammler's Planet,* he left little doubt of what he meant. Sammler, an old and impoverished survivor of the death camps, stands finally beside the body of his only benefactor, Elya Gruner. Tearless, he silently eulogizes the dead man: "'Remember, God, the soul of Elya Gruner. . . . At his best this man was much kinder than at my very best I have ever been or could ever be. He was aware that he must meet, and he did meet—through all the confusion and degraded clowning of this life through which we are speeding—he did meet the terms of his contract. The terms which, in his inmost heart, each man knows. As I know mine. As all know.'"[11] The novel has followed Sammler through several days in an utterly dystopian New York, where private lives are bottomless swamps of self-indulgence and public life is a war zone of street crime and disintegrating institutions. Yet his passage has been punctuated by a few moments of decency and beauty; and from what would seem to be the abyss of his own abandonment, Sammler speaks of a "contract" that defines responsibilities and bonds one human to another. Even in the wreckage of Manhattan, Bellow affirms the survival of a spiritual, existential space.

The grim vision of *Mr. Sammler's Planet* suggests that American city forms and American individualism are willfully averted from such spiritual affirmation. In *I and Thou,* Buber wrote the description of isolated modern consciousness with which this book begins. Modern man stands between two walls of pictures, one wall proclaiming the power of the Self to master experience, the other dissolving the Self in the tides of historical and physical necessity.[12] On the one hand, subjective consciousness is deified and then set apart

---

10. Ibid., 118.
11. Saul Bellow, *Mr. Sammler's Planet* (New York, 1977), 313.
12. Buber, *I and Thou,* 71–72.

in the Forbidden City of the private life, to occupy its hours with experiencing and consuming. On the other, the physical and social forms of public life, epitomized by our cities, have become so occluded as to baffle participation and reduce the individual to the role of an inert particle in their fatal workings. And then, says Buber, come those moments when the individual sees both sets of pictures at once, "and a deeper shudder seizes him." (As the mind, unable to unite the two images into one stereoscopic vision, recognizes: *this is not a world, but pictures on a wall*.)

As Whitman's poetry exemplifies that modern consciousness, both in its grand visions and in its moments of despair, Buber's metaphor describes his poetry with saddening accuracy. This passage concludes the middle part of *I and Thou*, in which Buber has discussed public life. In the third part, he moves from interhuman relationships to describe how these relationships are founded upon "The Eternal Thou." Later, he returns to his image of consciousness caught between a picture that says "I contain the world" and one that says "The world contains me"; and now he is ready to show how mankind may be delivered from this trap.

> Certainly the world "dwells" in me as an image, just as I dwell in it as a thing. But it is not for that reason in me, just as I am not in it. The world and I are mutually included, the one in the other. This contradiction in thought, inherent in the situation of *It*, is resolved in the situation of *Thou*, which sets me free from the world in order to bind me up in solidarity of connexion with it.
>
> I bear within me the sense of Self, that cannot be included in the world. The world bears within itself the sense of being, that cannot be included in the image. This sense of being, however, is not a "will" that can be thought, but simply the total status of the world as world, just as the sense of Self is not a "knowing subject" but simply the total status of the *I* as *I*.
>
> Only he who believes in the world is given power to enter into dealings with it, and if he gives himself to this he cannot remain godless. If only we love the real world,

that will not let itself be extinguished, really in its horror, if only we venture to surround it with the arms of our spirit, our hands will meet hands that grip them.[13]

Although Whitman spoke of the poet as the man of faith in an age straying toward infidelity (*CRE,* 713), he seldom really "believed in the world" on the terms set here by Buber, for all too often World became an object of experience over against the Self as "knowing subject"; and although his poems forever proclaim faith in God, Whitman's God is the reflex of the Self, or the epitome of the World, rather than an eternal Presence, a Thou distinct from both I and Not-Me. For this reason, he seldom discovers a solid connection with the world, seldom encounters another presence whose hand he might grasp. Instead, he envisions reality as a cloud of images that the Self possesses, or (in his later years) as an array of objects against which the Ego situates itself.

On a few occasions, his poetry does record an encounter with some actual presence—a row of bricklayers, a dying soldier, passengers, and harbor traffic at sundown. In these poems, he is able to effect a passage into an existential space that these presences occupy: a trade, a hospital, a city where the passengers dwell together. "Crossing Brooklyn Ferry" would be a powerful poem even if considered distinct from its time, nation, and author; when situated in those contexts, it is an extraordinary achievement. Whitman's poetry is seldom able to acknowledge such spaces, partly because it is so dominated by the spontaneous gestures of consciousness, partly because the American social order does not foster these spaces as it does not foster the enduring social and spiritual associations that might create them. But unless the space exists and can be recognized "in depth," its citizens shrivel into the stuff of consciousness, and the corroborated and mutual world vanishes.

In Buber's thought, the mutual world appears to be secondary to the moment of recognition in which I crosses over to personal Thou and ultimately to eternal Thou. These crossings are unmediated and unprompted. Returning from that recognition, I enters a world of connection with his or her fellow humans, a world mainly structured upon It, so that commerce and justice may be done, but always open to the possibilities of Thou. "Structures of man's communal life

13. *Ibid.,* 93–95.

draw their living quality from the riches of the power to enter into relation."[14] Can the structures of a mutual world work reciprocally to bring an indwelling self to the threshold of meaning, as Whitman says the "dumb beautiful ministers" waited upon him? Perhaps. Despite Buber's devotion to the Hasids' communal way of life and despite his commitment to an ideal Zionism, *I and Thou* includes admonitions against social and spiritual "forms" of communal life through which humans seek to provide continuity for the spirit of relation. The spirit, he says, will not be so contained: relation comes and goes, and when it goes the forms remain as mere cult, without power to summon back the spirit. "The authentic assurance of constancy in space consists in the fact that men's relations with their true *Thou,* the radial lines that proceed from all the points of the *I* to the Centre, form a circle."[15]

However, when those relations exist, they foster a bonded community and create an existential space, which Buber describes poetically as "a human cosmos with bounds and form, grasped with the spirit out of the universal stuff of the aeon, a world that is house and home, a dwelling for man in the universe."[16] He reiterated this sense of indwelling in "Distance and Relation" (1957): "man is . . . in the world as a dweller in an enormous building . . . to whose limits he can never penetrate, but which he can nevertheless know as one does know a house in which one lives."[17] In *Paths in Utopia,* he observes more prosaically that each person has "an eternal human need" "to feel his own house as a room in some greater, all-embracing structure in which he is at home, to feel that the other inhabitants of it with whom he lives and works are all acknowledging and confirming his individual existence."[18] The experienced community then fosters the realization of the larger community; as Buber puts it in another book: "man . . . must find his own self, not the trivial ego of the egotistic individual, but the deeper self of the person living in a relationship to the world."[19]

14. *Ibid.,* 49.
15. *Ibid.,* 114–15.
16. *Ibid.,* 118. The spatial imagery was excised by Buber in 1957.
17. Martin Buber, *The Knowledge of Man,* trans. Maurice Friedman and Ronald Gregor Smith (New York, 1965), 61.
18. Martin Buber, *Paths in Utopia,* trans. R. F. C. Hull (Boston, 1958), 140.
19. Buber, "The Way of Man According to the Teachings of Hasidism," in *Hasidism and Modern Man,* ed. and trans. Maurice Friedman (New York, 1958), 159.

Buber's terminology here is most important: *house, home, dwelling*. He does not say *map*. To profess that the angel's mouth is a passageway to meaning is not to claim access to some propositional truth or system. Steven Marcus, quoting Tommy Wilhelm's complaint against New York, says that the city once possessed "signifying potencies and structural coherences . . . made up of relations between social groups and of functions and symbols that related to social groups." But these "structures of signification" have decomposed: "The city is ceasing to be readable."[20]

Although there is a mythological element to this view of the city (the Genesis account of the Tower of Babel is one of its early ancestors), it is true that the impossibly oversized modern city destroys its own organic substructure, its tissue of association and membership. Nevertheless, to treat the city as a potentially "readable" text, which might be analyzed from an "overview" or penetrated to a "center" that affords a commanding "perspective," is to take a Cartesian view of the city and its space and of the kind of meaning that one might find there. When Whitman said, "What I promised without mentioning it, have you not accepted? / What the study could not teach— what the preaching could not accomplish is accomplished, is it not?" (§8, *V,* I, 223), he recognized that the "glory" into which he had stepped could not be translated into a proposition, but rather had to be experienced by dwelling within it. Christian Norberg-Schulz, the philosopher of architectural and urban design, distinguishes "cognitive" (*i.e.,* abstract) space from existential space.[21] Cities have often been grounded on cognitive space, whether imaginary cities like Atlantis or actual cities like Washington; but though these designs may give comfort to their overseers, they have seldom been much comfort to their inhabitants. We do not draw abstract, overhead maps of our homes; the meaning that Whitman, Buber, and Bellow all point to must be understood as sacramental rather than creedal. It gives a sense of situated membership rather than of universal intelligibility.

❖

20. Steven Marcus, "Reading the Illegible: Some Modern Representations of Urban Experience," in *Visions of the Modern City,* ed. William Sharpe and Leonard Wallock (Baltimore, 1987), 240. Several other essays in this collection reiterate Marcus' complaint.

21. Norberg-Schulz, *Existence, Space, and Architecture,* 9–14. In *Cognition and Reality,* Ulric Neisser speaks of "cognitive maps" in a different and contrary sense, as accounts of existential space.

Angels' Mouths and Existential Space

Denise Levertov is a poet with roots in Judaism, an emigrée from Great Britain who adopted the American—or modern—poetic situation defined by Whitman and Williams. She devoted her book *The Jacob's Ladder* (1961) to exploring the existential space of her own city-dwelling life in the light of a spiritual tradition in which Buber and the Hasids play an indispensable role.

It was through reading Williams that Levertov "naturalized" herself as a poet, when she came to America in her midtwenties. Williams' presence has never vanished from her poetry, and his direct influence is still evident in *The Jacob's Ladder*. Her imagination stirs with the same urban vitalities revealed in Williams' poems; she too delights in the jostle of incongruous surfaces; her lines breathe often with his excitement:

> The quick of the sun that gilds
> broken pebbles in sidewalk cement
> and the iridescent
> spit, that defiles and adorns!
> Gold light in blind love does not distinguish
> one surface from another, the savor
> is the same to its tongue, the fluted
> cylinder of a new ashcan a dazzling silver,
> the smooth flesh of screaming children a quietness, it
>   is all
> a jubilance, the light catches up
> the disordered street in its apron,
> broken fruitrinds shine in the gutter.
>
> (*JL*, 17)

Williams' "sharp eye for the material world" and "keen ear for the vernacular," she says, were her guide as she sought "to engage my capacities as a poet with the crude substance of dailiness."[22]

But Levertov had other guides as well, for Williams would never have said that "the light catches up / the disordered street in its apron." Not only is that too "womanly" for him; it bespeaks a different approach to the quotidian, one got from traditions neither Williams nor Whitman knew. These are religious traditions that foster a spiritual encounter with the here-and-now, through imaginative gestures that are intimate and redemptive rather than aesthetically

---

22. Denise Levertov, *The Poet in the World* (New York, 1973), 67.

detached. Her mother Welsh, her father a Russian Jew who became an Anglican priest, Levertov counts among her ancestors "Schneour Zalman, the founder of Habad Hasidism" and "Angel Jones of Mold, a Welsh tailor whose apprentices came to learn Biblical interpretations from him while cutting and stitching."[23] From this parentage, Levertov inherited a compound religious imagination that discovers the miraculous in the commonplace. This imagination is in part Christian; she has identified it as "Franciscan," reflecting Saint Francis' joyous vision of God incarnate in all physical beings,[24] and she has also connected it with Albert Schweitzer: "There can be no self-respect without respect for others, no love and reverence for others without love and reverence for oneself; and no recognition of others is possible without the imagination. The imagination of what it is to *be* those other forms of life that want to live is the only way to recognition; and it is that imaginative recognition that brings compassion to birth."[25]

More frequently she has associated this imagination with the Hasidic tradition that she learned from her father, "both learned Jew and fervent Christian."[26] "Hasidism," she writes, "has given me since childhood a sense of marvels, of wonder, . . . a recognition and joy in the physical world."[27] What Hasidism recognizes in the physical world is its divinity: "The strawness of straw, the humanness of the human, is their divinity; in that intensity is the 'divine spark' Hasidic lore tells us dwells in all created things."[28] As her reference to Schweitzer's imagination makes clear, the imaginative power that issues in poems also issues in transforming moral action. "The interaction of life on art and of art on life is continuous. . . . When words penetrate deep into us they change the chemistry of the soul, of the imagination."[29] Poems both report and foster the recognition of the "divine spark" that lives in commonplace persons and things. Moral life demands the same double recognition. Unimaginative life is neither poetic nor moral: "The world is / not with us enough," she once

---

23. Ibid., 70.
24. In an interview with Walter Sutton, quoted in Linda Wagner, *Denise Levertov* (New York, 1967), 26. The quoted passage does not appear in the interview as published in *Minnesota Review*, V (1965), 322–38.
25. Levertov, *The Poet in the World*, 53.
26. Ibid., 77.
27. Interview with Sutton, in Wagner, *Denise Levertov*, 26.
28. Levertov, *The Poet in the World*, 51.
29. Ibid., 112–14.

complained against an unworldliness that might be either Wordsworthian or Calvinist. "What I am talking about is . . . an ecstasy of attention, a passion for the thing known, that shall be more, not less, sensuous, and which by its intensity shall lead the writer into a deeper, more vibrant language: and so translate the reader too into the heavens and hells that lie about us in all seemingly ordinary objects and experiences: a supernatural poetry."[30] A Levertov poem then seeks to communicate an uncommon vision of the commonplace: a recognition of the other's being—its being-itself, its occupying its own space within a communal, shared world.[31]

Appropriately, then, she turns to Buber's *Tales of the Hasidim* for the epigraph and title of *The Jacob's Ladder,* for this imagination offers a passage between earth and heaven, the human and the divine, action and contemplation. But with equal appropriateness, the book's first poem, "A Common Ground," invokes Walt Whitman's 1855 Preface, in which an American poet sought to make poetry common not only by espousing commonplace materials but also by contending for its kinship with right action. This is the poem that Levertov chose to contribute to *Walt Whitman: The Measure of his Song:*[32]

> Not 'common speech'
> a dead level
> but the uncommon speech of paradise,
> tongue in which oracles
> speak to beggars and pilgrims:
>
> not illusion but what Whitman called
> 'the path
> between reality and the soul,'
> a language
> excelling itself to be itself.
>
> (*JL,* 3)

---

30. *Ibid.,* 97–98.
31. "The people we live with or meet with, the animals that help us with our farm work, the soil we till, the materials we shape, the tools we use, they all contain a mysterious spiritual substance which depends on us for helping it toward its pure form, its perfection" (Buber, "The Way of Man," 173). Here Buber affirms the spiritual mediation of the dwelt-in world much more clearly than he did twenty-five years earlier in *I and Thou.*
32. Jim Perlman, Ed Folsom, and Dan Campion, eds., *Walt Whitman: The Measure of His Song* (Minneapolis, 1981), 159.

Levertov's work implies a faith in the selfhood of persons, things, and acts. She spoke of the "strawness of straw," and here she describes poetry as language "excelling itself to be itself." The commonplace becomes the communal, as a loving eye discerns its selfhood and proclaims it in words. The ordinary becomes "the authentic," as she names it in another poem, "Matins," in *The Jacob's Ladder:*

> The authentic, I said
> breaking the handle of my hairbrush as I
> brushed my hair in
> rhythmic strokes: That's it,
> that's joy, it's always
> a recognition, the known
> appearing fully itself, and
> more itself than one knew.
>
> (*JL*, 57)

In a poem, she says, there are both epiphanies and communion.[33] "A Common Ground" depicts a group of office workers lunching in a park, surrounded by buildings and traffic. The redbud petals that drift down on them, falling in their coffee cups and on their sandwiches, she likens to the words of poems "entering / human lives forever, / unobserved, a spring element" (*JL*, 2). Her poems often begin with a striking visual image, but eventually pass over into images of taste and nourishment, sound and communion, as she finds "the authentic" within the experience. "The World Outside," for example, begins with a Sloan-like visual composition:

> On the kitchen wall a flash
> of shadow:
>   swift pilgrimage
> of pigeons, a spiral
> celebration of air, of sky-deserts.
> And on tenement windows
> a blaze
>   of lustered watermelon:

---

33. Levertov, *The Poet in the World,* 47: "The communion is triple: between the maker and the needed within the poet; between the maker and the needers outside him . . . and between the human and the divine in both poet and reader."

stain of the sun
westering somewhere back of Hoboken.

(JL, 4)

But the rest of the poem shifts into images of sound as she listens to someone nearby playing the flute and later hears from other apartments voices quarreling, more music making, words of pleasure and joy. Again like Sloan, or Whitman in his empathetic mode, she passes through the window to take an imaginative part in the lives she hears.

Like Whitman and Williams, as well as Sloan, Levertov delights in human encounters in the streets—a blind broom-seller, an old black man walking two contrary dogs in the rain, a burnet moth on the day of Pasternak's death. But these encounters are distinctively Levertov's, for they enter her world like angels or like those "strangers of great wisdom" of whom she had heard in her father's translation of *The Zohar,* who walk along with the rabbis and proffer resolutions to their arguments.[34] Revelatory encounters come not only with such strangers, but also with friends and intimates: with her husband, her son, with a friend, William Kinter, whom she addresses as "Zaddik" [a Hasidic rabbi] after he has explained to her the meaning of the Stations of the Cross in such terms that

>   I saw
> [. . .]
> a shadow of what
> might be seen there if mind and heart
>
> gave themselves to meditation,
> deeper
>
> and deeper into Imagination's
> holy forest.

(JL, 44)

Levertov's perception of "holiness" in her experience then comes from her affiliations with the world in which she dwells, rather than from being a simple separate person. Poetic vision is mediated for her through her being a city-dweller, a wife, a mother, a woman, a

34. Ibid., 76–77.

friend, a citizen. In all these roles, she can focus on the sensuously given, the here-and-now, seen "in depth" because it is related to those with whom she shares the experience.[35] As a citizen poet, the Denise Levertov of *The Jacob's Ladder* occupies existential space, a space that allows her to recognize how other persons and objects occupy their own volumes and orientations within the same communal space. It is natural for her poetry to draw maps of that space, as Whitman did in "Crossing Brooklyn Ferry." Although she has never achieved anything on the scale of Whitman's great poem, *The Jacob's Ladder* contains two mapping poems, one a memory of the countryside of her birthplace in Essex in England, the other an American city poem, "From the Roof."

"From the Roof" begins with another Sloan-like scene—Levertov on a rooftop taking in laundry from a line. It is a windy October night; expecting her husband's return from a trip, she remembers a time when they were not separated but alienated from each other. But

> . . . now alone in October's
> first decision towards winter, so close to you—
> >   my arms full of playful rebellious linen, a
> >   freighter
> >   going down-river two blocks away, outward
> >   bound,
> >   the green wolf-eyes of the Harborside Terminal
> >   glittering on the Jersey shore,
> and a train somewhere underground bringing you
>   towards me
> to our new living-place from which we can see
>
> a river and its traffic (the Hudson and the
> hidden river, who can say which it is we see, we see
> something of both . . .)
>
> <div align="right">(<i>JL</i>, 49)</div>

The "hidden river" is that current of greater being in which Levertov finds her place, from which come "angelic" emissaries such as the broom-vendor who appears a few lines later in her poem. This poem

---

35. When her sense of citizenship expanded, in the late 1960s, to encompass the United States and Vietnam, her poetry paid a Whitmanian price in shifting its ground from the sensuous to the rhetorical.

is about dwelling, about fully occupying space: it ends "by design / we are to live now in a new place." The space is defined by the city's geography, coincidentally close to that defined by Whitman more than a hundred years before. It is further defined by housekeeping with laundry and broom, by her private memories and anticipations, and by the poem, which serves as a public space itself in which they are brought into communion by Levertov's words. Her sense of membership and affiliation reaches out to husband (the "you" named in the poem), to broom-vendor, and to reader. This is Buber's "human cosmos." It is structured upon her sense of relationship; and from within it her imagination carries her toward new encounters with persons and things, which, in being themselves, shine with the glory of angels.

Later in the 1960s, this sense of intimacy and immediacy began to wane in Levertov's poetry as she committed herself to political issues that lay beyond her immediate horizon.[36] "City Psalm," from *The Sorrow Dance* (1967) dramatizes the stress of her attempt to keep faith with both. In the poem, Levertov is walking through a city, choked by its fumes, deafened by its jackhammers, oppressed by its squalor and injustice, while her thoughts are preoccupied by the daily killings in Vietnam. Nevertheless, she insists on the continuity of her vision of joy:

> . . . I have seen
> not behind but within, within the
> dull grief, blown grit, hideous
> concrete façades, another grief, a gleam
> as of dew, an abode of mercy . . . .
>
> [N]ot that horror was not, not that the killings did not
>   continue,
> not that I thought there was to be no more despair,
> but that as if transparent all disclosed
> an otherness that was blessèd, that was bliss.
> *I saw Paradise in the dust of the street.*[37]

Levertov clearly understands that there can be nothing innocent about her vision. Like Whitman in "Crossing Brooklyn Ferry," she

---

36. This waning is sketched by Robert Younkins in "Denise Levertov and the Hasidic Tradition," *Descant*, XIX (1974), 40–48.

37. Denise Levertov, *Poems, 1960–67* (New York, 1983), 222.

sees the dark patches that surround her and her adopted country. As Elie Wiesel's writings have repeatedly observed, the joy of the Hasidim was achieved in the memory of, and the anticipation of, the slaughter of the innocent. But the poem's final lines, with their monosyllabic, consonant-choked words and syntactical awkwardness, seem only to be words. She cannot find the selfhood in what she sees, and Paradise is found not in entering their space but in recoiling from them.

As Levertov has prolonged her American sojourn and as the fortunes of her own life have altered, she has lost much of her sense of a communal space within which it is possible to say "You" not only to oneself and to intimates, but also to strangers. She has entered more fully into the America that Whitman once envisioned—the simply separate spaces on which our anticommunitarian society long ago proved its claim.

❖

Perhaps Whitman recognized that the workings of sight both posed the "modern" problem of personal detachment and social disconnection, and at the same time suggested a response to that problem. In most of his poems, he sought to use the bridge of mediated pictorial images to communicate with his readers his delight in unmediated imaginative liberty. "The miracle of the eyesight," transforming objects into thoughts, might also transform separate readers into a responsive people. In "Crossing Brooklyn Ferry" he found, for once, a way to invoke the very process of seeing as he created a vision of a city where human beings occupy a communicable world. In that poem, he steps forth as one of Levertov's angels, leading us toward an America that we have not yet discovered.

Bibliography

Aaron, Daniel. *The Unwritten War: American Writers and the Civil War.* New York, 1973.
Abbott, Berenice. *Berenice Abbott: Photographs.* New York, 1970.
———. *Changing New York.* 1939; rpr. as *New York in the Thirties.* New York, 1973.
Abrams, Meyer H. "Structure and Style in the Greater Romantic Lyric." In *From Sensibility to Romanticism,* edited by Frederick W. Hilles and Harold Bloom. New York, 1965.
Adams, Stephen. "The Luminist Walt Whitman." *American Poetry,* II (Winter, 1985), 2–16.
Addams, Jane. *Twenty Years at Hull-House.* New York, 1912.
Alcott, Bronson. *The Journals of Bronson Alcott.* Edited by Odell Shepard. Boston, 1938.
Alcott, Louisa May. *Hospital Sketches.* 1863; rpr. Cambridge, Mass., 1960.
Alland, Alexander, Sr. *Jacob A. Riis: Photographer and Citizen.* Millerton, N.Y., 1974.
Allen, Gay Wilson. *The Solitary Singer.* Rev. ed.; New York, 1967.
Altick, Robert. *The Shows of London.* Cambridge, Mass., 1978.
Anderson, Quentin. *The Imperial Self.* New York, 1971.
Andrews, Malcolm. "Whitman and the American City." In *The American City: Literary and Cultural Perspectives,* edited by Graham Clarke. New York, 1988.
Askin, Denise. "Retrievements Out of the Night: Prophetic and Private Voices in Whitman's *Drum-Taps.*" *ATQ,* LI (1981), 211–23.
Asselineau, Roger. *The Evolution of Walt Whitman.* 2 vols. Cambridge, Mass., 1960.
Baudelaire, Charles. "Les Sept Vieillards." In *Les Fleurs du Mal,* edited by M. Mathews and J. Mathews. New York, 1953.
Beaver, Joseph. *Walt Whitman—Poet of Science.* Morningside Heights, N.Y., 1951.
Bellow, Saul. *Mr. Sammler's Planet.* New York, 1977.
———. *Seize the Day.* New York, 1987.
Benjamin, Walter. "A Short History of Photography." In *Classic Essays on Photography,* edited by Alan Trachtenberg. New Haven, Conn., 1980.

Berkeley, George. "An Essay Towards a New Theory of Vision." In *Works on Vision,* edited by Colin M. Turbayne. Indianapolis, 1963.

Betsky-Zweig, S. "An Uncommon Language: Crossing with Whitman." *Dutch Quarterly Review of Anglo-American Letters,* X (1979), 258–71.

Bloom, Harold. *The Ringers in the Tower: Studies in Romantic Tradition.* Chicago, 1971.

Bode, Carl. *The Anatomy of American Popular Culture.* Berkeley, 1959.

Bond, Reese Alexander. "Whitman's Visual Imagination." Ph.D. dissertation, University of Minnesota, 1971.

Bourne, George F. "The Night Guard." In *Poetical Pen-Pictures of the War,* edited by John Henry Hayward. 1863; rpr. Louisville, 1975.

Bové, Paul. *Destructive Poetics: Heidegger and Modern American Poetry.* New York, 1980.

Brasher, Thomas L. *Whitman as Editor of the "Brooklyn Daily Eagle."* Detroit, 1970.

Breitweiser, Robert Mitchell. "Who Speaks in Whitman's Poems?" In *The American Renaissance: New Dimensions,* edited by Harry R. Garvin and Peter C. Carafiol. Lewisburg, Pa., 1983.

Bremner, Robert. *From the Depths: The Discovery of Poverty in the United States.* New York, 1956.

Breslin, James E. "Whitman and the Early Development of William Carlos Williams." *PMLA,* LXXXII (1967), 613–21.

———. "William Carlos Williams and the Whitman Tradition." In *Literary Criticism and Historical Understanding,* edited by Phillip Damon. New York, 1967.

Brooks, Van Wyck. *John Sloan: A Painter's Life.* New York, 1955.

Buber, Martin. *I and Thou.* Translated by Ronald Gregor Smith. New York, 1958.

———. *The Knowledge of Man.* Translated by Maurice Friedman and Ronald Gregor Smith. New York, 1965.

———. *Mamre: Essays in Religion.* Translated by Greta Hort. Westport, Conn., 1970.

———. *Paths in Utopia.* Translated by R. F. C. Hull. Boston, 1958.

———. "The Way of Man According to the Teachings of Hasidism." In *Hasidism and Modern Man,* edited and translated by Maurice Friedman. New York, 1958.

Bucke, Richard Maurice. *Walt Whitman.* Philadelphia, 1883.

Buell, Lawrence. *Literary Transcendentalism.* Ithaca, 1973.

Cady, Joseph. "*Drum-Taps* and Nineteenth-Century Male Homosexual Literature." In *Walt Whitman Here and Now,* edited by Joann P. Krieg. Westport, Conn., 1985.

Carlisle, E. Fred. *The Uncertain Self: Whitman's Drama of Identity.* East Lansing, Mich., 1973.

Carlyle, Thomas. *Sartor Resartus.* Edited by Charles Frederick Harrold. New York, 1937.

Chase, Richard. *Walt Whitman Reconsidered.* New York, 1955.

Clarke, Graham. "'To emanate a look': Whitman, Photography and the Spectacle of Self." In *American Literary Landscapes: The Fiction and the Fact,* edited by Ian F. A. Bell and D. K. Adams. London, 1988.

Coffman, Stanley K. "'Crossing Brooklyn Ferry': A Note on the Catalogue Technique in Whitman's Poetry." *Modern Philology,* LI (1954), 225–32.

Coleridge, Samuel Taylor. *Samuel Taylor Coleridge.* Edited by H. J. Jackson. Oxford, Eng., 1985.

Coles, Robert. *William Carlos Williams: The Knack of Survival in America.* New Brunswick, N.J., 1975.

Collier, Peter. "Nineteenth-Century Paris: Vision and Nightmare." In *Unreal City: Urban Experience in Modern European Literature and Art,* edited by Edward Timms and David Kelley. New York, 1985.

Collins, Christopher. *The Uses of Observation.* The Hague, 1971.

Conrad, Peter. *The Art of the City: Views and Versions of New York.* New York, 1984.

Dijkstra, Bram, ed. *A Recognizable Image: William Carlos Williams on Art and Artists.* New York, 1978.

Dolis, John. "Hawthorne's Tactile Gaze: The Phenomenon of Depth." *MLQ,* XLIV (1983), 267–84.

Dougherty, James. "Broadacre City: Frank Lloyd Wright's Utopia." *The Centennial Review,* XXV (1981), 239–56.

———. *The Fivesquare City: The City in the Religious Imagination.* Notre Dame, Ind., 1980.

———. "Jane Addams: Culture and Imagination." *The Yale Review,* LXXI (1982), 363–79.

Eliot, T. S. *Collected Poems 1909–1962.* New York, 1963.

———. *The Waste Land: A Facsimile and Transcript of the Original Drafts Including the Annotations of Ezra Pound.* Edited by Valerie Eliot. New York, 1974.

———. "What Dante Means to Me." In *To Criticize the Critic and Other Writings.* London, 1965.

Emerson, Peter Henry. *Naturalistic Photography for Students of the Art.* 1889; rpr. New York, 1973.

Emerson, Ralph Waldo. *Selections from Ralph Waldo Emerson.* Edited by Stephen E. Whicher. Boston, 1957.

Erikkla, Betsy. *Whitman the Political Poet.* New York, 1989.

———. "Whitman as Revolutionary Son." *Prospects,* X (1985), 421–41.

Fanger, Donald. *Dostoevsky and Romantic Realism.* Chicago, 1965.

Folsom, Ed. "Whitman and the Visual Democracy of Photography." *Mickle Street Review,* X (1988), 51–65.

Frail, David. *The Early Politics and Poetics of William Carlos Williams.* Ann Arbor, Mich., 1987.

Frank, Joseph. *The Widening Gyre: Crisis and Mastery in Modern Literature.* New Brunswick, N.J., 1963.

Fredrickson, George M. *The Inner Civil War: Northern Intellectuals and the Crisis of the Union.* New York, 1965.

Friedman, Martin. *Charles Sheeler*. New York, 1975.
Friedman, Rohn S. "A Whitman Primer: Solipsism and Identity." *American Quarterly*, XXVII (1975), 443–60.
Galassi, Peter. *Before Photography: Painting and the Invention of Photography*. New York, 1981.
Gargano, James W. "Technique in 'Crossing Brooklyn Ferry': The Everlasting Moment." *JEGP*, LXII (1963), 262–69.
Gibson, James J. *The Perception of the Visual World*. Boston, 1950.
——. *The Senses Considered as Perceptual Systems*. Boston, 1966.
Gilpin, William. *The Mission of the North American People*. Philadelphia, 1873.
Glicksberg, Charles I., ed. *Walt Whitman and the Civil War*. Philadelphia, 1933.
Golden, Arthur. Introduction to *Walt Whitman's Blue Book*. Vol. II of 2 vols. New York, 1968.
Gombrich, E. H. *Art and Illusion: A Study in the Psychology of Pictorial Representation*. New York, 1960.
Goodrich, Lloyd, ed. *Edward Hopper*. New York, 1971.
——. *John Sloan*. New York, 1952.
Greenough, Sarah. "Alfred Stieglitz and 'The Idea Photography.'" In *Alfred Stieglitz: Photographs and Writings*, edited by Sarah Greenough and Juan Hamilton. Washington, D.C., 1983.
Greenough, Sarah, and Juan Hamilton, eds. *Alfred Stieglitz: Photographs and Writings*. Washington, D.C., 1983.
Greenspan, Ezra. *Walt Whitman and the American Reader*. Cambridge, Eng., 1990.
Hagstrum, Jean. *The Sister Arts: The Tradition of Literary Pictorialism and English Poetry from Dryden to Gray*. Chicago, 1958.
Hales, Peter B. *Silver Cities: The Photography of American Urbanization, 1839–1915*. Philadelphia, 1984.
Hartman, Geoffrey. *The Unmediated Vision: An Interpretation of Wordsworth, Hopkins, Rilke and Valéry*. New Haven, Conn., 1954.
Hayward, John Henry, ed. *Poetical Pen-Pictures of the War*. 1863; rpr. Louisville, 1975.
Heffernan, James A. W. *The Re-Creation of Landscape*. Hanover, N.H., 1984.
Heidegger, Martin. "Building Dwelling Thinking." In *Basic Writings*, edited by David Farrell Krell. New York, 1977.
Helmholtz, Hermann von. "Recent Progress in the Theory of Vision." In *Selected Writings*, edited by Russell Kahl. Middletown, Conn., 1971.
Helms, Alan. "'Hints . . . Faint Clews and Indirections': Whitman's Homosexual Disguises." In *Walt Whitman Here and Now*, edited by Joann P. Krieg. Westport, Conn., 1985.
Henri, Robert. *The Art-Spirit: Notes, Articles, Fragments of Letters and Talks* . . . . Compiled by Margery Ryerson. 1923; rpr. Philadelphia, 1960.
Hollis, C. Carroll. *Language and Style in "Leaves of Grass."* Baton Rouge, 1983.

Holloway, Emory, ed. *The Uncollected Poetry and Prose of Walt Whitman.* 2 vols. New York, 1932.

Holmes, Oliver Wendell. "The Stereoscope and the Stereograph." In *Photography: Essays and Images,* edited by Beaumont Newhall. New York, 1980.

Ivins, William. *Prints and Visual Communication.* Cambridge, Mass., 1953.

Johnston, John H. *The Poet and the City: A Study in Urban Perspectives.* Athens, Ga., 1984.

Kaplan, Justin. *Walt Whitman: A Life.* New York, 1980.

Kegan, Robert. *The Sweeter Welcome: Voices for a Vision of Affirmation: Bellow, Malamud and Martin Buber.* Needham Heights, Mass., 1977.

Killingsworth, M. Jimmie. *Whitman's Poetry of the Body: Sexuality, Politics, and the Text.* Chapel Hill, N.C., 1989.

Kouwenhoven, John A. *The Columbia Historical Portrait of New York.* New York, 1972.

Krausz, Sigmund. *Street Types of Great American Cities.* Chicago, 1896.

Krieg, Joann P., ed. *Walt Whitman Here and Now.* Westport, Conn., 1985.

Kroeber, Karl. *Romantic Landscape Vision: Constable and Wordsworth.* Madison, Wis., 1975.

Kwiat, Joseph J. "John Sloan: An American Artist as Social Critic, 1900–1917." *Arizona Quarterly,* X (Spring, 1954), 52–64.

———. "Robert Henri and the Emerson-Whitman Tradition." *PMLA,* LXXI (1956), 617–36.

Larkin, Oliver. *Art and Life in America.* New York, 1960.

Larson, Kerry C. *Whitman's Drama of Consensus.* Chicago, 1988.

Levertov, Denise. *The Jacob's Ladder.* New York, 1961.

———. *Poems 1960–67.* New York, 1983.

———. *The Poet in the World.* New York, 1973.

Levin, Gail, ed. *Edward Hopper: The Art and the Artist.* New York, 1980.

Lewis, R. W. B. *The American Adam.* Chicago, 1955.

Longfellow, Henry Wadsworth. *The Complete Poetical Works of Henry Wadsworth Longfellow.* Boston, 1902.

———. *Kavanagh: A Tale.* 1849; rpr. Boston, 1872.

Lynch, Kevin. *The Image of the City.* Cambridge, Mass., 1960.

———. *What Time Is This Place?* Cambridge, Mass., 1972.

MacGowan, Christopher J. *William Carlos Williams's Early Poetry: The Visual Arts Background.* Ann Arbor, Mich., 1984.

McGrath, Robert L. Introduction to *John Sloan: Paintings, Prints, Drawings.* Hanover, N.H., 1981.

Machor, James L. *Pastoral Cities: Urban Ideals and the Symbolic Landscape of America.* Madison, Wis., 1987.

———. "Pastoralism and the American Urban Ideal: Hawthorne, Whitman, and the Literary Pattern." *American Literature,* LIV (1982), 329–53.

McLuhan, Marshall. "The Aesthetic Moment in Landscape Poetry." In *English Institute Essays, 1951,* edited by Alan S. Downer. New York, 1952.

McNamara, Eugene. " 'Crossing Brooklyn Ferry': The Shaping Imagination." *Walt Whitman Quarterly Review,* II (1984), 32–35.
Marcus, Steven. "Reading the Illegible: Some Modern Representations of Urban Experience." In *Visions of the Modern City,* edited by William Sharpe and Leonard Wallock. Baltimore, 1987.
Mariani, Paul. *William Carlos Williams: A New World Naked.* New York, 1982.
Marling, William. *William Carlos Williams and the Painters.* Athens, Ohio, 1982.
Martin, Robert K. *The Homosexual Tradition in American Poetry.* Austin, Tex., 1979.
Matthiessen, F. O. *American Renaissance: Art and Expression in the Age of Emerson and Whitman.* New York, 1941.
Mayhew, Henry. *London Labour and the London Poor.* London, 1861–62.
Melville, Herman. *The Confidence Man: His Masquerade.* Edited by Hershel Parker. New York, 1971.
———. *Moby-Dick.* Edited by Harrison Hayford and Hershel Parker. New York, 1967.
Miller, Edwin Haviland, ed. *The Correspondence of Walt Whitman (1842–1867).* 6 vols. New York, 1961.
———. ["There was a Child Went Forth"]. In *Critical Essays on Walt Whitman,* edited by James Woodress. Boston, 1983.
Morse, Peter, ed. *John Sloan's Prints.* New Haven, Conn., 1969.
Nathanson, Tenney. "Whitman's Tropes of Light and Flood: Language and Representation in the Early Editions of *Leaves of Grass.*" *ESQ,* XXXI (1985), 116–34.
Neisser, Ulric. *Cognition and Reality.* San Francisco, 1976.
Newhall, Beaumont, ed. *Photography: Essays and Images.* New York, 1980.
Norberg-Schulz, Christian. *Existence, Space, and Architecture.* New York, 1971.
Norman, Dorothy, ed. *Alfred Stieglitz: An American Seer.* New York, 1973.
———. Introduction to *Alfred Stieglitz.* New York, 1976.
Novak, Barbara. *American Painting of the Nineteenth Century: Realism, Idealism, and the American Experience.* New York, 1969.
———. *Nature and Culture: American Landscape and Painting, 1825–1875.* New York, 1980.
Nygren, Edward J. "American Genre: Its Changing Form and Content." In *Of Time and Place: American Figurative Art from the Corcoran Gallery.* Washington, D.C., 1981.
O'Doherty, Brian. "Portrait: Edward Hopper." *Art in America,* LII (December, 1964), 68–88.
O'Neal, Hank. *Berenice Abbott: American Photographer.* New York, 1982.
Orvell, Miles. "Reproducing Walt Whitman: The Camera, the Omnibus and *Leaves of Grass.*" In *Prospects: An Annual of American Cultural Studies,* edited by Jack Salzman. Vol. XII. New York, 1987.
Pastore, Nicholas. *A Selective History of Theories of Visual Perception, 1650–1950.* New York, 1971.

Paul, Sherman. *Emerson's Angle of Vision.* Cambridge, Mass., 1952.
Paulson, Ronald. *Literary Landscape, Turner and Constable.* New Haven, Conn., 1982.
Perlman, Bennard B. *The Immortal Eight.* New York, 1962.
Perlman, Jim, Ed Folsom, and Dan Campion, eds. *Walt Whitman: The Measure of His Song.* Minneapolis, 1981.
[Pierrepont, Henry Evelyn.] *Historical Sketch of the Fulton Ferry, and Its Associated Ferries, By a Director.* Brooklyn, 1879.
Price, Kenneth M. *Whitman and Tradition.* New Haven, Conn., 1990.
Rawls, Walton, ed. *The Great Book of Currier and Ives' America.* New York, 1979.
Reynolds, David S. *Beneath the American Renaissance.* New York, 1988.
Riis, Jacob. *How the Other Half Lives.* New York, 1971.
———. *How the Other Half Lives: Studies Among the Tenements of New York.* 1890; rpr. New York, 1980.
Ringe, Donald. *The Pictorial Mode: Space and Time in the Art of Bryant, Irving and Cooper.* Lexington, Ky., 1971.
Rosenblatt, Jon. "Whitman's Body, Whitman's Language." In *Walt Whitman Here and Now,* edited by Joann P. Krieg. Westport, Conn., 1985.
Rosenfeld, Paul. "Alfred Stieglitz." In *Photography: Essays and Images,* edited by Beaumont Newhall. New York, 1980.
Rourke, Constance. *Charles Sheeler: Artist in the American Tradition.* New York, 1938.
Rubin, Joseph Jay. *The Historic Whitman.* University Park, Pa., 1973.
Ruskin, John. *Modern Painters.* 4 vols. New York, 1847.
St. Armand, Barton. "Transcendence Through Technique: Whitman's 'Crossing Brooklyn Ferry' and Impressionist Painting." In *The Arts and Their Interrelations,* edited by Harry R. Garvin and James M. Heath. Lewisburg, Pa., 1978.
St. John, Bruce, ed. *John Sloan's New York Scene.* New York, 1965.
Sayre, Henry M. *The Visual Text of William Carlos Williams.* Urbana, Ill., 1983.
Schmidt, Peter. *William Carlos Williams, the Arts, and Literary Tradition.* Baton Rouge, 1988.
Scott, David W. *John Sloan.* New York, 1975.
———. "John Sloan: His Life and Paintings." In *John Sloan 1871–1951,* edited by David W. Scott and E. John Bullard. Boston, 1976.
Scott, David W., and E. John Bullard, eds. *John Sloan 1871–1951.* Boston, 1976.
Scott, Dixon. "The Function of the Camera." In *Photography: Essays and Images,* edited by Beaumont Newhall. New York, 1980.
Sears, Stephen W., ed. *The American Heritage Century Collection of Civil War Art.* New York, 1974.
Sharpe, William Chapman. "City/Body/Text: Walt Whitman's Urban Incarnation." *Cycnos* [Nice], I (1984), 39–48.
———. *Unreal Cities: Urban Figuration in Wordsworth, Baudelaire, Whitman, Eliot, and Williams.* Baltimore, 1990.

Sharpe, William Chapman, and Leonard Wallock, eds. *Visions of the Modern City.* Baltimore, 1987.
Shloss, Carol. *In Visible Light: Photography and the American Writer, 1840–1940.* New York, 1987.
Shurr, William H. "Whitman and the Seduction of the Reader." *Mickle Street Review,* XI (1989), 71–79.
Sloan, John. *The Gist of Art.* New York, 1939.
———. *John Sloan: Paintings, Prints, Drawings.* Hanover, N.H., 1981.
Sontag, Susan. *On Photography.* New York, 1977.
Spacks, Patricia Meyer. *The Poetry of Vision.* Cambridge, Mass., 1967.
Stebbins, Theodore E., Jr. *Charles Sheeler: The Photographs.* Boston, 1987.
———. Introduction to *Charles Sheeler: The Photographs.* Boston, 1987.
Stevens, Patrick L. "Charles Sheeler, William Carlos Williams, and Precisionism: A Redefinition." *Arts Magazine,* LVIII (November, 1983), 100–14.
Stevens, Wallace. "Of Modern Poetry." In *The Collected Poems of Wallace Stevens.* New York, 1954.
Stieglitz, Alfred. *Alfred Stieglitz.* New York, 1976.
Stovall, Floyd. *The Foreground of "Leaves of Grass."* Charlottesville, 1974.
Sweet, Timothy. *Poetry, Photography, and the Crisis of the Union.* Baltimore, 1990.
Szarkowski, John, and Maria Morris Hambourg. *The Work of Atget.* New York, 1981.
Szasz, Ferenc M., and Ralph F. Bogardus. "The Camera and the American Social Conscience: The Documentary Photography of Jacob A. Riis." *New York History,* LX (1974), 409–36.
Taft, Robert. *Photography and the American Scene.* New York, 1938.
Tapscott, Stephen. *American Beauty: William Carlos Williams and the Modernist Whitman.* New York, 1984.
Tashjian, Dickran. *Skyscraper Primitives: Dada and the American Avant-Garde, 1910–1925.* Middletown, Conn., 1975.
———. *William Carlos Williams and the American Scene, 1920–1940.* New York, 1978.
Thomas, Alan. *Time in a Frame: Photography and the Nineteenth-Century Mind.* New York, 1977.
Thomas, F. Richard. *Literary Admirers of Alfred Stieglitz.* Carbondale, Ill., 1983.
Thomas, M. Wynn. *The Lunar Light of Whitman's Poetry.* Cambridge, Mass., 1987.
———. "Whitman and the American Democratic Identity Before and During the Civil War." *Journal of American Studies,* XV (1981), 73–93.
Thomson, James. "Spring." In *The Seasons,* edited by James Sambrook. Oxford, 1981.
Thomson, John, and Adolphe Smith. *Street Life in London.* 1878; rpr. New York, 1969.
Thoreau, Henry David. *The Correspondence of Henry David Thoreau.* Edited by Walter Harding and Carl Bode. New York, 1958.

Tocqueville, Alexis de. *Democracy in America.* Translated by Henry Reeve. 2 vols. New York, 1945.
Todd, Edgeley W. "Indian Pictures and Two Whitman Poems." *Huntington Library Quarterly,* XIX (November, 1955), 1–11.
Trachtenberg, Alan. "Whitman's Visionary Politics." *Mickle Street Review,* X (1988), 15–31.
———, ed. *Classic Essays on Photography.* New Haven, Conn., 1980.
Traubel, Horace. *With Walt Whitman in Camden.* Edited by Gertrude Traubel and William White. Vol. VI of 7 vols. to date. Carbondale, Ill., 1982.
Troyen, Carol, and Erica E. Hirshler, eds. *Charles Sheeler: Paintings and Drawings.* Boston, 1987.
Tsujimoto, Karen. *Images of America: Precisionist Painting and Modern Photography.* Seattle, 1982.
Waggoner, Hyatt H. *American Visionary Poetry.* Baton Rouge, 1982.
Wagner, Linda. *Denise Levertov.* New York, 1967.
Walker, Jeffrey. *Bardic Ethos and the American Epic Poem.* Baton Rouge, 1989.
Ward, J. A. *American Silences: The Realism of James Agee, Walker Evans, and Edward Hopper.* Baton Rouge, 1985.
Warren, James Perrin. *Walt Whitman's Language Experiment.* University Park, Pa., 1990.
Weaver, Mike. *William Carlos Williams: The American Background.* Cambridge, Eng., 1971.
Weisbuch, Robert. *Atlantic Double-Cross: American Literature and British Influence in the Age of Emerson.* Chicago, 1986.
Wertheim, Arthur Frank. *The New York Little Renaissance.* New York, 1976.
Whitman, Walt. *The Gathering of the Forces.* Edited by Cleveland Rodgers and John Black. 2 vols. New York, 1920.
———. *Leaves of Grass: Comprehensive Reader's Edition.* Edited by Harold W. Blodgett and Sculley Bradley. New York, 1965.
———. *Leaves of Grass: A Textual Variorum of the Printed Poems.* Edited by Sculley Bradley, Harold Blodgett, Arthur Golden, and William White. 3 vols. New York, 1980.
———. *New York Dissected.* New York, 1936.
———. *Notebooks and Unpublished Prose Manuscripts.* Edited by Edward F. Grier. 6 vols. New York, 1984.
———. *Prose Works, 1892.* Edited by Floyd Stovall. 2 vols. New York, 1963–64.
———. *Rivulets of Prose.* New York, 1928.
———. *Walt Whitman's Blue Book: The 1860–61 "Leaves of Grass" Containing His Manuscript Additions and Revisions.* Edited by Arthur Golden. 2 vols. New York, 1968.
Whittier, John Greenleaf. *The Poetical Works of John Greenleaf Whittier.* 2 vols. Boston, 1872.
Williams, Hermann Warner, Jr. *The Civil War: The Artists' Record.* Washington, D.C., 1961.
———. *Mirror to the American Past: A Survey of American Genre Painting, 1750–1900.* Greenwich, Conn., 1973.

Williams, William Carlos. "America, Whitman, and the Art of Poetry." *Poetry Journal*, VIII (November, 1917), 27–36.
———. "The American Background: America and Alfred Stieglitz." In *Selected Essays*. New York, 1969.
———. *The Collected Poems of William Carlos Williams*. Vol. I. Edited by A. Walton Litz and Christopher MacGowan. New York, 1986. Vol. II. Edited by Christopher MacGowan. New York, 1988.
———. *Imaginations*. Edited by Webster Schott. New York, 1970.
———. *In the American Grain*. New York, 1956.
———. *Life Along the Passaic River*. Norfolk, Conn., 1938.
———. *Paterson*. New York, 1963.
Younkins, Robert. "Denise Levertov and the Hasidic Tradition." *Descant*, XIX (1974), 40–48.
Zarobila, Charles. "Walt Whitman and the Panorama." *WWR*, XXV (June, 1979), 51–59.
Zweig, Paul. *Walt Whitman: The Making of the Poet*. New York, 1984.

Index

Aaron, Daniel, 82n
Abbott, Berenice, 280–85, 281n
—works: *Changing New York,* 280; *East Side Portrait,* 282; *The Financial District,* 281; *Hardware Store,* 280; *Model Early Tenement, east 70's,* 281; *Newsstand,* 280–81; *Washington Street,* 281; *West Street,* 281; *A. Zito's Bakery, New York, 1937,* 283–85
Abbott, Henry, 149n
Abrams, Meyer, 143–44, 143n, 154
Addams, Jane, 219–20, 220n
Aerial viewpoint, 157–59, 159–60n, 179, 191, 276
Alcott, Bronson, 60
Alcott, Louisa May, 88, 89, 90
Alienation, 4–5, 12, 13, 13n, 32n, 101–104, 140, 145n, 146, 201, 237, 272–73, 285, 286, 294–95
Altick, Robert, 166
America, Matter of, 1–10, 40, 47–48, 56–61, 84, 92–95, 114, 132–33, 139–40, 224, 289
Anderson, Quentin, 5n, 162, 170n
Apostrophe, 93
Arensberg, Walter and Louise, 246n, 250, 275
Artistic devices. *See* specific terms
Ashcan school, 224, 246, 246n. *See also* New York Realists
Askin, Denise, 82n

Asselineau, Roger, 85
Atget, Eugène, 211, 254, 279, 280
Atmospheric perspective, 115–16, 128n, 180
Auditory images, 21, 21n, 141, 303
Augustine, Saint, 255

Background. *See* Visual planes of attention
Banvard, John, 164, 164n
Barlow, Joel, 2
Bartholdi, Luigi, 93
Baudelaire, Charles, 32, 32n, 132, 239, 239n
Bellow, Saul: *Seize the Day,* 288–94, 298; *Mr. Sammler's Planet,* 294
Bellows, George, 223, 246, 256
Benjamin, Walter, 54n, 218, 221n
Berkeley, George, 25–26, 178, 186
Bierstadt, Albert, 166, 184n
Bill, Ledyard, 89
Bingham, George Caleb, 59, 67, 228
Blacks, 65–66, 66n
Blake, William, 22, 24, 32n, 50, 81
Bloom, Harold, 11
Bové, Paul, 30n, 163
Brady, Mathew, 117
Breitweiser, Robert Mitchell, 11
Brooklyn, 98, 141, 143–54, 156–63, 167–68, 169–70, 184, 190–98, 227, 233. *See also* New York City

317

Bryant, William Cullen, 41, 125, 126
Buber, Martin, 17, 17*n*, 39, 292, 299, 305
—works: "Distance and Relation," 297; *I and Thou*, 10–11, 16*n*, 38, 145*n*, 200–201, 272–73, 294–97; *The Knowledge of Man*, 297; *Mamre*, 292; *Paths in Utopia*, 297; *Tales of the Hasidim*, 301; "The Way of Man," 301*n*
Buell, Lawrence, 47*n*
Byron, George Gordon, Lord, 41, 43, 81, 123, 124, 134

Camera. *See* Photography
Canada, 78, 78*n*
Carlisle, E. Fred, 5*n*, 12, 16*n*, 17*n*, 146*n*, 154, 163*n*
Carlyle, Thomas, 11
Catalogs of images, 6, 39–40, 43–72, 47*n*, 84–85, 147*n*, 162–63, 167, 186, 205–206, 208, 224, 227, 228, 244, 247, 279
Catlin, George, 60
Cézanne, Paul, 264, 271
Chase, Richard, 5*n*, 30*n*, 59, 59*n*, 80*n*
Church, Frederic, 116, 166, 184*n*
Cities. *See* Urban life; and names of specific cities
Citizenship, 27, 55, 192, 193, 197, 212, 221, 247, 304, 304*n*
Civil War: in *Drum–Taps*, 28–30, 42, 71, 76–82, 84, 89–108, 110–17, 120–21, 133–34; Whitman's hospital service during, 30*n*, 42, 79, 82, 87–88; artwork of, 66*n*, 95, 96, 117–20, 118*n*, 119*n*; impact on Whitman's poetry, 71, 76–77, 134–35; in *Specimen Days*, 86–88, 90–91; in *War Memoranda*, 88; books of war "sketches" on, 88, 89, 90; in Hayward's *Poetical Pen-Pictures of the War*, 89, 105, 108–109; Whitman's reticence about realities of, 90–91*n*; newspaper accounts of, 91–92, 119*n*, 120; nation's response to death toll during, 99*n*; popular songs about, 109–10*n*; photographs of, 112*n*, 117, 118*n*
Civitas, 50–51, 141, 195, 238
Clarke, Graham, 21*n*, 47*n*, 174*n*, 281*n*
Coburn, A. L., 276*n*
Coffman, Stanley K., 163
Cole, Thomas, 112, 116
Coleridge, Samuel Taylor, 143, 144, 155–56, 185, 209, 242*n*, 249
Coles, Robert, 260*n*
Collier, Peter, 54*n*
Collins, Christopher, 32*n*
Conrad, Peter, 217, 230*n*
Constable, John, 123, 170, 199, 200
Cooper, James Fenimore, 27, 125
Cowper, William, 126
Cox, Kenyon, 224
Crane, Hart, 151, 259
Crawford, Thomas, 93, 94
Crevecoeur, J. Hector St. John, 9, 27
Cubism, 276
Currier and Ives, 63, 66*n*, 96, 118*n*, 222

Daguerre, L. J. M., 174
Daguerreotypes, 174–75, 179*n*, 208, 208*n*
Dante Alighieri, 40, 239
Daumier, Honoré, 226
Davis, Theodore, 95–96
Debs, Eugene, 234
Degas, Edgar, 175, 213, 224, 225, 286
Democracy, 1–9, 32, 40, 61, 64–65, 70, 73, 97, 99, 133, 134, 140, 153, 187, 195*n*, 199, 207*n*, 289
Demuth, Charles, 250
Denham, John, 122
Depth, sense of, 120–21, 133, 134, 166, 172–81, 183*n*, 184–87, 185*n*, 201, 214, 223, 264, 275
Dewey, John, 259
Dickens, Charles, 188, 207, 207*n*, 211, 212, 214, 217, 219
Dickinson, Emily, 12, 13, 20, 24
Dilations, 53–54, 53*n*, 59, 72, 141, 147, 183, 245, 261
Dioramas, 164, 168–70, 172, 174, 176, 179*n*, 184, 186, 188, 199, 223

Index

Dolis, John, 183*n*
Dostoevsky, Feodor, 188
Dramatic monologs, 97–107
Duchamp, Marcel, 250
Dutch painting, 61, 65, 214, 220

Eakins, Thomas, 224
Eastman, George, 268
Eastman, Max, 234
Egalitarianism, 3–7, 22–23, 48, 97, 195*n*, 198*n*, 208, 208*n*
Eliot, T. S., 241*n*, 255, 259*n*
—works: "Burnt Norton," 201; *Four Quartets*, 201, 240; "The Love Song of J. Alfred Prufrock," 237–38; "Preludes," 236–37, 238, 240, 257; "Rhapsody on a Windy Night," 237; *The Waste Land*, 238–40, 259, 262, 285; "What Dante Means to Me," 239*n*
Emerson, Peter, 180, 266
Emerson, Ralph Waldo: on conformism, 5; on "Me" and "Not-Me," 11, 12; and Whitman, 18, 71–72, 83, 243; as poet, 20; egalitarianism of, 22; on overseeing self, 32*n*; on industrial ugliness, 65; on vision and light, 65, 178, 190; transcendentalism of, 149, 150, 151; and Matter of America, 224
—works: "Experience," 12, 13; *Nature*, 10, 12, 149, 188; "The Poet," 22; "Self-Reliance," 144
Engravings, 27, 105, 118–20, 133
Erkkila, Betsy, 5*n*, 6*n*, 11, 95*n*, 145*n*, 192*n*
Expansionism, 48, 78, 160. *See also* Catalogs of images
Eyesight: as metaphor for spiritual discernment, 23–26, 26*n*; mystery of the eyesight, 24, 25, 106–108, 134, 141, 155, 160–63, 172–201, 306; Romantic eye, 24; touch and, 25–26, 177–78; communicative power of, 26–27; interest in, during nineteenth century, 174, 177–78; photography compared with, 174–75; 181; self-consciousness of, 176, 179*n*; Holmes on, 177, 178; Emerson on, 178, 190; Whitman's metaphor on, 178; physiology of, 179, 181, 184; Ruskin on, 179; and visual scanning, 182–83, 182*n*; and "saccadic" movements, 182*n*, 274*n*; and visual field, 187–89, 254. *See also* Visual images

Fantasy. *See* Phantoms
Female allegorical figures, 93
Fielding, Henry, 207*n*
"Flat" surface, 163, 172, 176, 177, 208, 218, 254
Folsom, Ed, 208*n*
Forbes, Edwin, 118, 119
Foreground. *See* Visual planes of attention
Francis, Saint, 300
Frank, Joseph, 172
Franklin, Benjamin, 27–28
Fredrickson, George M., 90–91*n*
Friedman, Martin, 279
Friedman, Rohn, 53*n*
Frost, Robert, 259*n*

Galassi, Peter, 210, 222
Genre painting, 61–63, 65, 73, 108, 112, 228
Gibson, James J., 182*n*, 187–90, 194, 195, 249
Gilpin, William, 46–47*n*
Ginsberg, Allen, 151
Glackens, William, 223
Golden, Arthur, 85*n*
Gombrich, E. H., 70, 174, 187, 189*n*
Goodrich, Lloyd, 227, 233, 266*n*
Greater Romantic Lyric, 143–44, 143*n*, 147, 153–54, 186
Greenough, Sarah, 271
Greenspan, Ezra, 13*n*, 18, 20
Grier, Edward, 117*n*
Gris, Juan, 250, 254

Hales, Peter, 214, 217*n*, 236*n*
Hamilton, Alexander, 259

Hartley, Marsden, 250, 271
Hartman, Geoffrey, 24–25, 53n, 155, 155n, 178
Hasidic Judaism, 292, 297, 299–301, 303, 306
Hassam, Childe, 223
Haussmann, G. E., Baron, 160n
Hawthorne, Nathaniel, 5, 175, 183n
Hayward, John Henry, 89, 105, 108–109
Heffernan, James A. W., 171
Helmholtz, Hermann von, 188, 189
Hemingway, Ernest, 222
Henri, Robert, 223, 224
Hine, Lewis, 246
Historical painting, 95, 96, 112
Hogarth, William, 219
Hollis, C. Carroll, 11, 13, 16n, 21, 45, 47n, 59
Holmes, Oliver Wendell, 132, 177–79, 199, 208, 211, 217, 224–25, 281
Homer, Winslow, 49, 117–19, 139, 142, 224
Homosexuality, 15, 15n, 82
Hopper, Edward, 282, 285–87, 286n
—works: *Approaching a City*, 285; "The City," 285; *Early Sunday Morning*, 285; *Nighthawks*, 285, 286–87; *Sunlight in a Cafeteria*, 285, 286
Hoppins, William J., 119n
Hudson River painters, 27

Idealism, 10, 188
Imagination: Whitman's interest in expansion of imagination of audience, 64–70, 73; primary, 185, 209, 242n, 246–47, 249; secondary, 246, 249; Williams on, 249–50, 251
Impressionism, 70, 175, 185n, 188, 224, 225, 271
Individualism, 4, 12–13, 32, 140, 190, 191, 273, 294. *See also* Alienation
Inness, George, 224, 225
Irony, 207–208, 219, 225, 226, 231, 237, 238, 255, 279
Irving, Washington, 27

Isolation. *See* Alienation
Ivins, William, 174

James, Henry, 43, 204, 205
Jarves, James Jackson, 184n
John, Saint, 240
Johnson, Eastman, 131n
Johnson, Samuel, 181, 240
Johnston, John H., 260n
Journalism: on Civil War, 91–92, 119n, 120; Whitman as journalist, 60, 91–92, 92n, 124, 124n, 125n, 156–57, 180, 198, 198n
Joyce, James, 258, 259, 261, 262, 282, 286
Judaism. *See* Hasidic Judaism
Juvenal, 206, 219, 238

Kaplan, Justin, 85
Kegan, Robert, 292
Kensett, John F., 173
Kinter, William, 303
Krausz, Sigmund, 216, 222

Lacan, Jacques, 24
Landscape painting, 112, 112n, 116, 123, 171, 179, 273–79
Landscape poetry, 121–26, 134, 142, 156
Lane, Fitz Hugh, 173
Language: gap between reality and, 18–19, 80, 144; Coleridge on, 155–56. *See also* specific literary techniques
Larson, Kerry C., 5n, 11, 16n, 21, 21n, 26n, 34n, 133, 146n, 154n
Lawson, Ernest, 256
Ledbetter, Huddie, 282
Lessing, G. E., 115, 156
Levertov, Denise, 299–305
—works: "City Psalm," 305–306; "A Common Ground," 301, 302; "From the Roof," 304–305; *The Jacob's Ladder*, 299, 301, 302, 304; "A Letter to William Kinter of Muhlenberg," 303; "Matins," 302; *The Poet in the World*, 299–301, 302n; "Six

Index

Variations," 299; *The Sorrow Dance*, 305; "The World Outside," 302–303
Libbey, Walter, 180
Lincoln, Abraham, 85, 86n, 99n, 114–15
Lippard, George, 28
Literary devices. *See* specific terms
Lithographs, 27, 61, 63, 65–66, 96, 100, 118, 127, 133, 158, 214
London, 166–67, 168, 207, 211
Longfellow, Henry Wadsworth, 2, 41, 124–26, 125n, 164n
Lorraine, Claude, 123
Luks, George, 223, 224, 266
Luminists, 27, 173
Lynch, Kevin, 191

Machor, James L., 30n, 161
McLuhan, Marshall, 207n
Magazine illustrations, 118–19, 131n, 223, 225, 235
Manet, Édouard, 224
Manhatta (film), 275–76, 281
Manhattan, 48–50, 51, 55, 77, 80–81, 93, 141, 143–54, 156–64, 167–68, 169–70, 184, 190–98, 225, 233, 247, 266–71, 275, 281. *See also* New York City
Marcus, Steven, 298
Marin, John, 271
Matisse, Henri, 271
Matthiessen, F. O., 59
Mayhew, Henry, 214–16, 228, 266
Melville, Herman, 64–65, 175, 199
Memory, 41–44, 42, 98, 101, 104, 106, 114n
Metonymy, 45, 59, 86
Middleground. *See* Visual planes of attention
Mill, John Stuart, 174
Miller, Alfred J., 59, 59n
Miller, Edwin Haviland, 181n
Miller, J. Hillis, 248
Milton, John, 142
Monet, Claude, 175, 185n, 225
Moody, David, 158

Moran, Thomas, 166
Morse, Samuel F. B., 174–75
Mount, William Sidney, 59, 65–67, 66n, 180, 214, 228, 246
Müller, Johannes, 177, 177n

Nathanson, Tenney, 19, 21, 147n
Neisser, Ulric, 191, 194, 195, 298n
New York City: and Civil War, 30, 77, 80–81; crowds as phantoms in, 31; in Whitman's "Mannahatta," 48–49, 55, 158; in Whitman's "A Broadway Pageant," 49–50, 51, 55; in Whitman's "Crossing Brooklyn Ferry," 141, 143–54, 160–63, 167–68, 169–70, 173, 184, 187, 190–98, 233; description of New York harbor, 156–57; aerial view of, 158–59; panoramas displayed in, 165; in Whitman's "There was a Child Went Forth," 173, 184, 185, 187; in Riis's photographs, 212–23, 224; in Sloan's paintings, 225–35, 230n; in Williams' works, 243, 254–56; in Stieglitz' photographs, 266–71; in film *Manhatta*, 275–76, 281; in Sheeler's works, 275–79; in Abbott's photographs, 280–85; in Bellow's works, 288–94, 298
New York Realists, 223–25, 236, 246, 246n, 271, 271n
Newspapers. *See* Journalism
Norberg-Schulz, Christian, 298
Norman, Dorothy, 271n
Norris, Frank, 223
Novak, Barbara, 184n

Objectivist poetry, 252, 266
O'Connor, William Douglas, 84–85, 88
O'Doherty, Brian, 286n
O'Keeffe, Georgia, 271, 272
Orvell, Miles, 165n

Painting: Hudson River painters, 27; Luminists, 27, 173; Whitman's familiarity with, 56, 59, 60, 60n;

Dutch painting, 61, 65, 214, 220; genre painting, 61–63, 65, 73, 108, 112, 228; and visual discovery, 70; Impressionism, 70, 175, 185n, 188, 224, 225, 271; historical painting, 95, 96, 112; landscape painting, 112, 112n, 116, 123, 171, 179, 273–79; apprehension of, 115; of Civil War, 117–18; panoramic paintings, 166, 184n; two- vs. four-dimensional, 172; photography compared with, 209–10; New York Realists, 223–25, 236, 246, 271, 271n; by Sloan, 224–35, 264–66, 269–71, 273, 274; modernist painting, 250, 264, 271; Precisionist painting, 266; by Sheeler, 273–79, 280; Cubism, 276; by Hopper, 285–87. See also names of artists and artistic techniques

Panoramas, 164–72, 174, 184n, 188, 190, 199, 208, 276

Paris, 168, 204, 205, 280

Pastoral life. See Rural life

Paterson, N.J., 248, 255–56, 258–62

Pathos, 207

Paul, Sherman, 178

Personifications, 93–95, 95n

Perspective, 115, 128n, 157–58, 160n, 179, 180, 191, 221, 264–65, 276, 278–79, 281

Phantoms, 31, 31n, 33, 47, 49, 50, 58, 81, 132, 140, 141, 172

Photography: by Riis, 69, 212–26, 228; of Civil War, 112n, 116, 117, 118n; replication of photographic images in 1860s, 118; first generation of, 155; significance of, 165, 174–75; eyesight compared with, 174–75; camera obscura and camera lucida, 176; flatness of images in, 177, 180–81, 208, 218; stereoscopic photography, 177; stereographic camera, 179; Holmes on, 208–209, 217; reactions to early photographs, 208–209, 208n; painting compared with, 209–10; with "detective" cameras, 211–12; by Stieglitz, 253, 253n, 266–73; mass reproduction of photographs, 268; by Sheeler, 274, 274n; in film Manhatta, 275–76; by Abbott, 280–85; portrait photography, 282; influence on Hopper, 286. See also Daguerreotypes

Pictorial planes. See Visual planes of attention

Pictorial poetry, 122–26, 134, 179, 185

Pictorialism, 76–77, 92–97, 102, 104–35, 105n, 141, 157–63, 167–68, 173–74, 176, 183–86, 185

Plato and Platonism, 148, 209, 240

Plumbe, John, 208, 208n

Poe, Edgar Allan, 12, 13, 50, 174

Pound, Ezra, 240, 259n, 259, 262

Poussin, Nicholas, 123

Poverty, 66–67, 207, 212–21, 213n, 235, 266

Precisionist painting, 266

"Prospect" poems, 122

Raphael, 56

Redpath, James, 88, 89, 99

Reform. See Social reform

Reincarnation, 149–50

Rejlander, Oscar, 131n, 214, 222, 266

Reynolds, David S., 23n

Riis, Jacob, 69, 212–26, 213n, 217–18n, 228, 236, 266, 268, 279, 281, 282, 286, 289

—works: *Bandit's Roost*, 221; *Home of an Italian Ragpicker*, 214, 215, 218, 219; *Street Arabs*, 214, 216, 218, 220

Roethke, Theodore, 24

Romanticism: American, 10, 22, 29; European, 10, 22, 24, 41, 123–24, 126, 143–45, 143n, 148–49, 151, 154–55, 161, 171; Greater Romantic Lyric, 143–44, 143n, 147, 153–54, 186

Roosevelt, Theodore, 212

Root, George F., 110n

Rosenblatt, Jon, 193n

Rosenfeld, Paul, 269n

Rural life: in Whitman's works, 28–35,

Index

30n, 59n, 99–100, 128, 128n, 206; in Stieglitz' photographs, 272; in Sheeler's paintings, 273–74
Ruskin, John, 155, 161, 174, 179–80, 179–80n, 183n, 188, 200
Rutherford, N.J., 241, 243–44, 246n, 247, 248, 251, 256–58, 289

St. Armand, Barton, 174n, 185n
Sargent, John Singer, 223
Sartre, Jean-Paul, 24
Satire, 207, 276
Sayre, Henry M., 255–56
Schweitzer, Albert, 300
Scott, David, 265n
Scott, Dixon, 211, 254, 282
Scott, Sir Walter, 125, 207n
Seeing. *See* Eyesight; Visual images
Shakespeare, William, 142
Sharpe, William Chapman, 14n, 17, 32n, 34n, 54n, 146n 221n
Sheeler, Charles, 271, 273–81, 274n, 276n, 279n, 280n, 285, 286
—works: *American Landscape*, 276; *Church Street El*, 276, 278; *City Interior*, 274–75, 276, 279; *Manhatta* (film), 275–76, 281; *Self-Portrait*, 279–80; *Skyscrapers*, 276, 277
Shelley, Percy Bysshe, 126
Shinn, Everett, 223, 224, 236
Shloss, Carol, 213n, 266
Shurr, William H., 17
Sight. *See* Eyesight; Visual images
Sinclair, Upton, 223
Sloan, John: excerpts from diary published in *John Sloan's New York Scene*, 225; socialism of, 234–35; Whitman's influence on, 69, 224, 227, 227n, 234; as New York Realist, 223, 225–36, 238, 245, 246, 250, 255, 265n, 266n, 269, 271, 279, 280, 282, 302, 303
—works: *Chinese Restaurant*, 228–29, 285, 287; *The City from Greenwich Village*, 264–66, 270, 273, 281; *The Gist of Art* (prose), 264; *Hairdresser's Window*, 231; *Man, Wife, and Child*, 230, 230n; *New York Life* series, 230; *Night Windows*, 230, 231; *Roofs, Summer Night*, 226; *Three A.M.*, 231–33, 274, 287; *Turning Out the Light*, 230; *A Window on the Street*, 231; *Women's Page*, 226
Socialism, 225, 234–35
Social reform, 210, 212, 219–20, 220n, 222, 281
Solipsism. *See* Alienation
Sontag, Susan, 269n
Stebbins, Theodore E., Jr., 274n, 276n
Stein, Gertrude, 222
Stella, Joseph, 279n
Stereographs, 177, 179, 208–10, 223, 224
Stereopticon, 188, 199
Stevens, Patrick L., 274n
Stevens, Wallace, 249, 260
Stieglitz, Alfred, 246n, 250, 266–73, 275, 281
—works: *Camera Work* series, 268, 269n; *The City of Ambition*, 268; *Equivalents*, 272; *The Hand of Man*, 268; *Old and New New York*, 269–70, 272; *Spring Showers*, 253, 253n; *The Terminal*, 267; *291* photographs, 269–71, 269n; *Winter, Fifth Avenue*, 267–68
Strand, Paul, 246, 275, 276n, 281
Surface, "flat," 163, 172, 176, 177, 208, 218, 254
Sweet, Timothy, 91n, 95n, 112n
Swift, Jonathan, 206, 240

Talbot, Jesse, 60n
Tapscott, Stephen, 259, 259n, 262n
Tashjian, Dickran, 279n
Thomas, Alan, 214, 215n
Thomas, M. Wynn, 5n, 8, 32n, 54n, 65n, 86n, 105n, 132n, 145n, 162, 195n, 200
Thomson, James, 122–23, 124n, 126, 134
Thomson, John, 211, 214
Thoreau, Henry David, 11, 12, 19, 24, 198

Time, 114, 167–71
Tocqueville, Alexis de, 4, 5, 199, 289
Touch, 25–26, 141, 177–78
Trachtenberg, Alan, 3, 17, 21*n*
Transcendentalism, 47*n*, 60, 149–50, 155
Traubel, Horace, 227*n*, 234
Trompe l'oeil, 167*n*, 174, 189*n*
Turner, J. M. W., 179, 179*n*
Twain, Mark, 99*n*, 165*n*

Umbricius, 206
Urban life: Whitman's focus on, 27–35, 32*n*, 140–41; during Civil War, 30, 30*n*, 77–78, 80–81, 86–87, 86*n*; in Whitman's "Mannahatta," 48–49, 55, 59*n*, 158; in Whitman's "A Broadway Pageant," 49–50, 51, 55; in pictorial art, 66–67; in Whitman's "Crossing Brooklyn Ferry," 143–54, 160–63, 167–68, 169–70, 173, 184, 187, 190–98, 200–201, 205, 233; as image of city of the mind, 162; in Whitman's "There was a Child Went Forth," 173, 184, 185, 187; and cognitive map of a city, 191, 194–96, 298, 298*n*; as shared space, 195–98, 195*n*; and equality, 198*n*; paradoxes of, 206–208, 255–56; Riis's photography of, 210–23; Sloan's paintings of, 224, 225–35, 264–66; Eliot's poetry of, 237–40; Williams' poetry of, 243–48, 254–63, 273; Stieglitz' photographs of, 266–73; Sheeler's paintings of, 274–79; Abbott's photographs of, 280–85; Hopper's paintings of, 285–87; Levertov's poetry of, 304–306. *See also* names of specific cities

Valéry, Paul, 25, 155, 155*n*, 178
Vision. *See* Eyesight
Visual images: in Whitman's earlier works, 20–27, 21*n*, 34–35, 39–42, 54–56, 59, 65, 70–71, 74–77; and mystery of the eyesight, 24, 25, 106–108, 134, 141, 155, 160–63, 172–201, 306; pictorial quality of, 76–77, 92–97, 102, 104–35, 105*n*, 141, 152, 155, 157–63, 167–68, 173–74, 176, 183–86; in pictorial poetry, 122–26, 134; in Whitman's late visualist poems, 126–35; and panoramas, 163–71; in Williams' poetry, 176, 246, 252–54, 261; in Levertov's poetry, 302–303
Visual planes of attention, 62–63, 69, 72, 105, 108, 111–12, 114–16, 121, 128*n*, 131, 160, 179, 222, 234, 274–75, 286
Volney, C. F., 56

Waggoner, Hyatt, 22*n*, 25*n*, 26*n*
Walker, Jeffrey, 5*n*, 18, 241*n*
Warren, James Perrin, 53, 85*n*, 181–82
Washington, D.C., 81, 84, 86, 86*n*, 93, 98, 197, 251, 298
Weaver, Mike, 246
Whitefield, Edwin, 158
Whitehead, Alfred North, 25*n*
Whitman, Walt: tension between public and personal in, 13, 82*n*; and citizen poet, 18, 20–22, 58, 71, 90, 141, 153, 197; on the American hero, 7–8; "I" and "Not-Me," 9–21; path between reality and the soul, 10, 13, 23–24, 32, 64, 75, 97, 106, 141, 165, 197, 242, 301; and pride/skepticism, 11, 14–16, 32; relationship with reader, 11–13, 16–18, 20–21, 21*n*, 83–84, 89, 99, 107, 133, 141, 146*n*, 149–50, 243; and sympathy/power, 11, 13, 13*n*, 32; doubt of, 13–16, 34–35, 75, 77, 80–84, 80*n*, 85, 134, 181, 182, 186; homosexuality of, 15, 15*n*, 82; failure to gain general appreciation, 18, 71, 83; faith of, 22, 27, 34–35, 60, 65, 200, 296; hospital service during Civil War, 30*n*, 42, 79, 82, 87–88; familiarity with pictorial art, 56, 59, 60, 60*n*, 180; as journalist, 60, 91–92, 92*n*, 124, 124*n*, 125*n*, 156–57, 180, 198, 198*n*; on light, 65–66; multiple identities

Index

as poet, 71, 76–77, 77n, 82–86, 85n, 116–17, 121–22, 126, 134–35, 141, 153; sexuality in, 71, 190; health of, 79; Satan in, 81–84, 86, 90, 116–17, 132, 135, 141; released from position of Department of Interior, 84; concessions to popular literary tastes by, 85, 96–97; in Washington, D.C., 86–87, 86n; interest in reaching larger American market, 88, 89, 134–35; sentimental narrative in, 99–102; on Nature, 132–33; on European compared with American poetry, 142; education of, 149n; relationship of spirit and body in, 149–51, 153; scientific and pseudo-scientific lore of, 149n; spirituality in, 199–201, 296

—works: "Aboard at a Ship's Helm," 130; "After the Sea-Ship," 127–28; "Ah Poverties, Wincings, and Sulky Retreats," 83; "Are You the New Person Drawn toward Me?," 15; "The Artilleryman's Vision," 102, 104; "As I Ebb'd with the Ocean of Life," 41; "As I Lay with my Head in Your Lap Camerado," 82–83; "A Backward Glance O'er Travel'd Roads," 2n, 17, 134; *Banner at Day-Break*, 88; "Bathed in War's Perfume," 93; "Beat! Beat! Drums!," 30n; "Beginning My Studies," 79; "Bivouac on a Mountain Side," 111–12, 114, 115, 121, 122, 173, 176, 186, 252; "A Boston Ballad," 207; "A Broadway Pageant," 49–51, 55, 56, 69, 78, 160; "By Blue Ontario's Shore," 4, 16n, 19, 78, 95n, 144; "By the Bivouac's Fitful Flame," 110–11, 113, 115–16; *Calamus*, 14, 31, 41, 73, 77, 80, 81, 132, 141; "Cavalry Crossing a Ford," 76, 113, 114, 116, 186, 252, 253; "The Centenarian's Story," 89, 97–98; "Chanting the Square Deific," 81, 132; "City of Ships," 30n; "Come Up from the Fields Father," 99–102;

"Crossing Brooklyn Ferry," 12, 114, 138, 141, 143–54, 145–47n, 154n, 155, 156, 162n, 167–68, 169–70, 170n, 171, 172–74, 176, 180, 183–88, 190–98, 200–201, 223, 227, 233, 247, 249, 263, 275, 285, 290, 292–93, 296, 298, 304–306; *Democratic Vistas*, 4, 132–33, 243; *Drum-Taps*, 28, 42, 76–90, 77n, 82n, 85n, 92–93, 95, 97, 102, 117, 120, 126, 128, 132–34, 139, 141, 142, 156, 157, 168, 176; "Faces," 54, 176, 208; "A Farm Picture," 128, 128n; "First O Songs for a Prelude," 30n, 77, 93, 93n; "From Paumanok Starting I Fly like a Bird," 78; "Give Me the Splendid Silent Sun," 28–30, 30n, 32, 49, 80–81, 206, 269; "A Glimpse," 73, 74; "How Solemn as One by One," 30n, 81; "I Saw in Louisiana a Live-Oak Growing," 41–42, 73; "I Saw Old General at Bay," 95, 118; "I Sing the Body Electric," 150; *Leaves of Grass* (1856 ed.), 44, 71, 89, 117, 141; *Leaves of Grass* (1860 ed.), 41, 44, 71, 88, 117, 141, 157, 243; *Leaves of Grass* (postwar eds.), 79, 126, 129–30, 262; "Letters from a Travelling Bachelor," 156–57; "Lo, Victress on the Peaks," 90, 93, 94n; "Mannahatta," 48–49, 55, 153, 158, 160, 163–64, 191, 255; "A March in the Ranks Hard-Prest, and the Road Unknown," 102–106, 108, 114, 115, 120, 141; "Mother and Babe," 128; "A Noiseless Patient Spider," 129, 131; *Notebooks and Unpublished Prose Manuscripts*, 19, 25, 25n, 31, 117; "Not Youth Pertains to Me," 87; "O Captain! My Captain!," 85, 97, 100; "Of the Terrible Doubt of Appearances," 14, 80, 186; "Old Ireland," 93, 93–94n; "O Me! O Life!," 83–84; "One's-Self I Sing," 140; "On the Beach at Night," 130, 173; "Our Old Feuillage," 43–44, 46, 70, 77,

144, 163; "Out of the Cradle Endlessly Rocking," 21, 41; "Over the Carnage Rose Prophetic a Voice," 78; "Passage to India," 47, 71; "A Paumanok Picture," 72–73, 97, 127; "Pensive on Her Dead Gazing," 93, 94n; "Pictures," 39–40, 54, 55–57, 59, 73, 174, 183; "Pioneers! O Pioneers!," 85, 97; "Poem of Walt Whitman, an American," 5–6, 8; Preface to 1855 Edition of *Leaves of Grass*, 1–10, 18, 19, 21–24, 27, 40, 59, 80, 95n, 132–34, 142, 154, 169, 187, 199–200, 242, 292, 296; "Rise O Days from Your Fathomless Deeps," 77–78, 93, 93n; "Salut au Monde!," 47, 54, 69, 71–74, 77, 97, 99, 113, 120, 127, 144, 147, 160, 183, 197; "Says," 129; "A Sight in Camp in the Day-Break Gray and Dim," 106–109, 111, 114; "The Sleepers," 62, 63, 66–70, 75, 97, 114, 198, 237; "Small the Theme of My Chant," 139, 198; "So Long!," 16n, 17, 250; "A Song for Occupations," 44, 60, 64, 104, 131, 205–206; "A Song of Joys," 46; "Song of Myself," 1, 3, 4, 6–8, 12, 13, 16, 18–21, 23, 24, 26n, 27, 28, 38, 45–46, 54–55, 57–59, 61–62, 63n, 64, 66–67, 72, 74, 78, 82, 87, 92, 97, 99, 104, 114, 120, 133, 134, 140, 142, 144–47, 150, 155n, 157, 162, 164, 165, 176, 183, 185, 186, 190, 191, 195, 198, 222n, 227–28, 234, 247, 249, 269, 275, 283; "Song of the Answerer," 17, 21n, 51, 53; "Song of the Banner at Daybreak," 89; "Song of the Broad-Axe," 50–54, 64, 70, 73, 104, 113, 121, 147, 152, 163, 167, 183, 191, 235, 245; "Song of the Exposition," 71; "Song of the Open Road," 3, 15–16, 26, 31–32, 45, 80, 176; "Song of the Redwood-Tree," 71, 133; "A Song of the Rolling Earth," 144; "Sparkles from the Wheel," 130–32, 191; *Specimen Days*, 86, 87, 88, 90, 91; "Spirit whose Work is Done," 84, 93, 94n; "Starting from Paumanok," 8, 46, 93, 262–63; "There was a Child Went Forth," 32–35, 80, 114, 140, 141–44, 155, 161, 172–73, 176, 180–87, 180n, 181n, 190–92, 194, 197, 201, 208, 243, 257, 285; "Thick-Sprinkled Bunting," 92; "This Compost," 142, 144; "Thoughts," 128–29; "Thou Mother with Thy Equal Brood," 71; "To a Certain Civilian," 82; "To a Locomotive in Winter," 130; "To the Leaven'd Soil They Trod," 79; "To Think of Time," 198; "The Torch," 128, 176; "Turn O Libertad," 93, 94n; "Vigil Strange I Kept on the Field One Night," 101–102, 113; *War Memoranda*, 88; "When Lilacs Last in the Dooryard Bloom'd," 93, 94n, 114–15, 121, 142, 165, 222; "The World Below the Brine," 73–75; "The Wound-Dresser," 42–43, 79, 98–99, 101, 102, 104, 108, 113; "Years of the Modern," 93, 93n

Whittier, John Greenleaf, 27, 31, 41, 99n, 125, 126, 132, 168–69

Wiesel, Elie, 306

Williams, William Carlos: visual images in, 176, 252–54, 261; as citizen poet, 241–42, 249; as physician, 241, 251; on Whitman, 241, 250n, 262–63; urban life in, 243–48, 254–63, 273, 289; on the imagination, 249–51; and modernist painting, 250; as Objectivist poet, 252, 266; and Sheeler, 275, 277–78; influence on Levertov, 299

—works: "Abroad," 244; *Al Que Quiere!*, 243–44, 246–49, 251, 260, 263, 278; "America, Whitman, and the Art of Poetry," 241; "The American Background," 241–42, 258, 268, 278; "Between Walls," 254; "Burning the Christmas Greens," 259; "The Catholic Bells,"

Index

257–58, 261; "The Clouds," 259; *The Desert Music,* 263; "Fine Work with Pitch and Copper," 245–46; "The Forgotten City," 246n; *In the American Grain,* 241, 247, 249, 260, 278; "January Morning," 248, 255, 261; *Kora in Hell,* 248–49, 255, 278; *Life Along the Passaic River,* 251–52; "Morning," 256–57, 258; "Pastoral," 244; *Paterson,* 258–63, 260n, 278; "Paterson," 259–60; "Perpetuum Mobile: The City," 254–56, 259, 261, 275; "Rain," 259; "Russia," 262n; *Spring and All,* 249, 250, 251, 278; "To Elsie," 243, 244, 251, 254, 291; "Tract," 244; "View of a Lake," 253; "The Wanderer," 247–48, 252, 259; "Woman Walking," 244–45; "Young Sycamore," 252–53

Wordsworth, William, 22, 24, 25n, 126, 199, 200

—works: *The Excursion,* 155–56; Intimations Ode, 148–49; "Michael," 41; *The Prelude,* 123–24, 166, 170, 221n; "Tintern Abbey," 42, 143, 144

Worringer, Wilhelm, 172n

Wright, Fanny, 56

Zarobila, Charles, 165
Zayas, Marius de, 271
Zukovsky, Louis, 252
Zweig, Paul, 20, 47n